17p

THE ARCHAEOLOGY OF CANTERBURY

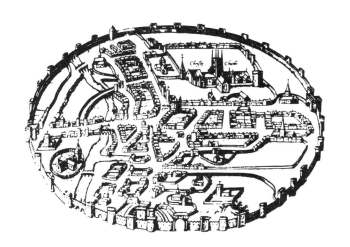

THE ARCHAEOLOGY OF CANTERBURY

General Editors: A.P. Detsicas, B.A., M.A., D.Litt., F.S.A., and T.W.T. Tatton-Brown, B.A.

VOLUME VIII

CANTERBURY EXCAVATIONS: INTRA- AND EXTRA-MURAL SITES, 1949–55 and 1980–84

BY

S.S. Frere, C.B.E., M.A., Litt.D., D.Litt., Litt.D., F.B.A., F.S.A.,
P. Bennett, B.A., M.I.F.A., J. Rady, and S. Stow, M.A.

WITH CONTRIBUTIONS BY

I. Anderson; M.M. Archibald, M.A., F.S.A., F.M.A.; J. Bayley, M.Sc.; J. Bird, B.A., F.S.A.; P. Blockley, B.Sc.; A. Brocklebank; R.J. Charleston, B.A., F.S.A.; the late D. Charlesworth, M.A., F.S.A.; J. Cherry, M.A., F.S.A.; B. Dickinson, B.A.; G. Egan, B.A.; B. Ellis; I.P. Garrard; the late P.H. Garrard, M.B.B.S.; M.J. Green; S. Greep, B.A., Ph.D.; K. Hartley, B.A., F.S.A.; F. Jenkins, M.A., Ph.D., F.S.A.; G. Lloyd-Morgan, B.A., Ph.D., F.S.A.; N. Macpherson-Grant; D.F. Mackreth, B.A., F.S.A.; D.M. Metcalf, M.A., D.Phil., D.Litt., F.S.A.; S. Morgan; D.E.M. Nash, M.A., D.Phil., F.S.A.; R.J. Pollard, B.A., Ph.D.; A.J. Price, B.A., Ph.D., F.S.A.; V. Tatton-Brown, B.A., D.Phil., F.S.A.; L. Webster, B.A., F.S.A.; and M.G. Wilson, F.S.A.

Published for the
Canterbury Archaeological Trust
by the
Kent Archaeological Society
Maidstone
1987

Produced by Alan Sutton Publishing, Gloucester
Printed in Great Britain

Published with the aid of a grant from the Historic Buildings and Monuments Commission (England).

ISBN 0 906746 10 8

CONTENTS

PART I: EXTRA-MURAL SITES

PART II: INTRA-MURAL SITES

PART III: THE FINDS AND POTTERY FROM CANTERBURY EXCAVATION COMMITTEE SITES 1946–60

PART IIIA: THE FINDS by Sally Stow

PART IIIB: THE POTTERY by M.G. Wilson

PART IIIC: THE ROMAN AND SAXON GLASS

PART IIID: THE POST-MEDIEVAL GLASS

APPENDIX 1

PART IV: THE FINDS AND POTTERY FROM THE
CANTERBURY ARCHAEOLOGICAL TRUST SITES 1980–84

LIST OF FIGURES

9

LIST OF PLATES

ABBREVIATIONS AND BIBLIOGRAPHY

Aldgate	Chapman and Johnson 1973.
Antiq. Journ.	*The Antiquaries Journal*, Society of Antiquaries of London.
Arch. Cant.	*Archaeologia Cantiana*, Transactions of the Kent Archaeological Society, Maidstone.
Barnard	F.P. Barnard, *The Casting-Counter and the Counting Board* (Oxford, 1916).
BAR	*British Archaeological Reports* (Oxford).
C.B.A.	Council for British Archaeology.
Canterbury I	Macpherson-Grant 1982.
Canterbury V	Pollard forthcoming.
Canterbury VII	Wilson 1983.
Camulodunum	C.F.C. Hawkes and M.R. Hull, *Camulodunum, First Report on the Excavations at Colchester 1930–39* (Oxford, 1947).
CHK	R.A.G. Carson, P.V. Hill and J.P.C. Kent, *Late Roman Bronze Coinage* (London, 1960).
Colchester	Hull 1963.
Dane John	Kirkman 1940.
Dover	Wilson 1981.
Gillam	J.P. Gillam, 'Types of Roman Coarse Pottery Vessels in northern Britain', *Archaeologia Aeliana* (4th series) xxv (1957), 180–251; 3rd edition (1970).
Gose	Gose 1950.
Jenkins	F. Jenkins, 'Canterbury Excavations June–December, 1947', *Arch. Cant.*, lxv (1952), 114 ff.
JBAA	*Journal of the British Archaeological Association*, London.
Ospringe	Whiting *et al.* 1931.
Proc. Soc. Ant.	Proceedings of the Society of Antiquaries of London.
RIB	R.G. Collingwood and R.P. Wright, *The Roman Inscriptions of Britain* (Oxford, 1965).
RIC	H. Mattingly, E.A. Sydenham, C.H.V. Sutherland and R.A.G. Carson, *The Roman Imperial Coinage* (London).
Richborough	Bushe-Fox 1932.
St. Dunstan's	Whiting 1927.
Skeleton Green	C. Partridge, *Skeleton Green* (*Britannia* Monograph Series no. 2, London, 1981).
Tyers	Tyers 1978.
V.C.H.	*The Victoria County History*, London.

Verulamium 1936	R.E.M. and T.V. Wheeler, *Verulamium, A Belgic and Two Roman Cities* (Oxford, 1936).
Verulamium	Wilson 1972.
Whitehall	Jenkins 1960.
Williams	A. Williams, 'Canterbury Excavations in 1945', *Arch. Cant.*, lx (1947), 87 ff.
Williamson	G.C. Williamson, *Trade Tokens in the Seventeenth Century*, i (London, 1889).
Young	C.J. Young, *Oxfordshire Roman Pottery BAR* British Series, no. 43 (Oxford, 1977).

Anderson *et al.* 1982	A. Anderson, M.G. Fulford, H. Hatcher, and A.D. Pollard, 'Chemical Analysis of Hunt Cups and allied Wares from Britain', *Britannia*, xiii (1982), 229–38.
Bennett *et al.* 1980	P. Bennett, N.C. Macpherson-Grant, and P. Blockley, 'Four Minor Sites Excavated by the Canterbury Archaeological Trust, 1978–79', *Arch. Cant.*, xcvi (1980), 267–304.
Bennett *et al.* 1982	P. Bennett, S.S. Frere, and S. Stow, *Excavations at Canterbury Castle, The Archaeology of Canterbury*, vol. i (Maidstone, 1982).
Blockley *et al.* forthcoming	K. Blockley, P. Blockley, M. Day, S.S. Frere and S. Stow, *Excavations on the Marlowe Car Park and associated Areas, The Archaeology of Canterbury*, vol. v (forthcoming).
Bushe-Fox 1932	J.P. Bushe-Fox, *Third Report on the Excavation of the Roman Fort at Richborough, Kent*, Reports of the Research Committee of the Society of Antiquaries of London, No. x (Oxford, 1932).
Chapman and Johnson 1973	H. Chapman, and T. Johnson, 'Excavations at Aldgate and Bush Lane House in the City of London, 1972', *Transactions of the London and Middlesex Archaeological Society*, xxiv (1973), 1–73.
Gillam 1970	J.P. Gillam, *Types of Roman Coarse Pottery Vessels in Northern Britain*, 3rd edition, (Newcastle-upon-Tyne, 1970).
Gose 1950	E. Gose, 'Gefässtypen der Römischen Keramik im Rheinland', *Bonner Jahrbücher Beiheft 1*, Kevelaer, 1950.
Hartley 1982	K.F. Hartley 'The Mortaria', in Bennett *et al.* 1982, 150–8.
Hull 1963	M.R. Hull, *The Roman Potters' Kilns at Colchester*, Reports of the Research Committee of the Society of Antiquaries of London, No. xxi, (Oxford, 1963).
Jenkins 1960	F. Jenkins, 'Two Pottery Kilns and a Tilery of the Roman Period at Canterbury', *Arch. Cant.*, lxxiv (1960), 151–162.
Jenkins 1962	F. Jenkins, 'Men of Kent before the Romans: Cantium in the Early Iron Age', *Canterbury Archaeological Society Occasional Paper*, iii (Canterbury, 1962).
Kirkman 1940	J.S. Kirkman 'Canterbury Kiln Site: The Pottery', in G.A. Webster, 'A Roman Pottery Kiln at Canterbury', *Arch. Cant.*, liii (1940), 118–33.
Macpherson-Grant 1980	N.C. Macpherson-Grant, 'Chaff-tempered Ware', *Kent Archaeological Review*, 61 (1980), 2–4.
Macpherson-Grant 1982	N.C. Macpherson-Grant, 'The Coarse Wares', in Bennett *et al.* 1982, 97–123, 133–49.
Mainman forthcoming	A. Mainman, 'The Early to Late Saxon Pottery', in Blockley *et al.* forthcoming.
Pollard 1981	R.J. Pollard, 'Two Cremations of the Roman Period from St. Augustine's College, Canterbury', *Arch. Cant.*, xcvii (1981), 318–24
Pollard 1982a	R.J. Pollard 'The Pottery, excluding Samian', in J.D. Ogilvie, 'The Hammill Ritual Shaft', *Arch. Cant.*, xcviii (1982), 160–6.
Pollard 1982b	R.J. Pollard, *The Roman Pottery of Kent*, unpublished Ph.D. thesis, University of Reading.

Pollard 1983   R.J. Pollard, 'The Pottery', in P.D. Catherall 'A Romano-British Pottery Manufacturing Site at Oakleigh Farm, Higham, Kent', *Britannia*, xiv (1983).

Pollard forthcoming   R.J. Pollard 'The Late Iron Age and Roman Pottery', in Blockley *et al.* forthcoming.

Tyers 1978   P.A. Tyers, 'The Poppyhead Beakers of Britain and their Relationship to the Barbotine decorated Vessels of the Rhineland and Switzerland', in (Eds.) P.A. Arthur and G. Marsh, *Early Fine Wares in Roman Britain* (BAR British Series, No. 57 (Oxford, 1978)), 61–108.

Whiting 1927   W. Whiting, 'A Roman Cemetery at St. Dunstan's, Canterbury', *Arch. Cant.*, xxxix (1927), 46–54.

Whiting *et al.* 1931   W. Whiting, W. Hawley, and T. May, *Excavation of the Roman Cemetery at Ospringe, Kent*, Reports of the Research Committee of the Society of Antiquaries of London, No. VIII (Oxford, 1931).

Wilson 1981   J. Wilson 'The Coarse Pottery', in B.J. Philp, *The Excavation of the Roman Forts of the Classis Britannica at Dover 1970–1977*, Kent Monograph Series Research Report No. 3 (Dover, 1981), 207–48.

Wilson 1972   M.G. Wilson, 'The Other Pottery', in S.S. Frere, *Verulamium Excavations I*, Reports of the Research Committee of the Society of Antiquaries of London No. xxviii (Oxford, 1972), 263–370.

Wilson 1983   M.G. Wilson 'The Pottery', in S.S. Frere and S. Stow, *Excavations in the St. George's Street and Burgate Street Areas*, *The Archaeology of Canterbury*, vol. vii (Maidstone, 1983), 192–311.

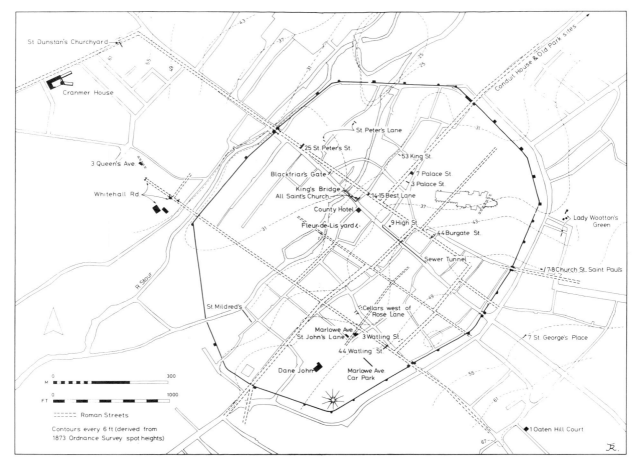

Fig. 1.   Plan of sites, dealt with in this volume, showing City Walls and known Roman streets (based on First Edition
Ordnance Survey, 1874). (Scale: 1:10,000)

INTRODUCTION

Canterbury Excavations Committee

An account of the genesis and character of the excavations carried out in the period 1946–60 by the former Canterbury Excavation Committee has been given in Vol. VII of this series. The design was to explore sites which had been laid bare by the bombing of 1942 before rebuilding should have removed the opportunity. Some of the sites then excavated have since been explored on a much larger scale by the Canterbury Archaeological Trust (see below); in these cases the results of the earlier work are being incorporated in the reports published by the Trust. Another group of sites explored in the area of Burgate and St. George's Streets, where there has been no more recent work, has been published in Vol. VII of this series. Of the 1946–60 programme there remains a number of somewhat scattered excavations in the central and north-western parts of the walled city and some outside the walls; it is these sites which are reproduced in the present volume. The opportunity has been taken to include accounts of the Roman and Saxon glass and of the post-medieval glass from all the 1946–60 excavations. The former is mainly the work of the late Dorothy Charlesworth and has been completed with assistance from Dr Jennifer Price. The latter is the work of Mr R.J. Charleston; to all three scholars grateful thanks are expressed.

The Extra-mural Sites

Between 1951 and 1955 one large and four small areas were examined outside the city wall.

The most extensive and most interesting was Site W, which occupied part of the western bank of the river Stour on the north-western side of the city. Here, in the Whitehall Road area, excavation was carried out in advance of the construction of a dual-carriageway road which was to form part of a new ring-road. In addition to finds of the Neolithic period, there was proof that in the late Iron Age Belgic occupation – already known below the Roman city on the east bank – had extended to this side of the river. A large group of stratified pottery was recovered, which considerably extends the range of late Iron Age forms already published from a site near Rose Lane (*Arch. Cant.* lxviii (1954), 104–14). Two contemporary buildings were examined. The Roman Watling Street was traced, and timber buildings of the first and second centuries were encountered; it seems that there were fairly extensive suburbs west of the river in the early Roman period, but that these were abandoned after the construction of the city's defences in the late third century.

On the opposite side of the city, at Lady Wootton's Green, outside the eastern defences and lying between the Cathedral and St. Augustine's Abbey, several Roman skeletons were found on C XX Site B; the presence of these, combined with the discovery in 1922 of a tombstone

(*RIB* 43) just outside the gate of the Abbey, indicates that there was a Roman cemetery here close to the road to Richborough. The other three sites were small. At Church Street (St. Paul's), beyond the Burgate, there was evidence for pre-Roman cultivation similar to that found beneath Roman levels here and there inside the walls (cf. vol. vii, pp. 70, 120); the site also showed that buildings extended this far east in the late first century, and from the late Roman period there were further traces of occupation.

At Old Park, some distance north-west of the city near the Sturry Road, an enigmatic late medieval structure was examined.

The Intra-mural Sites

Few areas were available for excavation in the central and north-western parts of the city in the post-war years. In order to gain some information about the extent and character of occupation there, advantage had to be taken of some small and isolated sites which it proved possible to investigate. Thus, a small excavation in the yard of the Fleur-de-Lis Hotel, near the presumed area of the forum, yielded an interesting group of miscellaneous Mediterranean marbles which had mostly been sliced for *opus sectile*. At no. 3 Palace Street, structures of both Belgic and Roman date were encountered. In St. Peter's Street a small trench yielded important information on the Roman street-plan, proving the presence of a Roman street in the vicinity of the West Gate – this was evidently a continuation of the street previously established south of Burgate Street. In King Street limited work proved Roman and medieval occupation in a part of the city of which previously nothing archaeological was known. A little further west, in St. Peter's Lane, the water-table was too high to enable much exploration of the Roman levels, but several phases of an overlying building of the later Middle Ages were examined.

The part played by Miss S. Stow in the study of the excavation records and in the preparation of draft reports which have then been revised by myself has been explained in the Introduction to Volume VII. She has drawn some of the plans published here and has been responsible also for the small finds report. The section-drawings and all the drawings of pottery and glass are the work of Miss M.G. Wilson; without her great contribution it would have been impossible to complete this report. The help received from Mr B.R. Hartley in the identification and dating of samian sherds and from Mrs. K.F. Hartley in those of mortaria will be readily apparent. Gratitude is also expressed to Mrs. Lynda Smithson for her immaculate typing of successive drafts of the text.

S.S. FRERE

Canterbury Archaeological Trust

The Canterbury Archaeological Trust sites included in this volume were nearly all rescue excavations in advance of mains service trenching, construction or refurbishment work from 1980 to 1984. Most of the observations were made by Trust personnel involved in large-scale excavations elsewhere, or engaged in post-excavation work, or by weekend volunteers. The success of these various operations owes as much to the interest and assistance shown and given to the Trust by the officers of the Canterbury City Council, by developers, architects and site workmen alike, as to the hard work and enthusiasm of our staff and loyal band of volunteers. Over the past seven years large-scale excavations in advance of development have taken place over a wide area of the historic city as well as in the Precincts of Canterbury Cathedral. Numerous smaller developments have nevertheless been continuously monitored by the Trust during this period and the results of at least some of this work (1976–80), published elsewhere.* Developments of any size within the walled city are of great importance, and our policy from the outset has been to excavate in advance of redevelopment or at the very least maintain watching briefs on every available site. In the final analysis, the success of this policy depends on many factors, not the least being time and finance. Unfortunately, very little money has been available for these emergency operations. Often the work has been undertaken as the archaeological deposits were being disturbed and, in some cases, after they had been removed. Sometimes developments in basements were only observed after work had begun, though more recently developers have been encouraged by the City Council's conservation staff to inform the Trust before such work gets under way. In the light of information recorded below, the need to maintain watching briefs on even minor development sites cannot be denied and this work *must* continue. Unfortunately, the acute lack of finance, which has consistently hampered the work of the Trust, today threatens the very existence of a full-time archaeological presence in the city.

Of the Trust's six extra-mural sites recorded in this volume, two were located in the Old Park area. An enigmatic stone building first recorded by Professor Frere in 1952 was revisited by members of the Trust in 1984. Considerable damage to the structure and the surrounding area had occurred since Professor Frere's excavation there and a survey of the surviving remains of this curious building appears below. Work undertaken on the Cathedral water-supply also appears in this section. This operation, conducted during an interlude between major excavations in the city, proved to be one of the most rewarding since, as a result of the Trust's efforts, the Dean and Chapter can now once again boast a functioning water-supply, first established by Prior Wibert over eight hundred years ago. On the east side of the city, construction-trenches for a new house in the back garden of no. 1 Oaten Hill Court revealed the remains of cellared structures associated with the little-known nunnery of St. Sepulchre's. A mixture of excavation, documentary and pictorial evidence has been combined below to reconstruct a tentative plan of this 'lost' establishment, famous in Kentish history for 'the Holy Maid of Kent.' West of the city wall and north-west of the Whitehall Road excavations of Professor Frere, part of a small Roman street or lane, perhaps associated with an industrial suburb west of the Roman town, was uncovered during a training excavation for the Canterbury Junior Archaeological Society. This hectic three-day operation, supervised by members of the Trust, is also included in this volume. The two remaining extra-mural sites were recorded during building operations south of the London Road and north-west of the city, in St. Dunstan's churchyard and at Cranmer House. Considerable gravel deposits for the Roman London Road

---

* See 'Some minor Excavations undertaken by the Canterbury Archaeological Trust in 1977–78' (*Arch. Cant.*, xciv (1978), 149–94) and 'Four minor Sites excavated by the Canterbury Archaeological Trust, 1978–79' (*Arch. Cant.*, xcvi (1980), 267–304).

were observed and recorded in the churchyard, and an extensive Roman cremation cemetery was revealed in foundation trenches during the construction of Cranmer House. Well over fifty individual cremations were salvaged during this development together with a small group of late sixth- or early seventh-century finds, indicating a re-use of the Roman cemetery in Anglo-Saxon times. These Saxon finds included a beautiful gold pendant inlaid with *cloisonné* garnets and decorated with filigree wire, described by Mrs. Leslie Webster as 'one of the most complex and splendid pieces of Anglo-Saxon jewellery to have been found since the discovery of the Sutton Hoo burial in 1939'.

Eight observations by the Trust and three excavations supervised by Mr J. Rady are included in the intra-mural section of the volume. At no. 7 Palace Street, during the laying of the basement, the remains of a mid-second century Roman metalworker's shop was recorded. The laying of a new water-main at the intersection of St. Peter's Street and The Friars exposed part of the foundation for a medieval gate which formerly gave access to the Blackfriars. The laying of a new gas-main from the junction of Best Lane and the High Street to beyond the block of shops called 'The Weavers' (nos. 1–3 St. Peter's Street) exposed part of the medieval fabric of the King's Bridge and parts of the church of All Saints. Up to three metres below the High Street, a continuation of the sewer tunnel, which exposed part of the fabric of the St. George's Roman bath-house (recorded in *The Archaeology of Canterbury*, vol. vii) was observed by the writer. This unusual and often hazardous operation revealed a further sixteen Roman walls, a major Roman street and elements of what may prove to be parts of Canterbury's Roman Forum. Part of a well-preserved stone-paved Roman portico with gutter blocks, discovered during building work at no. 9 High Street may also be associated with the Forum complex. Major Roman street-metallings were recorded during the lowering of cellars under nos. 14–15 Best Lane and no. 44 Burgate Street. A complex sequence of medieval cellars under no. 44 Burgate Street was also recorded. The final three sites included in this volume were excavated by the Trust in advance of redevelopment. Two sites close to the intersection of St. John's Lane and Marlowe Avenue produced a complex sequence of archaeological levels dating from the early Roman period to the present. The final site on the north-west side of the Dane John Gardens, though badly disturbed by extensive landscaping from the sixteenth to late eighteenth century, provided tangible evidence for the existence of a motte and bailey castle in the Dane John area.

A considerable vote of thanks is extended to all who took part in the work incorporated in this volume, and to the various experts who have provided the specialist reports on the finds. The small finds and pottery were drawn by Mark Duncan, Mark Ellam and Rebecca Mair, and most of the publication plans and sections are the work of Jonathan Rady and John Bowen. Gratitude is also expressed to Jane Elder for typing successive drafts of the text.

PAUL BENNETT

PART I: EXTRA-MURAL SITES

IA. OLD PARK, STURRY ROAD

In the summer of 1952 a trench coded C XXII OP was dug in old gravel-workings in Old Park along the Sturry Road about 1½ miles north-east of Canterbury. Concrete foundations had already been noticed here by Frank Jenkins, who drew the site to attention.

A wall 3 ft. 6 in. thick was found; it was built of gravel and flints set in mortar. The foundations were trench-built into a deposit of gravel (Fig. 2 (6)) and its inner face was rendered with white mortar except where it had been burnt and the facing had come away, leaving red burnt flints visible. The function of the building was difficult to determine but several considerations led to the initial supposition that it had been a reservoir: the surface inside the building was *c.* 4 ft. lower than that outside, the walls were very thick and the building was positioned above a large spring overlooking the city. But this solution was disproved by the discovery that the structure possessed only a loam floor 2–3 in. thick (5); this would have been incapable of holding water. Thus the function of the building remains obscure and its date is uncertain.[1] Three fragments of slightly curved coarse brick (Fig. 68, Nos. 37–39) were found in the floor (5), similar to those found roofing a tile-kiln at North Grange, Meaux (Yorkshire)[2] although these last were straight, not curved. The structure was probably erected in the mid fourteenth century, sherds of this date being found actually in the floor and beneath it in layer (6) (Fig. 81, Nos. 178–179).

No dating evidence was recovered from the destruction-layer (3), comprising mortar debris and large flints and chalk blocks, which overlay the northern part of the loam floor and ran up to the wall. Above this deposit lay dumps of earthy gravel (2 and 1), in which seventeenth- and eighteenth-century pottery was found.

IB. THE STONE BUILDING: SURVEY 1984

The building was revisited and surveyed by members of the Canterbury Archaeological Trust in February 1984[3] (Fig. 3 and Pl. 1). Considerable disturbance to the area surrounding the structure has taken place in the years following Professor Frere's excavation. Trenches cut around the outside of the building, probably by the military, have led to the erosion of a large part of the structure and the complete collapse of the north-east end and the north corner. The ground surface inside the building has also been reduced and a number of depressions showing at the present time indicate that holes may have been dug within the structure itself. The

---

1. There is no documentary evidence for a building here. Information from W. Urry.
2. *Med. Arch.*, v (1961), 137–68.
3. The survey was conducted by Messrs. J. Bowen, J. Rady and the writer.

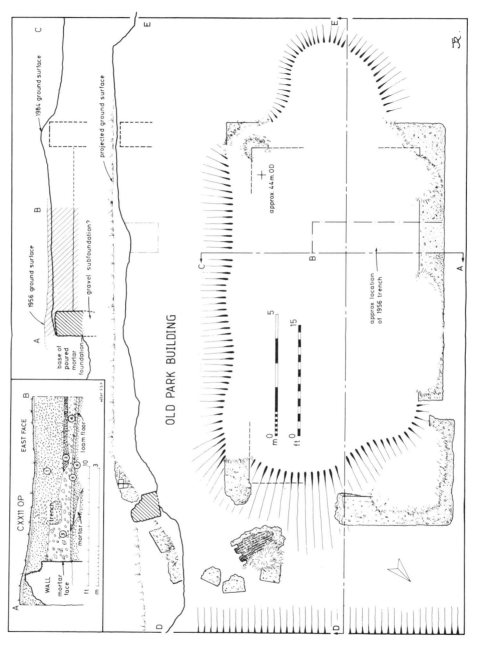

Fig. 2.   The Old Park Stone Building (Site C XXII OP): Plan, section and profiles. (Scale 1:150)

north-west wall of the building, exposed to the base of its footings, is badly weathered and will probably collapse in the near future.

The building aligned with its long axis north-east to south-west measures internally 13.65 m. (*c*. 45 ft.) by 6.65 m. (*c*. 22 ft.), with walls on average 1.00–1.10 m. thick (*c*. 3 ft. 6 in.). Internal stone quoins were observed in the south-east, south and south-west corners of the structure.

The collapsed portion of wall enabled an evaluation of the construction method. A large construction pit of vertical sides was cut and the walls built up from the base of the cutting. Flints were laid, defining the internal face of the wall and the wall-core of small flints and pebbles set in a hard mortar deposited behind the flintwork, up against the face of the cutting. Approximately four internal face-flint courses were laid at each stage of foundation construction.

The surviving fabric of the building represents only foundation work (no external face or external quoins survive), probably for a rectangular stone house of which only the cellar or undercroft survives. The considerable disturbances to the area surrounding the building have severely weakened the structure, and it is hoped a complete excavation of this curious building will take place in the near future.

II. THE CONDUIT HOUSE: THE CATHEDRAL WATER SUPPLY[4]

The Cathedral Conduit House is located approximately one kilometre (1,400 yds.) north-east of the cathedral precincts and some 35 m. (113 ft.) south-east of Canterbury Sports Centre (formerly the garrison indoor riding school) at the north end of Military Road (Fig. 3). Following repairs to the building in July 1981,[5] the Canterbury Archaeological Trust, with the encouragement of the Dean and Chapter of Canterbury Cathedral,[6] conducted a survey of the existing ducts, which formerly channelled spring water to the Conduit House. Three ducts extending north-east, east and south of the Conduit House were located, together with a number of brick-built catchment and filter tanks. The relocation of these conduits, which received water from springs situated on the 25 m. (82 ft.) contour inside the 'Old Park' and clearance of the various tanks, indicated that the entire system could be made operable. In early December 1982 a small team[7] financed by the Dean and Chapter commenced work on the north-eastern duct. This operation, which necessitated an excavation of the entire conduit and a replacement of the old timber drain with a plastic pipe,[8] lasted until February 1983. Repairs to the eastern and southern conduits were also undertaken at this time.

---

4. For a fuller discussion of the documentary evidence, see T. Tatton-Brown 'The Precincts Water Supply', in *Canterbury Cathedral Chronicle*, (1983), 45–52.

5. 'Interim Report on Excavations, 1981, by the Canterbury Archaeological Trust', in *Arch. Cant.*, xcvii (1981), 292–3.

6. Our grateful thanks are extended to Canon Derek Ingram-Hill, without whose enthusiastic encouragement, this work would not have been undertaken.

7. The hardworking team included Mike and Hilary Lubin, Simon Pratt and Ian Anderson. Much hard work was also carried out by Marion Green, Luc Lepers, Wes McLaughlin, Alan Ward and Andrew Webster.

8. The repairs to the water system were effected by members of the Cathedral Works Department. Our thanks are extended to Mr Brian Lemar and his staff for the considerable assistance they have given us at every stage of the work.

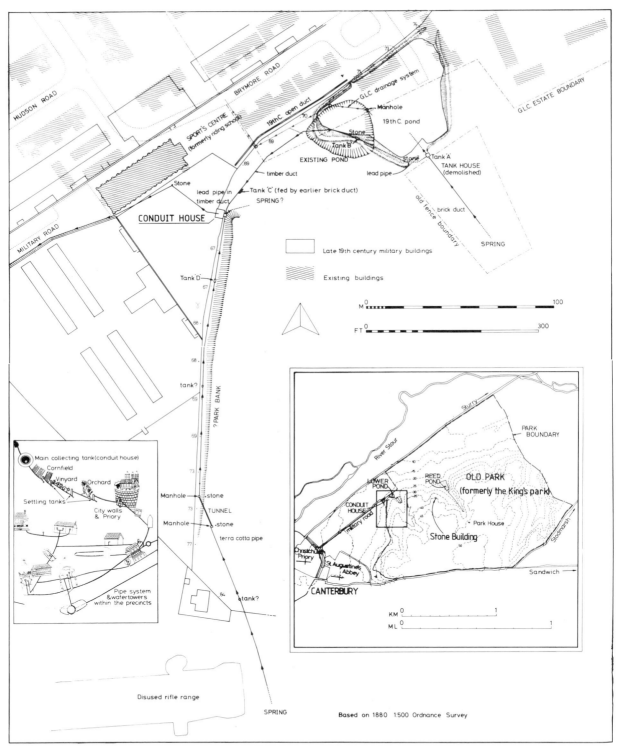

Fig. 3.   Location maps of the Old Park, with Cathedral Conduit House and pipe system. Inset map taken from the Wibert's Waterworks plan of *c.* 1160–65. (Scale: 1:2,000)

The refurbished system of ducts now produces a considerable head of water at Conduit House, sufficient to warrant the construction of an overflow system, which was completed by the cathedral works department late in 1983. In late January 1984, a final blocked pipe, east of the precincts under Broad Street was cleared and at the time of writing spring water once again flows through a system of conduits, tanks and pipes to the cathedral; a functioning water-supply that was first established by Prior Wibert over eight hundred years ago.

The Geology

The 1:50,000 geological map of the area,[9] shows that the escarpment and higher ground to the east and south-east of the Conduit House is formed of Palaeocene (Tertiary) Thanet Beds, capped to the east by a small area of Woolwich Beds. These are both overlain by middle-level gravels of the third terrace of the River Stour.

The memoir for the district notes that springs occur at the base of the escarpment, along the contact zone between clay and overlying sands within the Thanet Beds. The sands of both the Woolwich and Thanet Beds are up to 15 m. thick, fine-grained and generally poorly cemented. The Terrace deposits are usually of gravel or sand with rare lenses of brickearth. The whole hill contained within the 'Old Park' area therefore comprises good unconfined aquifer material. Further work on the geology of this area will eventually enable a detailed estimate to be made for the potential and consistency of the supply of spring water to the Conduit House.[10]

The Wibert System

Of the original twelfth-century system nothing has yet been found. Extensive disturbances to the landscape by the military in the nineteenth and early twentieth centuries and more recent developments in the area by the Greater London Council and others have probably removed most traces of it. The present Conduit House probably occupies the site of, and incorporates, part of the original Conduit House which appears in the famous Waterworks plan of *c*. 1160,[11] as a circular structure marked 'turris' (see Fig. 3). The original water source may have been a spring located approximately 820 m. (900 yds.) due east of the present Conduit House in the 'Old Park'. This spring issuing from the 35 m. (115 ft.) contour flowed north-westwards into a large pond, which still survives as the Reed Pond and may have been part of the medieval system. A second smaller pond, which survives today as an overgrown waterlogged depression, is shown on the 1880 Ordnance Survey map as a much larger earthwork which may also be part of the medieval system. The nineteenth-century pond, located 65 m. (213 ft.) north-east of the Conduit House had a break in the north-western bank indicating the possible location of a sluice. An open duct which flanked the north-western side of the pond may have originally carried water from the pond to the Conduit House. The upper and lower ponds may have originally been connected to one another by a similar duct which no longer survives. The southern end of this possible aqueduct joining the two ponds may have been constructed on a bank which was later re-used in part as the park boundary. The bank may, however, have been

9. *Geological Survey of Great Britain*, H.M.S.O. 1962. Geology of the country around Canterbury and Folkestone. I.G.S. Geological map, sheet 289. Solid and Drift Edition 1982.
10. My thanks to Mr D. Hone for supplying this information.
11. R. Willis, 'The architectural History of the Conventual Buildings of the Monastery of Christ Church in Canterbury', *Arch. Cant.*, vii (1868), 158–83.

constructed when the King's Park was laid out in the mid sixteenth century. Water from a second spring, located some 270 m. (295 yds.) south-east of the present Conduit House may also have been exploited in the medieval period. The Park bank (which is best preserved south of the Conduit House) may again have originally supported a duct linking the spring to the Conduit House.

The Waterworks plan indicates that the spring water was piped below ground from the Conduit House down the line of present Military Road to the Precincts (Fig. 3). The pipe, which in the mid twelfth century passed through agricultural ground (marked '*campus*' depicted with a representation of growing corn, '*vinea*' with growing vines and '*pomm*' i.e. *pommerium* shown as fruit trees) is also indicated as interrupted by five filter tanks, with the last tank of the series placed against the city wall, inside which is a crenellated tower.[12]

The Conduit House

The Conduit House, partly demolished by vandals in 1980, was cleared of rubble and prepared for renovation work in July 1981.[13] Although no traces of definite twelfth-century fabric were discovered, later medieval flintwork and dressed stones (e.g. the door jambs and a possible window lintel) were observed, together with brick, stone and flintwork (set in a sort of chequerwork, see Pl. II), which may date from the early seventeenth century. A major episode of repair probably took place in the early nineteenth century when the brick barrel-vaulted roof and supporting piers and the present brick-and-stone floor, lead-lined tanks and conduits were built. The plan of the late-medieval building was probably almost identical to that surviving today, with the exception of a door (now blocked and only partially surviving) which pierced the east wall, probably giving access to a separate filter tank attached to the east side of the Conduit House, and a possible window in the south wall. A timber-and-tile roof may have originally surmounted the late-medieval building.

The north-eastern Supply

The origin of the north-eastern supply is a spring located on the 25 m. (81 ft.) contour, 135 m. (440 ft.) due east of the Conduit House. A badly blocked and as yet uncleared brick-built duct with stone capping feeds water from the spring to a brick and iron filter tank (Tank A, Fig. 4), which is shown on the 1880 Ordnance Survey map. The tank (once covered by a small brick structure, now demolished) and the spring were until fairly recently contained within a fenced enclosure, of which only a few concrete posts survive. The tank is divided into two halves by a vertical iron plate. The northern half of the tank consists of an enclosed brick duct which extends northwards, possibly feeding water into the area formerly covered by the lower pond. The metal plate dividing the receiving tank from the duct has a U-shaped lip on its upper edge, presumably designed to inhibit flotsam from entering the duct. A lead pipe, located slightly lower in the tank than the filter lip, feeds water westwards, towards a second collecting tank (Tank B) situated some 40 m. west of Tank A. Although a link between the two tanks was not proven, a stone marked D.G.P. shown on the 1880 Ordnance Survey map (the stone in fact probably read D.C.P. – Dean and Chapter Pipe) and originally erected to mark the position of

12. For a detailed discussion of the waterworks drawing, see R. Willis *op. cit.*, 158–83.
13. *Arch. Cant.*, xcvii (1981), *op. cit.*, note 5.

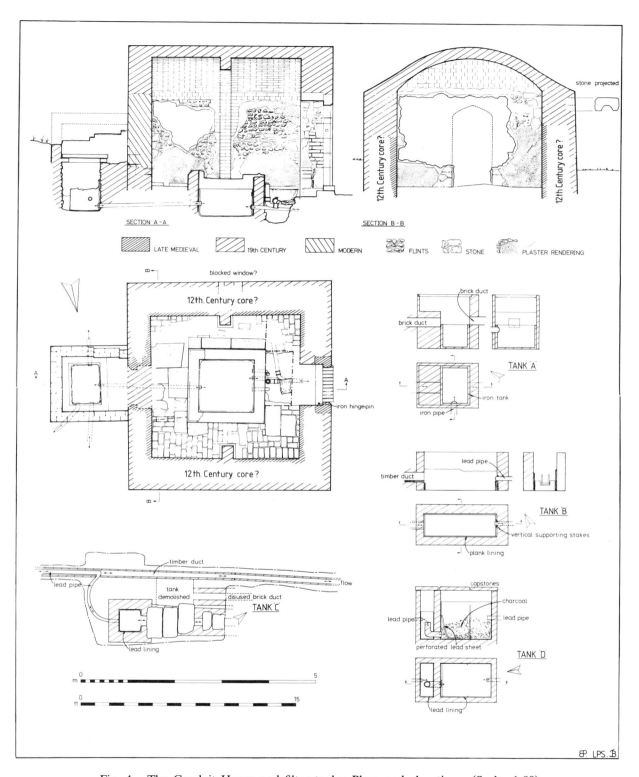

SECTION A - A

SECTION B - B

stone projected

12th. Century core?

12th. Century core?

LATE MEDIEVAL   19th. CENTURY   MODERN   FLINTS   STONE   PLASTER RENDERING

blocked window?

12th. Century core?

12th. Century core?

iron hinge-pin

brick duct

brick duct

TANK 'A'

iron tank

iron pipe

lead pipe

timber duct

TANK 'B'

vertical supporting stakes

plank lining

timber duct

flow

lead pipe

tank
demolished

disused brick duct

TANK 'C'

lead lining

capstones

charcoal

lead pipe

lead pipe

perforated lead sheet

TANK 'D'

lead lining

0   m   5

0   ft   15

BP LPS. B.

Fig. 4. The Conduit House and filter tanks: Plans and elevations. (Scale: 1:80)

an underground pipe from Tank A, follows a direct line to Tank B. This second tank, not shown on the 1880 map, is probably of late nineteenth- or more likely twentieth-century construction. The tank (Fig. 4), brick-built with a timber lining, has a lead pipe feeding water into it from the east and a 'French' drain of timber construction continuing the flow westwards. The location of the timber duct, which was of contemporary build with Tank B, is marked by an existing stone some 3 m. (9 ft. 10 in.) west of Tank B which is also shown on the 1880 map. In the area now contained within the fenced boundary of the G.L.C. housing estate (built in the 1970s) the timber duct was poorly preserved. Long sections of duct had been crushed and disturbed by earth-moving machinery and in one place the duct had been cut through by a cast-iron 'French' drain. This section of conduit (from Tank B to Tank C), which was probably damaged during the construction of the housing estate, was replaced with a plastic pipe in 1982. The old pond was probably infilled and substantially levelled when the estate was built and a new system of manholes and drains was built to take spring water away from the new buildings to a stormwater drain under Brymore Road. South-west of the estate fence, the duct survived intact, and continued on a south-west alignment for a further 20 m. (c. 66 ft.), to a point where a lead pipe had been inserted into the timber conduit. A larger-scale excavation was undertaken at this point, and two earlier brick conduits and tanks were encountered. The remains of a brick duct, which had been substantially removed, originally fed into a small square tank of which only the brick floor remained. A lead pipe may have connected this early tank to the Conduit House. The second brick tank survived substantially intact, with capstones still overlying both tank and duct. The tank had a lead lining and a lead pipe presumably connected it to the Conduit House. At a later stage, during the life of the timber 'French' drain, a new lead pipe was installed and a connection between this new pipe and the redundant tank was effected, presumably to take advantage of a supply of water which still flowed through the old conduit. The piped system then continued south-westwards to the collecting tank attached to the east side of the Conduit House. This lead-lined tank which is also of nineteenth-century brick construction, originally had a barrel-vaulted roof and may reflect continuity of a bi-partite system of tanks at the Conduit House from the late medieval period to the present day.

The eastern Supply
The area immediately east of the Conduit House was considerably disturbed by deep military trenches and earthworks which had undoubtedly severed the supply. Nevertheless, until recently, the only water entering the ruined Conduit House came from a surface spring flowing from this area. Attempts to locate the source of the spring close to the Conduit House revealed the remains of a partly demolished brick conduit and a severed lead pipe which had been subsequently inserted into the dismantled conduit. Although this pipe was only traced for approximately 7 m. (23 ft.), to the east, the clearance of this pipe was sufficient to divert the surface water into the pipe system to the collecting tank at the rear of the Conduit House.

The southern Supply
The source for the southern supply is a spring located on the 25 m. (c. 82 ft.) contour, situated some 270 m. (885 ft.) south-south-east of the Conduit House. A c. 15 cm. (6 in.) diameter terra-cotta pipe feeds water from the spring to a substantial brick-built manhole, which leads directly to a long brick-built tunnel 17 m. (56 ft.) (Pl. III) and a second manhole. This elaborate

duct probably built by the Army in the second half of the nineteenth century after damage to the water source by military activities,[14] carries water under the 'Old Park' bank to a point 155 m. (c. 508 ft.) due south of the Conduit House. A lead pipe continues the system from the second manhole to a filter tank (Tank D), situated 35 m. (115 ft.) south of the Conduit House. This brick-built tank with lead lining, divided by a brick wall into two unequal halves, contained a mass of charcoal in its southern half and had a removable perforated lead screen *in situ* against the partition wall. A U-shaped pipe, built into the dividing wall and protected by the lead screen, feeds water from the main tank (and the charcoal filter) into the second smaller lead-lined tank. A lead pipe then continues the flow northwards to the Conduit House.

The late nineteenth- or early twentieth-century Maps of the Water Supply
Besides the 1880 Ordnance Survey map, two other maps show details of the duct system feeding the Conduit House. These maps, probably drawn in the late nineteenth or early twentieth century by the military (at a scale of 1:1200) and the (now Mid-Kent) Water Company[15] (at a scale of 1:2500), were extensively used during the initial fieldwork. The 1:1200 map clearly shows the receiving tank for the north-eastern supply and a conduit leading from a spring to the south of it, but does not show either the lower pond or a tank interrupting the duct leading to the Conduit House. The eastern supply is shown as a 3-in. (7.6 cm.) lead pipe extending some 30.5 m. (100 ft.) into the disturbed ground behind the Conduit House. A further two 'catch pits' are shown interrupting the pipe for the southern supply, these being located 61 m. (200 ft.) and c. 119 m. (390 ft.) respectively from the Conduit House. Both tanks are shown with an additional pipe leading into them from the east. The pipe run continues from the second catch-pit on a south-east alignment for a further 97.5 m. (320 ft.), where it terminates in the area of a now disused rifle range. The 1:2500 map shows the collecting tank for the north-eastern supply, the lower pond and an intermediate (plank-lined) tank (noted as 'filter tank'). The eastern supply is not shown and a series of four tanks are depicted interrupting the southern supply, which also terminates in the area of the disused rifle range. Overall the two plans not only contain conflicting information, but the details on both maps are inaccurately plotted and do not agree with tank and duct positions found during the survey work. Despite these anomalies the approximate position of tanks shown on the drawings, but not found during the fieldwork, has been located on the overall plan (Fig. 3).

From the Conduit House a three-inch diameter (7.6 cm.) lead pipe runs out westwards towards the Sports Centre. Just before it reaches the building it turns abruptly south-west (the spot is marked by a stone inscribed D.C.P. – this stone is also shown on the 1880 Ordnance Survey map) and then runs down Military Road to a point some 375 m. (c. 1,230 ft.) north-east of the Precincts where a manhole containing two stop-cocks and an overflow pipe interrupt the pipe run. From this point the pipe continues to the city wall and beyond to a second stop-cock and overflow pipe just outside no. 5, The Forrens. A detailed survey of the water system within the Cathedral Precincts is currently being conducted.[16]

14. The Chapter Minutes record damage by the Army to a water pipe in 1868.
15. We are grateful to Mr Gordon Evans of the Mid Kent Water Company for supplying us (via the late John Hayes) with copies of these plans.
16. Briefly discussed by T.W.T. Tatton-Brown in *op. cit.*, note 4.

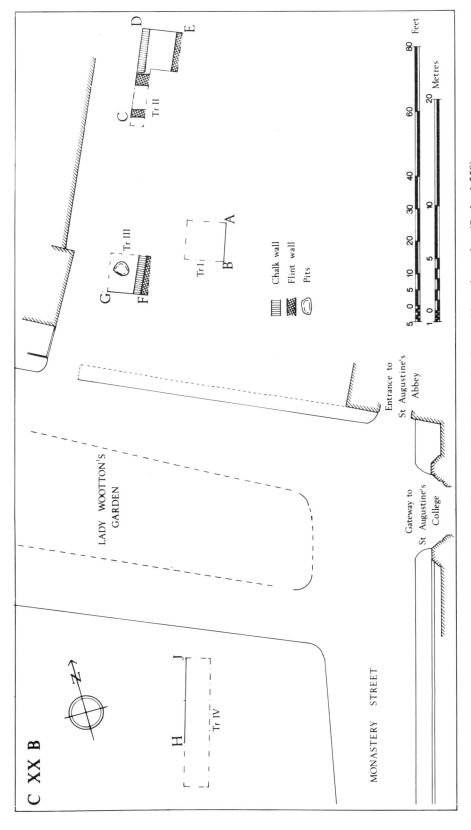

Fig. 5 Lady Wootton's Green (C XX B): Plan showing position of trenches (Scale: 1:350).

III. LADY WOOTTON'S GREEN

In the summer of 1951 four trenches were dug outside the Quenin Gate in Lady Wootton's Green (Fig. 5). The site code was C XX B.

Trench I

Only in Trench I was excavation continued below the thick medieval levels and here four Roman inhumations and a cremation burial were found (Fig. 6). These were evidently from a cemetery just outside the town adjoining the road leading to Richborough.[17] There was very little evidence for Saxon occupation in the area, contrary to expectation.

The Roman Burials (Fig. 6)

The earliest feature was an irregular shallow gravel-pit filled with brown gravelly loam (Fig. 7, Section A–B (11 and 18)) which yielded two samian sherds, Dr. 27, of probably Flavian date and Dr. 37 of *c.* A.D. 85–105 together with some coarse ware sherds of the late first or early second century (Fig. 80, Nos. 143–145). Into this filling had been cut the inhumation-graves. Inhumation 1 lay in a clearly-defined grave with a filling of dark sticky soil and was sealed by a layer of dark loam (10 and 14) which yielded late fourth-century sherds and also a Saxon cooking-pot sherd.

Dr H.A. Treble saw the skeleton *in situ* and thought that it was a male of fairly large stature aged between 25 and 30. The bones were lying naturally but the skeleton was disturbed; the left tibia was missing, the left arm was missing above the elbow, fragments of rib covered the knees and the head was bent forward. It is difficult to account for this disturbance since the grave filling itself and layer 10 above it seemed undisturbed; but the burial was sealed for a long period only by the 4 inches of layer 10, during which time cultivation may have occurred; alternatively, the burial was disturbed quite soon after inhumation by the insertion of the nearby cremation-burial over Inhumation 2.

The second inhumation (Fig. 7, Section A–B) also lay in a grave cut into layer 18 which was filled with dark damp loamy soil containing many pebbles. The skeleton, a male, was complete. The feet were horizontal and the position of the pelvis indicated that he was lying on his back. Into the top of the grave had been inserted a cremation-burial accompanied by a second vessel. The top of the cremation vessel (Fig. 80, No. 147) had been tightly packed with burnt flints; it is a beaker with date range of *c.* A.D. 120–200. The smaller vessel (Fig. 80, No. 148) is not closely datable but would seem to belong to the first half of the second century. Both lay about 1 ft. above the earlier skeleton.

Inhumation 3 lay just south of and parallel to Grave 2, by which it had probably been disturbed. The lower part of the skeleton was still in place but the upper part above the pelvis and three lower vertebrae were missing.

---

17.   The discovery of a Roman tombstone (*RIB* 43) outside the Great Gate of St. Augustine's Abbey in 1922 and of two cremations inside the Great Gate in 1981 (*Arch. Cant.*, xcvii (1981), 318–24) is further evidence for a cemetery here.

Grave 4 was very disturbed and all that remained was a pile of bones in the south-west corner of the trench; the pelvis and femur were detached and the vertebrae shattered. The cause of the disturbance was unknown.

Date of the Inhumations
Dating evidence was not plentiful, but the inhumations are later than the Flavian-Trajanic samian sherd in layer 18 and Inhumation 2 is earlier than the cremation burial whose outside limits are *c.* 120–200.

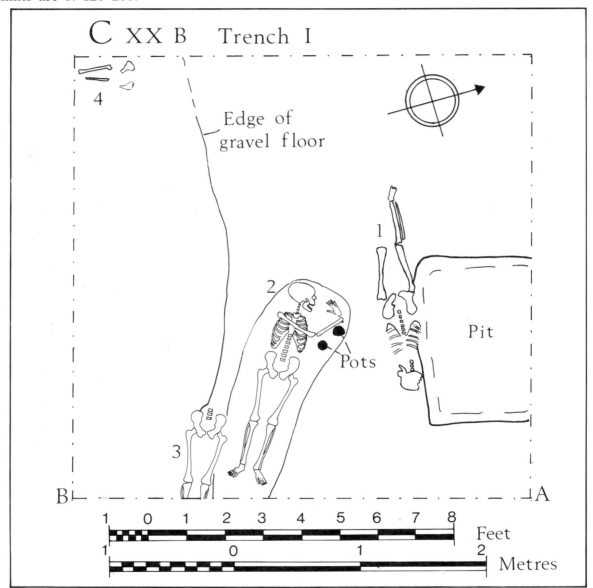

Fig. 6.   Lady Wootton's Green: Plan of Trench I (Scale: 1:30).

Post-Roman

Overlying layer 14 was a pebble floor (13) in the south part of the trench; it ended irregularly about 3 ft. from the edge of the excavation. On it lay Saxon cooking-pot sherds of ninth- to tenth-century date, including a rim as Canterbury Lane,[18] No. 345; but the occupation-soil (8) above it yielded a sherd of Group II cooking-pot[19] of the later eleventh century. In the north-east corner of the trench part of a second gravel floor appeared on which lay a thin deposit of sandy light-coloured loam (9); this yielded some sherds of late Saxon pottery of ninth- to tenth-century date including a rim as Canterbury Lane, No. 344. Above this was a thick accumulation of dark soil (7) containing many late eleventh-century sherds of Group II, and Pit 2 which cut the layer also yielded sherds of this date. Layer 7 was sealed by a cobbled surface (6) on which lay the remains of a fallen flint wall (5). Sherds of bright green-glazed yellow ware of Tudor date lay on the surface of 6, and suggested that the wall may have had some connection with the Monastery and have been demolished after the Dissolution.

The only other features in this trench were pits and the brick floor of a yard.

Trench II

At least two successive medieval buildings were observed in Trench II (Fig. 5 and Fig. 7, Sections C–D, D–E) The earliest had a chalk wall and a trodden earth floor (Section D–E (4)) which yielded a fourteenth-century jug sherd and on which there were three burnt loam hearths. This floor sealed a thick deposit of loam and gravel (5) and several pits which were cut into 5. One of these yielded several Group II sherds; similar pottery was found in another pit sealed by the footings of one of the chalk walls. This building was later replaced by one with flint walls. No obviously contemporary floor-levels were uncovered although a very disturbed trodden earth floor was found in the central part of the trench. Possibly the north–south flint wall was external and had a floor on its east side beyond the limits of the trench.

Later a building with brick walls and a brick floor was erected on the site.

Trench III

A similar sequence of medieval buildings was noted in Trench III (Fig. 7, Section F–G). No walls contemporary with the earliest building were found; it had a gravel floor (4). This sealed a black sticky occupation-material (5) beneath which was Pit 6. Layer 5 yielded a nearly complete Andenne jar of the twelfth or thirteenth century (Fig. 80, No. 149; Pl. XXX) together with a bone flute (Fig. 66, No. 22; Pl. XXVII); and Pit 6 contained cooking-pot sherds of the second half of the twelfth century. Above the floor was a thick chalk and flint deposit (3) yielding late thirteenth-century sherds; into this the chalk walls of the next building on the site were inserted. Any floors contemporary with this chalk building had been removed when later a building with

18. *The Archaeology of Canterbury*, vol. vii.
19. For some medieval pottery from Canterbury it is convenient to use the classification of the groups discussed in *Arch. Cant.*, lxviii (1954), 128 ff. The dating of these has been adjusted to be as follows:

Group I	*c.* 975–1025
Group II	*c.* 1050–1100
Group III	*c.* 1080–1150
Group IV	*c.* 1250–1300

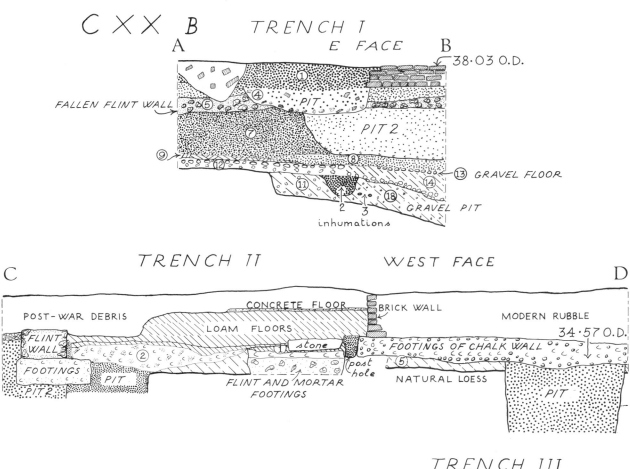

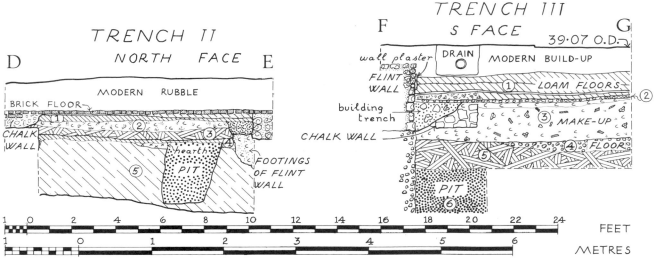

Fig. 7. Lady Wootton's Green: Sections. (Scale: 1:50)

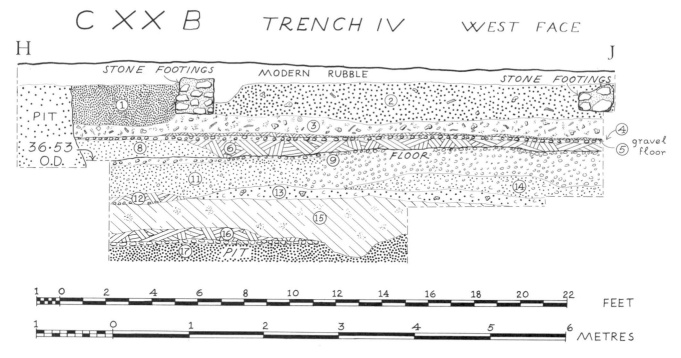

Fig. 8. Lady Wootton's Green: Section, Trench IV. (Scale: 1:50)

flint walls was erected. The foundation-trench of the new north–south wall largely destroyed the earlier chalk wall, the line of which had been *c.* 1 ft. to the west. Three successive stony loam floors (1) were contemporary with the flint wall. Subsequent levels were modern.

Trench IV (Figs. 5 and 8)

The excavation of Trench IV was incomplete because of bad weather and an unexpected depth of medieval deposits. The lowest level examined was a pit (17) which yielded a rim sherd of the eleventh century. It was filled with black sticky earth and was partly sealed by a chalk floor bounded by stake-holes 1½ in. in diameter and 8 in. deep and elsewhere by a pebble layer. Above this was a black charcoally layer (16), in which a Saxon gold pin of the seventh century (Pl. XXVII, F–H) was found together with sherds of the late twelfth or early thirteenth century; overlying 16 were thick yellow earth and yellow mortar fragments (15), earth and chalk (13) and pebbly layers (14) and (11), all containing sherds similar in date to those in 16. Two successive gravel floors, separated by an occupation layer (6), sealed 11. Layer 6 yielded only residual pottery, but layer 8, powdery earth also lying on the lower floor, contained sherds of the later thirteenth or the fourteenth century. The lower of these floors sealed a gully 7–8 in. deep and 10–11 in. wide which was filled with silty sand. The upper floor yielded thirteenth- or fourteenth-century jug sherds and on it was a thin occupation-deposit (4) containing many oyster shells. No walls contemporary with the floors were found.

Above 4 was a plastery layer of rubble (3) which yielded part of a brick 1.8 in. thick, and measuring 4.1 in. wide by more than 5 in. long, together with a fourteenth-century jug sherd; layer 3 was sealed by a spread of soft dark earth containing tile and flint fragments (2). Two lines of stone footings were cut into this but no contemporary floor-levels survived.

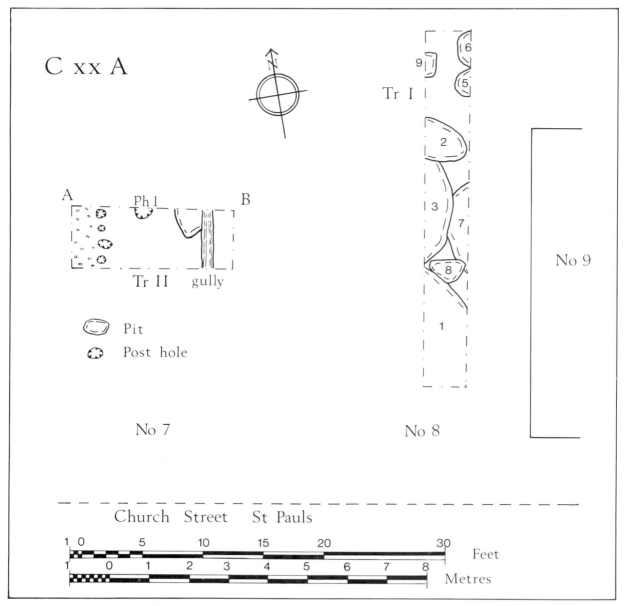

Fig. 9.   Church Street (St. Paul's) (C XX A): Plan (Scale: 1:95).

IV. NOS. 7 AND 8 CHURCH STREET (ST. PAUL'S)

In the summer of 1951 two small trenches were excavated opposite St. Paul's Church in Church Street outside the defences on the east side of the city. The site code was C XX A. The space available for excavation was small: Trench I was dug in the cellar of no. 8 and Trench II just behind the small cellar of no. 7 (Fig. 9).

There was evidence for two main periods of Roman occupation; the first at the end of the first century, the second in the fourth century.

Trench I

Between Pits 2 and 9 (Fig. 9) a layer of brown discoloured loam, 4–6 in. thick and containing chalk fragments and charcoal, overlay the natural subsoil. No dating evidence was recovered, but Belgic pottery was found in later pits and it seems probable that this layer was a Belgic field.

Nine pits were excavated. Pits 5, 6 and 7 were Roman; Pits 5 and 6 yielded sherds of Flavian samian Dr. 27 and Pit 7 a coin of Gallienus. Pit 4 produced a late Saxon sherd (Fig. 81, No. 169) as did Pit 9; Pit 3 was probably late thirteenth-century and Pit 1 fifteenth-century. Pit 2 (which yielded a halfpenny of the eighteenth or nineteenth century) and Pit 8 were relatively recent.

Trench II

A yellow gravel floor (Fig. 10 (9)), into which a post-hole (Fig. 9, post-hole 1) was cut, lay above a thin deposit of dirty loam covering the natural subsoil and similar to that in Trench I. At the west end of the trench this floor was covered with charcoally material (8A) which yielded sherds of samian dating down to early Flavian times (Dr. 15R, Dr. 30, Dr. 29) together with contemporary coarse wares (Fig. 81, No. 150). Above this was grey ashy occupation-earth (8) which at the east end of the trench lay directly on the floor. This deposit produced samian extending slightly later in date (Dr. 18R, 27, 18, 30 (early Flavian), 29 (c. A.D. 65–80) and 18, 27, 67 (Flavian)) together with a large group of coarse wares (Fig. 81, Nos. 151–162) of the period c. A.D. 80–110. Thus the floor represents a late first-century house. Above layer 8 was a possible loam floor (not visible on Fig. 10) overlying which was a deposit of dark earth (6B and 7) in which a coin of Constantine II and a number of sherds of late fourth-century pottery (Fig. 81, Nos. 163–167) were found. The western part of this was covered by a rather indistinct pebbly surface which may perhaps have been the rough floor of a late Roman hut; a line of four post-holes (Fig. 9) bordered its east edge. At the east end of the trench a pit and gully were cut into layer 6B. The gully yielded a red colour-coated bowl (Fig. 81, No. 168). These features, the post-holes and layer 6B itself were sealed by dark earth and charcoal (6) which yielded more fourth-century sherds and a coin of Valens.

The late Roman layers were covered by a thick medieval deposit of very dark brown soil (Fig. 10 (4)) which yielded a number of sherds of twelfth- and early thirteenth-century date (Fig. 81, Nos. 170–173) and into which Pit 1 and a post-hole were cut. This deposit was sealed by a layer of chalk and flint make-up (3) supporting a loam floor (2) in which several fourteenth-century sherds (Fig. 81, Nos. 176–177) were found. At the west end of the trench a layer of dirty green fine loam (3A) lay immediately below the floor; it yielded more fourteenth-century sherds (Fig. 81, Nos. 174–175).

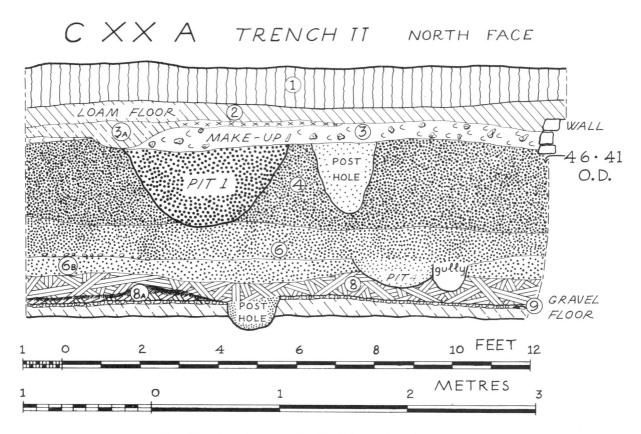

Fig. 10.   Church Street (St. Paul's): Section. (Scale: 1:30)

V. NO. 7 ST. GEORGE'S PLACE

In the summer of 1952 a north–south trench, coded C XXII G, was dug behind the cellar of no. 7 St. George's Place, below the concrete floor of a garden room.

Nothing of significance was uncovered and no plans or sections drawn. Two sherds of samian and several pieces of thirteenth-century pottery were found just above the natural subsoil, and it was clear that any Roman or medieval layers which may have existed had been destroyed by later gardening activity.

VI. NO. 1 OATEN HILL COURT

Introduction (Fig. 11)

In July 1983 during the cutting of foundation trenches for a new house in the back garden of nos. 1 and 2 Oaten Hill Court (a site fronting on to Cossington Road) elements of two late medieval chalk-block-constructed cellars possibly associated with St. Sepulchre's Nunnery were exposed. This site had been extensively disturbed in more recent times; no stratigraphy associated with the masonry structures was found and only the deeply cut features survived.

The Nunnery

The site is situated inside an area once covered by St. Sepulchre's Nunnery, in a position some 25 m. (81 ft.) south-east of the proposed location of the nunnery main gate. The nunnery was probably jointly founded by St. Anselm and William Cauldwell (Cauvel) in the late eleventh century,[20] on land belonging to St. Augustine's Abbey and had a parochial church attached to it under the patronage of Christ Church Priory. The small establishment, which was poor for the greater part of its life, housed a lady Prioress and five or six nuns. The nunnery was dissolved in 1536 and many of the major buildings were probably destroyed at that time and their exact location lost. The nunnery boundary wall and a range of buildings on the Oaten Hill frontage probably survived into the eighteenth century. One of the earliest maps of Canterbury showing this area (*c.* 1640), depicts two gates interrupting the boundary wall on the Oaten Hill frontage. The gate on the north-west, flanked by road-frontage buildings, may have been the main gate and gatehouse range giving access to the nunnery (located at the present intersection of Oaten Hill and Cossington Road). The second gate, situated in the south-west corner of the enclosure on the Oaten Hill frontage, may have given access to the parochial church and cemetery.

The Cellars

Two late medieval cellars and a wall foundation were exposed during trench-cutting for the new building. Both cellars had mortared chalk-block walls rendered on the internal faces with lime-washed plaster. The cellar located against the Cossington Road frontage (Fig. 11, Sections A–B and B–C) was probably aligned with long axis north-east to south-west and was 2.6 m. (8 ft. 6 in.) wide. The north-east and north-west walls were built of mortared chalk blocks faced internally with plaster. The south-east wall consisted only of plaster-rendered natural brick-earth, indicating that a light timber frame may have existed above this wall. A rebate cut back into the natural brickearth and lined with a mixture of roofing-tile and plaster originally housed a vertical post, which presumably supported the ground plate for the ground-floor frame. A stone pad on which the original post rested was found *in situ* at cellar floor level, some 1.60 m. (5 ft. 3 in.) below the present ground surface. The cellar backfill, a one-period dump of disturbed brickearth and loam, overlay a deposit of yellow sand which may have been a bedding for a tiled floor (a number of broken yellow glazed floor-tiles were recovered from the cellar backfill).

The second cellar, aligned with long axis north-west to south-east was 1.80 m. (*c.* 6 ft.) wide

---

20. *V.C.H.* (Kent), ii (1926), 142–4.

Fig. 12.   No. 1 Oaten Hill Court: Stone architectural fragments (Scale: approx. ⅛).

and survived to a maximum depth of 2.25 m. (7 ft. 4 in.) below the present ground surface. A fragment of the four-centred barrel-vaulted roof survived, indicating a maximum cellar height of c. 1.75 m. (5 ft. 8 in.). This cellar remained in use into the seventeenth century when a brick pier was constructed inside the cellar to support the north-west corner of a brick-built barn. The cellar was finally backfilled with domestic rubbish and hardcore in the nineteenth century.

The Wall Foundation

Of contemporary build with the second cellar was a crushed chalk wall foundation 0.90 m. (3 ft.) wide and 0.50 m. (1 ft. 8 in.) deep. The foundation, aligned north-east to south-west, abutted the cellar's north-east wall, and may have been for a building incorporating the cellar at its south-west end.

The Barn

The remains of a seventeenth-century barn built in English bonded-brickwork and incorporating a number of Caen stone blocks and architectural fragments (Fig. 12) was recorded on this site in 1980. One substantially intact wall, aligned north-west to south-east and probably the north-west wall of a building shown on W. and H. Doidge's (1752) map of Canterbury (inset in Fig. 11) was completely demolished early in the development process before a watching brief was established. This wall represented one of the few surviving fragments of a large seventeenth-century barn which may have re-used elements of other medieval buildings. A fragment of a medieval flint wall was observed buried in the barn's west wall in 1980. Sadly, no further details of this wall or the relationship between wall and cellar survived the demolition, as the barn walls were shallow–founded and were completely removed during the machine clearance of the site. The only surviving detail for this wall consisted of a brick pier built into the south-eastern corner of the second late-medieval cellar in the seventeenth century to support the north-west corner of the barn.

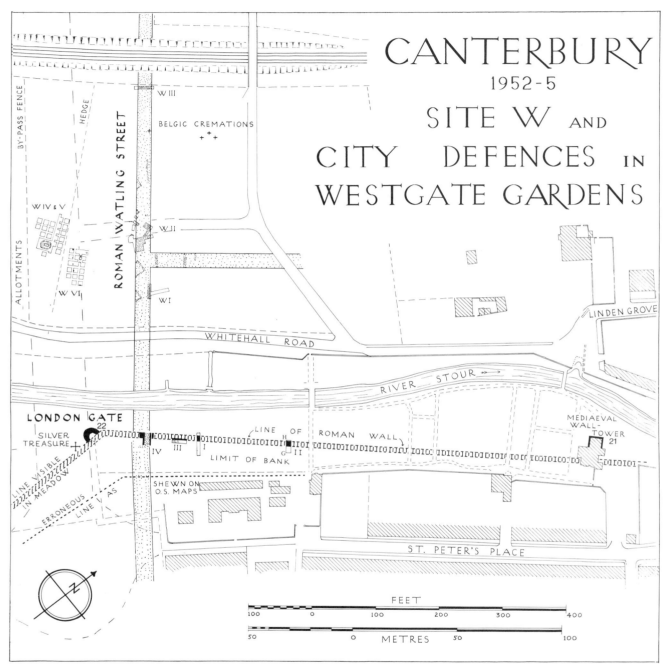

Fig. 13.   Whitehall Road (C XXIV–XXVII W): General plan showing Site W in relation to the city defences in Westgate Gardens (Scale: 1:1,810).

VII. THE WHITEHALL ROAD AREA

Between 1953 and 1955 a number of trenches was cut outside the city wall and beyond the Stour on the north-west side of Whitehall Road (Fig. 13). The area, then covered by meadows, is now occupied by a housing estate and the new ring road. The site codes were C XXIV, C XXV and C XXVI Site W.

Trenches W I–III encountered the Roman Watling Street as it ascended the valley-side from the crossing of the Stour towards Rochester. The dating evidence suggested that it had been built very soon after the conquest, for nothing Roman lay below the metalling. In Trenches W I and W III the street lay directly on the natural subsoil and this suggests that normally the top soil was cleared for the construction of Watling Street. In W II, however, the road overlay a thick Belgic occupation with traces of a building occupying a hollow in the natural brickearth. Two levels of Roman timber buildings bordering the north-east side of the street were found in Trench W I; in the second century there seems to have been a suburb here which may have extended northwards towards the tile and pottery kilns which were discovered near St. Stephen's Road by Dr F. Jenkins.[21] A street branching north-eastwards, at right-angles to Watling Street, was later observed by Dr Jenkins in builders' trenches (Fig. 13), and on the north-west side of this, near the railway a few yards north of the modern lane which crosses the line, two other pottery kilns and a tile kiln have also been recorded (*Arch. Cant.*, lxxiv (1960), 151–61).

Trench W IV, which lay south of and parallel with the hedge and later was developed into a series of squares (W V), revealed secondary Neolithic, Belgic and Roman occupation, including a hut which spanned the transition from Belgic to Romano-British times. Scattered Belgic cremation burials were traced in this area: the ashes were inurned in native butt beakers (Fig. 76, No. 118), and in one grave a second beaker accompanied the burial.

W VI is an area explored in 1956 by a summer school of the London University Extra-mural Department under the direction of Dr F. Jenkins and Mr R.A.H. Farrar. A short summary of this excavation was published by R.A.H. Farrar in *The Archaeological Newsletter*, vi No. 5 (1958), 126, from which it appears that a pottery kiln, pits, a small oven, and a late inhumation burial were discovered, together with some small finds which suggested the vicinity of a shrine.

The Excavations

A. Neolithic
The earliest occupation in the area was Neolithic B. In Trenches W IV and W V (Fig. 16, Section E–F; Fig. 17) shallow scoops filled with light brown and grey loam, rather iron-stained and much permeated by worm holes, were encountered. These produced several sherds of pottery (Fig. 71, No. 1) which belong to an early variety of Neolithic B, of Ebbsfleet type. Some of the scoops could perhaps have been post-holes, but they form no coherent pattern.

---

21. *Antiq. Journ.*, xxxvi (1956), 40–56.

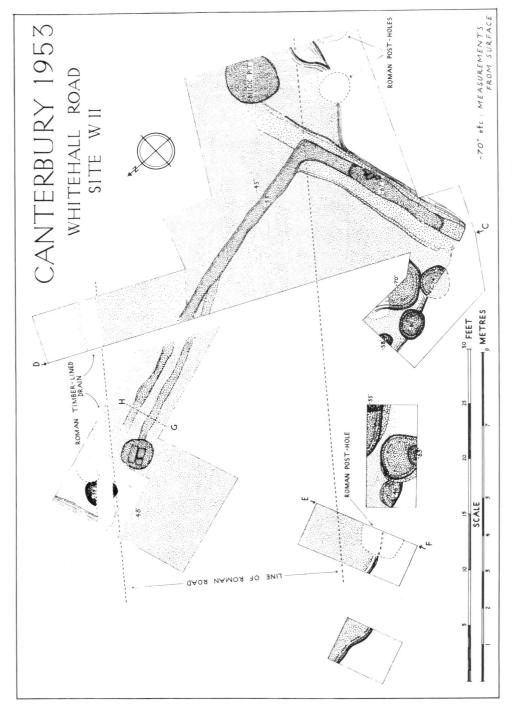

Fig. 14. Site W: Plan Trench II showing pre-Roman Belgic building (Scale: 1:100).

B. **Belgic**

The most interesting features discovered on Site W were Belgic.

Trench W II (Figs. 14, 15; Pl. IV)

Sealed by Watling Street in Trench W II was a thick layer of dark occupation of the pre-Roman Belgic period (Fig. 15, Section C–D (6)) consisting for the most part of grey or black sticky loam but containing ash, burnt daub, and – towards the south side – a layer of yellow loam, possibly collapsed wall-material. Across the top of 6, immediately below the road, was an inch of trampled charcoal and fine bits of daub and ash, suggesting the possibility of the demolition of a structure to make way for the road. When layer 6 had been removed a rectangular slot or foundation-trench was observed in the subsoil. It turned through a right-angle, and later its north-east side was further traced towards the north. It presented every appearance of being two sides of a rectangular building: but despite careful search no trace of the other two sides was found. At the south-west angle the south side ended abruptly. Nearby the excavated area was extended to the north and layer 6 was seen to end against a scarp of brickearth, deep yellowish red in colour and hard to trowel. It seemed to be and was taken for natural soil. It had been scarped away almost vertically, and what appeared to be two post-holes were partly cut through it. They were filled with creamy yellow loam and contained sherds and a few lumps of burnt daub; no hint of a post stain was seen within them, so that if they were post-holes, the post had been extracted and the holes filled with this disturbed clean loam. However, the 'natural' yellow loam was later found to overlie a band of ash seen at the base of post-hole –80 in. (Fig. 14). (These figures indicate depths of each feature from the surface.) The same phenomenon of two Belgic periods was found in Section E–F (Fig. 15) where two bands of ash were found in the yellow loam at a depth of over 6 ft. Time did not allow a full examination. It would seem at any rate that there had been deep disturbance of the natural brickearth in Belgic times all over the site, whatever its purpose, before the main occupation represented by layer 6 took place. If the brick-earth had been dug, e.g. for potters' clay, and the steep sides of the quarry-pits left to fall in, the results would be much as was found. In the next trench post-hole –63 in. (Fig. 14) was full of dark soil and ash and surrounded by hard yellow 'natural' loam: the depression in the eastern corner (–55 in.) seemed to be of earlier date. It is clear that these (?) post-holes make little sense in plan in relation to the foundation-trench, no trace of which was found on the western side. At the south-east end of the site was a Belgic pit sealed below Watling Street (Pl. V). It was about 6 ft. deep and circular, resembling an Iron Age storage pit: its filling consisted mainly of grey loam with charcoal flecks, but the lowest 9 in. of the filling was rather darker. The mouth had been sealed with a 4 in. clay plug before the road-metal had been laid, but this had nevertheless subsided into the top of the pit.

In the vicinity of this pit there was evidence of three Belgic phases: (i) a deep scoop filled with clean greyish-yellow loam; (ii) a shallower scoop above and cut into (i), containing occupation-material (6); (iii) the pit itself which cut through (ii) and whose upcast sealed it. Unfortunately, (i) yielded no useful finds, and the pottery from (iii) is indistinguishable from that from (ii).

With those three phases of occupation clear from the stratigraphy, we may feel confident that the Belgic occupation was a lengthy one; and this deduction is strengthened by the observation that phase (ii) itself lasted sufficiently long for alterations to become necessary to the 'building'. Along much of the east side there were two almost parallel slots of which the more westerly was

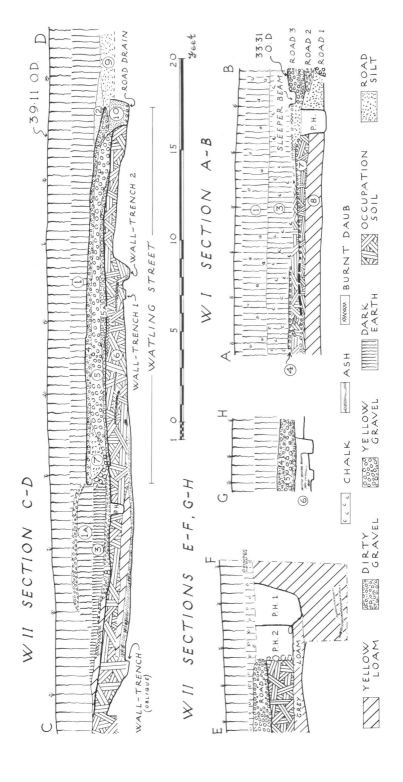

Fig. 15. Site W: Sections, Trenches WI and WII. (Scale:1:50)

the earlier. This conclusion was suggested by Section C–D and demonstrated in G–H (Fig. 15), where the eastern slot is seen to cut down through much of layer 6. In contrast the south wall of the 'building' did not show until the whole of 6 had been removed: the reason for this differential survival of the walls must be due to different treatment at demolition. The timbers of the south wall were removed and their site became silted over, whereas the east wall was more thoroughly burnt.

The later version of the east wall probably ended in a deep post-hole (–59 in.) filled with fine charcoal dust: the earlier ended at a shallower round post-hole which later had been sealed with Belgic tiles (1 ft. 6 in. × 8 in. × 1 in.) because of its softness. These terminal posts suggest that this end of the building had been open. Along the east side there was much ash and charcoal in both slots and especially immediately above the later one. A very large quantity of pottery was found along this side, especially in the more northerly of our trenches. In one place along the outer lip of the slot there was a little sticky creamy clay, which was probably unburnt daub *in situ* and which had not been burnt because it was below contemporary ground-level. There was a layer of burnt daub immediately beneath Watling Street in the south face of this cutting.

Elsewhere (e.g. Section C–D) there were deposits of yellow brick-earth within layer 6, which no doubt represent unburnt and disintegrated daub. The building thus was timber-framed with uprights bedded in the foundation-trench and the interstices plugged with daub. The building occupied a hollow in the brick-earth, perhaps partly caused by earlier quarrying, and when it had been burnt down the pottery and occupation-material settled in the hollow. But the construction of the Roman road must soon have sealed all below it. At the time of excavation such a rectangular building was almost unparalleled in an Iron Age context; recently, W. Rodwell has collected the scattered evidence for others.[22]

The pottery from 6 was in very great quantity (Figs. 72–3, Nos. 2–53) and considerably extends the range of forms already published from Belgic Canterbury.[23] The date-range, however, is comparable. The group includes imported pieces such as amphorae, *terra rubra, terra nigra,* and an Arretine platter, and examples of these occurred in the lowest levels. Moreover, the butt-beakers are of Tiberian rather than Augustan type. An overall span of *c.* A.D. 15–43 seems possible. Some slightly earlier butt-beakers appeared in W V.

Trenches W IV–V (Figs. 16, 17, 18; Pl. VI)
More Belgic occupation was found in Trenches W IV and V. After a preliminary trench (W IV) had revealed an area of occupation south-west of the hedge in the area allocated to the new ring road, a number of squares was opened up in August 1954. Below modern and medieval ploughsoil (1) (Fig. 16, Section C–D) which produced three silver pennies of the fifteenth century (p. 182), lay about 7 in. of brown soil (2) containing much Belgic ware but also a little Roman. It appears to have been cultivated during the Belgic period and to have formed a surface in Roman times: both Belgic and Roman features were cut through it, and if it had been cultivated in Roman times the former would have been obscured; but the presence of Roman sherds below the level of Belgic features cut through the layer implies that it continued to be a

22. Warwick Rodwell in (Eds.) B. Cunliffe and Trevor Rowley, *Lowland Iron Age Communities in Europe* (*BAR* International Series (Supplementary) no. 48 (1978)), 25 ff.
23. *Arch. Cant.,* lxviii (1954), 104–14.

trodden surface in the later period. Layer 3, a cleaner loam below, contained only Belgic material, mainly in its upper half. At its base occurred the small hollows containing Neolithic B sherds (p. 195), but these were confined to one area (Fig. 17).

A Belgic drainage ditch (Fig. 17, Ditch A) 2 ft. 6 in. deep ran down towards the river along the north-east edge of the site: in Square 22 four small stake-holes occurred in its upper filling. A second ditch (Fig. 17, Ditch C; Fig. 16, Section A–B) crossing Squares 25 and 24 was more slight; it drained probably towards the south. There was also a number of pits: none of these was as deep as that in W II, but some with vertical sides were quite possibly originally dug for storage: e.g. (i) Pit 26 (Fig. 16, Section E–F), which had a stepped floor 2 ft. 3 in. deep from the surface of (2) and rising to only 1 ft. 6 in; its lower filling was charcoally soil with occupation debris, capped by grey-brown loam. (ii) Pit 10, which was 1 ft. 8 in. deep and filled with dark occupation-material containing lumps of burnt daub, flint, and broken Belgic tile. (iii) Pit 22, only 10 in. deep, with charcoal and burnt daub at the bottom capped by grey loam with some daub. (iv) Pit 1, 1 ft. deep with grey loam filling containing flints. All these pits are admittedly somewhat shallow for storage-pits but they were well shaped and carefully cut. The remainder were rather too small or too shelving to be considered storage pits: e.g. Pit 3 (Fig. 16, Section A–B) was a scoop 10 in. deep at the centre with very oblique sides; its filling was dark brown loam with charcoal, burnt daub, Belgic tile fragments and occupation material: it resembled a small 'working hollow'. Most of the Belgic features contained flint flakes, some of them worked, and also burnt flints (Fig. 67, No. 29).

The principal feature of this site was a hut, substantially intact except where two Roman pits (Fig. 17, Pits 20 and 34) had cut its edges. It consisted of a sub-rectangular hollow almost 4 ft. deep from the base of the plough soil. In the dry summer of 1954 it was impossible to identify the post-holes of the structure in the dry loam; but more favourable conditions in April 1955 revealed a great number (Pl. VI). It was possible to distribute these post-holes into four phases of building (Fig. 18) partly by observing their relationship to later floors filling the hollow, and partly on the basis of their size, mutual intersections, content and alignment.[24] The successive rebuildings slowly enlarged the area enclosed (Fig. 18). It was not at first found easy to explain the original hollow as an intentional feature, for it is larger than the original hut and would probably have collected water; the loamy brickearth in which it was sunk becomes extremely sticky in wet weather and dusty in dry, and it seemed possible to suppose that the hollow might have been worn naturally and unintentionally by continued use, only later being made up with successive floors. But it is more probable that it was constructed as a straightforward sunken hut. Rodwell[25] has collected evidence for other pre-Roman examples. The original sunken hut would have been of the size of the Phase I building (Fig. 18), but the edges must have proved unstable, so that the hollow became saucer-shaped and gradually wider. There followed efforts to raise the level inside during successive rebuilds by adding new floors of loam over accumulated occupation debris (which could easily be done by the mere process of stripping down the walls). Below the original floor was the base of an earlier pit (36) containing a coin of Dubnovellaunus (c. B.C. 15–5 A.D.) and a butt-beaker rim in native fabric. The earliest floor and

24.   That the difficulties of the site were successfully unravelled owes much to the patient skill of Miss M.G. Wilson in its excavation.
25.   *Op. cit.* (note 22), 37.

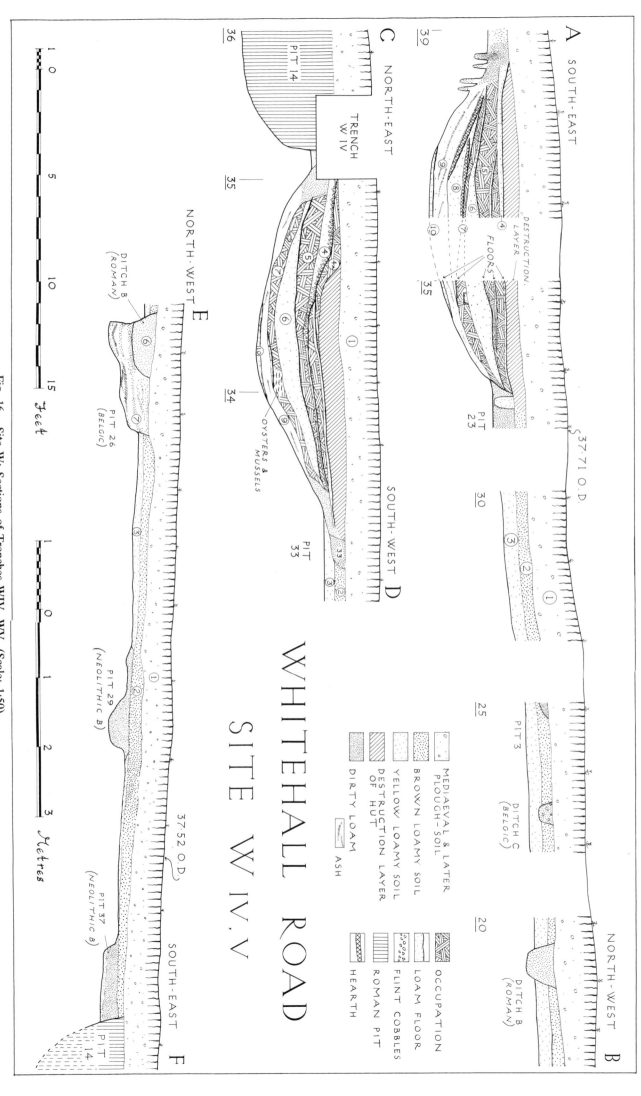

Fig. 16. Site W: Sections of Trenches WIV, WV. (Scale: 1:50)

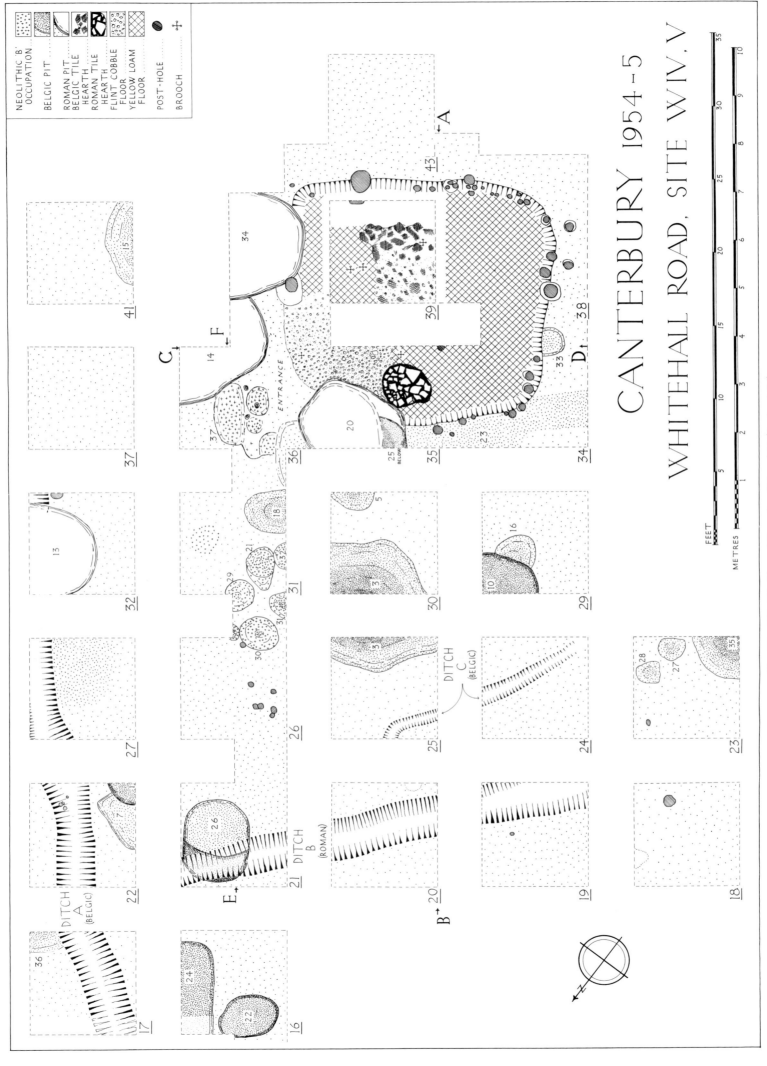

Fig. 17. Site W: Plan of Trenches IV and V (Scale: 1:76).

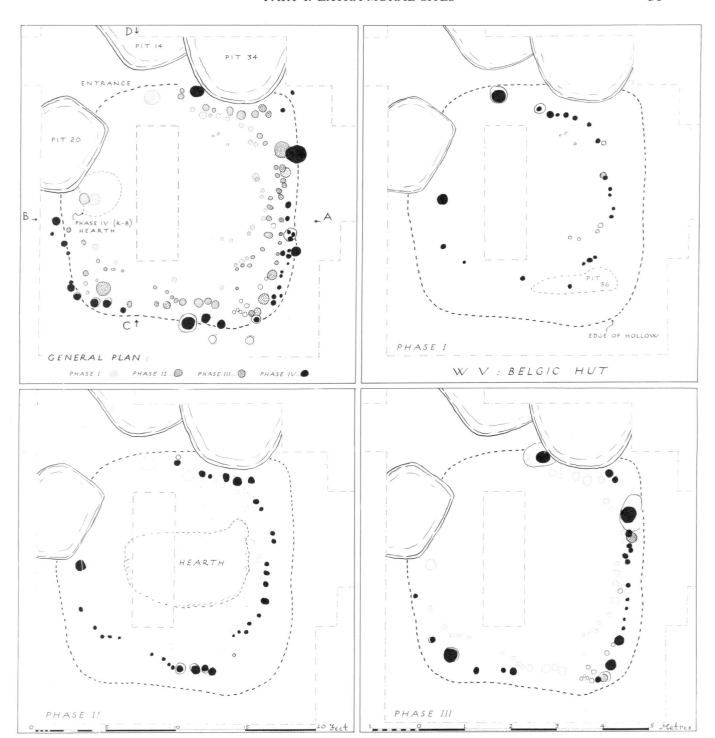

Fig. 18. Site W: Suggested phase plans of Belgic hut (Scale: 1:82).

occupation-layers contained local copies of butt-beakers and of *terra nigra* (Figs. 74–5, Nos. 54–83) which cannot be pre-Augustan and are more likely to date from *c*. A.D. 5–15 (e.g. Fig. 74, Nos. 71–2 copying *Camulodunum* form 1; Nos. 55–57 with rims not yet heavily bevelled internally). Layer 7 contained Fig. 75, No. 74, a *terra nigra* cup of *Camulodunum* form 54 stamped by Andecovilos. (Fig. 79, No. 1) which is probably Tiberian although not as late as some of the comparanda cited on p. 208. The hearth area, best seen in the phase (ii) plan (Fig. 18, and Section A–B (8), Fig. 16) was very large and mainly consisted of Belgic tiles which tended to disintegrate with the heat. The latest floor (4), belonging to phase (iv), had a much smaller hearth in a different position (Fig. 17), and it was made of broken pieces of Roman *tegulae* set flange-downwards in clay which was heavily burnt (Pl. VII). One of these pieces of *tegula* had mortar on its underside, and was thus re-used. The pottery associated with this floor was Claudian in date (Fig. 76, No. 107 in Romanized sandy fabric), and the destruction level above it, formed when this hut was burnt down, contained a samian form 27, Claudian: most of the pottery, however, was native. Roman tile is likely to have become available early at Canterbury, and a date late in the Claudian period perhaps *c*. A.D. 50 for this last hut is likely, and it will have been destroyed not long afterwards.

Some of the daub fragments were thinly coated with a white substance, kindly determined by Mr. H. Hodges as clay: it seems that the inner face of the walls was thus coated to resemble plaster. Pit 10 contained a Belgic tile fragment similarly coated: tiles were mainly used for hearths in Belgic levels, but this one may have been incorporated in a wall.

C. **Roman**

Trenches W IV–V
The only Roman features in this area consisted of Ditch B (a drainage gully) and a number of rubbish pits which mainly date from the first and second centuries. Later Roman material was noticeably rare, existing as a thin scatter over the site and collecting in the mouth of Pit 20 (Fig. 77, No. 130). Two coins of Cunobelin were found in later contexts (Pit 20 and layer 2), and the following coins were found in or just below the plough-soil: Agrippa (Pit 14); Hadrian; a radiate; Constans (two); and Constantius II.

Trenches W I–III were more productive of Roman remains.

Trench W I (Figs. 13, 15, 19)
This trench was sited on the crest of the river-terrace; there was considerable lynchet-accumulation of plough-soil protecting the remains below it. The trench was divided into two parts by the position of the large storm-water drain, the laying of which in 1953 had first attracted attention to the site.

The north edge of the Roman Watling Street was encountered at the south end of W I A (Fig. 15, Section A–B). It had three successive layers of metalling, and road-silt had accumulated beyond its edge. The old plough-soil (8), through which the first road had been inserted *c*. A.D. 43, had remained open and contained material down to the Flavian period. Overlying 8 was some dark earthy loam (7), an occupation-layer containing charcoal and pottery (Fig. 77, Nos. 131–133) dating to the period *c*. A.D. 80–115, and this was sealed by a floor bounding a row of post-holes along the street. The floor was of pebbles with a large area of amphora-sherds. Its

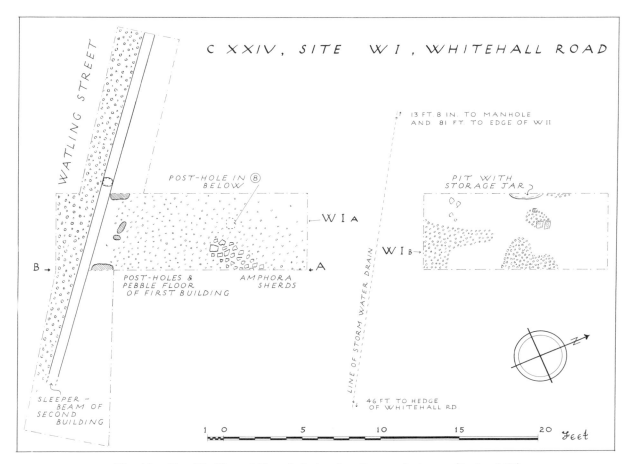

Fig. 19. Site W: Plan of Trench I showing Roman features. (Scale: 1:73)

date was probably *c.* A.D. 110–130 to judge by the pottery sealed in layer 7 and in the second road-surface in Trench W II which yielded a Flavian-Trajanic piece of samian (Dr. 33). In a pit cut through the floor was a very large storage jar and a first-century mortarium (Figs. 77–8, Nos. 134, 142); the floor was covered by a layer of occupation material. After a pause during which its southern part was sealed by silt from the street, it was succeeded after the middle of the second century by a second pebble floor (Section A–B, 4); this was disturbed by ploughing which had entirely removed it in Trench W I B. This second building was associated with the sleeper-trench of a timber-framed wall contemporary with the third street-surface. On the upper floor were two sherds (Fig. 77, No. 135) of the period A.D. 160–200 together with earlier pottery. The sleeper-trench, which yielded a number of nails and a sherd of ?Antonine samian, was traced for *c.* 23 ft. north-westwards along the road-edge; to the south-east it had been ploughed out on the crest of the terrace 7 ft. from Trench W I A. It was extremely difficult to trace owing to the nature of the soil, and further work was abandoned owing to developments in W II.

Trench W II (Figs. 13, 14, 15)

A first trench here sectioned Watling Street which proved to be 17 ft. 6 in. (5.32 m.) wide (Fig. 15, Section C–D; Pl. IV); here again there were three road-surfaces. The first surface (5A) was bordered on the south side by a timber building with pebble floor (8) which contained Claudian samian (Dr. 15/17) and an early group of coarse pottery. The second road-surface, of clean yellow gravel (5) contained a sherd of Flavian-Trajanic samian (Dr. 33) and coarse pottery of the first half of the second century (Fig. 77, Nos. 136–7) and was laid perhaps in the reign of Hadrian. This road was bordered on its north side by a timber-lined drain (Section C–D (10)), 17 in. wide and 8 in. deep (further north-west it deepened to 18 in). The drain contained a large number of small nails and a group of mid second-century pottery, including samian form 37, Central Gaulish, A.D. 125–150 and form 27, Central Gaulish, Hadrianic-Antonine, and Fig. 77, Nos. 138–141. Along the south edge of the second road-surface was a mortary robber trench, probably of a timber-framed building. Both the drain and robber trench were sealed by a third road-surface, probably not later than the Antonine period to judge by the pottery found at this level in W I. The metalling was remarkable for the large number of iron nails (up to 2 in. long) which it contained. Above the level of this road-surface on the south side traces of a pebble floor perhaps of the third century were found. Layer IA below it contained Antonine samian (forms 31, 33) as well as a large group of coarse wares, mainly residual. Some large post-holes along this side of the road seemed to go with this floor (plan, Fig. 14; Section E–F, Fig. 15).

There was a marked absence of late third- or fourth-century material on Site W. This may be partly due to plough damage, but it seems certain that once the city walls had been built, or probably even earlier, occupation of this whole area beyond the river was greatly reduced. At this time it may have come under cultivation once more; but if so later ploughing has disturbed the evidence.

VIII. No. 3 QUEEN'S AVENUE

A training excavation for the Canterbury Junior Archaeological Society took place in the back garden of no. 3 Queen's Avenue from 26 to 28 October, 1981. The site was chosen because of its proximity to Roman Watling Street (30 m. (100 ft.) south of the site) and the chance find of a number of Roman *tegulae* during the laying of a new garden path by the owners of the property, Mr and Mrs. L.D. Lyle.[26] The excavation, supervised by members of the Canterbury Archaeological Trust,[27] was only partially completed, and it is hoped that further investigations of this area will take place in the future.

The earliest feature, only partially located in the excavated area and at a depth of 0.65 m. below the present ground surface, was a well-metalled, single-phase Roman lane or track with shallow side-gutter, aligned north-north-west to south-south-east. A few sherds of late first- and second-century pottery were recovered from the road gutter and the lane metalling (Fig. 20).

The alignment of this track is at variance with the line of Roman Watling Street (aligned north-west to south-east) and of a second street (aligned north-east to south-west), located by

26. Mrs. Lyle was also Chairwoman of the Junior Society at this time.
27. The author was assisted by Mr Ian Anderson and Miss Marion Green.

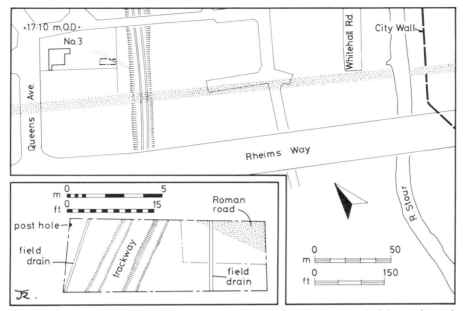

Fig. 20. No. 3 Queen's Avenue: Location plan of Roman lane and eighteenth- and nineteenth-century features. (Scale: 1:2,500)

S.S. Frere (see above p. 45). Nevertheless, the metalling may have been part of a small track laid to service an industrial suburb of the Roman town, east of Roman Watling Street and south of the St. Dunstan's Roman cemetery.

The Roman levels were sealed by deposits 0.30 m. (*c.* 1 ft.) thick of discoloured 'turned over' brickearth, which probably accumulated from the late medieval period, when this area was part of the pasture of Westgate Court Farm. Associated with agricultural activity and probably pre-dating the mid-nineteenth century were two field drains and a roughly paved (in brick, pebbles and flints) and wheel-rutted track (Fig. 20). These late farm features and the 'plough-soil' were sealed by a layer 0.15 m. (6 in.) thick of garden loam.

IX. ST. DUNSTAN'S CHURCHYARD

A service trench cut along the west side of St. Dunstan's churchyard (see Fig. 1) in March 1984, exposed a thick deposit of compacted Roman street metalling immediately south of and partly under the present London Road. The service trench, cut to connect the new Church Hall (presently under construction), with the main sewer under London Road, was excavated on a sloping gradient from the new Church Hall to a maximum depth of 3 m. (10 ft.) below the present surface, at the intersection with the main sewer under London Road. The northern end of the trench was cut in unstable ground and closely-set shuttering, erected for reasons of safety, made it impossible to draw a detailed section through the truncated archaeological deposits.[28]

28. The writer was assisted by Messrs. P. Blockley, J. Rady, M. Herdman and Miss J. Curtis.

Much of the trench cut only into upper cemetery deposits. The natural brickearth and Thanet sands were only encountered from a point 30 m. (*c.* 100 ft.) south of the centre of the London Road. Although a substantial layer 0.80 m. (2 ft. 8 in.) thick of dark brown silty brickearth flecked with carbon and burnt clay of possible Roman date overlay the natural deposits south of the Roman street, no contemporary burials or features were located. A small number of abraded, undatable Roman pot sherds were recovered from the deposit.

The Roman street was located at the north end of the service trench and consisted of compacted and banded gravels 1.20 m. (*c.* 4 ft.) thick. The primary metalling, a mixture of fist-sized, water-rounded cobbles capped by rammed gravel, had been set into a terrace, cut approximately 0.30 m. (*c.* 1 ft.) below the surface of the natural Thanet sands. The edge of the terrace was located 1 m. (3 ft.) north of the present cemetery wall, on the line of the southern kerb of the London Road. This first street was approximately 5.5 m. (*c.* 19 ft.) wide; the south edge of the street was defined by a V-shaped road gutter (which was only partially visible). A complex sequence of metallings extended over the early terrace, increasing the street width to at least 8 m. (*c.* 25 ft.). The final road surface was located 0.60 m. (*c.* 2 ft.) below present ground level.

The Roman levels were sealed by a complex sequence of soil deposits 1.20 m. (*c.* 4 ft.) thick associated with the development of the St. Dunstan's cemetery, which was probably established in the late eleventh century.

X. CRANMER HOUSE, LONDON ROAD

Introduction (Figs. 21–22)

During February and March 1982 machine-cut foundation-trenches for a new building, on the corner of London Road and Prince's Way[29] brought to light fifty-three Roman cremation burials and a number of early Saxon finds, including a very fine early seventh-century gold pendant.

The site, formerly Westgate Court Farm, is situated south of the London Road and approximately ½ km. west of the Westgate of the city. Unfortunately, this development was considered to be outside the area of the known Roman cemetery and no excavation took place in advance of the building work. The new building with elaborate trench-laid foundations and a wide, deep service duct linking all parts of the new complex (see Pl. VIII) considerably disturbed the archaeological levels.

The first three stages of machine work consisted of the removing of topsoil, the cutting of foundation-trenches for the north-east wing and the cutting of foundations for the south-east wing of the new building. Only a part-time watching brief was maintained during these operations, usually at the end of the working day after the machine had ceased digging. The excavated soil was for the most part loaded directly into a lorry and transported off site. No burials were located *in situ* during the first three stages of the development, and only a scatter of amphora sherds (34) was recovered from discarded soil flanking the north side of the south-east wing. The watching brief, established after these stages had been completed, showed that only

---

29. Warden-assisted homes for the aged, built by Wiltshiers for the Canterbury City Council.

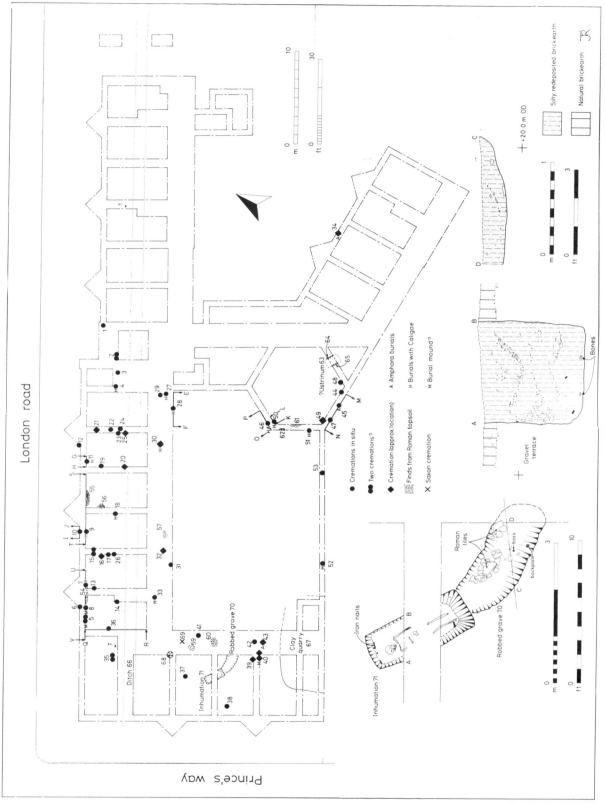

Fig. 21. Cranmer House, London Road: Builder's trench plan with location of burials. (Scale: 1:400) Detailed plans (Scale: 1:80) and sections (Scale: 1:40) of Anglo-Saxon features.

by monitoring the cutting and checking the discarded soil as it was removed could one locate and salvage the burials. Any number of burials could therefore have been lost during the cutting of foundation-trenches for the north-east and south-east wings of the new building. Only after a complete cremation urn was uncovered by the workmen did the full-time monitoring begin.[30] Many of the burials, truncated during the cutting of foundations, were recorded *in situ* and in section. Others were uncovered almost intact and rapidly exhumed by members of the Trust.[31] A number of burials were retrieved from discarded soil and in some cases rescued from the machine bucket itself.

Although this hectic salvage operation saw both archaeologists and contractor working effectively together without retarding the progress of the development, it can only be regretted that an area-excavation of such an important site did not take place. Any future developments in this area (an adjacent site may become available for excavation in the near future) should undoubtedly be investigated more thoroughly.

The Roman Cremation Burials

The inventory set out below comprises four sections for each burial:

   (i)   the cremated bones (report pp. 263–71).
  (ii)   A brief inventory of the vessels found in the burial and approximate dating (report pp. 284–98 and Figs. 107–114). Unless otherwise stated, all vessels are coarse wares.
 (iii)   Other associated non-ceramic finds (report pp. 271–84, and Figs. 102–106).
 (iv)   A brief description of the burial.

Burial 1   (i)   Adult (report p. 263);
          (ii)   A.   Jar containing cremation (Fig. 107, report p. 285);
                 B.   Jar (rim only);
                 C.   Body sherds.
                 Date: Mid second to third century.
         (iii)   No associated non-ceramic finds.
         (iv)   This burial was recovered by the workmen, who reported that other pots may have been present. Sherd C may represent a fragment of at least a third pot. A well-defined Roman ground surface was noted nearby, at +19.75 m. O.D. The lowest level of the grave pit survived the machine cutting and lay at +18.95 m. O.D.
Burial 2   (i)   Young adult male (report p. 263).

30.   Much of the credit for the early discoveries must go to the workmen and their supervisors, who with care and enthusiasm recovered a number of burials and allowed a full-time monitoring of the foundation cutting to take place. Special thanks are extended to the skill and patience of the driver of the mechanical excavator, whose keen eyesight and uncanny anticipation of the unexpected often saved burials from complete destruction.

31.   Particular thanks are extended to Mr John Rady, who worked long and taxing hours on this site. Thanks are also extended to the many volunteers who helped maintain the hectic watching brief, especially Ms M. Taylor and Messrs. S. Pratt, I. Anderson, W. McLaughlin and R. Stokes.

(ii) A. Jar containing cremation (Fig. 107, report p. 285);

       B. One-handled flagon;

       C. Base of a possible bowl;

       D. Base of a possible jar;

       E. Body sherd of a possible flagon;

       F. Body sherd of a possible bowl;

       G. Base of a possible jar;

       H. Indented glass flask fragment;

      Date: Mid second to third century.

(iii) Pot A contained hobnails and an iron nail (S.F. 46).

(iv) All the pots, except E, were recovered by the workmen, who reported that other pots may have been removed by the machine. The remains of pot E was recovered *in situ* from a partially surviving grave pit, the sump of which was at +18.90 m. O.D. These pots may constitute an incomplete collection from at least two or possibly even three closely-set burials. D and G may be the fragmentary remains of two other cremation urns.

Burial 3 (i) Adult, probably male (report p. 263).

         (ii) A. Jar containing cremation (Fig. 108, report p. 285);

              B. Flask;

              C. Glass flask fragments.

             Date: Mid second to third century.

         (iii) The remains of a circular *speculum* mirror (S.F. 4) was found outside and to the west of A (report p. 271, Fig. 102). Two iron nails were recovered from within the cremated bones in A.

         (iv) Pl. IX. This burial was partially truncated during machining and excavated by members of the Trust. A possible Roman ground-surface horizon was noted in nearby sections, this lay at +19.70 m. O.D. The lower level of the grave pit survived intact. The mottled redeposited natural infill contained no finds. The sump of the grave pit lay at +19.20 m. O.D.

Burial 4 (i) Adult, probably male (report p. 264).

         (ii) A. Jar, containing cremation (Fig. 108, report p. 285).

             Date: Mid second to third century.

         (iii) Fragments of a hobnailed boot or boots were recovered, overlying the cremated bones. Two iron nails were found with the cremated bones.

         (iv) Pl. IX. The burial was discovered by the workmen, and recorded *in situ*. The workmen reported that other pots may have been present. The base of the burial pit lay at +19.10 m. O.D. The pit infill was excavated by the workmen and no associated finds were recovered.

Burial 5 (i) No cremated bones recovered.

         (ii) A. Fragmented jar possibly for cremation (report p. 286);

              B. Samian Dr. 37, Central Gaulish (base and lower body);

              C. Fragmented jar;

              D. Body sherds of a jar, possibly from A or C.

             Date: Mid second to third century.

         (iii) No other associated non-ceramic finds.

         (iv) Fig. 22, Section U–V. This group of pots was also located by the workmen. No cremated bones were recovered. The presence of at least two coarse ware jars A and C may indicate possibly two incomplete and badly damaged cremation burials. Vestiges of a distinct low 'mound' were discerned covering the burial. Pot C may have been incorporated in the 'mound' or in the grave backfill.

Burial 6 (i) No cremated bone recovered.

         (ii) A. Oxfordshire brown colour-coated flagon (report p. 286);

              B. Body sherds;

              C. Body sherds.

             Date: Mid third to early fourth century.

          (iii) No other associated non-ceramic finds.

(iv) Fig. 22, Section U–V. This burial was almost entirely removed by the machine. Pot A was recovered *in situ*. Body sherds B and C from the discarded soil. No cremation urn was recovered.

Burial 7 (i) Adolescent, age thirteen to sixteen years (report p. 264).

(ii) A. Base of cremation jar (report p. 286).
Date: Flavian to early fourth century.

(iii) Hobnailed boots (S.F. 1) from the grave backfill.

(iv) Fig. 22, Section U–V. The burial was almost entirely removed by the machine, with only the base of the cremation urn recovered from the discarded soil, together with cremated bone.

Burial 8 (i) No cremated bone recovered.

(ii) A. Fragments of a jar possibly for cremation (report p. 286);
B. BB2 dog-dish;
C. BB2 pie-dish;
D. Miniature beaker;
E. BB2 sherds, possibly from B or C or another vessel.
Date: Late second to third century.

(iii) Iron nails (S.F. 15) were recovered from the grave backfill.

(iv) Fig. 22, Section U–V. This burial was truncated by the machine. Pots A, B, C and E were recovered from the discarded soil, D from the remaining grave backfill. Vestiges of a distinct, low 'mound' overlying the remains of the buried Roman ground surface. Fragments of a jar were recovered in two separate caches from the 'mound' (8a and 8b).

Burial 9 (i) Only a few fragments of burnt bone were recovered (report p. 264).

(ii) A. Fragmented jar containing the remains of the cremation (Fig. 109, report p. 287);
B. Colour-coated beaker.
Date: Late second to third century.

(iii) Hobnails (S.F. 17) were recovered from pot B.

(iv) Fig. 22, Section S–T. Pot A was truncated by the machine and most of the cremated bones lost. No other ancillary vessels were found, though others may have existed.

Burial 10 (i) Adult (report p. 264).

(ii) A. Jar containing cremation (Fig. 109, report p. 287).
Date: Mid second to third century.

(iii) A fragment of bone or antler box inlay (S.F. 47, report p. 273, Fig. 102) was recovered from A.

(iv) Fig. 22, Section I–J. Only part of the burial pit, containing A, was located; other vessels may have been removed during machine work.

Burial 11 (i) Young adult male (report p. 264).

(ii) A. Jar containing cremation (Fig. 109, report p. 287).
Not closely datable.

(iii) Hobnailed boots (S.F. 20) from grave backfill.

(iv) Fig. 22, Section G–H. This burial was truncated by the machine. The vertical soil stains noted in the backfill of the grave pit may indicate that the burial was contained within a wooden structure, perhaps a box. The badly fragmented remains of a roofing-tile covered the cremation urn. Hobnailed boots flanked the sides of the possible 'box'. Powdered glass was noted in the grave backfill, but not recovered.

Burial 12 (i) No cremated bone recovered.

(ii) A. Base of jar, possibly for cremation;
B. Samian Dr. 33, Central Gaulish;
C. Beaker.
Date: Late second to third century.

(iii) No other associated non-ceramic finds.

(iv) This badly fragmented burial had been disturbed and crushed in antiquity. The samian vessel may have originally covered the cremation jar. The burnt bone was dispersed in the grave backfill, which was largely removed by machine. The bottom of the grave pit lay at +19.70 m. O.D.

Burial 13 (i) Young adult male (report p. 265).

(ii)   A. BB2 jar containing cremated bones (report p. 288).

Date: Late second to early fourth century.

(iii) No other associated non-ceramic finds.

(iv) Only a fragment of the burial pit survived. Pot A was truncated by the machine. No other associated pots were retrieved. The bottom of the burial pit lay at +19.66 m. O.D.

Burial 14 (i)   Adult (report p. 265).

(ii)   A. Jar containing cremated bones (report p. 288).

Date: Second century.

(iii) Iron nail (S.F. 19) from cremated bones in A.

(iv) Pot A was truncated by the machine. No other pots were retrieved; it is quite possible that only one existed. The bottom of the burial pit lay at +20.17 m. O.D.

Burial 15 (i)   a. Young adult from A (report p. 265).

b. Adult from J (report p. 265).

(ii)   A. Jar containing cremation a. (Fig. 110, report p. 288);

B. Jar;

C. Flagon;

D. Rim sherd of jar;

E. Colour-coated beaker;

F. Base of flagon;

G. Samian Dr. 40, Central Gaulish;

H. Beaker;

J. Jar containing cremation b. (Fig. 110, report p. 288).

Date: Second half of second century (possibly early third century).

(iii) Bone or antler box inlay (S.F. 22) from A (report p. 274, Fig. 102). Rectangular *speculum* bronze mirror (S.F. 5) covering pots J and F (report p. 273, Fig. 102).

(iv) Pl. X. This large group of pots partly truncated by the machine represents at least two burials. Pots B and D may have been incorporated in the grave backfill, or may indicate a third burial. No soil stains indicating grave pits were observed. The base of pot A lay at +19.63 m. O.D. Pot C was stoppered with a large water-rounded flint and G was covered by an *imbrex* fragment. Pots J and F were covered by the bronze mirror. The burial, or burials, was cut by a recent feature (73), which contained a worn bronze coin of Claudius I (A.D. 41–54) in its backfill. This coin could have been originally associated with the burial.

Burial 16 (i)   No cremated bones recovered.

(ii)   A. Jar possibly containing cremation.

Date: Mid second to third century.

(iii) No associated non-ceramic finds.

(iv) This burial was almost completely removed by the machine. No trace of the burial pit was located and only an approximate location is shown on Fig. 21. The jar sherds were recovered from the discarded spoil.

Burial 17 (i)   Adult male (report p. 266).

(ii)   A. Jar containing cremated bones (Fig. 110, report p. 288);

B. BB2 dog-dish.

Date: Late second to early fourth century.

(iii) No associated non-ceramic finds.

(iv) The burial was truncated by the machine. Sherds of a third pot, possibly a flagon, were recovered from the spoil-heap, but could not definitely be associated with the burial. A well-defined Roman ground surface was noted nearby, at +20.15 m. O.D. The bottom of the burial pit lay at +19.75 m. O.D.

Burial 18 (i)   Adult, probably male (report p. 266).

(ii)   A. Two-handled flagon containing cremated bones (Fig. 111, report p. 288).

Date: Second century.

(iii) Hobnail from bottom of grave pit (S.F. 58).

(iv)   The burial pit and pot A were truncated by the machine. Other pots may have been present, but were not found. The pot was stopped by a large water-rounded cobble. The hobnails may indicate the presence of a pair of boots placed on either side of the flagon. The bottom of the burial pit lay at +19.67 m. O.D.

Burial 19 (i)   Adolescent, aged approximately twelve years (report p. 266).

(ii)   A.   Jar containing cremated bones (Fig. 111, report p. 288);
     B.   Flagon;
     C.   BB2 dog-dish, possibly a 'miniature';
     D.   Samian Dr. 31, Central Gaulish;
     E.   Base of beaker.
     Date: Mid second to mid third century.

(iii)   Bronze ring with bone object attached, possibly a bangle or amulet? (S.F. 18), from pot A (report p. 274, Fig. 103). Two iron nails from cremated bones in pot A (S.F. 16).

(iv)   Though damaged by the machine, the pots noted above represent the entire contents of the burial. The bottom of the burial pit lay at +19.73 m. O.D.

Burial 20 (i)   The cremated bones from Burials 20a and 23a were accidentally mixed during analysis. The cremated bones from Burial 20, therefore, represent either:
     a.   Adult, probably male (report p. 266).
     b.   Young adult, probably male.

(ii)   A.   Jar containing cremated bones (Fig. 111, report p. 288).
     Date: Second century.

(iii)   A few iron nails were recovered from the cremated bones of either burial 20 or burial 23.

(iv)   This pot was recovered from the machine bucket. No trace of a burial pit was observed, and only an approximate position for this burial is shown on Fig. 21.

Burial 21 (i)   No cremated bones.

(ii)   A.   Beaker (Fig. 112, report p. 288).
     Date: Second half of second century to third century.

(iii)   No associated non-ceramic finds.

(iv)   This pot was recovered from the machine bucket. No trace of a burial pit was observed and only an approximate position for this burial is shown on Fig. 21.

Burial 22 (i)   Adult (report p. 267).

(ii)   A.   Jar containing cremated bones (report p. 288);
     B.   Flagon;
     C.   Samian Dr. 31, Central Gaulish;
     D.   Single body sherd.
     Date: Mid second to third century.

(iii)   No associated non-ceramic finds.

(iv)   This burial was badly disturbed by the machine. Sherd D may have been incorporated in the grave backfill. A well-defined Roman ground surface was located at +20.05 m. O.D. The base of the burial pit lay at +19.65 m. O.D.

Burial 23 (i)   The cremated bones from Burials 23 and 20 were accidentally mixed during analysis. The cremated bones from Burial 23, therefore, represent either:
     a.   Adult probably male (report p. 266).
     b.   Young adult, probably male.

(ii)   A.   Jar containing cremation (Fig. 112, report p. 288);
     B.   Flask;
     C.   BB2 pie-dish;
     D.   Colour-coated beaker;
     E.   Jar;
     F.   Beaker;
     G.   Lamp (found inside A over cremated bones).
     Date: Late second to early third century.

(iii) No associated non-ceramic finds.

(iv) This burial, clipped by the machine was mostly recovered from the section shortly before the new concrete wall foundations were laid. Though the pots mentioned above probably represent the entire grave contents, all the pot sherds were not recovered. The base of the burial pit was located at +19.64 m. O.D.

Burial 24　(i)　Adult male (report p. 267).

(ii) A. Jar containing cremation (report p. 290).
Date: Second century.

(iii) No associated non-ceramic finds.

(iv) This pot, crushed in antiquity, was truncated by the machine. No associated vessels were located and none may have existed. The bottom of the burial lay at +19.60 m. O.D.

Burial 25　(i)　Adult (report p. 267).

(ii) A. Jar containing cremation (report p. 290);
B. Single body sherd.
Date: Second century.

(iii) No associated non-ceramic finds.

(iv) This pot was retrieved from the machine bucket. No trace of the burial pit was located and only an approximate position for this burial is shown on Fig. 21.

Burial 26　(i)　Adult (report p. 267).

(ii) A. Jar containing cremation (report p. 290).
Date: Mid second to third century.

(iii) No associated non-ceramic finds.

(iv) This burial was largely removed by the machine. The remains of the jar was recovered from the section. No associated vessels were located and none may have existed. A well-defined Roman ground surface was noted at +20.10 m. O.D. The bottom of the grave pit lay at +19.68 m. O.D.

Burial 27　(i)　Adult (report p. 267).

(ii) A. Jar containing cremation (Fig. 112, report p. 291);
B. BB2 dog-dish;
C. BB2 dog-dish;
D. Flask;
E. Beaker;
F. Colour-coated beaker;
G. Pot sherds.
Date: Late second to third century.

(iii) Hobnailed boots (S.F. 57) were located on the bottom of the grave pit flanking pot A. (Fig. 103, report p. 276).

(iv) This collection of pots, uncovered by the machine, represents the complete content of the burial. Sherd G may have been from the grave backfill. The bottom of the burial lay at +19.40 m. O.D.

Burial 28　(i)　Adult, probably young male (report p. 267).

(ii) A. Jar containing cremation (Fig. 113, report p. 291);
B. BB2 dog-dish;
C. Beaker.
Date: Late second to third century.

(iii) Hobnailed boots were found on the bottom of the grave pit, flanking pot A. A coin of Antoninus Pius (A.D. 138–161) was recovered from within the cremated bones in pot A.

(iv) Fig. 22, Section E–F. This burial was truncated by the machine. Pot B was inverted over pot A. A fragment of tegula covered pot C.

Burial 29　(i)　Adult, probably male (report p. 268).

(ii) A. Bowl containing cremation (report p. 292).
Date: Mid first to early second century.

(iii) No associated non-ceramic finds.

(iv) This burial consisted of a single pot. The base of the grave pit lay at +19.50 m. O.D.

Burial 30 (i)   Adult, male (report p. 268).

(ii)   A.   Jar containing cremation (Fig. 113, report p. 292).
Date: Mid first to early second century.

(iii)   Hobnailed boots flanked either side of the cremation jar.

(iv)   This burial contained only a single pot, flanked by a pair of hobnailed boots. The complete burial was recovered from the machine bucket. Only an approximate location is shown on Fig. 21.

Burial 31 (i)   Adult male (report p. 268).

(ii)   A.   Jar (badly shattered) containing a cremation (report p. 292);
B.   Jar.
Not closely datable.

(iii)   No associated non-ceramic finds.

(iv)   This burial contained only a single pot. Sherd B may have been incorporated in the grave backfill. The base of the grave pit lay at +20.08 m. O.D.

Burial 32 (i)   No cremated bones.

(ii)   A.   Jar or bowl sherds (Fig. 113, report p. 293);
B.   Small beaker or cup.
Not closely datable.

(iii)   No associated non-ceramic finds.

(iv)   This collection of sherds recovered from discarded soil indicates the presence of a possible cremation burial. Carbon and a few fragments of cremated bones were noted in the same upcast, but were not recovered for analysis. Only an approximate location for this possible burial is shown on Fig. 21.

Burial 33 (i)   Adult, probably a small female (report p. 268).

(ii)   A.   Jar containing cremation (report p. 293);
B.   Flask;
C.   Colour-coated beaker.
Date: Late second to early fourth century.

(iii)   An oval pewter dish or bowl (S.F. 10) (report p. 276, Fig. 103) was recovered from under the cremated bones in pot A. Hobnails (S.F. 48) were found overlying the cremated bones in pot A. Iron nails (S.F. 21) and a flint flake (S.F. 14) (report p. 276) were located in the grave backfill.

(iv)   This burial, uncovered and partly crushed by the machine, may have contained other pots. The base of the grave pit lay at +19.95 m. O.D.

Burial 34 (i)   No cremated bone.

(ii)   Fragment of a Dressel 20 amphora (report p. 293).

(iii)   No associated non-ceramic finds.

(iv)   These amphora sherds, recovered from discarded soil, may have been from an amphora burial. Only an approximate location is shown on Fig. 21.

Burial 35 (i)   Young male, aged eighteen to twenty years (report p. 268).

(ii)   A.   Jar containing cremation (Fig. 113, report p. 293);
B.   Beaker;
C.   Beaker;
D.   Beaker;
E.   Flagon;
F.   Jar (base only);
G.   Samian Dr. 33, Central Gaulish.
Date: Late second to third century.

(iii)   No associated non-ceramic finds.

(iv)   These pots, badly disturbed and broken by the machine, may have been from two closely-set burials. Pot F may have contained a second cremation, but no cremated bones were recovered. Traces of at least one grave pit were detected. This lay at approximately +20.00 m. O.D.

Burial 36 (i)   Child under nine years (report p. 269).

(ii)   A.   Jar containing cremation (Fig. 113, report p. 293);

              B.   Beaker;

              C.   Flagon.

              Date: Mid second to mid third century.

     (iii)   Fig. 22, Section Q–R, Pl. XII. A bronze object (S.F. 13) (report p. 276, Fig. 104) was recovered from the grave backfill. Irrecoverable powdered glass fragments were noted close to pot C in the grave backfill.

     (iv)   The group of pots represents the entire contents of this burial.

Burial 37   (i)   Adult (report p. 269).

     (ii)   A.   Jar containing cremation (report p. 293);

              B.   Single sherd.

              Date: Late second to fourth century.

     (iii)   No associated non-ceramic finds.

     (iv)   This burial, partly truncated by the machine may have contained only one pot. Sherds B were recovered from the grave backfill. The bottom of the grave pit lay at +20.46 m. O.D.

Burial 38   (i)   Adult male aged twenty-five to thirty years (report p. 269).

     (ii)   A.   Jar containing cremation (report p. 293);

              B.   Flagon;

              C.   Body sherds.

              Not closely datable.

     (iii)   Fragments of a corroded object (S.F. 30) (report p. 276) were recovered from the grave backfill.

     (iv)   The top of this burial was sheared off by the machine. At least three pots may have accompanied this burial. The bottom of the grave pit lay at +20.50 m. O.D.

Burial 39   (i)   Adult (report p. 269).

     (ii)   A.   Jar (base only) containing cremation (report p. 293);

              B.   Body sherds;

              C.   Body sherds.

              Not closely datable.

     (iii)   No associated non-ceramic finds.

     (iv)   This burial was located close to Burial 40. Both were badly truncated by the machine and crushed. No trace of the grave pits for Burials 39 or 40 was found. Only pots A and B were definitely part of a separate burial. Body sherds C may belong to Burial 40A.

Burial 40   (i)   Adult (report p. 269).

     (ii)   A.   Jar (base only) containing cremation (report p. 293);

              B.   Sherd of Dressel 20 amphora;

              C.   Flagon;

              D.   Bowl;

              E.   Samian Dr. 31, Central Gaulish;

              F.   Jar;

              G.   Jar;

              H.   Beaker or flask;

              I.   Figurine of *Dea Nutrix* (S.F. 9) (report p. 276 ff., Fig. 104).

              Date: Mid second to third century.

     (iii)   Hobnails from the cremated bones in pot A (S.F. 31 and 28).

     (iv)   This burial, situated close to Burial 39 was badly disturbed by the machine. Some of the pots may have been covered by amphora sherds as no amphora burial is suspected here. A number of jar sherds from Burial 39C may belong to pot A. Both burials were crushed by the machine, and it is quite likely that sherds from one burial were mixed with the other. Only pots A and B in Burial 39 are definitely part of a separate interment.

Burial 41   (i)   Young adult male (report p. 269).

     (ii)   A.   Jar containing cremation (report p. 293).

               Not closely datable.

     (iii)   No associated non-ceramic finds.

(iv)   The top of this burial was truncated by the machine. It is quite likely that this burial contained only a single pot. The bottom of the grave pit lay at +20.45 m. O.D.

Burial 42 (i)   Adult (report p. 270).

(ii)   A.   Jar (report p. 294);
        B.   Flagon;
        C.   Body sherd.
        Not closely datable.

(iii)   No associated non-ceramic finds.

(iv)   This burial was very badly crushed by the machine. Only elements of a possible third pot were found. The bottom of the grave pit lay at +20.50 m. O.D.

Burial 43 (i)   Adult (report p. 270).

(ii)   A.   Dressel 20 amphora (bottom half) (report p. 294);
        B.   Flask;
        C.   Iron Age sherd.
        Not closely datable.

(iii)   No associated non-ceramic finds.

(iv)   The upper half of the amphora burial was cut away by the machine. Only the bottom half of the amphora survived, with the cremated bones and the body sherds of a flask. Sherd C was contained within the brickearth infill of the amphora, overlying the cremated bones. The bottom of the grave pit lay at +20.35 m. O.D.

Burial 44 (i)   Adult (report p. 270).

(ii)   A.   Jar containing cremation (report p. 294);
        B.   Flagon;
        C.   BB2 dog-dish;
        D.   Jar body sherds (possibly from A);
        E.   Jar (base).
        Date: Mid second to third century.

(iii)   Tanged flint arrowhead from brickearth infill overlying the cremated bones in A (S.F. 34) (report p. 279, Fig. 104).

(iv)   The top of this burial was sheared off by the machine. The burial probably contained three pots. Jar sherds D may have belonged to A. The base of a second (or third) jar E was recovered from the grave backfill. A well-defined Roman ground surface was noted at +20.10 m. O.D.

Burial 45 (i)   Adult (report p. 270).

(ii)   A.   Dressel 20 amphora containing cremation (report p. 294).
        B.   Fabric IV (p. 294) body sherds.
        Not closely datable.

(iii)   A lead plug (S.F. 36) was found sealing a small hole in the body of the amphora.

(iv)   Fig. 21, Section M–N, Pl. XIII. This amphora burial was recovered almost intact. The machine clipped the top of the pot, breaking off only small fragments. The handles and neck of the amphora were broken off in antiquity, to insert the remains. Very few cremated bones were recovered from the burial. The amphora was infilled with clay and soil, before the backfilling of the grave pit.

Burial 46 (i)   Two adults including one male (report p. 270).

(ii)   A.   Dressel 20 amphora containing cremation (Fig. 113, report p. 294);
        B.   Flagon;
        C.   BB2 pie-dish;
        D.   Body sherds of jar;
        E.   Body sherd;
        F.   Glass unguent bottle (report p. 280).
        Date: Mid second to early third century.

(iii)   A miniature sword (S.F. 40 and 53) (report p. 279, Fig. 104). An iron knife (S.F. 54) (report p. 280, Fig. 104). An iron knife blade (S.F. 49). Hobnails (S.F. 59). Round-headed iron nail (S.F. 35).

(iv) Fig. 22, Section O–P, Pl. XIV. This amphora burial was recovered intact. The handles and neck of the amphora were removed in antiquity, to insert the burial. Body sherds D and E were recovered from the backfill of the amphora. The burial was set in a wide and deep burial pit. A post-hole (46A), cut from the Roman ground surface, was noted in section, and may have been a grave marker.

Burial 47 (i) No cremated bones.
(ii) A. Flagon
Not closely datable.
(iii) No associated non-ceramic finds.
(iv) Fig. 22, Section M–N. This burial had been crushed in antiquity, and was almost entirely removed by machine. Part of the grave pit containing A was recorded in section.

Burial 48 (i) Adult (report p. 270).
(ii) A. Jar containing cremation (report p. 294);
B. Indented glass flask (report p. 281, Fig. 105).
Date: Late second to fourth century.
(iii) Flint flake (S.F. 41) recovered from grave backfill.
(iv) This burial was crushed in antiquity and was partly cut away by the machine. The base of the grave pit lay at +19.90 m. O.D.

Burial 49 (i) No cremated bones.
(ii) A. Colour-coated beaker (report p. 294);
B. Flask or jar;
C. Flagon.
Date: Second century.
(iii) No associated non-ceramic finds.
(iv) This burial was cut by a farm wall foundation and by the machine. No obvious grave pit was located.

Burial 50 (i) Adult (report p. 271).
(ii) A. Jar containing cremation (Fig. 113, report p. 294);
B. Jar sherds;
C. Lid;
D. Cup;
E. Samian, Dr. 37, Central Gaulish.
Date: Late second to fourth century.

Burial 51 (i) No cremated bones.
(ii) No pottery.
No datable finds.
(iii) A hobnailed boot was located in the bottom of the grave pit (S.F. 60) (report p. 281, Fig. 105).
(iv) This possible burial was entirely removed by the machine. No pots were recovered. The bottom of the grave pit was located at +19.83 m. O.D.

Burial 52 (i) Child aged seven to ten years (report p. 271).
(ii) A. Jar containing cremation (report p. 294);
B. Flagon.
Date: Late first to early second century.
(iii) Hobnails (S.F. 45) were recovered from the cremated bones in pot A.
(iv) This burial was disturbed in antiquity and was truncated by the machine. The base of the grave pit lay at +19.76 m. O.D.

Burial 53 (i) Adult (report p. 271).
(ii) A. Jar containing cremation (report p. 295);
B. Beaker;
C. Jar sherds.
Date: Second century.
(iii) No associated non-ceramic finds.

(iv)   This burial was exposed by the machine and contained only one pot, A, which was covered by a *tegula* fragment. Sherds B and C were recovered from the pit backfill. The base of the cremation pit lay at +19.79 m. O.D.

THE BURIED ROMAN TOPSOIL AND OTHER ROMAN FEATURES

A well-defined buried Roman soil horizon, which appeared as a thin dark grey band studded with occasional pebbles, flints and broken tile, was noted across almost the entire site. This deposit, never more than 0.05 m. thick, overlay a layer of leached brickearth which, in turn, either sealed hard orange natural head brickearth or gravel. The horizon which sloped gently downwards from south-west to north-east may have been buried turf over an undisturbed leached natural subsoil, which often contained either patches or flecks of carbon and in a few places burnt clay. A number of pot scatters and isolated finds (including human bones (60)) were recovered from the horizon. (Feature 54: see Fig. 22, Section U–V; Feature 55, Section S–T and Features 58–61).

A number of features cut from the Roman horizon may have been associated with the use of the area as a cemetery. These comprised:

Feature 62   A small pit containing a large deposit of carbon, fragments of at least three jars and a number of other sherds (report p. 295).
Date: Late second to fourth century.

Feature 63   A large shallow depression containing carbon and burnt clay. Evidence for burning extended around this feature, and it was flanked by at least two large post-holes (64) and (65) of diameter 0.17 m., cut to a depth of 0.35 m. from the contemporary Roman ground surface. A number of iron nails (S.F. 43) were recovered from the carbon. This feature may have been an *ustrinum* (place of cremation).

Feature 66   A large V-shaped ditch (Fig. 22, Section Q–R) was located in all the construction trenches aligned north-west to south-east fronting on to the London Road. The ditch, on average 1 m. wide, was cut to an average depth of 0.65 m. from the contemporary Roman ground surface. The ditch which was probably parallel to the line of the Roman street, now under the London Road, undoubtedly represented a major boundary within the cemetery. A small group of pottery, dating from the late first to third century A.D., was recovered from the ditch fill (report p. 295). No burial was found cutting the ditch fill and no burials were cut by the ditch.

Feature 67   A very large and deep pit was located in the extreme south-west corner of the site. This feature, which cut through the natural head brickearth and bottomed on the gravel terrace, may have been a clay quarry. The pit, which contained redeposited grey silty brickearth with pebbles, flints, fragments of tile and oyster shells, may have been cut to extract clay for pot or brick manufacture. The small quantity of pottery recovered from the backfill, dating from the mid first to the mid third century (report p. 296), suggests that this feature may predate many of the burials found on the site and may have never been deliberately backfilled. A single sherd of Saxon grass-tempered pottery found in the uppermost fill of the pit may indicate that the pit was only partly infilled and that it probably showed as a hollow as late as the seventh century.

THE SAXON FEATURES

Besides a single sherd of Saxon pottery recovered from a possible Roman clay quarry (67), two features and two burials of Saxon date were located at the west end of the site, fronting on to Prince's Way. These comprised:

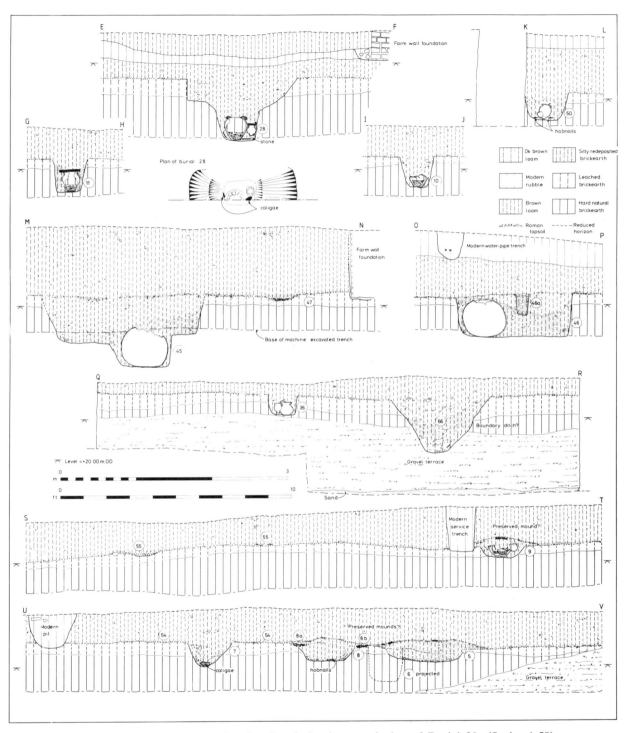

Fig. 22. Cranmer House, London Road: Sections, and plan of Burial 28. (Scale: 1:50)

Feature 68   The remains of a shallow pit, mostly removed by the machine, containing a thick deposit of carbon, mixed with lumps of burnt clay. A *sceatta, c.* A.D. 690–725 (S.F. 8, report p. 281), was recovered from the carbon. The bottom of the pit was located at +20.40 m. O.D.

Feature 69   A possible Saxon burial, containing:

     (i)   No inhumed or cremated bones.

     (ii)   A. Flagon (Fig. 114, report p. 297);

           B. Samian Dr. 31, Central Gaulish;

           C. Samian Dr. 31, Central Gaulish.

     (iii)   a. Saxon glass palm cup (report p. 281, Fig. 114);

           b. Saxon glass palm cup (report p. 281, Fig. 114).

     (iv)   This group of pots was removed entirely by the machine and rescued from the machine bucket. No trace of an inhumation or grave was discovered. Only an approximate location is shown on Fig. 21.

Feature 70   A shallow 'grave-shaped' cutting, backfilled with redeposited brickearth. The bottom of the cutting contained some large flints and fragments of Roman brick. A very fine early seventh-century gold pendant was found lying on the bottom of the feature in two pieces – the boss having been detached from the rest of the pendant (report p. 282, Fig. 106, Pls. XVI and XVII). The feature also contained some iron nails (S.F. 38). This shallow cutting may have been a grave which had been robbed in antiquity. An Iron Age sherd and some miscellaneous Romano-British sherds were recovered from the backfill (report p. 297).

Feature 71   An inhumation burial. The burial, that of an adult male aged thirty to thirty-five years (report p. 271), was in a very poor condition, because of the acidity of the subsoil. The machine cut away all but the upper and lower parts of the skeleton (Pl. XV). The grave, aligned roughly north-west to south-east, was cut well into the natural gravel. Six large iron nails (report p. 284, Fig. 105) recovered in position around the body suggest that it may have originally been contained within a stout wooden coffin (Fig. 21). The grave cut the feature containing the seventh-century pendant.

THE WESTGATE COURT FARM

The old Westgate Court Farm, formerly administrative centre of the archbishop's great Manor of Westgate, was located just outside the West Gate of the City on the south-west. Nearby was also the Archbishop's Mill. In 1846, the Ashford to Ramsgate railway was built and a new farmyard was established north of the railway on the south side of the London Road and just to the south-west of St. Dunstan's Church. An accurate plan of the new farm complex first appears on sheet 3.7 of the 1:500 Ordnance Survey of 1894. The farm buildings, located south of Cogan's Hospital and west of the St. Dunstan's National School, were built in the mid nineteenth century, west of a large *c.* 1830 housing estate. They consisted of the farmhouse, set back from and parallel to the line of the London Road, flanked to the south by a range of buildings set round an open yard. The western range with a small circular structure attached to the external north-west corner was probably an oast house and barn. The building blocks flanking the other three sides of the yard were probably stables and byres. Gates were located in the north-east and south-east corners of the yard. Other small farm buildings are also shown on the survey.

The brick-built foundations of the Westgate Court Farm house together with elements of the northern range of the farmyard buildings, including the small circular structure attached to the oast house, were exposed when topsoil and rubble were mechanically removed before the cutting of the new building's foundation trenches. Time did not allow a thorough survey of the building foundations and associated features and only two pits associated with the farm are noted on the plan (Fig. 21, (72) and (73)).

The Westgate Court Farm was demolished in the early 1960s when a housing estate was built over much of the farmyard complex, and a new road (Prince's Way) constructed to service the new estate. Since the 1960s the remaining area of the Westgate Court Farm has been open ground, awaiting redevelopment.

DISCUSSION

The fifty-three or more Roman cremation burials salvaged during the construction of the new building fronting onto the London Road came from an area considered to have been outside the well-known St. Dunstan's and London Road Roman cemetery. The Roman road to London, aligned south-east to north-west, passed through the west gate of the town and ran for a distance of approximately 450 m. to a point where it turned south-westwards (aligned north-east to south-west). The cemetery seems to have flanked either side of the Roman street and the new burials now indicate that interments extend at least 600 m. north-west of the town wall. The south-western limit of the cemetery may extend as far as the line of the Rheims Way and the Victoria Sports Ground, as four burials were recorded there by Dr F. Jenkins during road and drain construction in 1951–2,[32] and at least two burials are recorded to have been found in the same area early in this century.[33] The cemetery extended north of St. Dunstan's Street. Dr Jenkins noted two inhumation burials from under the forecourt of Hallet's Garage in 1951.[34] More recently (July 1983) an inhumation burial was uncovered by workmen laying a new gas pipe under Kirby's Lane close to the line and north of the London Road. Other burials noted in the area defined by these boundaries include 'a bottle of red Roman ware . . . portions of pottery (broken urn), bones (burnt) and a coin' from 'The Orchard' in the 'upper part of Church

32. The four burials located by Dr F. Jenkins during the digging of a drain south-west of the line of the present Rheims Way, from the London Road to the bank of the Stour were:
    (1) A Belgic furrowed-ware jar containing cremated bones, standing in a small cylindrical pit *c*. 1 ft. 9 in. (*c*. 0.54 m.) deep and 2 ft. (0.61 m.) diameter. Found on the 5th December, 1951, at 95 ft. (*c*. 28.96 m.) east of the railway cutting.
    (2) A carinated black ware bowl containing only three minute pieces of human bone, standing in the base of a coarse ware jar, with a similar base covering the cremation urn. A flagon, lacking mouth and handle, bearing the remains of a cream-coloured slip was found with the urn. The vessels were recovered from a pit similar to that of burial 1, located 46 ft. 3 in. (*c*. 14.08 m.) east of the approach road to the Victoria Recreation ground. Found on 3rd January, 1952.
    (3) An incomplete jar (containing burnt bones), upper part missing, apparently broken in antiquity, and a complete 'poppy-head' beaker. The base of the burial pit, found on 4th January, 1952, 13 ft. (*c*. 3.96 m.) east of the approach road to the Victoria Recreation Ground, was 3 ft. 6 in. (*c*. 1.07 m.) below the modern surface.
    (4) This burial was found 2 ft. (0.61 m.) below the approach road to the recreation ground on the 9th January, 1952, and consisted of a simple cremation urn which had been truncated by a modern waste pipe. My thanks to Dr Jenkins for this information.
33. Hereabouts on the 7th March, 1906:
    (1) A complete samian Dr. 37 was found. The bowl bears the retrograde signature **BIILSA M** in a small label within the decoration; see A.P. Detsicas, *Antiq. Journ.*, xliv (1964), 153–6, Fig. 2.
    (2) A red earthenware bottle was found under the approach road in March 1913. (Pers. comm. Dr Jenkins.)
34. Pers. comm. Dr Jenkins.

Road', found by James Pilbrow in 1867–68 (possibly near the intersection between Cross Street and Church Street south of St. Dunstan's Church).[35] Eight to ten cremation burials were recovered in 1926, when a Telephone Repeater Station was erected immediately south of the National School and fronting on to St. Dunstan's Terrace,[36] and three inhumation burials were recovered from the cellar of no. 8 New Street in 1976.[37] Many other unsubstantiated reports of Roman burials in the St. Dunstan's area exist, together with a number of unprovenanced finds, probably from Roman burials, found in the general area and housed in the collection of the Royal Museum, Canterbury.

The natural deposits encountered during the cutting of the foundation trenches were hard brickearth overlying gravel and sand. The natural brickearth horizon rises gently from north-east to south-west, with gravel-terrace deposits outcropping through the brickearth in the extreme north-west corner of the site. Overlying the hard natural clay was a leached, pale-orange subsoil, which was in turn capped by a thin layer of brown silty buried topsoil. Most of the burials were sealed by this topsoil, which was heavily flecked with carbon and burnt clay specks. Patches of carbon, burnt clay and scatters of pot sherds were observed in a number of machine-cut sections and are noted on Fig. 22. One thick deposit of carbon contained within a shallow cutting with fired orange edges (63) and associated with at least two substantial post-holes (64) and (65) may indicate the position of an *ustrinum* (place of cremation). At least three burials (5, 8 and 9) bore traces of a raised mound, and it is possible that others existed but were not noticed during this extremely hectic salvage operation. One other burial pit containing an amphora (46) may have been marked by a post.

A number of cremation urns contained iron objects mixed with the cremated bones, particularly nails and studs from *caligae* (Roman shoes). Many of the larger nails were bent and were presumably from waste baulks of timber and planking used in the funerary pyre, accidentally gathered with the cremated bone and placed in the urn. Other nails, including hobnails, may have derived originally from household furniture and clothing laid on the pyre with the deceased. At least seven burials contained hobnails, indicating that whole shoes had been laid in the cremation pit; these nails were usually placed alongside or either side of the funerary urn.

The greatest concentration of interments was situated close to the London Road. These burials flanked either side of a V-shaped ditch (66), which was aligned parallel to the Roman road. Unfortunately, no burial was found cutting or cut by the ditch and insufficient material was recovered to date its cutting or backfill. Nevertheless, it seems likely that the ditch was originally designed to define the cemetery, south of the line of the London Road.

The possible clay-quarry (67), located in the south-west corner of the site contained a wide range of pottery dating from the mid first to perhaps the fourth century. This feature, perhaps originally dug to extract clay for pottery or tile manufacture, may have remained only partially backfilled for a long period. Indeed, the presence of a single Saxon grass-tempered sherd from

35. J. Pilbrow, 'Excavations at Canterbury in 1868', *Archaeologia*, xliii (1871), 151–64, note 90.
36. W. Whiting, 'A Roman Cemetery at St. Dunstan's, Canterbury', *Arch. Cant.*, xxxix (1927), 46–54.
37. P. Bennett, 'Excavations at 8 New Street, Canterbury', in 'Some Minor Excavations by the Canterbury Archaeological Trust in 1977–78', *Arch. Cant.*, xciv (1978), 149–52.

the upper infill of the pit suggests that the cutting may have remained as a hollow into the seventh century A.D.

Dr Pollard's analysis of the pottery (pp. 284–98) indicates that the main period of burial was from the mid second to the third century, with only three burials belonging to the mid first to early second century. The cremation burials recovered from under the nearby Repeater Station in 1927 were of Flavian to Antonine date with only one burial of a definite first-century date. Only the three earliest burials from the London Road site, therefore, need overlap in date with the Repeater Station interments. It is, therefore, tentatively suggested that the cremations recovered from this development site represent burials in a cemetery north-west of the town which was gradually extending up the London Road through time.

The small group of late sixth- or early seventh-century A.D. finds intimates a possible re-use of the old Roman cemetery in Saxon times and may indicate that other burials of a similar date may exist under and beyond Prince's Way. The Saxon burials, which include a possible cremation (69) containing two very fine glass palm cups and two re-used Roman vessels, an inhumation burial (71) of an adult male containing no associated grave goods, and a possible 'robbed' grave (70) containing the gold pendant, may be part of a possible Saxon annexe to the Roman cemetery. Two other finds, a silver *sceatta* (68) found in a shallow carbon-filled pit dated to *c.* A.D. 700 (report p. 281) and a single sherd of grass-tempered pottery recovered from the upper fill of the possible clay-quarry (67), were both found close to the burials at the north-west end of the site and may have been deposited at roughly the same time. Other than the well-known burials of the early Kentish Kings and Archbishops at St. Augustine's Abbey, this is the first time that evidence suggesting the presence of an early Saxon secular cemetery has been found near the Roman town.

Overall, the large *corpus* of finds recovered during this brief and hectic salvage operation not only indicates the size and complexity of the Roman cemetery north-west of the Roman town, but intimates a re-use of that cemetery in early Saxon times.

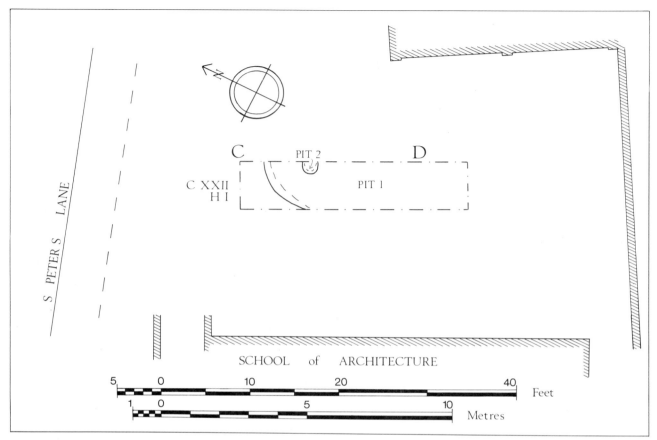

Fig. 23.   St. Peter's Lane: Plan of Trench I. (Scale: 1:130)

PART II: INTRA-MURAL SITES

XI. ST. PETER'S LANE

In the summer of 1952 two trenches, coded C XXII H, were dug at separate points in St. Peter's Lane (Figs. 23 and 24). Waterlogged conditions at both made excavation difficult, and it was found to be impossible to excavate the Roman levels satisfactorily without the aid of a water-pump.

Trench I

Nothing of significance was uncovered here and there were very few finds. Overlying the natural gravel and brickearth was a layer of light grey loam (7) (Fig. 25, Section C–D) which yielded a Belgic sherd. This was overlaid in the centre of the trench by a layer of yellow loam (6), 5 in. thick, and at the north-west end by dark grey soil (5).

Both these layers were probably Roman and were cut by a small pit, 2, in which one Roman sherd was found. At the extreme north-west end of the trench layer 5 was covered by a (?) medieval loam floor (4), which was partially burnt and overlaid by a thick occupation-layer (3). This was cut by a very large rubbly pit, 1, which extended over the central and eastern part of the trench. It contained large flints, medieval and Roman tile, bones, oyster shells and thirteenth- and fourteenth-century pottery and was probably dug to bury the demolition debris of a building. Pit 1 was overlaid by mortary black medieval soil and gravel (2) in which part of a jug of similar date was found. A yellow loam floor (1) overlay this, sealed by stiff black soil above which was modern concrete make-up and rubble.

Trench II

In Trench II several phases of medieval building were found *c.* 2 ft. 6 in. above waterlogged Roman deposits. Only the latest Roman level could be excavated. This consisted of brown pebbly earth (22) (Fig. 25, Section A–B) containing Antonine samian Dr. 38 and a number of dish sherds (Fig. 82, Nos. 17, 18). It lay below the water-level and was overlaid by a thick layer of fine-grained wet black mud (17A) containing pottery covering a date-range of the first to fourth century but probably deposited as make-up in the medieval period to raise the ground well above the water-level for the construction of buildings.

No walls were found contemporary with the earliest building, which had a loam floor (20). This overlay a medieval pit (21) and was covered by a dark charcoally and daub layer (17 = 16) yielding fourteenth-century jug sherds. It was into this that the walls of the Phase 2 building were cut. This had a chalky loam floor (14) which extended both east and west of the contemporary north–south wall and yielded a sherd of a fourteenth-century cooking-pot. It was

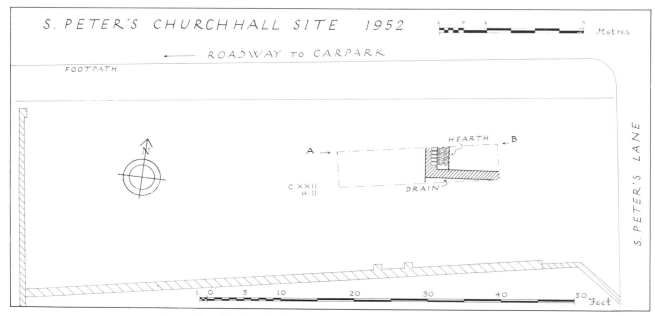

Fig. 24.   St. Peter's Lane: Plan of Trench II. (Scale: 1:155)

covered in part by a scatter of flat tiles. This building was probably functional for only a short time; the wall and floor were sealed by an occupation-layer (13) consisting of dark earth and loam and containing a fourteenth-century rim (Fig. 83, No. 19); into this layer the walls of the next (Phase 3) building were cut. Only the south-west corner of this lay within the trench. The building had a rough cobbled floor (12) which yielded fourteenth-century sherds and was covered by a layer of brownish earth (11 = 9). At the east end of the trench layer 9 had been cut away by Pit 4 which yielded fourteenth-century pottery (Fig. 83, Nos. 20–23). Layer 9 and Pit 4 were sealed by a thin loam deposit (8) which was probably a secondary floor. This was covered in turn by an occupation-deposit (6). The building then went out of use and the walls, which may have been timber on stone sills, were demolished down to the bottom three stone courses. A layer of mixed earth and loam (10), in which a penny of Edward II was found, was piled up against the west edge of the north–south wall, the surviving top of which it partially sealed. The building was soon rebuilt (Phase 4, Fig. 24). A tiled drain ran along its south side (Pl. XVIII) overlying the earlier east–west wall which was rebuilt slightly to the north; the new north–south wall lay very slightly west of the previous line. The building was floored with thick yellow loam (2) and in the south-west corner lay a tiled fireplace (Pl. XIX). By the seventeenth century the building was out of use; a layer of loam (5) yielding sherds of seventeenth- to early eighteenth-century date sealed the tiled fireplace and extended over part of the demolished north–south wall, to the west of which was a layer of dark earth (3) containing much rubble and many tiles, mostly broken and probably from the roof, together with a whole cooking-pot and other fourteenth-century sherds (Fig. 83, Nos. 24–35). Above this a thick deposit of dark soil (1) accumulated and was overlaid by modern make-up, concrete and a brick floor.

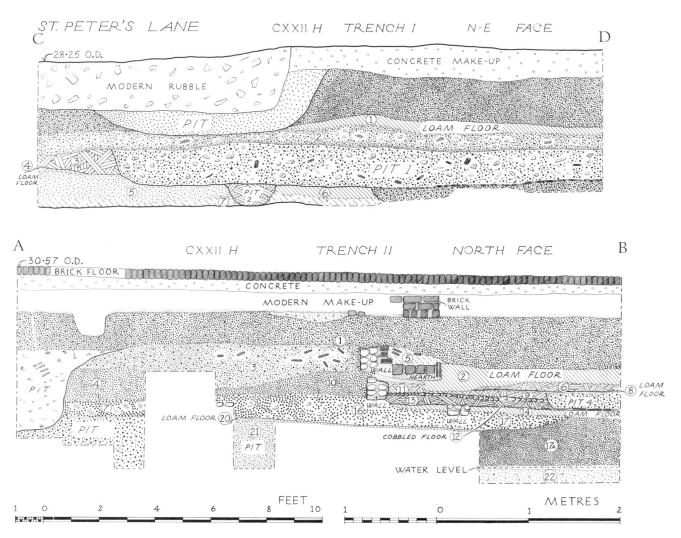

Fig. 25. St. Peter's Lane: Sections. (Scale:1:40)

XII. No. 25 ST. PETER'S STREET

In August 1953 two very small trenches, coded C XXIV, were dug in the cellar of no. 25 on the north side of St. Peter's Street (Fig. 1). The surface of a Roman street was found c. 1 ft. 3 in. below the surface of the brick floor of the cellar, at a depth of c. 8 ft. 3 in. (2.5 m.) below the level of the present pavement. This metalling lies on a line joining the West Gate to the alignment of the street along the south side of Burgate Street and therefore probably represents a principal artery of the Roman city. It is perhaps significant that St. Peter's Church appears to be aligned along the edge of this street rather than along the medieval street and may perhaps be of late Roman origin although no Roman fabric is detectable. The present chancel is not earlier than the fourteenth century, but the west end of the church contains substantial early Norman (or even Saxo-Norman) elements.[38]

XIII. No. 53 KING STREET

In the summer of 1952 a trench, coded C XXII K, was dug on the site of no. 53 King Street (Figs. 1 and 26). A succession of floors, occupation-levels and pits of Roman, medieval and post-medieval date were uncovered. The trench was divided by a north-east to south-west brick partition, 6 in. wide, and to the north-west of this a strip 1 ft. 6 in. wide was left unexcavated.

At the north-west end of the trench (Fig. 27, Section A–B) the earliest Roman levels had been destroyed by later pits; but to the south-east of the brick partition (Fig. 27, Section C–D) a Roman building with at least two phases of occupation was found. Part of two rooms was uncovered. The primary floor in the north-west room was of chalky loam. A post-hole, 2, was cut into it and burnt daub lay on its surface. This floor was divided from a contemporary gravel floor (10) to the south-east by a north-east–south-west sleeper-trench which would have held a timber partition. Layer 10 yielded a sherd of Flavian-Trajanic samian Dr. 37 which provides a *terminus post quem* for Phase 1 of the late first to early second century; but it also yielded a dish rim (p. 211, No. 1) of a type uncommon before 150, so that a rather later date in the second century is more likely. The partition later went out of use; both floors and the sleeper-trench were covered by grey-green gritty loam (7) which contained pieces of mortar, tile, oysters and charcoal, a sherd of Hadrianic-Antonine samian Dr. 31 and another fragment of a dish (of the type shown in Fig. 82, No. 18). Above it at the north-west end was a second gravel floor (7a) and at the south-east end a thick clay floor. Layer 7a yielded a sherd of Antonine samian and part of a colour-coated beaker (Fig. 82, No. 3) dated to the late second or early third century; these provide a *terminus post quem* for Phase 2. On the surface of the floor, which was cut by Pits 5 and 10, was an occupation-deposit and bones. These were covered by a destruction-layer of fallen daub and burnt wood. Above it was another gravel floor on the surface of which a pipe-clay figurine of Venus (Pl. XXVII:E) was found. The floor was covered by dark occupation-soil (5) which contained many bones. This layer sealed Pit 7 which, in the western sector of the trench (Section A–B), had destroyed the earlier Roman levels. It was filled with dark soil, fragments of painted plaster, charcoal and burnt clay and yielded much pottery which suggests a date of the first quarter of the third century. Layer 5 which thus has a *terminus post quem* of the early third century was covered with black soil (3); but it and subsequent layers were badly disturbed by Pit 1 containing seventeenth-century pottery (Fig. 82, Nos. 9–10) as well as by Pits 2, 4, 6 and 8 and a well.[39]

---

38. There is documentary evidence for a church being here by *c.* 1180. W. Urry, *Canterbury under the Angevin Kings* (London, 1967), Rental C 31. See also T.P. Smith 'The Church of St. Peter, Canterbury', *Arch. Cant.*, lxxxvi (1971), 99–108, for a discussion of the earliest parts of the church.

39. Pit 8 was probably late Roman and this was cut by Pit 4 which yielded a sherd of a ninth- to tenth-century Saxon cooking-pot. Pit 2, which cut Pit 4, produced Medieval Group II sherds. Group II pottery is discussed in *Arch. Cant.*, lxviii (1954), 129–31 and in the Lanfranc's Dormitory report (forthcoming publication); it is now dated *c.* 1050–1100. No datable material was found in Pit 6.

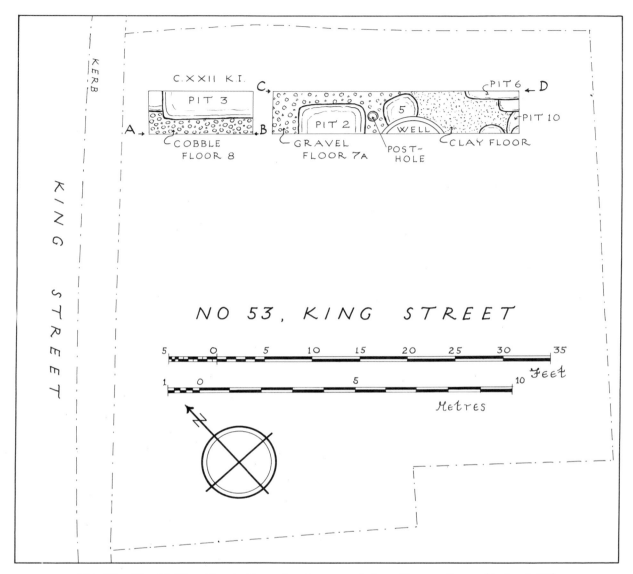

Fig. 26. No. 53 King Street: Plan, showing second-phase Roman floors. (Scale: 1:120)

To the north-west of the brick partition the levels above Pit 7 were slightly better preserved. The pit was sealed by grey-black loam (9) (Section A–B), above which was a black layer (5a) in which a barbarous radiate of c. 270 was found. Layers 9 and 5a were both cut by Pit 9 which was filled with grey-black loam. This and layer 5a were covered by late Roman cobbling of a floor or yard (8), on the surface of which were lumps of iron slag and a large patch of charcoal. This floor was cut by Pit 3 which yielded a sherd of Medieval Group IV pottery, dated to the second half of the thirteenth century. Black gravelly soil (4), which yielded pottery probably also datable to

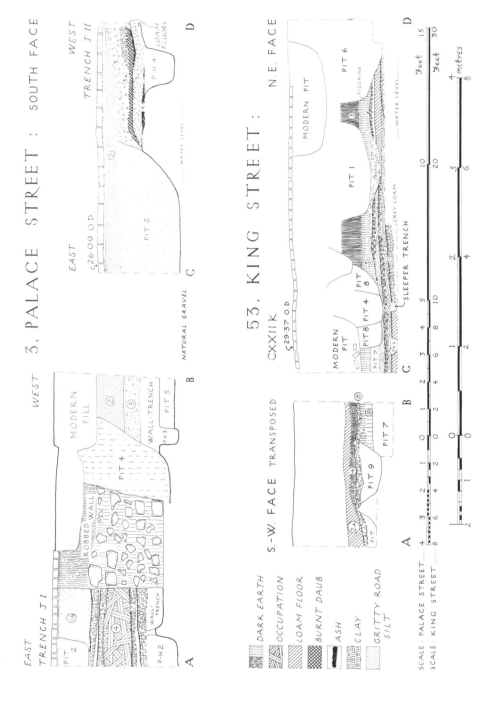

Fig. 27.   No. 3 Palace Street and No. 53 King Street: Sections. (Scales: 1:40 and 1:80)

the second half of the thirteenth century, covered both layer 8 and Pit 3, and was overlaid by a loam floor (2a) yielding seventeenth-century stone ware and much residual thirteenth- to fourteenth-century pottery. A hearth which contained the base of a black cooking-pot was cut into the floor, and to the south-east of it was an irregular spread of broken roof-tile, covered by a burnt deposit.

Thus, despite inability to reach natural subsoil because of the high water-table, occupation of the site was shown to be continuous from the mid second century to some point in the fourth; and thereafter occupation resumed from late Saxon to modern times.

XIV. No. 3 PALACE STREET

This site, which was coded C XXII J (Figs. 1, 27–29), was dug in 1952 in a deep cellar which was on two different levels and encumbered by struts shoring neighbouring buildings; but remains of three successive Belgic houses were found, and above them was an area of gravel metalling bordered by a large Roman building. The gravel was taken to represent a street running from south-west to north-east, and to be heading for the North Gate. At the time it was believed that this street, although here a few yards west of the direct line, represented the *cardo maximus* of the city directly connecting the north and south (Worth) gates; for in *c.* 1950 further street-metalling on the alignment was observed beneath the cellar of the former Guildhall.[40] However, recent work by the Canterbury Archaeological Trust has shown that the street system in the centre of the city does not form a rectangular grid, and any direct line between the two gates is interrupted. It is probable, therefore, that other explanations of the observed areas of metalling of No. 3 will be found necessary.

Belgic Houses
It was not possible to determine the plans of the pre-Roman buildings because the area available for excavation was very limited both by the size of the cellar and by substantial timbers shoring the adjacent houses; moreover, the robber-trench of a later Roman building had caused considerable damage to earlier levels. Parts of three successive Belgic houses were found in Trench I (Fig. 28). Of House 1 a wall-trench, into which post-holes were set at intervals, ran along the south side of Trench I (Fig. 28 and Fig. 27, Section A–B). This had held one of the timber walls of a rectilinear building; in the centre of Trench I it had been destroyed by the later robber-trench, but it was picked up again to the west of this where it overlay a shallow Belgic pit (Fig. 27, Section A–B, Pit 5). The wall-trench was *c.* 8 in. (20 cm.) deep with sloping sides, and was filled with gravelly earth which contained lumps of burnt daub and charcoal which presumably accumulated when the building burnt down. It was not clear which floor-levels were contemporary with this timber wall, but one floor was probably represented by a gravelly loam layer (9) which overlay the natural subsoil at the east end of Trench J I. This was the equivalent of layer 10 at the west end, but neither layer is visible in Section A–B. A little fragmentary pottery of pre-Roman Belgic type was associated with these floors. This house was later rebuilt;

40. *Arch. Cant.*, lxxxiii (1968), 10–11.

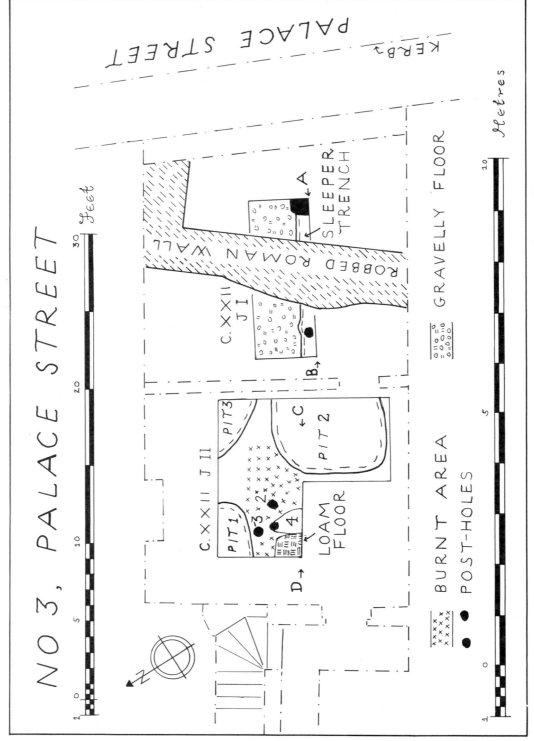

Fig. 28.   No. 3 Palace Street: Plan of Belgic features. (Scale: 1:72)

the south-eastern part of the wall-trench was sealed by a gravel floor (8). The floor was not found to the north-west of the Roman robber trench, where the wall trench was sealed by brown gritty soil (5) yielding Neronian-Flavian samian and sherds of coarse ware covering a date-range of *c*. 50–120; this seems to indicate that the second house did not extend as far west as its predecessor and that the Roman robber trench had destroyed its front. This house, too, was burnt down: on the surface of layer 8 was a deposit of grey soil and burnt loam and charcoal (8A) in which a flagon-handle of Belgic fabric was found; this accumulation was clearly the result of a fire. The house was again rebuilt and had a gravel floor (7), on the surface of which was a patch of yellow loam and a number of oysters, together with a sherd of a jar probably of Claudian date. This third house, like its predecessors, was burnt down, after which the area seems to have lain open for about a century. A thick dark brown occupation-layer (4), in which charcoal and tile fragments were found, covered 7 and yielded pottery with a date-range of *c*. 50–170, including Flavian samian Dr. 37, and a coarse ware dish and bowl (Fig. 82, Nos. 13–14). Above this were two more floors; the first was of gravel and yellow loam (3A). This was covered by a thin layer of greenish mortary occupation-soil above which was a second gravel floor (1) yielding Antonine samian Dr. 31, 33 and 31R. These floors belonged to a late second-century building about which no more information was obtained unless they belonged to the stone-walled building discussed below.

More evidence of the Belgic houses was found in Trench II. Very little information was obtained about the earliest, for all that remained of it here was a small expanse of loam floor and three post-holes (Fig. 28, Post-holes 2–4). Post-hole 2 was circular and 8 in. in diameter; it had been deliberately filled with large burnt flints around which was gravel packing, giving a total diameter of 14 in. Post-hole 3 was 6 in. in diameter and filled with grey earth. Post-hole 4 was rather irregular, measuring 1 ft. 10 in. by 1 ft. 6 in. with a possible post-pipe, 6 in. in diameter, at its north end. The floor and post-holes were sealed by a thin layer of burning (4) which reinforces the evidence in Trench I that this building was burnt down. This layer yielded purely Belgic pottery (Fig. 82, No. 11) and in post-hole 2, below the burnt flints, was most of a large crushed Belgic jar (Fig. 82, No. 12). After the fire reconstruction took place and a gravel floor (3C) was laid down; it was 4 in. thick and yielded several sherds of Belgic pottery. Above it in the south-west corner of the trench was a clay floor; both floors were sealed by a layer of burnt wood covered by burnt daub (3B) – evidence of the final conflagration (Fig. 27). This destruction-deposit contained Belgic sherds, though probably now of Claudian date.

The history of the Belgic structures in the two trenches is uniform, and can be taken to indicate that in the first and third phases there was only one building on the site, and that these houses were of fair size (at least 23 ft. = 7 m. long), substantial build and rectangular shape. Two of the buildings appear to be of pre-Roman date; the last is of about the period of the Roman Conquest.

The part played by large well-built rectangular structures in Belgic architecture has recently been stressed by Warwick Rodwell,[41] who has listed a number of examples, including one at Canterbury. The present site adds to the number.

41. In (Eds.) B. Cunliffe and T. Rowley, *Lowland Iron Age Communities in Europe* (*BAR* International Series (Supplementary) no. 48, (1978)), 25–41.

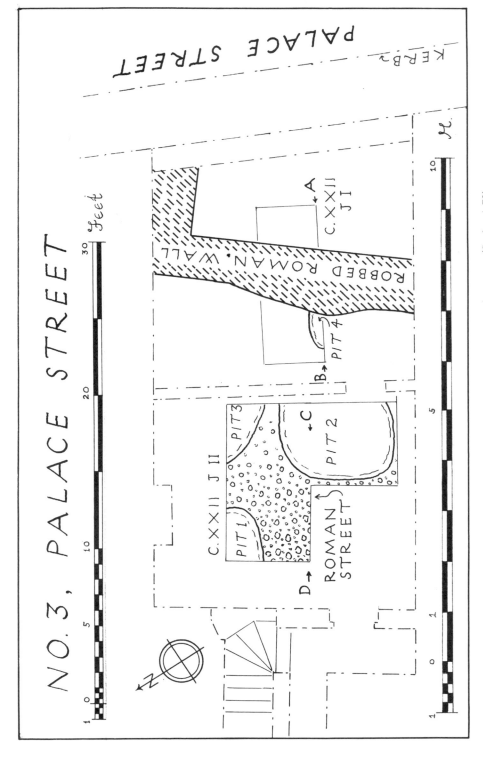

Fig. 29. No. 3 Palace Street: Plan of Roman features. (Scale: 1:72)

Street

At some time perhaps in the third quarter of the first century an area of metalling, taken to be a street, was laid over the houses in Trench II (Fig. 29 and Fig. 27, Section C–D). Burnt layer 3B had been sealed by 3A, which was a muddy layer 3 in. thick containing charcoal and oyster fragments. It was overlaid by compact yellow gravel and small stones (3) which yielded Neronian-Flavian samian and was clearly metalling. This sloped down towards the east becoming dirtier and looser. The loose gravel marked the east edge of the street area, which was covered with silty road-wash (2), yielding Antonine samian and a coin of Magnentius, probably intrusive. Pits 2 and 3, aligned with the edge of the metalling, were filled with similar silt. It is improbable that there should have been open pits along the side of a street or yard and more likely that the pits were cut into the silt and quickly refilled with their original material. Pottery from them suggests a date *c*. A.D. 200–240 (Fig. 82, Nos. 15, 16). If this is the correct interpretation, they may have held posts supporting part of a colonnade belonging to the Roman building discussed below, or to a timber predecessor.[42]

Roman Building

Only two walls of the third-century masonry building were found within the area excavated; both had been badly robbed either in the late Roman or medieval period so that only the robber trench survived. This was cut through a layer of make-up (Fig. 27, Section A–B (1A)) and through the earlier floors below it (1, 3, 7 and 8) as well as through Pit 4 which had very probably also been cut by the original wall. This pit yielded Antonine samian and its contents went down to the end of the second century; this provides an early third-century *terminus post quem* for the masonry building. The robber trench was flat-bottomed and square cut; it was 2 ft. deep and 3 ft. wide except where pits had caused it to bulge, and it was filled with Roman building-rubble, very large flints and blocks of Kentish ragstone some of which were burnt, as was the pottery. The floor of this building was indistinct but was probably represented by a spread of mortar immediately below the cellar floor above a thick layer of make-up (1A). Floors 3A and 1, the latter containing Antonine samian Dr. 31, 33 and 31R and capped by a thin spread of mortar, may have belonged to this building; but it is more likely that they relate to a second- or early third-century predecessor perhaps in timber, to which the possible post-pits (Fig. 29, Pits 2 and 3) may be related. If so, they will have supported a verandah outside a timber-framed wall on the line of the later stone one, for the floors referred to did not extend west of the robber trench (Section A–B).

---

42. Possibly this was one of the buildings observed by James Pilbrow. In 1868, a stretch of wall, 130 ft. (39.6 m.) long, was found in Sun Street, and *c*. 100 ft. (30.5 m.) to the west of this a similar wall *c*. 95 ft. (29 m.) long was found running along Guildhall Street (*Archaeologia*, xliii, p. 162, nos. 57 and 58; *V.C.H.* (Kent), iii, 73, (21)). If extended these walls would have met in Palace Street at an angle of 30°. It is more likely that they belong to two different buildings and the substantial robber trench found under no. 3 Palace Street may have formed part of one of them. Alternatively, it could be connected with finds observed by Pilbrow actually in Palace Street *Archaeologia*, xliii, Pl. XXII, No. 59; *V.C.H.* (Kent), iii, 73 (23).

XV. No. 7 PALACE STREET

INTRODUCTION

During recent repairs and modifications to no. 7 Palace Street, the large cellar under the premises was lowered by approximately 0.45 m. In normal circumstances the Canterbury Archaeological Trust would have been informed by the City Council's conservation department that such an operation, in a potentially important part of the city, was to take place. Unfortunately, the developer did not apply for the relevant planning permission and, as a result, an opportunity to examine systematically some remarkably well-preserved archaeological levels was lost.

The rapid lowering of the cellar was first noted by Mr K. Reedie, Curator of the Royal Museum, who informed the Trust on 6th December, 1982. A hectic three days were then spent salvaging the information given below.[43]

Our thanks are extended to the workmen who allowed access to the cellar, despite the speed with which they were expected to complete the lowering process.

SUMMARY

The original cutting of the cellar, which was roughly 7 m. sq. with a brick floor (the surface being at 2.10 m. below the present pavement of Palace Street), had removed all post-Roman stratigraphy and perhaps some of the latest Roman levels (see Fig. 30). Only two large and deep post-medieval post-holes (39) and (40) were found cutting the intact levels. The south half of the cellar had been largely removed by the workmen and hardcore laid down, before the salvage operation began. Large quantities of pottery, particularly amphora and flagon sherds recovered by the workmen (some later accidently discarded by them), together with verbal evidence for banded layers indicated intensive Roman occupation in this part of the cellar. Only the levels in the northern half of the cellar were observed in any detail by the authors. Initial observations indicated the presence of the south-eastern verge of a street aligned north-east to south-west, leading directly to the Roman North Gate and located at the western end of the cellar. Subsequent work to the east of the street, accomplished in extremely poor lighting conditions, revealed a series of drains separating the road from the remains of at least one Roman timber building.

THE ROAD

A sequence of at least four major street surfacings separated by layers of silt (2), (4), (5) and (7), together with three intercutting road drains (8), (9) and (37) were noted in the north-west corner of the cellar (Fig. 30, Section A–B). The road, aligned roughly north-east to south-west

---

43.   The writer was assisted in this work by Mr J. Rady.

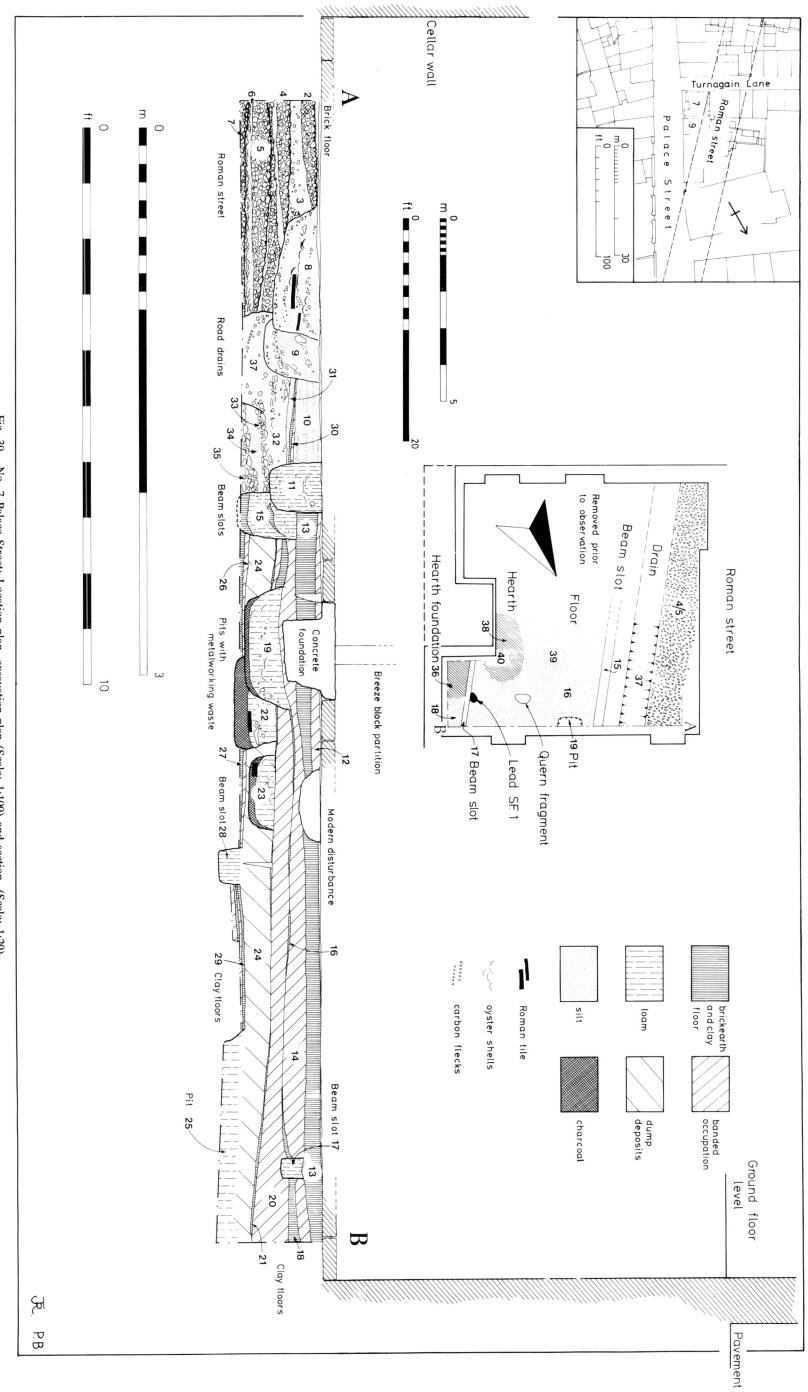

Fig. 30. No. 7 Palace Street: Location plan, excavation plan (Scale: 1:100) and section. (Scale: 1:20)

leads directly to the Roman North Gate, and may be a continuation of the road recently discovered under the east end of the Poor Priests' Hospital[44] and during the cutting of a sewer tunnel in the High Street.[45] Later street metallings undoubtedly existed, but were removed when the cellar was constructed. Earlier street metallings and road silts in gutters were exposed and removed when deeper foundations were cut from the finished levels of the new cellar floor. No trace of the natural horizon (head brickearth) was encountered by the workmen during the cutting of the deeper trench for underpinning the cellar walls. The surviving Roman stratigraphy, must have therefore been at least 1 m. thick.

THE BUILDING

Aligned parallel to the street were two intercutting beam-slots (11) and (15) possibly representing the frontage of a Roman timber building. A remarkably well-preserved sequence of floors and internal features was examined to the east of the road-frontage beam-slots, indicating at least four phases of clay floors. The Phase III floor (16) is shown in Fig. 30.

The earliest floors were observed at the lowest level of the reduced cellar, though earlier floors may have existed below this. Although no road-frontage beam-slot was located, one must have existed in a similar position, but at a lower level than the later ones. Bisecting the early building was an internal beam-slot (28). A clay floor (27) extended west of this feature to the road frontage and a second floor of two phases (29) extended east of the slot. Cutting this floor in the north-east corner of the cellar was a large pit (25) of which only the upper few centimetres were extracted. The upper pit fill yielded a small number of sherds dating from the mid second century. Sealing the earliest floor was a considerable dump of grey-green sandy silt and pebbles (24). This compact deposit, void of finds, was cut by two small sub-rectangular shallow pits (22) and (23) which also contained no finds. A road-frontage beam-slot (15) cut this deposit and a new clay floor (21) was laid over it. Sealing the floor were layers of compact, banded occupation material (20) which contained ash and charcoal and yielded a large number of mid to late second-century sherds (report p. 302). Capping the banded occupation and re-using the same road-frontage beam-slot (15) was a further clay floor (16) bounded to the east by a new beam-slot (17). A patch of burnt clay (38), possibly an internal hearth, was noted on the floor close to the internal slot. A large lump of lead waste (S.F. 2) was recovered from the surface of the floor, lying against the internal beam-slot. The floor east of the internal slot (18) contained the remains of a heavily burnt stone, rubble and tile foundation, possibly an industrial hearth (36). Cutting the road-frontage floor (16) was a small rectangular pit (19). This pit, similar in fill to the earlier pits (22 and 23) contained a few sherds of second-century pottery and a quantity of metalworking waste, which included a complete brass-making crucible.[46] Sealing this floor and abutting the internal beam-slot was a complex sequence of trodden and banded deposits of ash

44. *The Archaeology of Canterbury*, vol. vi (forthcoming) 'Excavations in the Castle Street and Stour Street Areas', and *Arch. Cant.*, xcviii (1982), 216.
45. *Arch. Cant.*, xcviii (1982), and Canterbury Archaeological Trust's *Topographical Maps of Canterbury A.D. 400, 1050, 1200, 1500 and 1700* (revised edition 1982).
46. See below p. 299 and J. Bayley 'Roman Brass-making in Britain', in *Historical Metallurgy*, 18 (i) (1984), 42–3.

and charcoal (14), which also yielded a large number of mid- to late second-century sherds (report p. 301). A new road-frontage beam-slot (11) and a thick clay floor (13) cut and sealed the earlier deposits. A thin layer of ash and charcoal sealed the lowest levels of the floor. Both floor and surviving occupation were capped by the brick floor of the cellar.

CONCLUSIONS

The information salvaged during the lowering of the cellar throws important light on an area of the Roman city that has been little studied because of a lack of suitable sites for excavation. The location of another main Roman street adds more evidence to our growing knowledge of the Roman street plan. Perhaps more important is the location of the small timber building. The complex and thick sequence of floors with internal features indicates an intense occupation of the building during the mid to late second century. The high percentage of ash and charcoal within the occupation deposits, taken together with the possible hearths on the Phase III floor and the metalworking waste, strongly suggests that the building may have been a workshop, probably that of a metalworker or smith. It can only be regretted that this extremely important evidence was retrieved in such unfortunate circumstances, since a systematic excavation of the levels removed during the lowering of the cellar would have produced much more supportive evidence for this supposition.

XVI. BLACKFRIARS' GATE

On 20 February, 1984, the main southern gate to the Blackfriars[47] was cut through during the laying of a new mains water pipe. This part of the gate foundation, located close to the intersection of St. Peter's Street and The Friars and east of no. 11 St. Peter's Street, had previously been extensively disturbed by numerous service trenches including the mains sewer installed when James Pilbrow was the City Engineer in 1868.[48]

The wall foundation, 1.32 m. (4 ft. 4 in.) wide and 0.30 m. (1 ft.) below the present pavement, was constructed of roughly-coursed chalk rubble, faced front and back with a mixture of small greensand blocks and knapped flint. The wall, standing to a height of 0.55 m. (1 ft. 10 in.) overlay a foundation 1.68 m. (5 ft. 6 in.), which projected 0.30 m. (1 ft.) in front of the wall face. The foundation cut a sequence of earlier street metallings and was sealed by construction debris of spent mortar and chalk rubble. Extensive dumps of gravel capped the debris and abutted against the face of the wall. The contemporary levels east of the wall had been severely truncated by recent service trenches and by a large pit cut against the back face of the wall. Traces of compact gravel and mortar, cut by these disturbances, may have been associated with a lane running through the gate to the friars' buildings.

The gate, built by 1356,[49] was demolished in 1787. Information, taken from a print showing

47. See Margaret Sparks with Tim Tatton-Brown, *The Blackfriars in Canterbury* (1984).
48. *Archaeologia*, xliii (1871).
49. A.R. Martin, 'The Dominican Priory at Canterbury', in *Arch. J.*, lxxxvi (1929), 157.

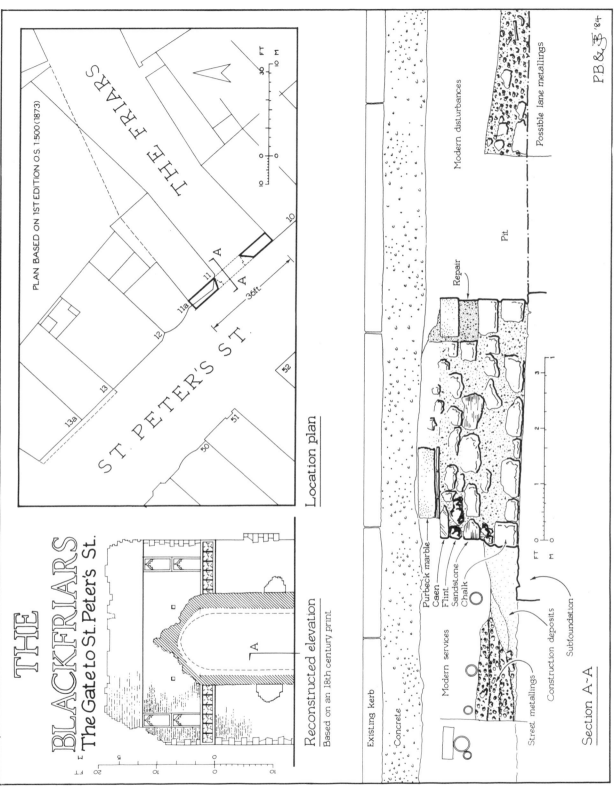

THE BLACKFRIARS
The Gate to St. Peter's St.

Location plan

PLAN BASED ON 1ST EDITION O.S. 1:500 (1873)

THE FRIARS

ST. PETER'S ST.

Reconstructed elevation
Based on an 18th century print

Section A~A

Existing kerb

Concrete

Modern services

Street metallings

Construction deposits

Subfoundation

Purbeck marble
Caen
Flint
Sandstone
Chalk

Modern disturbances

Repair

Pit

Possible lane metallings

PB & JS '84

Fig. 31. Blackfriars Gate: Reconstructed elevation (Scale: 1:200), location plan (Scale: 1:400) and section. (Scale: 1:20)

the gate shortly before 1787 and from the 1st Edition Ordnance Survey 1:500 map of 1873, has been used in a tentative location of the gateway itself (Fig. 31).

The wall foundation, initially considered to be part of the western abutment of the gate, was thought more likely to be a foundation spanning the gate jambs, set below contemporary ground level. The present opening from St. Peter's Street to The Friars probably bears no relation to the original width of the gate. Indeed, it is quite likely that the boundary between nos. 11 and 11a St. Peter's Street represents the western end of the gate. The gate shown on the contemporary print (see insert drawing, Fig. 31) is undoubtedly of some size and covers a greater area than that surviving today between nos. 10 and 11 St. Peter's Street.

Corroborative evidence for this exists in the form of a bird's-eye view map of the Blackfriars area originally drawn in 1595[50] which shows the Friars as a wide curving road of unchanging width. The 1873 Ordnance Survey plan of the area therefore suggests that no. 11 St. Peter's Street was built partly over the original wide street leading into the Blackfriars and partly over the demolished gate. If one accepts that no. 11 St. Peter's Street was built over the gate foundations, then a total gate width of 10.98 m. (36 ft.) is indicated. If the foundation did represent the western abutment of the gate, an opening no more than 2.13 m. (7 ft.) wide would be indicated. Given that this gate was one of the main points of access into the Blackfriars, such a width does not seem plausible. A comparison with other Canterbury gates (e.g. the Fyndon Gate at St. Augustine's, Parker's Gate on Palace Street and the Mint Yard Gate) indicates a much wider opening, certainly in excess of 7 ft. and perhaps as much as c. 10 ft. (3.05 m.) wide. The reconstructed plan shown on Fig. 31 has therefore been based on the assumption that the overall width of the gate measured 36 ft., that the gate opening was at least 10 ft. wide, and that the foundation observed during the cutting of the service trench was set below contemporary ground level.

XVII. THE KING'S BRIDGE AND ALL SAINTS' CHURCH

During May and June 1982 the laying of a new 12 in. gas main from the junction of Best Lane and the High Street to beyond the block of shops called 'The Weavers' (nos. 1, 2 and 3 St. Peter's Street) exposed part of the medieval fabric of the King's Bridge and parts of the church of All Saints (Fig. 32).[51]

In a trench cut down the centre of Best Lane close to the intersection with the High Street, parts of the east and south walls of the church of All Saints (a church with a nave, north aisle and a tower at the west end of the south wall – in existence by c. 1200)[52] were exposed, together with the massive greensand quoins of the south-east corner (Fig. 32). In a second trench in the

50.   Bird's-eye view map of the Blackfriars by T. Langdon (1595) now lost but engraved in c. 1790 by J. Robson of Bond Street, London, and an engraving, also by Robson, of the gate 'lately taken down'.

51.   Thanks are extended to the Segas workmen, particularly Mr Tom Iverson, who brought to our attention their encounter with the King's Bridge, and particularly for their efforts to avoid damaging the surviving fabric. Thanks are also extended to Messrs. I. Anderson, S. Pratt and A. Ward for their assistance during the recording operation.

52.   W. Urry, *Canterbury under the Angevin Kings* (London, 1967).

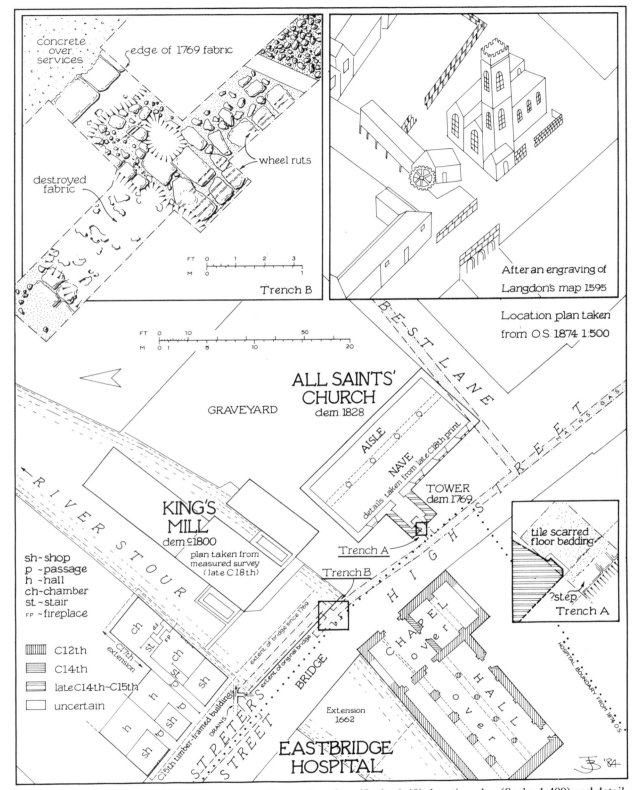

concrete over services

edge of 1769 fabric

wheel ruts

destroyed fabric

FT 0 1 2 3
M 0

Trench B

After an engraving of *Langdon's map 1595*

Location plan taken from O.S. 1874 1:500

FT 0 10 50
M 0 1 5 10 20

BEST LANE

ALL SAINTS' CHURCH
dem. 1828

GRAVEYARD

AISLE

NAVE

details taken from late C18th print

TOWER
dem 1769

Trench A

Trench B

RIVER STOUR

KING'S MILL
dem c.1800

plan taken from measured survey (late C18th)

sh ~ shop
p ~ passage
h ~ hall
ch ~ chamber
st ~ stair
FP ~ fireplace

|||||| C12th
▭ C14th
▭ late C14th–C15th
▭ uncertain

ch
ch
FP
st
st
sh
h
sh
p
h
sh
p
sh

C17th extension

C15th timber-framed buildings

DRAINS

ST PETER'S STREET

BRIDGE

extent of bridge since 1769
extent of original bridge

HIGH STREET

MAINS GAS

CHAPEL over HALL over

EASTBRIDGE HOSPITAL

Extension 1662

tile scarred floor bedding

?step
Trench A

HOSPITAL BOUNDARY FROM 1874 O.S.

JB '84

Fig. 32.   King's Bridge and All Saints' Church: Excavation plans (Scale: 1:40), location plan (Scale: 1:400) and detail of engraving *c.* 1595.

High Street a little further to the west, the west side of the principal medieval south door was exposed (with external flat chamfer and no 'stops'), together with the original threshold which lay some 1.20 m. (*c.* 4 ft.) below the present street (Fig. 32, Trench A). The tower to the medieval church (and the doorway) was demolished in order to widen the street and bridge in 1769. In 1828, the rest of the medieval church was demolished and rebuilt in yellow brick. This church (closed in 1902), was in turn taken down in 1937[53] and is largely covered by the present Gasboard showroom (no. 23 High Street). Part of the original graveyard (with headstones) still survives as a small public garden behind the showroom.

A third trench cut from the intersection of the High Street with Stour Street to 'The Weavers' exposed an extensive sequence of medieval and post-medieval street metallings; many of the earlier streets were mixed with or sealed by floor-silt. Flooding was a great problem in this area in the medieval period and was particularly troublesome when mills were operating down-stream. Flooding continued to be a problem into more recent times and was only finally solved when large quantities of hardcore were laid – particularly lumps of vitrified furnace-lining from the gasworks – to raise the level of the road. At the western end of the trench (Fig. 32, Trench B), opposite the Surgery (no. 24 High Street) the workmen exposed the tough well-constructed fabric of the top side of the King's Bridge. The bridge, a triple-arched structure almost certainly of late twelfth-century build (the underside of which can still be seen from a boat), was remarkably well-preserved and considerable wear to the Greensand blockwork fabric of the bridge was evident, as were a number of pronounced wheel-ruts (Pl. XX). The triple-arched bridge had the main stream going under it on the west and a mill-leat on the east.

That part of the bridge exposed by the service trench covered the eastern arch used by the King's Mill, first mentioned in a charter of King Stephen of *c.* 1144. The present doctor's surgery (no. 24 High Street) is a *c.* 1800 house sitting on the site of the mill with the mill-tail still intact underneath. Two stone-lined drains located during the work on the bridge may have fed effluent· into the river, and may have been linked to the 'common Forrens' or public toilet that was situated on the bridge from the late medieval period to the early eighteenth century. In 1769, the bridge was widened on the north side by ten feet and the roadways either side of the bridge were raised and thickly metalled to prevent flooding. Much of the material used in the widening derived from a triple-arched section of the northern city wall over the river called the Water Lock (near Abbots' Mill) demolished in the same year. A print of the widened bridge drawn shortly after its completion[54] is reproduced on Pl. XXI.

A section of a 'bird's-eye view' map of the Blackfriars area drawn in 1595[55] (inset on Fig. 32) shows the King's Bridge before widening, the mill and medieval All Saints' Church and tower (with south door). A plan showing the disposition of buildings in the area in *c.* 1595 (based on the 1874 1st Edition Ordnance Survey 1:500 map), together with the location of the various gas trenches is shown on Fig. 32.

53. My thanks to Mrs. M. Sparks for this information.
54. J. Duncombe and N. Battely, 'The History and Antiquities of the three archiepiscopal Hospitals at and near Canterbury', *Bibliotheca Topographica Britannica*, (London 1785).
55. Bird's-eye view map of the Blackfriars by T. Langdon (1595) now lost, but engraved in *c.* 1790 by J. Robson of Bond Street, London.

XVIII. COUNTY HOTEL AND FLEUR-DE-LIS YARD: THE FORUM AREA

The exact location of the Canterbury forum and basilica is unknown, but a number of Roman features very probably connected with public buildings have been recorded in the area between Stour Street and White Horse Lane (Fig. 33) in the eighteenth, nineteenth and twentieth centuries and it seems very likely that the forum lay in this vicinity.

A mosaic measuring 4 ft. by 8 ft. (1.22 by 2.44 m.) was found in 1758, 3 ft. below the surface, while making a cellar for a house which is now part of the County Hotel (Fig. 33, Site a).[56]

James Pilbrow, during his observation of drainage-trenches in 1867–68 noted three walls (Fig. 33, walls 26–28) crossing the High Street at right angles near the County Hotel;[57] 28 was 4 ft. (1.22 m.) wide and lay 4 ft. east of Stour Street; 27 was also 4 ft. wide and lay 14 ft. (4.27 m.) east of 28; 26 was 8 ft. (2.44 m.) wide and 15 ft. (4.57 m.) east of 27. The tops of these walls lay 7 ft. (2.13 m.) below street-level and beyond 26 was a layer of concrete and loose stones.

A fourth wall 25 was found c. 85 ft. (25.9 m.) east of 26 in front of no. 35 High Street, just north-east of the former Fleur-de-Lis Hotel (now the Wimpy Bar). This was 4 ft. wide and had shallower foundations than the other three. It 'ended in a pavement of solid stone 12 in. (0.3 m.) thick and 5 ft. below the surface'. This extended as far as White Horse Lane and some distance up it.

Another wall 12 ft. (3.66 m.) long, built of squared stones and running parallel with the High Street was observed opposite All Saints' Church, but this was thought to be medieval.[58]

Architectural fragments of oolite had been found in 1861 in the same area as wall 25.[59] These consisted of 'bases of columns with ornamented cornices which were whole in eight or ten instances' and 'bases of a cornice with chamfer moulding and three half-roll mouldings'. All are now lost, but their presence suggests a public building.[60]

More recently Dr Frank Jenkins has recorded Roman features in this area. In May 1949, the Post Office Engineering Department dug a trench for an underground cable jointing-chamber at the junction of Stour Street and High Street (Fig. 33, Site b); a spread of gravel 2 ft. 6 in. (0.76 m.) thick was uncovered.[61] This, Jenkins suggested, was part of a street flanking the forum. It

56. *Arch. Cant.*, xv (1883), 338 ff. and colour-engraving between pp. 126–7. *V.C.H.* (Kent), iii, 67 and 68 (2). The site is marked only approximately on Fig. 33. The exact position is unknown.

57. *Archaeologia*, xliii (1871), 154, nos. 73–76; *Arch. Cant.*, xv (1883), 338 ff.

58. *Archaeologia*, xliii (1871), 154, no. 72.

59. *Arch. Cant.*, iv (1861), 35; *JBAA*, xvii (1861), 59; *Proc. Soc. Ant.*, Ser. ii 1 (1861), 327; *V.C.H.* (Kent), iii, 68 (2).

60. *V.C.H.* (Kent), iii, 68 (2) suggests a temple on the grounds that these remains were found too near to the limits of the inhabited area on the west side of the city, then thought to be the King's Bridge branch of the River Stour, to belong to any other public building. This argument is no longer valid, for the area is now known to be in the centre of the Roman city.

Urry in *Arch. Cant.*, xciv (1978), 1 ff. has published a transcript from the Hasted papers in Canterbury Cathedral Library which records the discovery of an oval structure in Jewry Lane in 1689 in and around which were found many Roman coins together with two heifer skulls and a number of boar-tusks; it was thought at the time to be a temple of the goddess Diana. (*Note*: In the eighteenth century the name Jewry Lane was still applied both to the present lane of that name and to the section now called White Horse Lane).

61. *Arch. Cant.*, lxiv (1951), 63.

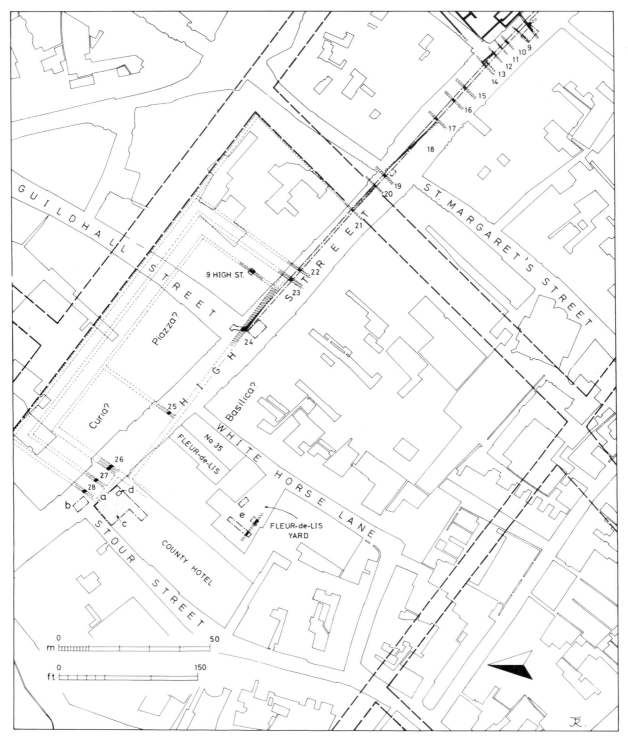

Fig. 33. Sewer tunnel and suspected forum area: Location plan of observed and excavated remains. (Scale: 1:1,250)

sealed a deposit of water-logged soil in which Flavian samian (Dr. 18, 15, 27 and 37) was found together with an *as* of Titus. But in 1951 and again in 1953 more Roman gravel was exposed during enlargement of the County Hotel cellars (Pl. XXIII, Fig. 33, Site c). If this was continuous with the gravel just mentioned, it was now too extensive for a street and could be interpreted as forming part of the forum courtyard. The gravel had a level surface and was sealed by black medieval earth. In 1953, traces of a wooden pipe-line, 3 in. in diameter, with an iron junction-collar, were found running north–south across the gravel, which was *c.* 4 ft. thick, at a depth of *c.* 18 in. There was no sign of any disturbance in the gravel above and it was thought to be contemporary.

As a result of these discoveries an archaeological trench 5 ft. by 4 ft. was dug by S.S. Frere in 1953 in the centre of the cellar (Fig. 33, Site d). This showed that there were two periods of metalling. Waterlogged conditions made full excavation impossible and no datable finds were recovered; but the lowest level excavated was a deposit of loose sandy gravel which in view of the depth of the natural subsoil elsewhere was clearly not natural. Above this was a deposit of yellow loam which had a hard trampled surface; this was covered by a second deposit of gravel *c.* 3 ft. (0.9 m.) thick. More gravel was observed in this area in 1958.

This area of Canterbury did not suffer greatly from bomb damage and thus areas available for excavation were limited. One such area did exist in the yard of the former Fleur-de-Lis Hotel and three trenches, coded C XXVIII B, were dug there in 1955 (Fig. 33, Site e and Fig. 34). The Fleur-de-Lis was demolished in 1958 and the western part of the yard is now covered by the County Hotel extension. There was much disturbance, but remains of walls and part of a substantially bedded, very worn tessellated pavement were found together with much Roman building debris which included wall-veneers of various marbles[62] (Pls. XXVIII, XXIX). This seemed to confirm the presence of a public building in this area.

The earliest feature, which was not fully excavated, was a wide shallow ditch located in Trench I (Fig. 35, Section A–B (14)). This had been cut into the natural gravel and was packed with large flints. It was probably *c.* 10 ft. wide but not more than 30 in. deep. Sealing this was a loam deposit (13) in which many animal bones were found. Above this was a gravel make-up (12) covered by a layer of *opus signinum* (11). Set on this, immediately to the north-east of a south-east to north-west wall, was a thin strip of worn tesellated pavement. The *tesserae*, which were large (measuring $1\frac{1}{2}$ by $1\frac{3}{4}$ in.), petered out *c.* 2 ft. 2 in. from the wall and beyond this only their *opus signinum* base (11) survived. This was very soft and decayed, possibly because of the proximity of wet pit-filling. In places layer 11 was covered by a thin charcoally layer (10), above which was a second deposit of quite good quality *opus signinum* (8), very likely a secondary floor.

The south-east to north-west wall on the south-west side of the tessellated pavement was *c.* 17 in. (0.43 m.) wide and built of flint and mortar on gravel footings. It was found in Trenches I and II but in the latter was only seen at the extreme south-east and north-west edges since all the Roman levels within the trench had been destroyed by medieval and later cess-pits. The wall of one of these incorporated a fragment of column-drum with a dowel-hole. Traces of quarter-

---

62.   The marble is reported on in Appendix 1 of this report (p. 250).

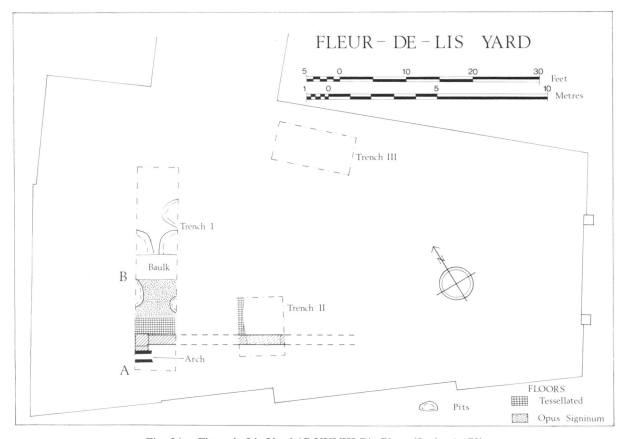

Fig. 34.   Fleur-de-Lis Yard (C XXVIII B): Plan. (Scale: 1:172)

round moulding were found on the north-east side of the wall, but there was a 2-in. gap between it and the wall where the plaster or marble facing had disappeared.

Trench I was less disturbed and the wall was seen to be of two periods. The Period I wall, which was bonded with white mortar, had fallen into disrepair and had been covered by a debris layer (3) containing bones, flints, pieces of marble – both cornice and wall-veneer – and yielding a sherd of a flanged bowl of the same type as Fig. 77, No. 130, dating to the second half of the fourth century. The wall had later been rebuilt with yellow mortar above layer 3; this rebuild is thus dated to the second half of the fourth century at the earliest.

At the west side of Trench I the first-period wall turned south. The corner was turned in tile and immediately adjacent was a hypocaust arch turned in tile (Pl. XXIV, Fig. 35), and resting on the surface of natural gravel. There was no floor to support the pillars of a hypocaust in the area exposed; possibly the hypocaust lay on the other side of the arch, the area excavated representing merely the stoke-hole. However, there was no sign that firing had ever taken place. The space in front of the arch and south-west of the south-east to north-west wall was filled to the intrados of the arch with a layer of sticky light brown earth (9) containing building-rubble

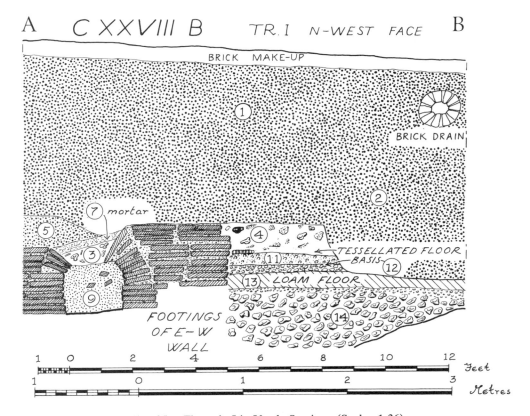

A C XXVIII B   TR. I N-WEST FACE   B

BRICK MAKE-UP

① ②

BRICK DRAIN

⑦ mortar

⑤ ④

③ ⑪ TESSELLATED FLOOR
BASIS

⑫

⑨ ⑬ LOAM FLOOR

FOOTINGS
OF E-W
WALL ⑭

Feet

Metres

Fig. 35.   Fleur-de-Lis Yard: Section. (Scale: 1:36)

and a few pieces of marble. Above this, up to the top of the surviving tile-work lay a deposit of darker brown earth (3) yielding many marble fragments together with pieces of flint, ragstone and tile. Layer 3 was earlier than the reconstruction of the wall and evidently represented a phase of demolition. A number of bones, described in Appendix 2, was found in layers 9 and 3.

Dating evidence for the construction of the building was negligible; but there was little occupation beneath it. In Trench II the tessellated floor lay only 12 in. above the natural subsoil; this probably indicates that it was erected or at least planned early in the Roman period: a site near the centre of the city is unlikely to have been left vacant for long. The chocolate-coloured loam, which is typical elsewhere of the Claudio-Neronian period in Canterbury, was absent on this site. The rebuilding of the south-east to north-west wall dates to the second half of the fourth century and it is thus unlikely that the building went out of use until the very end of the fourth century or later. Only residual pottery was found in a debris-layer (4), which accumulated over the tessellated pavement and *opus signinum*.

Trench III, like Trench II, was greatly disturbed. At a depth of 5 ft. 6 in. (1.7 m.) was a layer of Roman building debris containing much mortar together with some lumps of ragstone and *tegulae* and a large slab of marble-veneer. This layer also yielded many fragments of wall plaster with a plain pink surface. This debris was 1 ft. 8 in. thick; below it at a depth of 7 ft. 2 in. lay a clay hearth resting on a foundation of stone and tile fragments set into a layer of clean loam. A medieval pit in this trench yielded a Saxon sherd (Fig. 84, No. 36), and Pit 1 in Trench I yielded fourteenth-century sherds together with an imported jug from western France of late twelfth- to thirteenth-century date (Fig. 84, No. 37).

The function of the Roman building is not clear; the hearth in Trench III (Fig. 34), c. 20 ft. (6 m.) to the north of Trench II, may perhaps indicate a house or a shop, but this may belong to another building. The presence of marble fragments, which included thin wall-veneers in red porphyry from Egypt, Giallo Antico from Algeria or Numidia and Carrara marble from Italy (Pls. XXVIII, XXIX and see Appendix 1), makes it certain that there was a public building somewhere here. The site lies over 400 ft. (122 m.) north-north-west of the known area of the public baths in St. Margaret's Street and is unlikely to have formed part of that establishment. Whether it formed part of the forum is impossible to decide in view of the small area examined and of the narrowness of the wall found. This wall, however, was only an internal one, and certainly the richness of the marble veneers suggests a public function.

XIX. THE HIGH STREET SEWER TUNNEL

The Sewer Tunnel (Fig. 33)

During November and December 1982 the sewer tunnel driven under parts of the Parade and St. George's Street[63] was continued north-westwards under the Parade, and the High Street to the intersection with Guildhall Street. Eight Roman walls, a drain and the southernmost end of the St. George's Street Roman bath-house were cut through and recorded during the first stage of tunnelling. A further sixteen walls, a major Roman street and a metalled area, possibly a courtyard, were truncated and recorded during the cutting of the second stage. The driving of the tunnel began on 8 November, from a shaft dug opposite nos. 41 and 42 High Street.[64] A second 'emergency' shaft, cut as a result of the workmen encountering toxic gases in the heading, was established opposite the High Street intersection with Mercery Lane.[65] The tunnel was then extended to a third shaft opposite no. 16 The Parade.[66] The final stage, connecting the new sewer to the existing service under Guildhall Street, was completed on 2 December. Our thanks are extended to the contractors, D. Justice Ltd., and to the officers of the City Engineer's Department of Canterbury City Council.

The walls are described from south-east to north-west:

(a)   Wall 9 was 0.60 m. wide, built of fist-sized 'fresh' flints in a tough yellow mortar on a compacted gravel foundation 0.38 m. deep. This wall, which was also located in a G.P.O.

---

63. *The Archaeology of Canterbury*, vol. vii, S.S. Frere and Sally Stow, *Excavations in the St. George's Street and Burgate Areas*, vol. vii (1983), 322 ff.
64. The shaft was excavated to a depth of +7.50 m. O.D., 3.75 m. below the present road level.
65. The shaft was excavated to a depth of +8.45 m. O.D., 4.00 m. below the present road level.
66. The shaft was excavated to a depth of +9.05 m. O.D., 4.15 m. below the present road level.

service trench in 1976,[67] is undoubtedly part of the south wing of the Butchery Lane Roman house.

(b) Between Walls 9 and 11 a bedding of flints and mortar was noted in the roof of the tunnel; it was perhaps the basis for a mosaic pavement, which was partly uncovered during the cutting of the G.P.O. service trench in 1976.[68]

(c) Wall 10 was probably an early wall foundation pre-dating the Butchery Lane house. The foundation, 0.40 m. wide and 0.30 m. deep was of rammed gravel, and was overlain by the flint and mortar bedding noted above.

(d) Wall 11, 0.55 m. wide with a rammed gravel foundation 0.45 m. deep, was built of fair-sized 'fresh' flints and lumps of sandstone. This wall was flanked to the south-east by the bedding for a mosaic pavement and to the north-west by bedding deposits for an *opus signinum* floor, and had also been located in the G.P.O. trench. This wall and the associated bedding deposits are also part of the Butchery Lane house.

(e) Between Walls 11 and 12 a further bedding of flints and mortar was noted in the roof of the tunnel; this was perhaps the basis for an *opus signinum* floor, since a well-preserved section of *opus signinum* was truncated when the G.P.O. trench was cut nearby in 1976.

(f) Wall 12, approximately 0.50 m. wide on a gravel foundation, was built of fist-sized 'fresh' flints in a tough yellow mortar. The wall was cut by a robber trench and at least one large pit. This wall, partially located in the G.P.O. trench, may be the east wall of the west wing of the Butchery Lane house. Wall 13 may be the west wall of the same wing.

(g) Wall 13, approximately 0.50 m. wide on a gravel foundation, had been almost completely quarried away. A wide robber trench noted near the roof of the tunnel extended down to within the first courses of the wall foundation. This wall, together with Wall 12 may be a continuation of the parallel walls for the paved corridor flanking the west side of the Butchery Lane house.

(h) Wall 14 consisted only of a gravel-filled foundation trench extending down 0.35 m. from the roof of the heading. This foundation, 0.42 m. wide, may have been for a wall pre-dating the Butchery Lane house.

(i) Between Walls 14 and 15 (a distance of approximately 9.40 m.) was a thick layer of occupation deposits, including layers of gravel and tile rubble, consistent with courtyard surfacings, or the paving of an area between two buildings. These deposits, which were cut by a number of rubbish pits and a modern drain, sealed the natural brickearth, which lay at +8.80 m. O.D.

(j) Wall 15, 0.70 m. wide, with a rammed gravel foundation 0.50 m. deep, was built of flints in a tough yellow mortar. A single tile bonding course was noted near the roof of the tunnel. This well-preserved wall may have been an external wall for a separate building located west of the Butchery Lane house and facing on its west side onto a major Roman street (see below, Walls 16–20).

(k) Between Walls 15 and 16 were earlier banded occupation deposits. These consisted of layers of black-brown loam with fragmented roofing-tile and oyster shells capped by bands of redeposited brickearth. Over the banded deposits, close to the roof of the

67. S.S. Frere and Sally Stow, *op. cit.*, *supra* note 63, 322.
68. *Arch. Cant.*, xcii (1976), 240 and Pl. II (opposite p. 244).

tunnel, was a layer of flint which was perhaps the basis for an *opus signinum* floor. The banded deposits and flint layer were cut by a number of medieval pits.

(l)   Wall 16 was 0.65 m. wide on a gravel foundation; it was built of fist-sized 'fresh' flints in tough yellow mortar. The wall was partly cut by a robber trench or pit and only two or three courses of flintwork survived.

(m)   Between Walls 16 and 17 were deposits undoubtedly pre-dating both walls. These consisted of a thick 'dump' of redeposited brickearth (located close to the roof of the heading), overlying a deposit of banded dirty gravel containing a few broken tiles. The gravel deposit, which may have been a paved area associated with an earlier building, overlay a grey (topsoil) clayey loam, which in turn sealed the natural brickearth. The natural brickearth lay approximately at +9.00 m. O.D.

(n)   Wall 17 was 0.70 m. wide, made of flints in a tough off-white mortar, resting on a rammed gravel foundation 0.45 m. deep. Only three courses of flintwork showed below the roof of the heading. This foundation together with Walls 16 and 15 may have been for an eastern wing of a building with an internal courtyard (see below).

(o)   Between Walls 17 and 18 and close to the roof of the tunnel were layers of banded gravel, possibly for a courtyard. The gravel flanked the northern side of Wall 18 but was not found to the south of it. The banded gravel deposits overlay deposits similar to those noted above (see (m)).

(p)   Wall 18 was approximately 0.60 m. wide and, though badly disturbed by at least two pits and a modern sewer trench, ran at right angles to Wall 17. The wall, built of fist-sized flints in a tough off-white mortar on a rammed gravel foundation 0.40 m. deep, was flanked to the north, as just described, by the gravel of a possible courtyard. The gravel did not extend south of the wall, where no diagnostic stratigraphy was observed. This longitudinal wall may have been for a southern range of rooms surrounding the suggested internal courtyard.

(q)   Between Walls 18 and 19, the archaeological deposits were severely disturbed by medieval and modern pits.

(r)   Wall 19 was 0.70 m. wide and consisted almost entirely of a rammed gravel and flint foundation 0.45 m. deep. A probe inserted into the roof of the heading indicated the presence of either solid masonry or a stone block. This foundation may have therefore supported either a wall or the stylobate of a colonnade, flanking the possible courtyard.

(s)   Between Walls 19 and 20 a layer of flints sealing banded occupation deposits was noted close to the roof of the heading. This layer of flints may have been a basis for an *opus signinum* floor. The banded occupation deposits probably predate the flanking walls.

(t)   Wall 20 was 0.46 m. wide. The wall, built of fist-sized 'fresh' flints in a tough off-white mortar, rested on a compacted gravel foundation 0.30 m. deep. The wall-foundation cut into the verge of a Roman street. Walls 20 and 19 may have been a western portico or corridor wing for a hitherto unknown building with a possible internal courtyard. A southern range may be indicated by Wall 18 and a western range by Walls 17, 16 and 15. The metalling flanking the north side of Wall 18 (see (o)) may have been the remains of an internal courtyard.

(u)   Between Walls 20 and 21 was a major Roman street. The thick banded metallings were recorded in the full height of the tunnel. The natural brickearth underlying the street was located at approximately +8.40 m. The street was approximately 10.5 m. wide.

(v)   Wall 21, approximately 0.50 m. wide, was built of 'fresh' flints and lumps of sandstone in a tough yellow-brown mortar on a gravel and cobble foundation 0.35 m. deep. The foundation-trench cut road-tailings and silting and flanked the west side of the street. This wall may have surrounded a large courtyarded enclosure (see below).

(w)   Between Walls 21 and 22 was a considerable expanse of banded metalling (at least 27.5 m. wide). The metalling, comprising gravel and cobbles, with occasional fragments of sandstone and broken tile was at least 0.75 m. thick; at least four major phases of surfacing were noted in the matrix.

(x)   Wall 22 was approximately 1.05 m. wide and was built of greensand rubble in a tough yellow mortar. The wall filled the whole height of the heading and no foundation deposits were exposed. This wall flanked the west side of the courtyard and may have been a load-bearing wall for another major Roman building.

(y)   Between Walls 22 and 23 were banded clay floors and occupation deposits. The floors extended up from the bottom of the tunnel at +8.20 m. for a height of 0.70 m. At least six major refloorings were noted.

(z)   Wall 23 was 1.25 m. wide and was built of greensand rubble in a tough yellow mortar. This wall also filled the full height of the heading and no foundation deposits were exposed. Walls 22 and 23 with the internal floors noted above (see (y)) may have been for a range of rooms or corridor fronting the open courtyard (see (w)).

(zz) Wall 24 was approximately 2 m. wide and was built of greensand rubble. Though extensively robbed for much of its length, a small section of wall 3 m. long survived at its eastern end, (at the point of intersection with Wall 23). The foundations of this substantial wall, set roughly at right angles to Wall 23, were not exposed during the cutting of the tunnel. This wall was again encountered when a short length of tunnel was driven from the shaft outside nos. 41 and 42 High Street to the existing sewer in Guildhall Street. A short section of the south edge was revealed in the shaft and a part of the north wall edge was revealed in the tunnel extension to Guildhall Street. No traces of intact stratigraphy flanking the wall were observed. These walls (22, 23 and 24) indicate the presence of a major public building, set in a courtyard (see (w)) with a precinct wall to the east fronting onto a major north-east to south-west Roman street (see (u)).

Other possible elements of the same building complex were observed by James Pilbrow, who supervised the laying of Canterbury's sewer-pipe system in 1867–68.[69] The large walls discovered by him (marked as Walls 25–28 on Fig. 33) '. . . were of the Roman period, and appeared . . . to mark the site of some extensive public building.' In 1861 Brent[70] recorded many architectural fragments found opposite the Fleur-de-Lis Hotel (demolished in 1958 and now 34a High Street). Other possibly related finds, including a fine mosaic found in 1758 under what is now part of the County Hotel, and courtyard metallings excavated more recently by Dr F. Jenkins and Professor S.S. Frere, are recorded in full above (p. 93). The remains of a substantial masonry, portico and drain aligned north-east to south-west, recently uncovered

69.   *Archaeologia*, xliii (1871), 154.
70.   *Arch. Cant.*, iv (1861), 35.

during building work under no. 9 High Street (see below, p. 102) are also undoubtedly associated with the same building complex.

The new walls and extensive courtyard metallings discovered during the cutting of the sewer tunnel add yet more important evidence to the observations of Pilbrow and Brent and the excavations of Frere and Jenkins and suggest that these remains may have been part of Canterbury's Roman forum.

XX. No. 9 HIGH STREET

On 14 February, 1984, workmen[71] cutting a small foundation-pit in the road-frontage basement of these premises (now a travel agents) revealed the well-preserved remains of a Roman portico.

The foundation-pit was cut through a block of intact stratified deposits between the road frontage cellar and a second cellar located at the rear of the property. A narrow slot, 0.34 m. (1 ft. 1½ in.) wide, was cut vertically through the fabric of the rear wall of the road frontage cellar to the level of the basement floor, (c. 2.40 m. (7 ft. 10 in.) below the ground floor) where the foundation-pit, measuring 2.05 m. (c. 6 ft. 9 in.) by 1.75 m. (c. 5 ft. 9 in.) was dug to a maximum depth of 1.50 m. (c. 4 ft. 11 in.). During this operation stone blockwork was encountered, and some of the large stones had been removed before the Trust was informed of the find by Mr Clive Bowley of the City Council Conservation Section.

The portico foundation was aligned north-east to south-west and consisted of a 'buried' stylobate wall surmounted by bedding deposits and large paving blocks, flanked to the north-west by gutter blocks. The elaborately laid foundations consisted of a wide raft of carbon-coated, fire-fractured sandstone chippings (many coloured orange and cherry red by the fire) set in a wet and sticky black-brown clay (19). This raft of unknown depth extended across the excavated trench to form a foundation for both portico and drain.

The stylobate wall (16), 1 m. (c. 3 ft. 3 in.) wide, was constructed over the foundation raft and a poured mortar scree (18) sealed the raft either side of the wall. The stylobate wall, built 0.43 m. (1 ft. 5 in.) high, also of fire-fractured sandstones, set in a tough yellow mortar, was edged with larger flat-sided lumps of fired sandstone. A thick layer of compact sandy gravel (17), laid either side of the wall, was capped by a sticky yellow brickearth (15), which formed a bedding for the portico floor and drain. The stylobate wall, which did not project above the level of the floor, was also capped by a thin layer of brickearth bedding, surmounted by large paving blocks. No trace of a column base was observed on any of the large blocks overlying the wall. The substantial blockwork of the portico floor (14), the largest block of which was 1.20 m. (3 ft. 11 in.) long and 0.35 m. (1 ft. 2 in.) thick, extended over the stylobate wall as a flat and even horizon. The stylobate gutter blocks (12) were laid at the same time as the portico floor, with the base of the gutter-groove lying approximately 0.35 m. (c. 1 ft. 2 in.) below the level of the floor. A number of paving blocks (13) flanking the north-west side of the gutter and laid over the compact gravel deposit (17), indicated that blockwork paving extended some way beyond the

---

71.   Grateful thanks are extended to Messrs. John Hammond and Pete Franklin of Wiltshiers who greatly assisted the recording work.

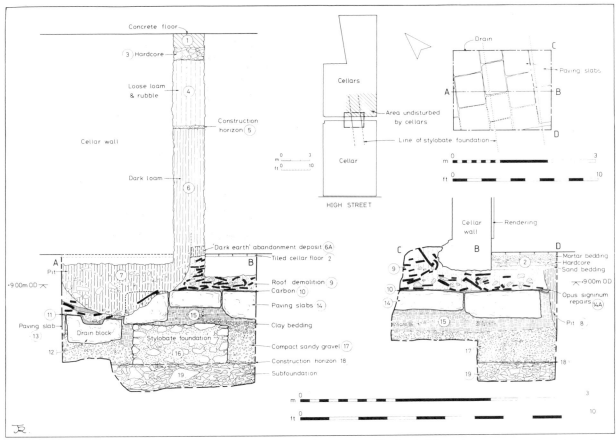

Fig. 36.   No. 9 High Street: Location plan (Scale: 1:400), sections (Scale: 1:40) and reconstructed paving plan.
(Scale: 1:80.)

line of the portico, suggesting a paved courtyard. The portico floor-slabs showed considerable signs of wear (some of the blocks were 'polished' smooth, others were slightly concave, and stones that projected slightly above the level of the floor had rounded edges) and in one small area (Fig. 36) a gap between two paving slabs was repaired with *opus signinum* mortar (14a).

A 0.2 cm. ($\frac{3}{4}$ in.) lens of sticky black carbon (10) sealed the floor and a similar deposit (11) filled the gutter groove. This deposit was capped by a demolition layer (9) 0.35 m. (*c.* 1 ft. 2 in.) thick, consisting almost entirely of *tegulae* and a few *imbrices*, together with mortar (some still adhering to the tiles) and loose-textured dark brown loam with much carbon. The demolition deposit, which extended over the gutter blocks and paving north-west of the portico, probably derived from the collapsed and perhaps burnt portico roof. Sealing the Roman levels was a considerable layer 1.30 m. (4 ft. 3 in.) thick of dark brown loam (6). Cut from within this deposit were two medieval pits (7) and (8).

The sequence of soil deposits capping the dark loam (5) and (4) shown on Fig. 36 may have accumulated when the cellared buildings were constructed in more recent times. These deposits were capped by hardcore and concrete (3) and (1) associated with the present ground floor of no. 9 High Street.

The extremely well-preserved portico, which probably extends relatively intact under the remaining cellared area of the property, may well be associated with a number of substantial Roman walls found during the digging of the sewer tunnel under the High Street in 1982 (see above p. 98) and with discoveries made in the County Hotel area by Professor S.S. Frere and others (see above p. 93). Taken together, all these discoveries indicate the presence of major public buildings, possibly the Roman forum complex.

The fire-fractured stones utilised in the foundations of the portico, may have been re-used from an earlier building which had perhaps been destroyed by fire. The level of the portico floor, set higher than the stones tentatively identified as paving for the forum *piazza* (see below), indicates a slight step down from the portico floor to the level of the courtyard paving, a standard relationship for a portico and courtyard arrangement. The quantities of carbon, found overlying the portico floor and filling the gutter groove, taken together with the considerable collapse of roofing furniture, may also indicate a final destruction by fire of at least this part of the building complex.

An attempt to reconstruct at least the northern part of the proposed forum *insula* utilizing all known building elements, was recently published by the author in *Arch. Cant.*, c (1984). This tentative assessment of the area, has in part been incorporated in Fig. 33. Professor Frere in correspondence has kindly suggested that, on the basis of the various elements so far discussed above, a normal *principia* type building cannot exist here and that a more unusual plan for the overall complex, like that at Verulamium, should therefore be suspected. On the strength of observations at no. 9 High Street and observations by Pilbrow opposite the White Horse Lane intersection with the High Street (possible paving slabs similar to those seen at no. 9 High Street and other slabs at the north end of White Horse Lane, which may belong to another part of the building complex), he suggests that the forum *piazza* may have existed west of no. 9 High Street and north of the line of the High Street. Professor Frere further observes that the *curia* may have been located north-west of this, flanked by the walls located by Pilbrow in 1868. The basilica, he indicates, may have been situated south of the High Street although he does admit that lack of structural evidence under the County Hotel creates interpretational problems. One solution to this may be that the Pilbrow walls turn in front of the County Hotel, creating some sort of porch in front of the basilica. A range of heated rooms incorporated into the basilica may be indicated by the structural elements found in the Fleur-de-Lis yard, but they may equally be part of a range of rooms along the outside of the basilica as at London or Verulamium, or alternatively may represent elements of a separate building. The large circular Roman structure discovered in the Jewry Lane area in 1689 (discussed above p. 93), may have been part of a temple or shrine associated with the general building complex, but this may equally have been a *laconicum* associated with perhaps another public bath-house located in the proposed forum *insula* south of the basilica.

It is hoped that more work in nearby cellars, will perhaps add sufficient information to tie together the random elements and form a more cogent picture of this intriguing area of the Roman town.

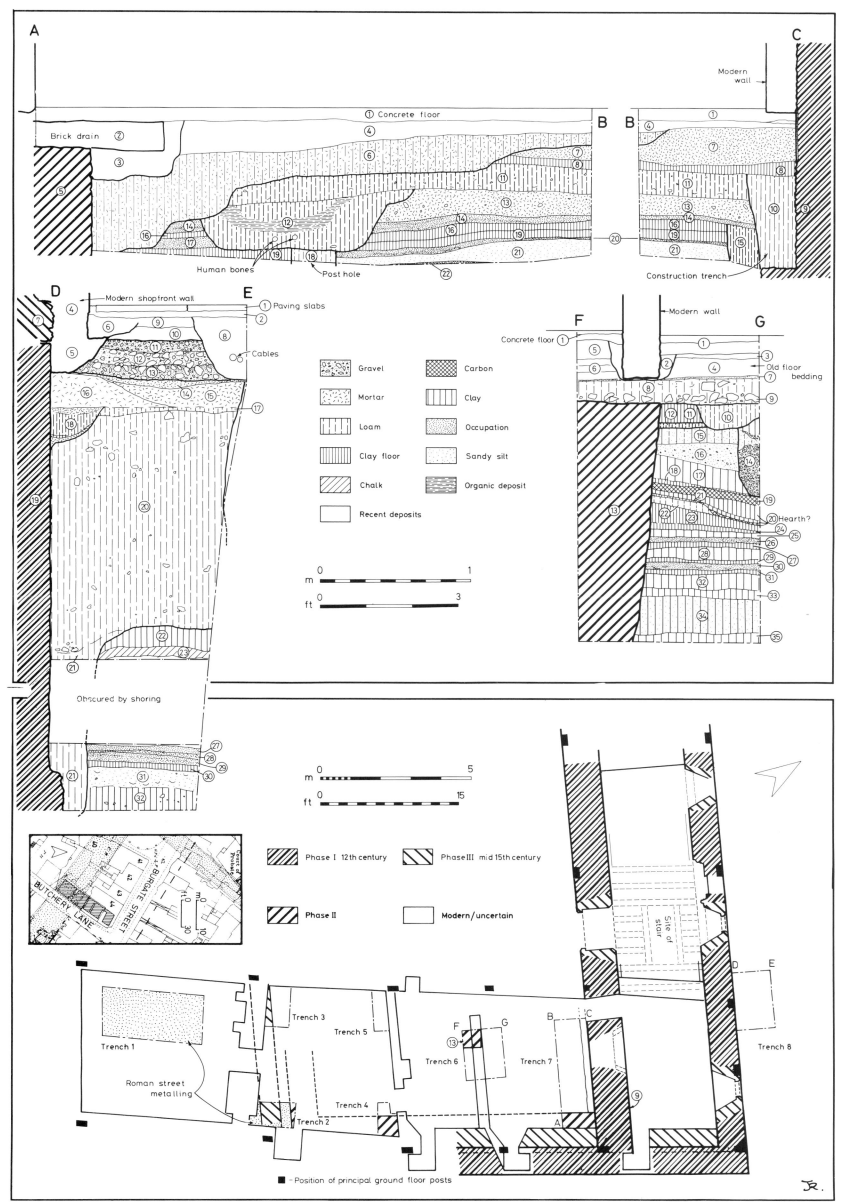

Fig. 37. No. 44 Burgate: Location plan (Scale: 1:1,250), phased cellar plan (Scale: 1:125) and sections. (Scale: 1:25)

XXI. Nos. 14 AND 15 BEST LANE

During renovation work on nos. 14 and 15 Best Lane and the construction of extensions to the rear of these properties, contractors cut into the Roman street running between Westgate and the Burgate. The trenches were observed by the Canterbury Archaeological Trust, but no excavation work was possible.

Street metallings were exposed to a depth of c. 1 m. over an area 8 m. wide across the line of the Roman street, but no road edges were seen. This street forms one of the main north-west to south-east arterial routes through Canterbury and would have been up to 10 m. in width. At no point did the contractors' trenches reach the base of the street metallings.

A layer of fine loam covered the latest street metalling. This level produced a large block of Kentish ragstone c. 20 cm. across, which lay on the street surface. The fragment may have come from the forum which lay to the south-east of this street.

An extension to the rear of no. 20 High Street, observed by Dr F. Jenkins in the 1950s to the south-west of no. 14 Best Lane, also exposed an area of street metalling, presumably part of the same street.

XXII. No. 44 BURGATE

During renovation work in June and July 1984 at no. 44 Burgate, seven trenches (numbered T1 to T7) in the cellars and one (T8) immediately in front of the premises, under Burgate Street, exposed stratified deposits indicating the presence of a major north-west to south-east Roman street and a Roman timber building. Masonry walls associated with earlier cellars dating from the late twelfth to the fifteenth century were also exposed. The present part brick and part late medieval chalk-block cellar underlies a substantially intact mid fifteenth-century timber-framed building.[72]

A large trench (T1) dug in the cellar at the south-western end of the building (under no. 3 Butchery Lane) exposed a thick deposit of layered, rammed gravel for a major Roman street aligned north-west to south-east. The metalling, disturbed in places by later activity, extended into the adjoining basement, where it was cut through by the chalk-block walls of the fifteenth-century cellar. The road gravels were not completely cut through by the new foundation-trenches and a total depth for the metallings was not established.

A trench dug at the north-east end of the central cellar (T7) cut through a well-preserved sequence of stratified deposits (Fig. 37). At the base of the cutting, traces of a worn clay floor mixed with occupation loam (T7, 22) were exposed. Though only a small area of floor was observed in the cutting, considerable subsidence had undoubtedly occurred during the life of the compact surface, perhaps indicating the presence of rubbish pits or similar disturbances under the floor. This settlement may have been the reason for the deposition of a thick layer of pale grey sandy silt (21) found covering the earlier floor. The soil dump was sealed by a sequence of

---

72. This building has been surveyed by Mr J.A. Bowen of the Canterbury Archaeological Trust and will be published in full in a forthcoming volume in the *Archaeology of Canterbury* series, on Canterbury buildings.

floors which were also considerably affected by subsidence. A compact layer of clay and occupation (20) capped the dump. This was in turn sealed by a further two clay floors ((19) and (16)) separated in part by a lens of occupation loam (17). At least two post-holes, (15) and (18), were found in association with the floors. A final floor (14) capped the earlier floors and post-holes, and was in turn sealed by a dump of clay and mortar (13) which may have been debris associated with the building's destruction.

A similar sequence of Roman layers was examined in a large square foundation-pit (T6) cut in the centre of the central cellar. Here the lowest deposits were of discoloured redeposited brickearth (T6, 35), and grey silty clay (34) containing lumps of burnt and unburnt clay. Two layers of wet sticky clay flecked with carbon and burnt clay (33 and 32) sealed these deposits and were in turn capped by a yellow clay floor (31). A sequence of clay floors, interspersed with occupation deposits, overlay the primary floor. The fifth clay floor (21), which was laid on a bedding of grey loam (22), was associated with a fired and partly vitrified hearth or industrial feature (20). A thick laminated deposit of burnt clay and carbon containing metalworking waste (19) covered these levels and was in turn sealed by a sixth and final floor (18). The occupation levels were sealed by a layer of clay-wall demolition (17) and a deposit of pale green sandy silt (16), which may have been 'wash' from the nearby Roman street. A final layer of clay-wall demolition (15) completed the sequence of Roman layers. This was cut by a possible late Roman wall sub-foundation (14), aligned parallel to the Roman street and filled with compact gravel and capped by a thin lens of poured off-white mortar.

A complex sequence of Roman levels was also observed in the foundation-pit (T8) cut immediately outside and to the north-east of no. 44 Burgate. Here a sequence of floors and occupation deposits (T8, 26–30) was laid over successive layers of redeposited brickearth and grey green silty loam (31 and 32). Overall, the stratified Roman deposits located in the three foundation pits (T6, T7 and T8) were probably part of one building, possibly an industrial workshop. A few sherds of pottery recovered from the stratified Roman deposits in Trench 6 dated from the late first to the late third or early fourth century (see p. 303).

The Roman deposits in Trenches 6 and 7 were sealed by a layer of dark brown loam (T6, 11 and T7, 12). In Trench 5 a single pit (12), cut from within the black loam and through the Roman levels, was located in section. A number of human bones recovered by the workmen during the digging of the trench may originally have come from this pit. In Trench 8, part of a late Saxon rubbish pit (36), which had been largely removed by the late twelfth-century cellar, was observed. A small *corpus* of late eleventh-century sherds (report p. 303) was recovered from this pit by the workmen, together with one complete loom-weight (Fig. 123, No. A) and a fragment of a second.

Cutting the surface of the black loam in Trench 7 was the construction trench (T7, 10) for the late twelfth-century cellar wall (9), (the rear wall of the road frontage cellar). The wall, constructed entirely of well-coursed, small fresh flints, was built on an offset foundation, set 0.65 m. (c. 2 ft.) below the top of the construction trench. The construction trench was capped by a beaten earth and clay floor (8), which also sealed the surface of the dark loam (11). The cellar wall was plaster-faced above the level of the floor. The external face of the road frontage wall of the same cellar was exposed in Trench 8. The edge of a large construction trench (T8, 20), 1.15 m. (3 ft. 9 in.) wide was located during the cutting of the new foundation pit. The construction trench, backfilled with a mixture of sticky dark loam and redeposited Roman soils, was capped by construction and levelling deposits (14–18). The road frontage wall (19) was built free-standing in a second offset foundation trench (21), cut from the floor of the larger trench and through construction deposits of compacted chalk and mortar (22 and 23) which sealed the floor of the large foundation trench.

The original twelfth-century cellar probably extended under adjacent buildings fronting Burgate, and is best preserved under no. 43 Burgate. Here the fragmentary remains of a twelfth-century string-course survived in the north-east and south-west walls of the cellar. The nature of the fabric surviving above string-course level suggests the presence of a barrel-vault which had been subsequently cut back. A distinct change in cellar frontage wall fabric discerned in Trench 8 may be associated with vault removal and a rebuilding of the surviving fabric (T8, 7). The original cellar undoubtedly exists under no. 44 Burgate, but was not fully exposed during reconstruction work. One puzzling detail was noted, however, in the rear wall of the Burgate frontage cellar. This was an *in situ* timber lintel, indicating the presence of a splayed opening, possibly a window. Later refacing on both sides of the wall had obscured corroborating details. Two problems arise if a window does exist in this position. If one accepts the presence of a barrel-vault in the road-frontage cellar, then a window in this position can only be a secondary feature and must indicate that the barrel-vault had been removed before the window was inserted. Walls indicating the presence of a second medieval cellar at right angles to the Burgate frontage cellar, fronting Butchery Lane, were found during renovation work. Again, if one accepts that this second cellar is a medieval feature, then a window in this position (with a window giving light from one cellar to another), seems totally implausible. Further still, a window in this position can only indicate that the earliest cellarage existed only on the Burgate frontage. This does not agree with the identification of a clay floor (T7, 8) capping the construction trench for the primary cellar (T7, 10) and the plaster facing of the wall above floor level – these features suggest either adjoining early cellars or some sort of structure overlying the floor south-west of the cellar and therefore obscuring the proposed window. The problem will remain unsolved until a total excavation of the area can be undertaken.

Sealing the clay floor (8) in Trench 7 was a thick deposit of crushed mortar with some flints (T7, 7). This deposit may have been laid deliberately to raise the floor level or may have been residue from a phase of reconstruction. Cutting this deposit and the earlier levels was a wide stepped feature (6), sloping from the south-east to the north-west across the contractor's trench. The feature, backfilled with a mixture of light brown loam and mortar, may have been a construction trench for a new cellar wall (5), built at right angles to the Burgate frontage cellar, fronting Butchery Lane. The wall, of small well-coursed fresh flints and a few lumps of chalk, was built over the offset foundation of the earlier cellar wall (9) but was bonded into the wall superstructure, indicating that at least part of the earlier wall was demolished to offset level prior to the construction of the new cellar. Two other fragments of the same cellar were also located in Trenches 2 and 4. A third fragment of wall, possibly a load-bearing cross-wall but more likely a load-bearing pier foundation, was located in Trench 6 (T6, 13). Taken together these wall fragments indicate the presence of a second medieval cellar, built some time between the late twelfth and fifteenth centuries. A small area of intact beaten earth and clay floors associated with this cellar was observed in Trench 6 (T6, 11).

The existence of a third cellar was indicated when a large chalk-block wall was located in Trenches 2 and 3. This wall was undoubtedly part of the fifteenth-century cellar, which was eventually extensively modified in brick in more recent times (at least two phases of brick cellar were observed). The masonry walls associated with the Period II cellar were probably demolished or modified during the mid fifteenth-century rebuilding. The razed foundation located in Trench 6 (T6, 13) was sealed by a sequence of post-medieval and modern deposits, consisting of a possible flint paving (9), a deposit of brown loam (8) and a thick layer of banded, trodden floors of dirty yellow sand mixed with coal dust (4). These layers were sealed by make-up (3 and 4), and by hardcore and concrete (1) for the present floor. The stratified deposits in Trench 7 were also sealed by make-up (T7, 4) and concrete (1) for the existing cellar floor. In Trench 6 the compacted gravel metallings for Burgate Street (T8, 11–13) were capped by a dirty yellow sand bedding (10) for an earlier pavement, and by a dirty brown loam (9). These layers were cut by a construction trench (6) for the foundations of the recent shop front (4–6). The sequence of layers observed in Trench 8 was completed by a sand bedding and concrete slabs for the existing pavement (1 and 2).

The earliest reference to stone houses on the site of no. 44 Burgate dates back to c. 1180.[73] By c. 1200 a 'great stone house'[74] existed on the site, paying a rental of 20 pence per annum to Christ Church Priory by 1370[75] (and by then called 'The Bull' or 'The White Bull'). During the Priorate of Goldstone I (1449–1468)[76] the present timber-framed building (which also includes nos. 40–42 and 43 Burgate and nos. 1–3 Butchery Lane), also called 'The Bull', was erected around three sides of a courtyard as lodgings, divided into at least ten and possibly twelve separate units with stairs up to each from the ground floor. Shops (over the stone cellars) may have existed on the ground floor, with lodgings above.[77]

XXIII. ST. MILDRED'S

In April 1953 two trenches were cut to a depth of 4 ft. by a mechanical excavator at right angles to the River Stour on a site lying south-west of the Tannery and north-east of St. Mildred's School (Fig. 38). The site code was C XXIII K. It was hoped to find a north–south Roman street,[78] but waterlogged and muddy conditions impeded the excavations and the results were inconclusive.

Trench II was waterlogged and produced nothing of note.

The lowest level reached in Trench I was a layer of gravel (Fig. 39, Section A–B). This was thought to be natural, but there was a thin deposit of occupation material and bones on its surface and it is possible that it was part of a Roman street. Mud and water prevented full investigation despite the use of a pump.

Above the gravel was a deposit of black pebbly mud (8) about 4 ft. 6 in. (1.37 m.) thick. This

73. W. Urry, *Canterbury under the Angevin Kings* (London, 1967) Rental C24 and Map 1, Sheet 5.
74. W. Urry, *op. cit.*, Rental D107 and Map 2, Sheet 6.
75. Cathedral Library and Archives, Canterbury. Rental 71.
76. H. Wharton, *Anglia Sacra* (1691) 145. The obituary of Prior Goldstone I (1449–68).
77. My thanks to J.A. Bowen and T. Tatton-Brown for this information.
78. The next north–south street west of Castle Street was thought to lie on this line.

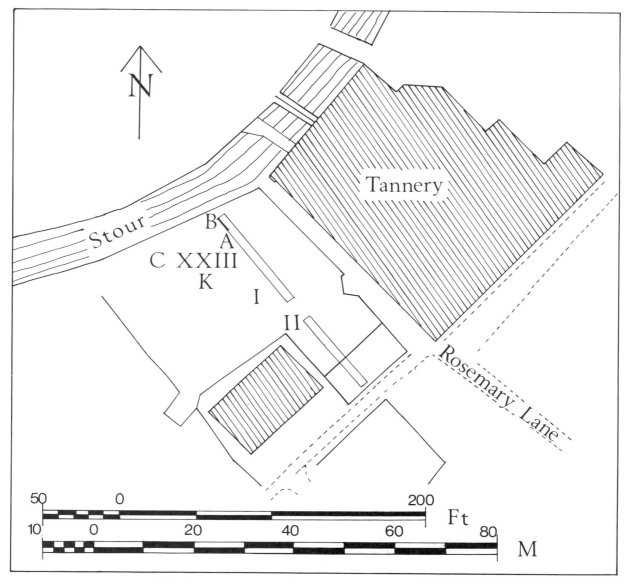

Fig. 38. St. Mildred's (C XXIII K): Plan. (Scale: 1:750)

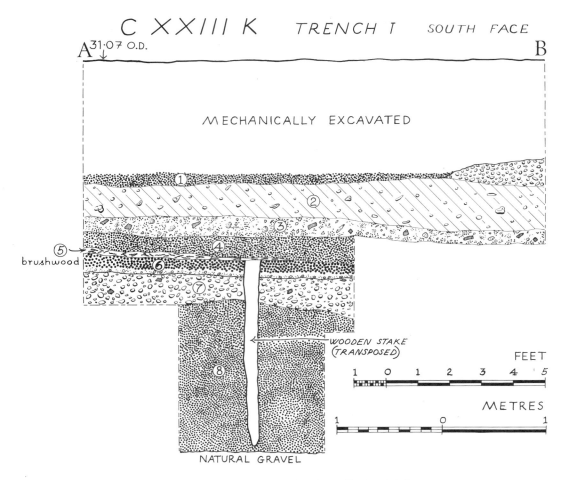

Fig. 39. St. Mildred's: Section. (Scale: 1:36)

was probably the product of flooding[79] rather than a stratified layer since it contained mixed pottery dating from the Belgic to late Antonine periods, including a sherd of a Belgic cordoned jar, a Belgic base and flagon handle, a rim sherd of a Belgic butt beaker and several sherds of Neronian-Flavian samian (Dr. 27, 24/25), Flavian samian (Dr. 27, 18, 37, 36), and late Antonine samian (Dr. 31R, 79). This deposit was sealed by a layer of fairly hard gravel (7) comprising large and small flints, many fragments of Roman tile and a very worn mortarium rim. The top 4 in. of the gravel yielded a sherd of eleventh- to twelfth-century Rhenish ware and pottery of

79. Dr Frank Jenkins had encountered similar waterlogged conditions during his observation of the area being excavated for the extension to the gas works in February to May 1951, cf. *Arch. Cant.*, lxiv (1951), 67; *Archaeological Newsletter*, April 1951, 166. He found indications of Belgic occupation; just above the natural brickearth small quantities of Belgic pottery were observed which is unlikely to be later than the mid first century A.D. (*Arch. Cant.*, lxiv (1951), 64, Fig. 2). There was no trace of Roman buildings in this area; several earthy deposits were seen which yielded pottery ranging from the first to the fourth century.

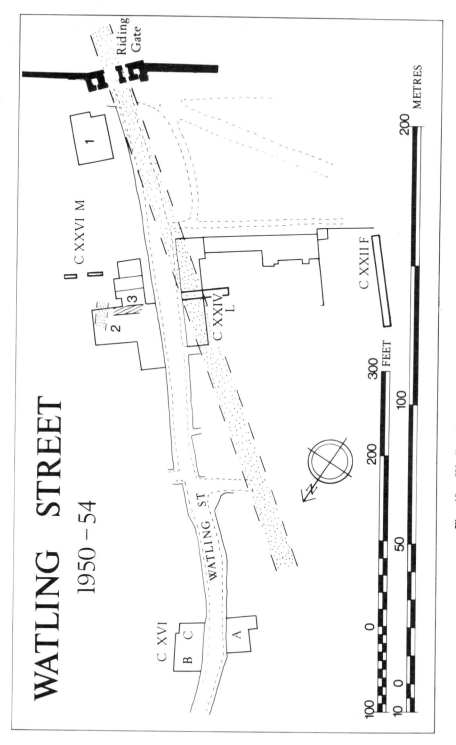

Fig. 40. Watling Street area: General plan. (Scale: 1:1250)

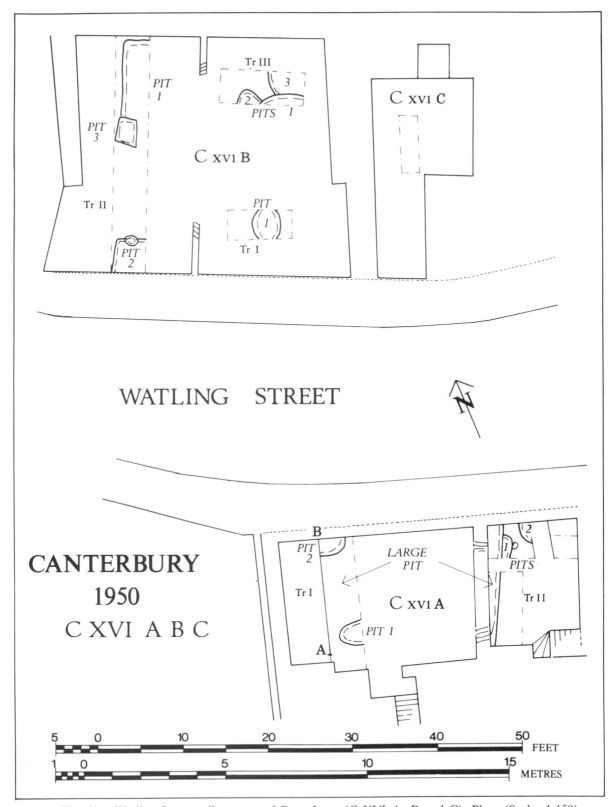

Fig. 41. Watling Street cellars west of Rose Lane (C XVI A, B and C): Plan. (Scale: 1:150)

Medieval Group II.[80] This layer was found again, at a depth of *c.* 7 ft. from the modern ground level in Trench I B, a further *sondage* within the mechanically excavated area of Trench I, 65 ft. south-east of A on Figs. 38 and 39. The surface which seemed cambered was worn as if by traffic and it was probably part of a twelfth-century east–west street.

Above the gravel was a sandy layer containing pebbles and oysters (6a) in which several residual mortarium sherds were found as well as a rim sherd of a late thirteenth-century jug. Above this was a layer of black mud (6) yielding Group IV medieval pottery of the late thirteenth century. There was a number of wooden stakes driven into layers 6, 7 and 8, possibly representing a revetting along the bank of the River Stour. These and layer 6 were sealed by a peaty deposit (5) which contained many seeds and twigs and several sherds of thirteenth-century pottery. This was overlaid by a deposit of dark mud (4) on top of which was dark earth mixed with fine mortar together with a few large lumps of mortar and general building debris (3). Hard yellow clay and gravel (2) overlaid by black mud (1) covered this.

XXIV. CELLARS WEST OF ROSE LANE

In April 1950 three cellars (C XVI A, B and C) fronting Watling Street, east of its junction with St. Margaret Street and west of Rose Lane were excavated (Fig. 40). Cellar A lay on the south side of the street; the other two on the north.

C XVI A

Two trenches were excavated. At the north end of Trench I a peaty deposit (Fig. 42, layer 8) was found overlying the natural subsoil. This was the base of a very large pit and the peaty material probably accumulated when it lay open and waterlogged for a time. Well-preserved fragments of a leather shoe (Fig. 69, No. 7) were found in the peat, which also yielded a storage-jar sherd probably datable to the first half of the second century. The eastern edge of this great pit was found in Trench II (Fig. 41) where it post-dated a Belgic pit (Pit 1) and traces of other early pits.

Above the peat was a series of mortar and loam tips (Fig. 42 (1)–(7)) which yielded several sherds of Antonine samian Dr. 33, and coarse ware of a similar date (Fig. 85, Nos. 1–9). These sloped down to the south-west and were presumably deposited to fill and level off the pit in the mid or late second century, possibly for the erection of a building, although no trace of this was found. The pit – to judge from its size – was probably a quarry to obtain brickearth for a pottery or tile-kiln.

Two other pits were found in Trench I. Pit 1 was filled with black sticky soil beneath which was decayed vegetation, and may have been an earth-closet. This yielded a sherd of Saxon cooking-pot, probably of the ninth century, and a residual sherd of third-century mortarium.

80. For some medieval pottery from Canterbury it is convenient to use the classification of the groups discussed in *Arch. Cant.*, lxviii (1954), 128 ff. The dating of these is now considered to be as follows:

Group I	*c.* 975–1025
Group II	*c.* 1050–1100
Group III	*c.* 1080–1150
Group IV	*c.* 1250–1300

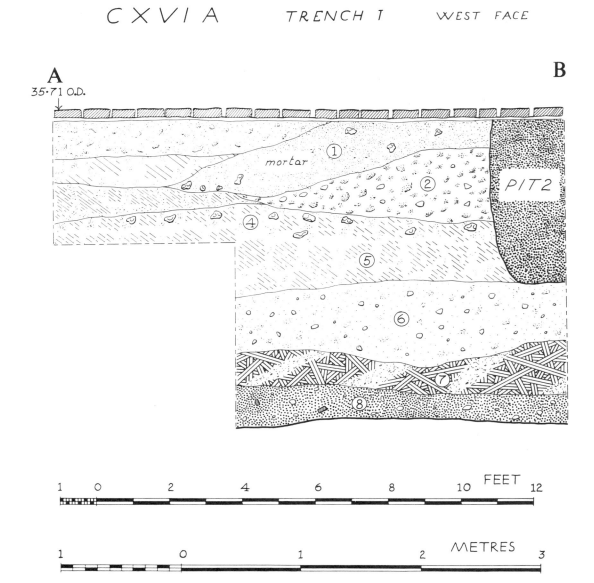

Fig. 42.   Watling Street cellars (C XVI A): Section. (Scale: 1:30)

Pit 2 which was cut through layers (1)–(5) (Fig. 42) yielded a number of sherds of medieval pottery (Fig. 85, Nos. 26–28) all of which belong to, or are associated with, the Group II material discussed in *Arch. Cant.*, lxviii (1954), 129–31 and now dated to *c*. 1050–1100.

Trench II was very disturbed by a modern drain and sump; apart from the edge of the large pit, already discussed, the only features were a post-hole adjoining Belgic Pit 1, and a second pit yielding three sherds of Roman pottery. This pit had been largely destroyed by a modern drain.

C XVI B and C XVI C

It was hoped that Sites C XVI B and C would pick up the line of Roman Watling Street. The modern street curved to the south at this point, but in 1950 it was still thought that the Roman street ran straight on, continuing the line of Beer Cart Lane[81] beneath which Pilbrow had observed solid street-metalling.[82]

Three small trenches were opened in cellar C XVI B (Fig. 41). The only feature in Trench I was a pit yielding a sherd of a hand-made Saxon cooking-pot (Fig. 85, No. 29). Four pits were found in Trench II. An early Roman Pit 1 lay at the north end of the trench. It was not fully excavated but its upper layers, dark purplish loam and charcoal (1), beneath which was more pebbly material (2), yielded first-century samian Dr. 29, 27, 15/17, a coin of Cunobelin and a number of sherds of first-century coarse pottery (Fig. 85, Nos. 10–13). A second pit (No. 2) lay at the south end. This yielded late second- or early third-century samian Dr. 37, late Antonine samian Dr. 79 and a number of coarse sherds of third- to fourth-century date (Fig. 85, Nos. 16–19). It was cut by a small medieval pit (No. 4), only the very bottom of which was found as it had been truncated by the cellar. This yielded a thirteenth-century cooking-pot (Fig. 85, No. 30).

Pit 3, in the centre of the trench, yielded a rim sherd of a thirteenth-century cooking pot and a glazed jug sherd of thirteenth- or fourteenth-century date.

Three Roman pits were found in Trench III. Pit 1 was filled with soft grey charcoally material. This seemed to be later than a shallow scoop to its west, Pit 2. Antonine samian Dr. 31 and much coarse pottery were recovered from these two pits but were not differentiated (Fig. 85, Nos. 20–25).

Pit 3 was filled with dirty loam above which was a layer of pebbles overlaid by more dirty loam, burnt daub and charcoal. This pit was earlier than the other two and yielded first-century pottery (Fig. 85, Nos. 14–15).

The small trench dug in cellar C XVI C was very disturbed by drains except at the north end; there, overlying a deposit of dark charcoally occupation-earth (3) which yielded Belgic sherds, was a loam floor of Roman date. This was covered by a layer of dirty occupation material (1) in which samian, Dr. 36, probably of Flavian date, and the rim of a jar (Fig. 86, No. 31) were found.

---

81. The discovery in this same year that the Roman theatre lay at the junction of Beer Cart Lane, St. Margaret's Street, Castle Street and Watling Street (*Britannia*, i (1970), 83 ff.) showed the error of this supposition; and in 1953 the true line of the Roman street was found south of the existing one at Site C XXIV L (Fig. 40, and pp. 117–21 below).

82. *Archaeologia*, xliii (1871), 156.

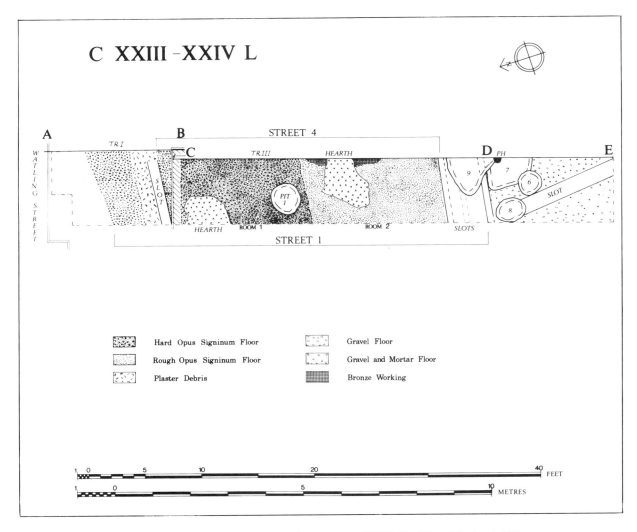

Fig. 43.   No. 44 Watling Street (C XXIII–C XXIV L): Plan. (Scale: 1:100)

XXV. No. 44 WATLING STREET

In April and August 1953 the cellar and grounds of no. 44 Watling Street were investigated. This site lay south of the street opposite Lady Huntingdon's Chapel (Fig. 40) and the trenches were coded C XXIII–C XXIV L.

Roman Watling Street was found, and to the south of it a timber-framed building. The street had clearly been closed or diverted during the second half of the second century when the entire width of the first three surfaces of metalling was overlaid by an *opus signinum* floor; this was associated with a timber sleeper-beam trench and must have been part of a building. The building was later demolished and Watling Street resumed its earlier course.

Pre-Watling Street Levels (Fig. 43)
The earliest occupation on the site occurred in the mid first century A.D. and was connected with bronze-working. In Trench III below the street-metalling (Fig. 44, Section C–D) a yellow loam floor (17) overlay the natural subsoil. This yielded Belgic pottery including part of a flat coarse base. Two bronze working hearths (Fig. 43) were cut into the floor, one of which was very ashy and of several periods. Associated with these were very small bronze fragments, drops of metal and pieces of crucible. The hearths and floor were sealed by a thick occupation-layer (15) which contained patches of reddish purple compact clay, small pieces of red burnt daub and fragments of charcoal. This was presumably debris from a hearth. This deposit yielded two scraps of first-century samian, some Belgic coarse ware (Fig. 86, Nos. 32–38) and a copper coin of the Gallic tribe of the Meldi dating from about the forties B.C.[83] Above layer 15 but not visible on Section C–D was a spread of fallen plaster and more building debris; this was sealed by the earliest metalling of the Roman street. Similar layers (12) and (11) containing plaster were found in Trench I (Fig. 44, Section A–B); these layers also yielded Belgic sherds including Fig. 86, Nos. 39–40.

Early Watling Street
The south edge of the primary street was found in Trench III, just north of Pit 7 (Fig. 44, Section D–E) and the north edge in Trench I (Section A–B); its overall width, therefore, was *c.* 33 ft. The metalling was only 2 in. thick, but being of compacted pebbles was very hard (Fig. 44, Section C–D III Street 1, and Section A–B I (10)). Belgic sherds and a rim-sherd of an early Roman cordoned jar were found in the metalling, suggesting that it was laid down fairly soon after the conquest. This street was resurfaced on two occasions (Fig. 44, Section C–D Streets 2 and 3) and its width reduced by *c.* 14 ft. on the north side. Here a layer of road silt (Fig. 44, Section C–D III (13A); Section A–B (8)) accumulated over the primary surface, and filled a shallow scoop (9) just beyond the north edge (Section A–B). Trench III layer 13A yielded second-century samian Dr. 37 and 36; it was overlaid by more similar silt (III (13)) which covered the northern edge of Streets 2 and 3, and yielded Trajanic samian Dr. 18/31 and 27. The make-up for Street 3 yielded Flavian samian Dr. 18 and 36, and Street 3 itself part of a

---

83. S. Scheers, *Traité de Numismatique celtique*: II *La Gaule belgique* (Paris, 1977), 138.

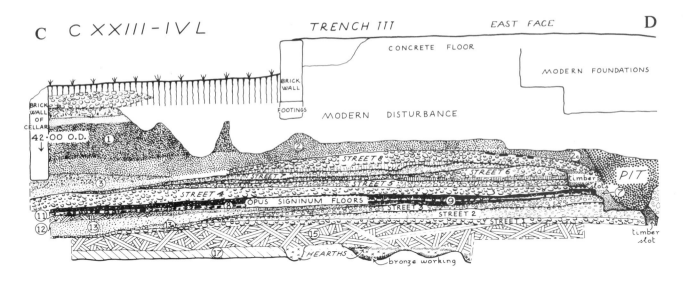

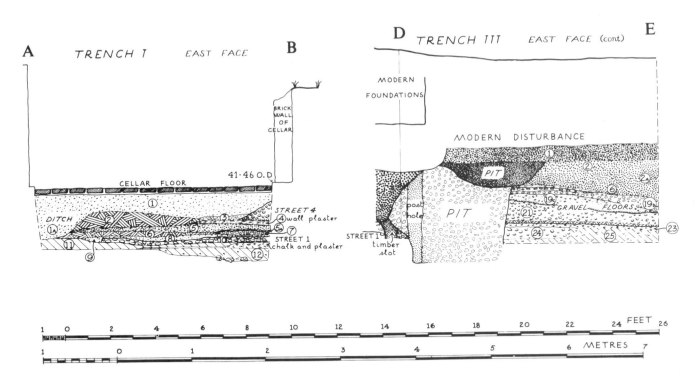

Fig. 44.   No. 44 Watling Street: Sections. (Scale: 1:50)

mortarium dated to the second century, possibly between 140 and 200 (Fig. 86, No. 41) and a number of sherds of coarse pottery (Fig. 86, Nos. 42–44).

Building overlying Early Watling Street

In the second half of the second century Watling Street was either blocked or diverted, for a building with an *opus signinum* floor was laid down over almost the entire width of the former street. A *terminus post quem* for this building is provided by Antonine samian Dr. 37 and 31 found in the silty occupation layer (12) below the floor at the north end of Trench III (Fig. 44, Section C–D) and Dr. 37 (A.D. 160–190) found in the floor make-up (layer III 8). Variation in the texture of the *opus signinum* seemed to indicate that it covered two rooms (Fig. 43); but no dividing slot or post-holes were found. The northern Room 1 was bordered on the north side by a timber sleeper-beam trench, full of green silt. Its floor was hard, *c.* 3 in. thick, and rested on mortar lumps and tiles (Section C–D III (8)); it showed only one period. The floor in Room 2, to the south, was at a slightly lower level and was rough and worn and full of large projecting tile fragments; it had later been repaired with *c.* ½ in. of well-trodden cemented sand.

This building was later demolished and most of the building debris cleared away down to floor level, except to the north of Room 1 where a hard plastery layer (4) containing tiny fragments of *opus signinum* was found; this was probably a consolidated layer of tumbled wall. Watling Street now reverted to its former course and remained on this line with successive re-metallings until the late Roman period.

Watling Street

The first surface of the relaid street (Street 4) was laid directly over the *opus signinum* floor. It consisted of small pieces of well-compacted gravel and yielded residual Hadrianic-Antonine samian Dr. 31. It was *c.* 25 ft. wide, *c.* 6 ft. wider than Streets 2 and 3, but was subsequently resurfaced on four occasions (Streets 5, 6, 7 and 8) with a reduction in width. The latest Street 8, in which nails and lumps of corroded iron were found, was only 19 ft. wide and steeply cambered. It ended on a definite ledge along the north side, beyond which was yellow silt (III (3)) sealing the northern edge of the wider Street 4 below. A similar silty layer (1) was found in Trench I (Section A–B) where it filled a ditch cut through occupation-soil (2). A number of sherds of residual samian was found in and on these streets. A sherd of a third-century mortarium (Fig. 86, No. 45) lay on the surface of Street 6 and flanged-bowl sherds were found in Streets 7 and 8 (Fig. 86, Nos. 46, 47).

Building to the south of Watling Street

Immediately to the south of the street was a succession of east–west timber-slots (Fig. 44, Section C–D; plan, Fig. 43); these yielded several sherds of Antonine samian and belonged to a timber-framed building at least twice rebuilt, bordering the street during much of the Roman period. It was badly disturbed by late Roman Pit 7, but a room divided – at least in its latest phases – by a north–south partition 18 in. wide was partially excavated.

The primary floor (24), which yielded Flavian samian Dr. 37, overlay a stony grey clay layer (25) also containing Flavian samian (Dr. 29, 18R) and was covered by a secondary gravel floor (23). Above this was a thin occupation layer containing oysters, in turn overlaid by a thicker floor (21) yielding Antonine samian. Above this again was a little occupation material covered

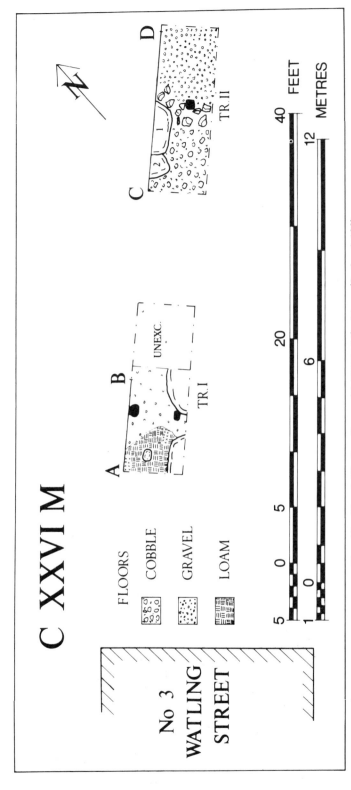

Fig. 45. No. 3 Watling Street (C XXVI M): Plan. (Scale: 1:100)

by more gravel floors (19c and 19d) which also yielded Antonine samian (Dr. 33 and 31). Contemporary with 19c and 19d was a north–south timber slot 1 ft. 6 in. wide, to the west of which were rough mortary and pebble floors 18a, b and c.

At the end of the Roman period the timber-framed building went out of use and the street ceased to be maintained. The whole area was sealed by a layer of dark soil similar to that found on other sites in Canterbury and elsewhere at this period (Fig. 43, Section C–D–E, 6, 2A, 2, 2C, 2D). This deposit yielded a number of sherds of late fourth-century date (Fig. 86, Nos. 48–55) and six fourth-century coins, including one of Arcadius (A.D. 395–408). A similar deposit of dark earth (1), of medieval date, sealed III (2); this yielded a residual amphora stamp (Fig. 87, No. 64). Subsequent levels were very disturbed and the only features surviving in identifiable form were several medieval pits.

XXVI. No. 3 WATLING STREET

In the summer of 1954 two trial trenches coded C XXVI M were cut to the rear of no. 3 Watling Street, *c.* 50 ft. to the east of Lady Huntingdon's Chapel (Fig. 40).

Traces of two huts, one of first-century date, the other of the late fourth century were found in Trench II. The area had been extensively cultivated and the Saxon and medieval levels were very disturbed.

The lowest level excavated in Trench I was a gravel surface (Fig. 45 and Fig. 46, Section A–B, layer below (10)) which was very disturbed in the northern part of the area. Further south it was more substantial and is probably a continuation of the metalled path found by Audrey Williams at the north end of her trench on the site of Lady Huntingdon's Chapel.[84] The metalling was overlaid by dirty grey loamy material (10) which yielded a sherd of a Saxon cooking-pot and a rim sherd of a medieval cooking pot probably to be dated to the second half of the twelfth century. Above (10) at the south end of the trench, and sealing the Saxon sherd, was a yellow loam floor (11) in which the remains of two hearths were found. The only pottery recovered from the floor was residual Roman material. Dark powdery soil and charcoal (9) sealed the floor and (where the floor was absent) layer 10 as well. Layer 9 yielded a sherd of a hand-made Saxon cooking-pot (Fig. 86, No. 58) (and a coin of Constantius II), and was overlaid by fine dark earth (8) into which two post-holes, containing fragments of red daub, were cut. Layer 8 was covered by thick deposits of cultivated soil (1)–(7) in which was found a number of thirteenth- and fourteenth-century cooking-pot sherds. The only other feature of note in this trench was Pit 2, which yielded a Saxon cooking pot, probably of the later tenth century (Fig. 86, No. 59).

Trench II

The surface of a gravel floor was the lowest level excavated in this trench (Fig. 45 and Fig. 46, Section C–D). Its limits did not lie within the small area exposed and no wall post-holes were found; but it was thought to belong to a Belgic or early Roman hut. The floor was covered by a layer of loamy earth and stones (10) containing several sherds of Belgic pottery (Fig. 86, No. 56)

---

84. *Arch. Cant.*, lx (1947), 87 ff. It may also be connected with metalling found by Dr Frank Jenkins in the north-west corner of his site at no. 1 Watling Street, cf. *Archaeological Newsletter*, May 1951, 181.

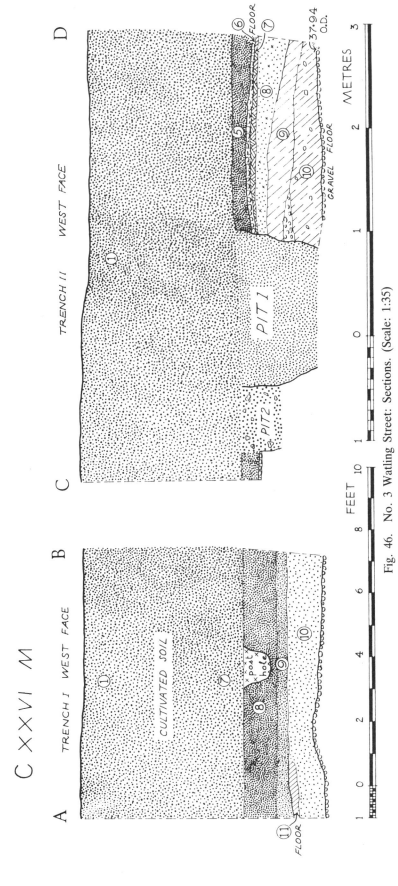

Fig. 46. No. 3 Watling Street: Sections. (Scale: 1:35)

and above this was a deposit of yellowish-brown mottled loam (9) which may have come from a collapsed loam wall. Hadrianic samian Dr. 18/31 and much coarse pottery, including a second-century mortarium sherd (Fig. 86, No. 57) and other pieces of second-century type, were found in this layer, indicating that the hut went out of use during the second century. Light loamy earth (8), which yielded late second- or early third-century East Gaulish samian and a red colour-coated bowl sherd not earlier than *c.*A.D. 260 overlay (9) and was sealed by a thin layer of dark earth (7). This produced much late Roman pottery and eight late third- and fourth-century coins:

1 – Tetricus I	1 – Helena
1 – Claudius II	1 – Constans
2 – radiates	2 – Theodosian

One of the Theodosian issues was sealed by a cobble floor (6), on the surface of which were five more fourth-century coins:

1 – barbarous FEL TEMP REPARATIO	1 – Theodosius I
1 – Valentinian I	2 – late fourth century – uncertain type

This floor, which thus has a *terminus post quem* after 379, presumably belonged to a very late Roman hut. The floor was absent in the central part of the trench, and in this area layer 7 was covered by large building flints (some with mortar attached) and a few Roman tile fragments – debris from a collapsed wall. A deposit of dark earth (5), which in addition to late Roman material yielded three small medieval cooking-pot sherds, covered the wall-debris and floor; cut into it was Pit 1 filled with fine dark earth and producing a Saxon sherd with stamped rosettes (Fig. 87, No. 65) and Medieval Group II sherds. This post-dated Pit 2 which also yielded several sherds of Medieval Group II pottery[85] (Fig. 86, No. 63). Layer 5 and the pits were sealed by thick deposits of garden soil (1)–(4) which yielded more Medieval Group II material and two thirteenth-century jug sherds.

XXVII. MARLOWE AVENUE CAR PARK

In the summer of 1952 an east–west trench *c.* 107 ft. long by *c.* 12 ft. wide (coded C XXII F) was dug to a depth of 4 ft. by a mechanical excavator in the south-east corner of the Marlowe Avenue Car Park (Figs. 40 and 47).

Four 10 ft. squares divided by baulks 8 ft. wide were excavated in the eastern part of the area, but with disappointing results. The natural subsoil lay only 4 ft. 6 in. from the surface and the sole features found were pits. Trench V which lay at the west end of the area, beyond an A.R.P. shelter which was not removed, was more interesting; two or three of the pits found there may have been connected with a Saxon hut.

The only feature found in Trench I was a large circular medieval pit. It was not fully excavated

---

85. Cf. *Arch. Cant.*, lxviii (1954), 129–31; it is now dated *c.* 1050–1100.

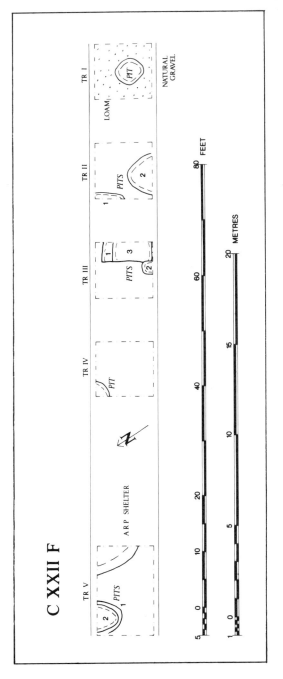

Fig. 47. Marlowe Avenue Car Park (C XXII F): Plan. (Scale: 1:200) (For position, see Fig. 40.)

and the only finds were two small unglazed sherds, probably of twelfth- to thirteenth-century date. The natural gravel outcropped in this area, becoming mixed with loam and capped by it towards the west end of the trench.

Two pits, one Roman, the other of sixteenth- or seventeenth-century date were excavated in Trench II. The Roman pit (2) was *c.* 3 ft. 6 in. deep. It was filled with tips of dirty loam and yielded a coin of Gratian and much Roman pottery (including Antonine samian Dr. 33 and 31, and a late second- or third-century mortarium sherd) but this was mostly residual. Fragments of a large light-yellowish Roman tile *c.* 2½ in. thick which probably came from a hypocaust were also found.

Most of Pit 1 lay under the west baulk, its straight eastern edge protruding *c.* 6–9 in. into the trench. The filling was black and yielded a small orange sherd probably of the sixteenth to seventeenth century.

Three pits were found in Trench III. Pit 1 was a shallow scoop filled with black soil and was of probable thirteenth-century date. Its south-west side was cut by medieval Pit 2. Pit 3 lay beneath part of Pit 1 and was filled with mixed loam and earth.

The only feature found in Trench IV was a segment of a black-filled pit. It had an inner filling of chalk rubble with mortar near the top and contained Medieval Group II pottery.[86]

Three pits were found in Trench V. Pit 1 was large and had a dark filling which yielded a sixth-century grass-filled Saxon sherd (Fig. 86, No. 62), residual late Roman pottery and a coin of Gallienus. It was cut by Pit 2 which occupied almost the same position but was slightly smaller. This had a ring of daub around the edge and dark earth in the middle. The top levels contained many oysters, bones and fragments of Roman brick. A coin of Alfred and sherds of two Saxon cooking-pots of probable ninth-century date[87] were found (p. 218, Nos. 60, 61). Pit 3 lay just to the south of Pits 1 and 2. It was filled with loose daub and sooty earth above which were dipping layers of soil. These contained a twelfth- to thirteenth-century base sherd (but this is probably intrusive) and two sherds of ninth-century Saxon ware. Fragments of wattle-impressed daub were found in both Pits 2 and 3 and it seems likely that they were connected with a ninth-century Saxon house.

Another pit, or possibly the butt-end of a ditch, lay in the north-east corner of this trench. It was 3 ft. deep with sloping sides and was filled with light dirty loam (5) above which was dark earthy loam (3c) in the top of which were many gravel flints and small lumps of *opus signinum*, tile and painted wall-plaster. Above this was clean yellowish loam (3b) overlaid by dark earthy layer (3a). Layer 5 yielded Claudian samian Dr. 18 and layers 3a and 3c joining pieces of samian Dr. 33 which suggest a mid second-century date for the filling.

86. *Arch. Cant.*, lxviii (1954), 129–31; it is now dated to *c.* 1050–1100.
87. The pottery found was similar to that found in Canterbury Lane (*The Archaeology of Canterbury*, vol. vii), where it was associated with ninth-century Badorf ware and is presumably also of ninth-century date.

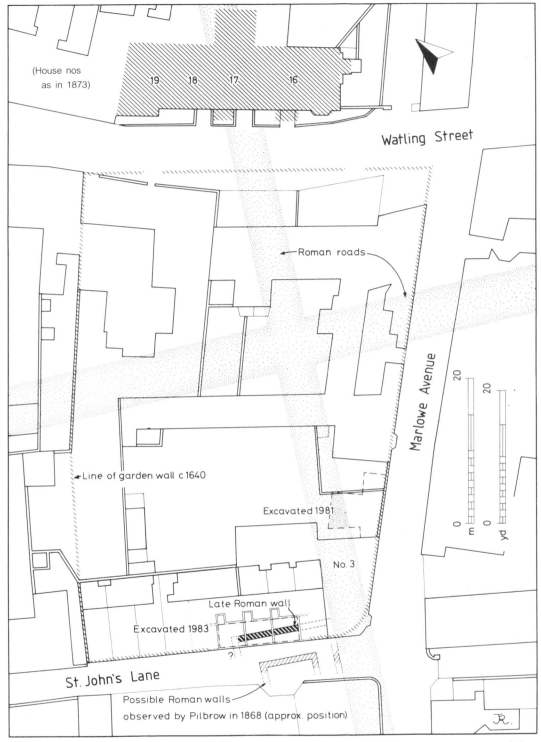

19 18 17 16

Watling Street

Roman roads

Marlowe Avenue

Line of garden wall c 1640

Excavated 1981

No. 3

Late Roman wall

Excavated 1983

?

St. John's Lane

Possible Roman walls
observed by Pilbrow in 1868 (approx. position)

20

20

0

m

0

yd

Fig. 48.   Marlowe Avenue and St. John's Lane sites: General plan, showing Roman streets and the
seventeenth-century garden walls of no. 16 Watling Street. (Scale: 1:500)

XXVIII. MARLOWE AVENUE AND ST. JOHN'S LANE SITES

INTRODUCTION

Between September and November 1981 a small excavation was carried out in an area of open ground immediately north of no. 3 Marlowe Avenue (Fig. 48). The land, due for redevelopment, was owned by Mr J.F. Berry and thanks are due to him for financing the work. Excavation, in advance of development, resumed on 4th July, 1983, about 14 m. west of the 1981 dig on the site of a row of early nineteenth-century half-cellared cottages (demolished in the late 1960s) which fronted onto St. John's Lane. The month-long excavation was confined to the cellars of nos. 5, 6 and 7, the rubble fill of which was removed by machine. Consequently, the main deposits investigated were of Roman date. Thanks are due to Colin Tomlin Associates, owners and developers of the site, who financed the excavation.

EXCAVATIONS AT MARLOWE AVENUE (1981)

Summary

The most important structure found during the excavation was a major Roman street which ran approximately north-east to south-west across the north-west side of the excavated area. This street is a continuation of that first found by Professor S.S. Frere on excavations to the north. Six phases of metalling were discerned altogether and, although little datable material was recovered from the road-surfaces themselves, the dating of associated deposits indicates that the road had a life-span extending from the late first or early second to the fourth (and possibly early fifth) century.

Sequences of road ditches and post-hole lines ran parallel to the road through much of the Roman period. The post-holes probably represented fences bordering the road but, due to extensive medieval disturbance in this area, the possibility that some belonged to buildings or other structures fronting the road could not be ruled out. During most of the period, however, the area immediately adjacent to the road appeared to be unoccupied open ground, in which rubbish pits were dug.

The latest road-surface was contemporary with a metalled courtyard of flint and tile, found in the south-east of the site and which had fronted onto the open road (Fig. 51). The courtyard sealed very late fourth-century deposits, was certainly extant in the fifth century and was probably the forecourt of a late Roman building that remains undiscovered to the south-east of the excavated area.

The courtyard was sealed by a deposit of black loam, a layer that has been found elsewhere in the city and which may represent a period of post-Roman abandonment prior to the Saxon resettlement. No sign of any Saxon occupation was found on site, although a number of sunken featured buildings was found on some of the Marlowe excavations situated about 50 m. to the north-east.

The pre-Norman levels were all extensively disturbed by later pits, the digging of which continued intermittently up until the seventeenth century, along with agricultural activity including possible ploughing.

In the late thirteenth and early fourteenth centuries a number of very large, shallow intercutting pits was dug on the site (Fig. 52). It is possible that these subrectangular features were quarries, either for the extraction of gravel from the Roman street, or for the location of Roman masonry for robbing. In the backfill of one of these features was found a thirteenth-century silver-gilt finger ring with a blue sapphire setting.

The quarries and associated stratigraphy were sealed by an horizon of scattered peg-tiles which may represent a period of abandonment during and after the Black Death in the middle of the fourteenth century. Although the site is adjacent to a road (now called Marlowe Avenue, but originally St. John's Lane) that possibly existed here as early as the twelfth century, no signs of any buildings or direct evidence for occupation were discovered at this point. It appears therefore, that the area was always open ground until the nineteenth century. During the post-medieval period the area was a walled garden (from c. 1625 belonging to a large house at no. 16 Watling Street) and rubbish and cess-pits were dug.

In the early to mid-eighteenth century a large rectangular cess-tank, constructed out of re-used stone, was built on the site, near the road frontage (Fig. 52). The life of this feature was fairly complex, but two main phases, probably separated by the re-erection of a wall between the site and the street could be determined. The cess-tank was eventually backfilled with large quantities of domestic refuse, including hundreds of sherds of late eighteenth- and early nineteenth-century pottery. This may have taken place in the early 1830s at the same time as the construction of no. 3 Marlowe Avenue which still stands adjacent to the site. Layers relating to the building's construction, and various trenches containing services to it, were excavated.

One of the latest features exposed was the foundation of a circular structure (Fig. 52) that was situated between no. 3 Marlowe Avenue and a contemporary boundary wall. During the nineteenth century there was a large brewery immediately opposite the site on the other side of the street. It is likely, therefore, that the structure was a building connected with brewing, maybe an oast- or malt-house.

Natural Deposits

The top surface of natural brickearth was fairly horizontal over the site area at a level of about +11.00 m. O.D. The natural gravel terrace under this was not exposed.

Period I – Pre-Conquest to Flavian Soil Build-up

A thick layer of pale orange yellow to buff brown clay (excavated in two spits (147) and (154)), slightly flecked with carbon and daub, overlay the natural brickearth across most of the trench (Fig. 53, Sections A–B, B–C; Fig. 54 F–G; E–H–A; Fig. 55).

The deposit contained pottery ranging from pre-conquest to Flavian in date, some animal bone and a number of flint flakes. Eight stake-holes, aligned approximately north-west to south-east, were encountered in the south-west area of the site (Fig. 49A). They cut the lower spit (154) and may represent a fence. No other features were identified.

Conclusions

The nature of the earliest levels suggests a gradual accumulation of soil on the site, probably

Fig. 49. Marlowe Avenue: Period plans: (A) Periods I and IIA; (B) Period IIB – plan 1 Road I, ditches
and post-holes. (Scale 1:60)

extending from before the Conquest up to the Flavian period. The absence of features may indicate a lack of occupation in the area during most of the first century.

Period II – Phase A: Construction of Roman Road (Fig. 49A)
At some time between the Flavian period and the early second century a major Roman street aligned approximately north-east to south-west was laid across the north-western half of the excavated area (see also Fig. 48).

Prior to the deposition of the road-metalling, the earlier deposits had been removed down to the natural brickearth in the area of the street and the resulting depression built up with hard redeposited brickearth. These deposits (125), (152), (160), Fig. 53, Sections A–B, B–C; Fig. 54, Section E–H–A), yielded Iron Age, pre- and early-Flavian pot sherds and a number of flint flakes, all probably residual.

The road-metalling (Road I (119)) directly sealed these deposits and consisted of pink sandy clay and gravel surfaced by hard compacted gravel. The only find recovered from the metalling matrix was a bronze object (S.F. No. 169).

Two parallel, longitudinal gullies and a line of eighteen stake-holes were found cutting the pre-metalling dump deposits but almost certainly pre-dating the road-metalling. Both the gullies and the line of stake-holes were aligned with the street. The gullies (142 and 153) were of irregular profile and 10 cm. deep. Gully 142 was directly sealed by Road I, and contained a fill similar to the earlier matrix of the road. Gully 153 was sealed and filled by the dump deposit (152). The stake-holes were about 1 cm. to 2 cm. in diameter, and usually of shallow depth (on average 10 cm.). These features were immediately sealed by the Road I metalling (119).

Conclusions
Although there was little evidence from pre-street deposits for the date of street construction, the dating of deposits associated with the road metalling (see below p. 132), suggests that it occurred at sometime between the end of the Flavian period and the early second century (see p. 133 for a fuller discussion). Before the metalling was laid the ground was reduced to a solid level and a brickearth raft deposited to stabilize the ground and to produce the *agger* of the road. After this stage, but before the metalling was deposited, a number of features was cut into the raft. The exact purpose of these features is not clear. The gullies may have been cartwheel tracks but they appeared to be fairly regular. The stake-holes may relate to the setting out of the road, but if this is so, their close spacing seems rather unnecessary. The alignment of the features and their position imply some relation with the street, however.

Period II – Phase B: The Roman Street and its initial Re-metallings (Figs. 49B and 50A and Pl. XXXI)
Although the surface of Road I did not appear to be particularly worn in this area, it was eventually re-metalled. A total of five later re-metallings in the road matrix was excavated, two of which have been placed in this phase (Road II (112), Road III (110)).

Between Road I and Road II was a very thin lens of sterile grey silt (118). The first re-metalling (Road II (112), not shown on plan) was composed of rammed gravel similar to that of the primary street. The edge of this road-surface was considerably eroded, and did not extend as far east as the primary street. The matrix contained no finds.

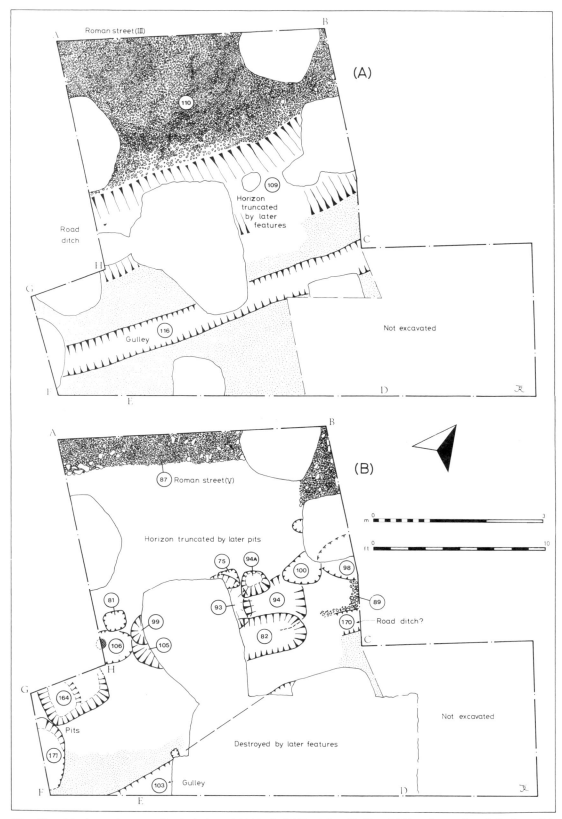

Fig. 50. Marlowe Avenue: Period plans (A) Period IIB – plan II, Road III and associated ditches; (B) Period IIC, Road V, post-holes and pits. (Scale: 1:60)

Overlying Road II was a very thin band of grey-green silt and yellow clay (111), which contained small quantities of pottery dating from c. A.D. 70 or 90 to 120. Overlying this deposit was another metalling (Road III (110)), of similar composition to the earlier metallings although it contained larger flints in some areas. Sealing this road was another thin layer of silt (107)/(108).

A number of drainage ditches to the east of the road was excavated. However, correlation between the metallings, and the ditches and stratigraphy to the east of the road was difficult (and sometimes impossible) because of heavy disturbance by later features in this position. The earliest ditch excavated was (120) (Fig. 53, Section B–C; Fig. 54, Sections F–G, E–H–A). The true width of this feature and its exact relationship to the first two metallings were destroyed by a later ditch belonging to Road III. However, the feature was almost certainly for drainage of the first two metallings (Roads I and II). This flat-bottomed ditch was at least 0.9 m. across, parallel to the roads, and contained a fill of light yellow brown silty clay, redeposited brickearth and gravel. A fair amount of late first to early second-century pottery was also recovered.

The west side of the ditch was cut and truncated by feature 109/114. This was a wide, fairly deep depression rather than an actual road-ditch, but it almost certainly served the same purpose. It ran parallel to Road III and contained a homogeneous fill of dirty greenish-yellow silt interspersed with some tip-lines of small flints, pebbles and oysters. The upper backfill appeared to be contiguous with the layers of silt 107/108 spilling off Road III. These road-silt deposits yielded a large quantity of pottery which dated to the late first or early second century. A coin of the late first century (S.F. No. 121) was also found in silt layer 107.

Over most of its area, the fill of the ditch was truncated and sealed by medieval features. Much of the road silt 107/108 suffered the same reduction.

To the east of these road ditches was layer 115 (see also Fig. 55). This deposit directly overlaid layer 147, and appeared to seal ditch 120. The exact relationship between 115 and the later road ditch 109/114 was not clear even in section (Fig. 53, Section B–C), and the horizon itself was greatly disturbed by later features. It seems likely that the cutting of ditch 109/114 took place after the partial deposition of 115.

Layer 115 consisted of a light brown loamy clay flecked with oyster shells, carbon and daub and contained pottery from the late first to late third or early fourth century.

Six post-pits were found in this area, all sealed by layer 115, (124, 155, 157, 172, 175, 176). Two of these (175 and 176) were cut by the first road ditch 120. Post-pit 175 was cut by 155. The post-pits were mostly circular, and formed a line running approximately parallel to the roads and ditches. Their depth varied from between 25 cm. and 50 cm. They all contained slightly different fills, usually grey or light brown clays and most were packed with large flints. Small amounts of late first-century pot sherds were recovered from some of them.

Three other shallow post-holes were excavated (143, 144 and 145). These cut ditch 120 and were sealed by the later ditch (109/114). They all contained a similar fill of yellow/brown silty clay and a few probably residual sherds of pottery. One other feature was excavated. This was a longitudinal U-shaped gully (116) running parallel to the other ditches, but over 0.5 m. further to the east. The feature was cut from within layer (115), and was filled with very similar soil. The fill also yielded large quantities of pottery dating from the first to the late second century.

Conclusion

Two ditches ran parallel to the edge of the road. The earlier (120) was almost certainly for drainage of the first two metallings. This was replaced, probably when the third metalling was laid, by another ditch which was wider and less regular. The cutting of this feature removed the edge of the second metalling. Feature 116 could have been another later road ditch, but may have served some other purpose since it was positioned rather a long way from the edge of the road itself.

No interpretation can be given for the group of three post-holes (143), (144) and (145). The post-holes further to the east, which ran parallel to the road, may represent a fence line along it. The post-pits would have contained fairly large posts, and it is just conceivable that they were part of a building fronting the road; but no other remains that could have been from a building were encountered.

Layer 115, which sealed these posts, almost certainly represented a gradual build-up of soil to the east of the street. The date-range of pottery recovered from it suggests that its deposition may have started shortly after the construction of the road, continuing up to the late third or early fourth century. Unfortunately, this deposit cannot be directly related to any of the metallings.

Very little dating evidence was recovered from the roads or road-surfaces themselves, apart from small quantities of late first- or early second-century pot. However, the chronology of related deposits suggests that the first three road-metallings were laid in fairly quick succession. A late first- or early second-century date for the original metalling is supported by late first- or early second-century date of the original ditch (120). Although pottery of a similar period was found in the later ditch (109/114), the fill of which sealed Road III, this may be residual by a short period. The possible third ditch (116) contained pottery of a late second-century date. The layer to the east of the road (115) was obviously still accumulating in the late third or even early fourth century, and much of this deposition must have occurred well after the construction of Road III.

It is very likely, therefore, that the lifetime of the first three road-surfacings extended well into the second century, but it is not possible to be more specific. Originally, the road and its ditches may have been bordered by a fence, or just possibly by a timber building. This structure became redundant shortly after road-construction and a gradual build-up of soil, possibly representing unoccupied open ground, began. This build-up may have continued after the life of Road III, extending into the late third or early fourth century.

Period II – Phase C: Third- to fourth-century Road-metallings, Pits and Post-holes (Fig. 50B)
The later Roman levels were completely cut away in the centre of the site by medieval features; consequently, the remaining stratigraphy at the north-west of the site was severed from the stratigraphy to the south-east.

1. *Roman Street*
The Roman road was eventually re-metalled for a third time (Road IV (102)). The metalling sealed substantial earlier silt deposits (108), (107) and (109) and was composed of hard, rammed sterile natural gravel. This was sealed by a layer of dark brown or black clay/silt (101), which contained a coin of the late third or early fourth century (S.F. No. 119).

This deposit was sealed by Road V (87), which only remained along the north-west side of the trench, destroyed elsewhere by medieval features. Metalling 87 was composed of large rounded pebbles in hard compacted sandy gravel and was covered by a very thin lens of silt and pea-grit (86), which contained a coin of *c.* A.D.270–90 (S.F. No. 118). In the western corner of the site this deposit was partially sealed by a thin lens of very dark grey to black silty clay (84).

In the eastern part of the site, layer 115 was sealed by a thin layer of very mottled mid-dark brown clay loam flecked with mortar, carbon and shell ((97), Fig. 54, Section E–H–A; Fig. 55). The top few centimetres of this deposit were excavated separately as a spit (91). These deposits contained pottery ranging from the late third to the fourth century and some Roman bricks and *tegulae*. A coin of *c.* A.D. 270–90 (S.F. No. 151) was recovered from layer 97. Spit 91 which was directly sealed by a later courtyard ((79), see below), also contained coins dating to A.D. 394–5 and A.D. 388–402 (S.F. Nos 178A and 178B).

A small portion of contemporary stratigraphy survived along the north-east section of the trench (Fig. 53, Section B–C). Most of it was probably equivalent to layer (97), but the upper part was composed of a thin metalling (89), bordered by a shallow, possibly longitudinal, feature (170). This gully, which appeared to be parallel to the road, contained a fill of mid olive-brown clay and pebbles, and was sealed by a layer of dark brown loam (169) which was stratigraphically identical to layer 91. A coin of A.D. 367–75 (S.F. No. 171) was found in this deposit.

Conclusion

Road V is given a *terminus post quem* of the late third or early fourth century by the coin (S.F. No. 119). No good dating for Road IV was recovered, but the thickness of the silt deposits both overlying and underlying it, and the chronology of the earlier roads suggest that it was in use during the third century. It is conceivable that this road was constructed in the late second century, but the thickness of the silt build-up between this surface and the earlier roads suggest a fairly long period between them and, therefore, a later date for construction.

The small patch of metalling (89) cannot be stratigraphically related to either of these roads, but the section (Fig. 53) indicates that it may be part of the final phase of metalling (Road VI, see below). It was bordered on the east by a small gully (170) that may have been a late road-ditch. This gully cut layer 97, the deposition of which may have spanned the fourth century. The top of this level, (91), was almost certainly deposited at the end of the fourth or even in the early fifth century.

2. *Other Features*

Two pits and another gully were encountered, partially within the eastern area of the trench. The pits (164) and (171) were probably cut from within layer 97. Pit 164 (section not published) was completely truncated by a medieval feature, but definitely cut layer 115 and contained a fill of dark olive-grey silty clay flecked with oyster, carbon and mortar. The pit yielded pottery of the late third and fourth centuries. Pit 171 (Fig. 54, Section F–G), was just to the east and contained two main fills, a very dark grey-brown glutinous clay in the base and very mixed yellow brown and dark brown clay loams above. Pottery ranging from the late first to the fourth century and coins of A.D. 321 and *c.* A.D. 270–90 (S.F. Nos 189 and 195) were recovered from it. The pit was definitely sealed by the later courtyard (79). Only a small part of the gully 103 was

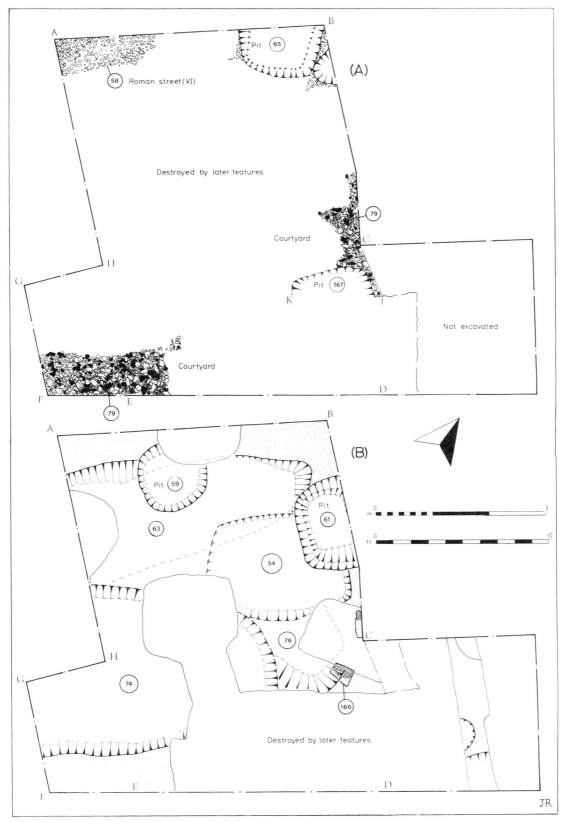

Fig. 51. Marlowe Avenue: Period plans (A) Periods III and V, late-Roman road and courtyard and twelfth–thirteenth-century pits; (B) Period VIA fourteenth-century quarries. (Scale: 1:60)

excavated, but it appeared to run approximately parallel to the Roman street. The feature was cut from within layer 97 and contained a fill of mottled mid brown and dark grey clay loams, flecked with orange clay, carbon and oyster shells (Fig. 54, Section E–H–A and Fig. 55, D–E–F). Sherds of the late third to fourth century were recovered from it.

A number of other features has been included in this phase. They cut through the road-silt deposits already described, but because they were nearly all completely truncated by medieval features they could not be stratigraphically related to any of the roads, or (with the exception of one (98)) to the stratigraphy to the east of the site.

The features were all post-pits (75, 81, 93, 94, 98, 99, 100, 105, 106), which formed a line running parallel to the street, in the position of the earlier road-ditch (109/114), through which they all cut. Three of the posts, (93), (99) and (105), were almost completely removed by a medieval pit. These intercutting post-pits were mostly large and deep and contained fills of redeposited road silt and gravel mixed with clay, and large flints and Roman tiles, obviously packing for the posts. Post-pit 106 contained a circular post stain nearly 20 cm. across.

The post-pits yielded pottery ranging in date from the late second to the mid-third century. Coins of c. A.D. 260–90 and A.D. 268–70 (S.F. Nos 113 and 114) were found in 98 and a coin of c. A.D. 270–90 (S.F. No. 110) in 75.

Post-hole 98 was the only one of the group that could be related to any of the stratigraphy to the east of the road, but the exact level from which it was cut was not clear, even in section (Fig. 53, Section B–C). It appeared to cut through most of deposit (115), and may have been related to or possibly sealed by the third re-metalling (Road IV, see below). It was definitely sealed by the later courtyard dating to the very late fourth or even fifth century.

Conclusion
These features probably all originate in the last quarter of the third century, and show that by this time the earlier road-ditch had become completely silted up. Although not proved, the posts may be contemporary with the third or fourth re-metalling of the street. The possibility that they represent a timber building fronting the street cannot be definitely ruled out; the post-pits were certainly big enough to represent a structure of this sort. However, no other traces of a building were seen (although these may have been removed by the medieval features) and the regular recutting and replacing of the posts suggests that they may have been part of a substantial fence. The stratigraphical position of post 98, and the number of replacements of the posts, suggest that whatever structure they represent may have remained in position well into the fourth century.

Period III – Late Roman Road and Courtyard (Fig. 51A)
Probably in the fourth century the major street was re-metalled for the last time (Road VI (58)). This metalling (heavily disturbed not only by medieval features, but also by possible later agricultural activity) was composed of loose cobbles in a matrix of almost sterile very dark grey brown to black loamy clay. In some areas the matrix contained patches of better-preserved metalling containing more gravel, in others the metalling was virtually non-existent. It was sealed by stratigraphy containing medieval material.

It is possible that this road was equivalent to the patch of metalling (89) mentioned above (p. 134).

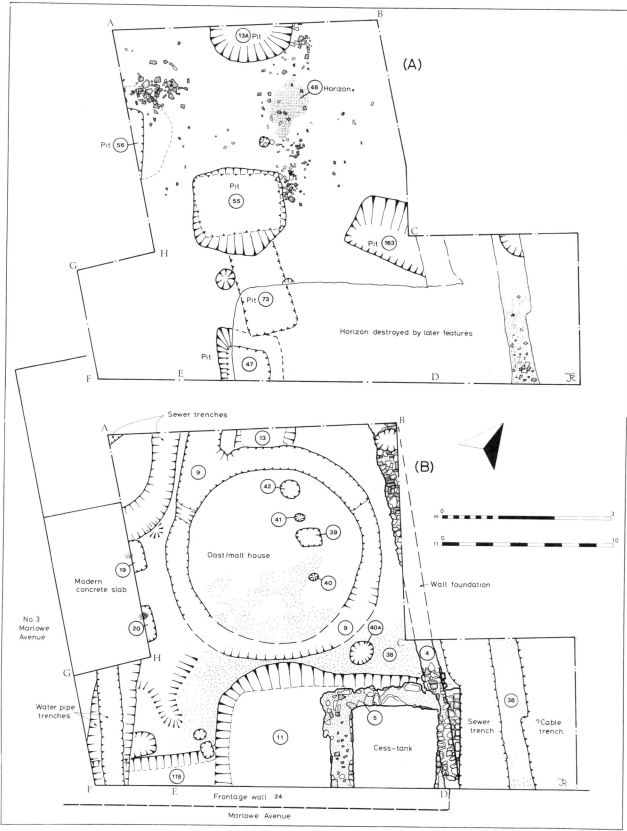

Fig. 52. Marlowe Avenue: Period plans (A) Periods VIB and VII, late fourteenth-century horizon and post-medieval pits; (B) Periods VII and VIII, post-medieval and modern features. (Scale: 1:67)

Only a few small 'islands' of stratigraphy of this period survived later disturbances. Adjacent to the road all earlier deposits were sealed by a courtyard ((79) Fig. 53, Section B–C; Fig. 54, Sections F–G and E–H–A; Fig. 55). This well-defined level was composed of *tegulae*, bricks and flints of varying size. Small quantities of animal bone, nails and late Roman pottery were also present.

Conclusion

The courtyard is given a *terminus post quem* of the very late fourth or even early fifth century by the coins that were found immediately underlying it. If the patch of metalling (89) is part of Road VI, the courtyard also post-dates the latest street, being laid over its silted edge. It is quite likely that the street was open and still in use at this time. The coins may have been washed off its surface.

These results suggest that the Roman street was still extant in the early fifth century. Fronting it was a courtyard, laid in the very late fourth or early fifth century, which may represent the forecourt of a late Roman building as yet undiscovered to the south-east of the site.

Period IV – Post-Roman Abandonment

Only very small areas of post-Roman stratigraphy had survived the destruction caused by medieval features. Courtyard (79) was sealed by a deposit 20–30 cm. thick of very dark grey-brown or black clay loam (77). This material was in turn sealed by medieval layers. The deposit was slightly flecked with carbon, daub and oyster shells and contained some Roman building materials, animal bone, a coin of A.D. 341–46 (S.F. No. 146) and a few sherds of pottery, including late Roman wares, and one sherd of Saxon Group 4 (seventh–eighth century). A few possibly early medieval sherds were also recovered from the top of the deposit.

Conclusion

Similar dark earth levels have been found in numerous other excavations in Canterbury and probably represent a period of abandonment post-dating the Roman occupation and, in other areas of the city, predating the Saxon resettlement. Although only a small amount of this level existed in the trench, the paucity of Saxon pottery and complete lack of early Saxon wares in particular imply that little or no Saxon occupation took place here. No sunken featured buildings were found during the excavation, although a number was excavated on the Marlowe sites (situated only 50 m. to the north-east).[88] The black loam did not exist over the Roman street. The level here was higher because of the road *agger*, and the layers consequently disturbed by later agricultural activity, probably ploughing.

The conditions prevailing in the area during the post-Roman period are clear. Eventually, possibly in the fifth century, the Roman street went out of use and its position was lost under the gradually accumulating deposits of black loams. The area was probably unoccupied throughout the rest of the millenium, although subsequent agricultural activity may have begun during this period.

88. *The Archaeology of Canterbury*, vol. v, forthcoming.

Period V – Early medieval Deposits

Levels associated with this period did not exist as distinct layers over the excavated area. The small 'islands' of stratigraphy that survived later disturbance suggest that the gradual post-Roman accumulation of soil continued; the few sherds of early medieval pottery found within the top of the black loam imply that the deposition of the layer continued up to that period. The layers over this deposit and the latest Roman road-metalling ((53), (62) and (64), Fig. 53, Section A–B, B–C; Fig. 54, Section E–H–A), all contained fair quantities of early medieval pottery, but also sherds of a slightly later date.

The area was certainly under the plough by this time, and this agricultural activity not only disturbed the latest street-metallings and the black loam, but also any soils deposited during this period. No distinct separation of the layers occurs until the mid-fourteenth century.

The only features of this period located were two cess- or rubbish-pits ((65) and (167), Fig. 51A; Fig. 53, Section A–B; Fig. 55, Section J–K). Pit 65, only partially within the excavated area, cut through the Roman street in the north-western corner of the site. It was sealed by a later deposit (62). The lower deposits in the pit consisted of numerous lenses of brown organic material, washed brickearth and grey loams. Most of the upper layers were dark brown or black loamy clays containing pebbles and flecks of chalk, mortar, carbon and burnt clay. Pottery from the pit dated to the eleventh to mid twelfth century. Pit 167 was sealed by a complex of later medieval features, and was also partially removed by a post-medieval cess-tank. The fill of this feature contained lenses of organic material with very loose grey and dark brown loams. These deposits yielded a large quantity of pottery of the early to mid thirteenth century.

Conclusion

Although little stratigraphy of the period survived, it suggests that agricultural use of the area possibly with ploughing, which may have begun earlier, continued through the Saxo-Norman period and up to the mid to late thirteenth century. During this time rubbish- or cess-pits were dug, which implies occupation nearby.

From at least the middle of the twelfth century, the site fronted a street (originally St. John's Lane, now called Marlowe Avenue).[89] Across this street, virtually opposite the site, was St. John's Church, which became a malt-house in the seventeenth century.[90]

Period VI – Phase A: Late thirteenth and early to mid fourteenth-century Quarries and Pits (Fig. 51B)

The levels (also mentioned above p. 138) between the black loam (77) and the next definite horizon (48), were very similar (53, 62, 64, 70);, see also Fig. 54, Section F–G, Fig. 55). The stratigraphy only survived as a number of small segments, divided up by later features, and generally consisted of a layer of dark brown loamy clay flecked with carbon, oyster shells and mortar. The level contained medieval roof-tiles and quantities of residual pottery, as well as sherds ranging in date from the early medieval period to the fourteenth century. A small

89. W. Urry, *Canterbury Under the Angevin Kings* (London, 1967), Map 1(b), sheet 5 and Map 2(b) sheet 8.
90. *Ibid.*, 210.

segment of similar stratigraphy was excavated in the north-east corner of the site, between two modern trenches.

Cut from within these deposits was a group of large intercutting pits or quarries ((54), (63), (74) and (76)) no deeper than 0.50 m. These features removed nearly all of the late and immediately post-Roman levels on site. The intersecting edges of the pits were very indistinct (the edges marked on plan are only tentative) and the fills were virtually homogeneous, being mainly dark brown grey loams incorporating patches of green silt and pebbles redeposited from the Roman street, quantities of residual and medieval pottery, peg-tiles, burnt clay lumps, slag and clinker (Fig. 54, Section F–G, E–H–A). One of the pits (54) also contained two coins of Henry III (mid thirteenth century) (S.F. Nos. 77 and 80) and a thirteenth-century silver-gilt finger ring with a sapphire setting (S.F. No. 63) in the upper fill (Fig. 117).

The large size and shallow depth of these features, the high proportion of residual material and the relatively small concentration of medieval domestic refuse within them suggest that they were not rubbish-pits. This, together with the fact that they were all probably contemporary, and may have been dug consecutively before being backfilled, strongly suggests that they were quarries, possibly for the extraction of road gravel or, since some were off the area of the road, an attempt to locate Roman masonry for quarrying.

Two pits 59 and 61 were also excavated. Pit 59 (section not published) was shallow and contained a fill of mid-brown silty loam and pebbles. Late thirteenth- or early fourteenth-century pottery was recovered from it. The pit was cut from within layer 53 and cut one of the quarries (63). Pit 61 was cut from the top of layer 62, and was about 1.6 m. deep (Fig. 53, Section B–C). The fill was a very loose, homogeneous dark brown loam which incorporated a quantity of residual pottery and other sherds dating to the mid to late fourteenth century. The pit cut two of the earlier quarries (54 and 63).

One other feature from this phase was excavated, a possible hearth or oven (166). This feature was truncated and cut in two by a later pit, and to the south was completely destroyed by quarry 76. The feature consisted of a floor and wall of brickearth, burnt on the inside; but not enough of it remained for its shape, size or function to be determined.

The quarries, pits and associated stratigraphy, were overlaid by a distinct but patchy horizon of scattered peg-tiles, flints and lenses of redeposited brickearth (48). The matrix of the tile scatter also contained pottery, most of which dated to the later fourteenth century. Towards the south-east of the site the tile scatter disappeared, but the horizon was probably represented by the top surface of layer (70).

Conclusion

The stratigraphy suggests that the gradual post-Roman accumulation of soil, possibly partly the result of agricultural activity, continued up to the late thirteenth century. A hiatus in the cultivation is implied by the presence of the large quarries and by the distinct tile scatter. This almost certainly began around the late thirteenth or early fourteenth century when the quarries, possibly for the extraction of road gravel, or location of masonry walls, were dug. The tile scatter may indicate a subsequent period of abandonment which may have lasted into the fifteenth century (see below p. 141). It is conceivable that this abandonment started in the mid fourteenth century, perhaps as a result of depopulation engendered by the Black Death.

Period VI – Phase B: Late medieval Pits (Fig. 52A)

The horizon of scattered tiles was sealed by a layer (46/49), over most of the trench area (Fig. 54, Section F–G; Fig. 55). This deposit was very similar to the levels both under and over it, and was mainly excavated as a spit. This deposit consisted of medium to dark brown clay loams flecked with oyster shells, mortar, carbon, chalk and tile. The matrix incorporated medieval peg- and floor-tiles and pottery which included a fair proportion of residual material as well as sherds of the late fourteenth and fifteenth centuries.

Directly overlying these deposits was a virtually identical layer, also excavated as a spit (43A; see also Fig. 53, Section A–B, B–C; Fig. 54, Section E–H–A), and an amorphous lens (only found in the extreme south-east corner) of medium brown loam heavily flecked and mottled with orange yellow clay (45). These deposits contained pottery dating to the fifteenth and sixteenth centuries.

Three pits were cut from within these levels, (13A), (47) and (73). Pit 13A, sectioned by the north-west edge of the trench, was circular and probably cut layer 46. It contained a uniform fill of very dark brown clay loam incorporating small quantities of animal bone, pottery of possibly the fifteenth century, and a larger proportion of residual early medieval sherds. Pit 47 was partially truncated by a post-medieval cess-tank, but almost certainly cut layer 49 and possibly layer 45. The basal layers of the feature consisted of lenses of brown loamy clays. The upper fill was a fairly homogeneous mid to dark brown loam. A useful *corpus* of pottery including a number of almost complete vessels, the majority of which were fifteenth-century in date, was recovered from it.

Pit 73 was situated towards the centre of the site and was cut to just below the water-table (approximately +10.00 m. O.D.). Due to the condition of the pit and the immediately surrounding levels, its exact shape and stratigraphical position could not be precisely determined. The edges were very unstable and collapsed on all sides while the pit was being excavated (the shape on plan should be regarded as showing the position of the pit, rather than its outline). The edge of the pit as cut was probably lost in antiquity, since a band of water-bearing sand in the natural brickearth at this point made the natural deposits very unstable and had resulted in a large undercut and void at the base of the pit which extended for well over 0.50 m. beneath the Roman stratigraphy. This had caused extensive collapse possibly shortly after the digging of the pit, for it was almost entirely filled with substantial lumps and layers of collapsed brickearth interspersed with bands of brown loam and organic material. Very little datable material was recovered from the backfill. The pit has been placed in this phase since it appeared to be cut from a similar level as Pit 47 and contained two medieval (possibly fifteenth-century) sherds as well as a number of medieval peg-tiles.

Conclusion

The horizontal deposits overlying the tile scatter suggest a resumption of horticultural or agricultural activity in this area, maybe after a short period of abandonment. The site may well have been a garden during the fifteenth and sixteenth centuries as it was for most of the later post-medieval period (see below p. 144). The digging of cess- or rubbish-pits was resumed in the fifteenth century, with a consequent continuity of pit digging up until the seventeenth century.

Period VII – Post-medieval Pits and Cess-tank (Fig. 52B)

The earlier levels were sealed by similar deposits of dark brown clay loam (43) which were heavily flecked with chalk, mortar and small lumps of coal and orange clay. Ceramic material from the layer included pottery ranging from the medieval period to the early to mid eighteenth century and a quantity of clay pipe fragments, mainly stems. Similar deposits were also excavated in the small segment of stratigraphy between two modern trenches in the far north-east corner of the site.

1. *The Pits*

Three pits were cut from or from within this level. Pit 50 (section not published), extended to a depth of about 0.50 m. below the brickearth. To the east it cut Pit 73. The pit was mainly filled with a mid grey loamy clay, with lenses of ash and yellow clay. It contained no preserved organic material, but a number of coprolites was found as well as a sixteenth- or seventeenth-century knife (S.F. No. 188). A large quantity of pottery was also present, the majority of it being of the sixteenth or seventeenth century.

Pit 56 was only partially within the excavated area, being cut by the south section (Fig. 54, Section E–H–A). Its shape could not be determined but it was probably rectangular. The pit had a bell-shaped profile, the bottom being almost twice the width of the top. This profile was caused by the collapse of the brickearth edges at the base of the pit. This collapsed brickearth was not found in the pit, and therefore must have been removed while the pit was being dug or before it was finally filled in. Subsequent settling of the fill had left a large void in the undercut, which in places was filled by intrusions of slumped earlier stratigraphy. The bulk of the pit contained a complex sequence of very thin layers, mainly different deposits of ash, orange clay, carbon and charcoal and ashy loams, covered by deposits of light grey and brown clays. Tip lines of oyster shells and peg-tiles were frequent and animal bone, nails, slag and clinker, a fairly large quantity of coprolites and large numbers of iron and bronze objects were recovered. These included pins, boot-lace tags and part of a bronze sieve (S.F. No. 149). Pottery in the fill dated the pit to the sixteenth or seventeenth century.

Pit 163 was shallow and filled with a uniform dark grey-brown loamy clay flecked with oyster shells, carbon, mortar and peg-tiles, which yielded animal bone, iron nails, slag and clinker, decorated floor-tiles as well as pottery (Fig. 53, Section B–C). Much of this was residual early medieval or medieval in date, but a fair proportion of late-medieval and some post-medieval sherds was present. The pit probably dates to the sixteenth or possibly seventeenth century.

2. *Eighteenth- and nineteenth-century Cess-tank and associated Levels* (Figs. 52B, 55 and Pl. XXXII).

By this period the street-frontage side of the site was almost certainly bounded by a garden wall (see below p. 144). None of this *original* wall survived on site because of the construction of a two–phase cess-tank up against it. The relationship of the garden wall to the original cess-tank could not be determined because the construction of the second phase included a complete rebuild of the garden wall at this point. The original cess-tank, parts of which (24A) were incorporated into the second phase, was built in a large construction-pit (11), which cut layer 43. The surviving reduced east wall of this structure was constructed of re-used, possibly Roman tufa, bricks and large shale and limestone blocks bonded with a pale yellow lime mortar. Scars

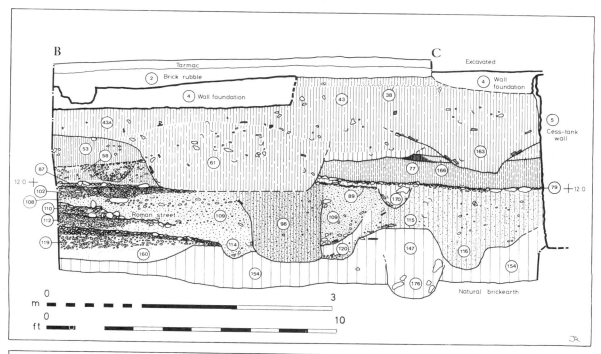

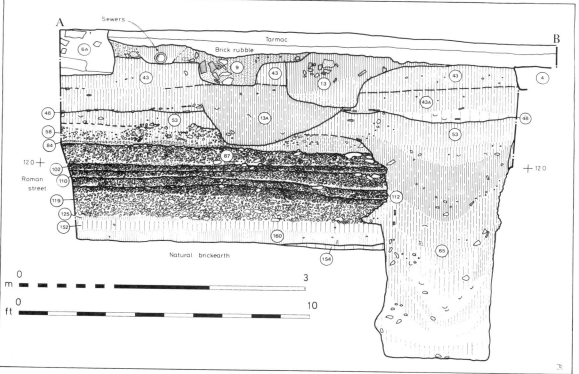

Fig. 53. Marlowe Avenue: Sections A–B and B–C. (Scale: 1:40)

from the original side walls could be seen at either end. Sealing layer (43) around the structure was a thin lens of mortar (38), possibly construction debris.

The original cess-tank was demolished and rebuilt on a smaller scale. This process almost certainly entailed the demolition and re-erection of the garden wall at this point. The second phase cess-tank was built in two distinct stages (5) and (5A), between which the void left by the extraction of the original structure was partially backfilled and the road-frontage garden wall rebuilt. This new garden wall (24) extended along the whole east side of the site and to the south was constructed within a trench ((11B); Fig. 54, Section F–G). The two 'builds' of the cess-tank and the new road frontage wall were all of similar construction, mainly flint courses with bricks, sandstone, limestone, chalk and shale blocks set in a yellow lime mortar.

After the completion of the cess-tank, the construction trenches were completely backfilled and also the gaps around the new tank. This backfill (12) contained a George II farthing of 1749 (S.F. No. 145).

Layer 43 and the mortar spread (38) were sealed by a layer of dark brown loamy clay heavily patched with light brown clay, carbon, brick and mortar (37). This level was sealed by modern deposits and contained clay pipes and eighteenth-century pottery.

Cutting this level was a line of post-holes ((13), (40A) and (39) to (42)) aligned approximately east–west. Some of these were sealed by modern deposits, others by nineteenth-century construction-levels for no. 3 Marlowe Avenue. The posts, which were of varying shape and depth, probably belonged to a late eighteenth-century fence.

Conclusion

In *c.* 1625 a large house (the present no. 16 Watling Street), belonging to the Mann family, was built. The area of land in front of the house between Watling Street and St. John's Lane in which the site is situated became a walled garden belonging to this property (Fig. 48) and is shown on a coloured map of Canterbury dating to *c.* 1640.[91] The map indicates that this garden functioned as a kitchen garden, and the pits excavated on site suggest that the south corner may have been reserved for rubbish disposal.[92]

The dating of the excavated deposits and later maps of Canterbury (e.g. Doidge's of 1752) suggest that the area remained as gardens or allotments for most of the post-medieval period, although digging of rubbish-pits appears to cease after the seventeenth century. By the middle of the eighteenth century the garden seems to have been formalized to some extent, since an avenue of trees running its length from north to south is shown on Doidge's map.

The stone cess-tank probably dates from this period. The construction and life of this feature was fairly complex, but two main phases were evident. The construction of the second phase appears to have necessitated the re-erection of the garden wall in this area. The coin of 1749 found in a deposit relating to the construction of the final structure gives a *terminus post quem* for the second phase.

91. Map 123 in the Cathedral Archives and Library, Canterbury.
92. The property also possessed an ornamental garden at the rear, part of which was excavated in 1978; see *The Archaeology of Canterbury*, vol. v, forthcoming.

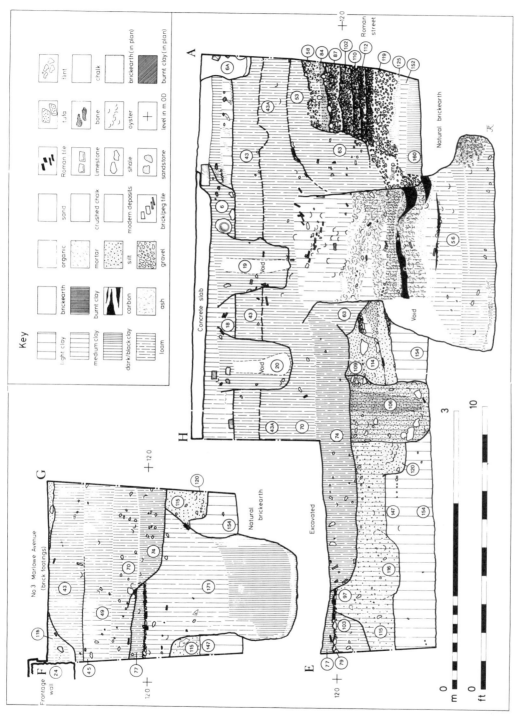

Fig. 54. Marlowe Avenue: Sections F–G and E–H–A and key to sections. (Scale: 1:40)

The sequence can be summarised as follows. A large cess-tank, near the road-frontage was originally built within a construction trench in the early to mid eighteenth century. The construction of this feature produced a mortar spread (38). Sometime in the second half of the century three sides of the structure were demolished, and the garden wall along the street frontage reduced. A new, smaller cess-tank was then built in two distinct stages. Between these stages of construction the wall separating the site from the road was probably rebuilt, partially on top of the reduced cess-tank wall. The upper part of the cess-tank was then completed, butting up against this wall. The building of the cess-tank in two stages may have been to facilitate the reconstruction of the frontage wall. The surviving frontage wall in some ways resembles the cellar walls belonging to the row of cottages excavated on St. John's Lane, but appears to be of an earlier date, (see p. 156). It is likely that much of the masonry in these walls was obtained from the original boundary wall which surrounded the No. 16 Watling Street garden.

Period VIII – Nineteenth- and twentieth-century Features (Fig. 52B)
Over most of the southern area of the trench, layer 43 was truncated and sealed by deposits (18) relating to the construction of no. 3 Marlowe Avenue, which was immediately adjacent to the site (Fig. 54, Section E–H–A). These levels also incorporated a number of service trenches for the building. The construction levels were in turn truncated and sealed by twentieth-century crushed brick levelling rubble and road tarmac (1) and (2), which also sealed layer (43) to the north.

No. 3 Marlowe Avenue was built in the early nineteenth century (see below), and its flimsy brick footings were exposed at one point. The road-frontage wall (24) and the cess-tank were almost certainly demolished to below ground level upon its erection since the front wall of the house was built on the road frontage wall (Fig. 54, Section F–G).

Layer 18 was a levelling dump laid after the initial construction of the footings and consisted of deposits of yellow clay and brick rubble. The south section bisected two large post-holes ((19) and (20)) which cut the construction deposits. The 1st Edition Ordnance Survey map of 1873 shows a conservatory built against the north wall of the house, and it is likely that these post-holes relate to this structure.

The stone cess-tank was eventually backfilled, probably as a single event. This backfill (10) consisted of a complex sequence of lenses and layers of coke, carbon, ash, mortar and plaster, variously coloured loams, brick and tile rubble and some organic material which may have been decayed wood or vegetable matter. Large numbers of complete vessels dating from *c.* 1790 to 1835 were recovered (Pl. XXXIII). Some of these vessels must have been produced after *c.* 1820 (see pottery report p. 309). Other ceramic material included clay pipes and small bone, bronze and iron objects were also present. The bone objects included a possible syringe (see report, p. 307). Buttons, a keyhole plate and hinges and pins were found and glass objects included a quantity of pharmaceutical bottles.

After this backfilling and once the fabric of the cess-tank had been reduced to below ground level, a wall was built running approximately east–west across the site from the road frontage and directly over the reduced north wall of the cess-tank. The brick-rubble trench-built foundation of this wall (4) was sealed by modern levels.

No. 3 Marlowe Avenue was almost certainly constructed after 1802 when the owner of no. 16

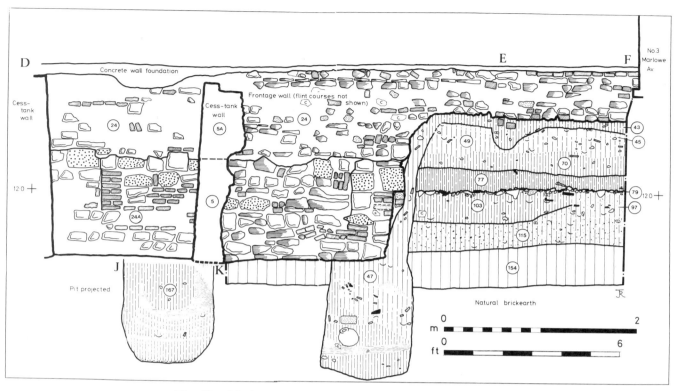

Fig. 55.   Marlowe Avenue: Sections D–E–F. (Scale: 1:40)

Watling Street, a William Scott, died and the house and grounds sold by lots.[93] In 1807, the main house was bought by John Hodges, the first of a number of solicitors who subsequently owned the property.[94] The selling of the garden in lots probably engendered the construction of the numerous buildings shown on the 1873 Ordnance Survey, of which no. 3 Marlowe Avenue was one. The brick wall (4) was almost certainly contemporary with no. 3, and probably divided separate properties. This wall sealed the demolished cess-tank and, therefore, must date to after *c.* 1830–35. It is likely that no. 3 Marlowe Avenue and the boundary wall (4) were erected at the same time as the backfilling, i.e. in the early 1830s.[95]

The large *corpus* of pottery recovered from the cess-tank may derive either from solicitors in residence at no. 16 Watling Street from 1807, or possibly from people living in the former 'Great Stable' in the garden (which was a domestic residence from at least 1762),[96] who may have been moved or evicted upon the selling of the land.

93. Title deeds abstract 1802.
94. E.g. Shersby, *History of Kingsford, Arrowsmith and Wightwick* (unpublished).
95. This agrees with what is shown on two maps of Canterbury dating to 1825 and 1843 respectively (3rd Edition Doidge and T.W. Collards).
96. Title deeds abstract 1802.

Between Wall 4 and no. 3 Marlowe Avenue, the trench-built foundations (9) of a circular structure nearly 4 m. in diameter, were excavated. The foundation was filled with brick, tile, chalk and flint rubble in a matrix of dirty yellow mortar and grey clay. Another foundation extended eastwards at a tangent from the main body of the structure. The foundations cut layer 43, but appeared to be contemporary with the construction of no. 3 Marlowe Avenue, since the fill of the foundation was contiguous with the construction layers (18).

A brewery existed opposite the site on the other side of Marlowe Avenue during this period.[97] The size and plan of the circular structure are similar to oast- or malt-houses of the period and, therefore, it is quite likely that the foundations were of such a building related to the brewery. The building is not shown on the 1873 edition of the Ordnance Survey maps and must have been demolished by that time.

The remaining features excavated were all service trenches. Feature 6 contained a disused sewer, possibly an original service to no. 3 Marlowe Avenue. This had been replaced by a modern sewer (6A), just clipped by the south-west corner of the trench. A modern water-pipe trench (32) ran into the house from the road in the south-east corner. This may have replaced an earlier water-pipe trench (32A). The small extension to the north of the site was almost completely filled by two modern trenches. One (3) was a main sewer, the other (8), which was not excavated, may have been for telephone cables.

EXCAVATIONS AT ST. JOHN'S LANE (1983)

Summary

Apart from truncated pits and other features, all the levels investigated were of Roman date.

The earliest features all dated to the mid first century, or possibly just before. These included a ditch, and a very large feature which was probably a clay quarry. Other features were of Flavian date and most were rubbish-pits.

In the late first or early second century a major Roman street was laid a few metres to the east of the site. The stratigraphy suggests that the area may have been levelled at this time. For the next century a gradual build-up of soil occurred, with little change in land use. Large pits were dug close to the street in the second century and this and the absence of any structural remains imply that no buildings fronted onto the road at this time.

Roman levels of a later period were heavily disturbed and only survived in a few places. They did, however, suggest the possibility that some construction may have taken place in the vicinity during the late second or third century. The sub-foundation of a large wall ran approximately east–west across the site. Its west end was completely removed by later features, but the wall almost certainly turned south at this point. Dating for the wall was not conclusive, but a *terminus ante quem* provided by one of the features that cut away the corner suggested that it was late Roman. Since the wall was perpendicular to the Roman street, it was almost certainly part of a building fronting onto it. The line of the wall or even the wall itself, may have been preserved into the early medieval period, since a row of eleventh- or twelfth-century rubbish- and cess-pits ranged down its south side.

Also excavated was a late fourteenth- or fifteenth-century stone cess-tank, situated against the St. John's Lane frontage. This may have belonged to properties on Watling Street.

97. Ash and Company's Dane John Brewery.

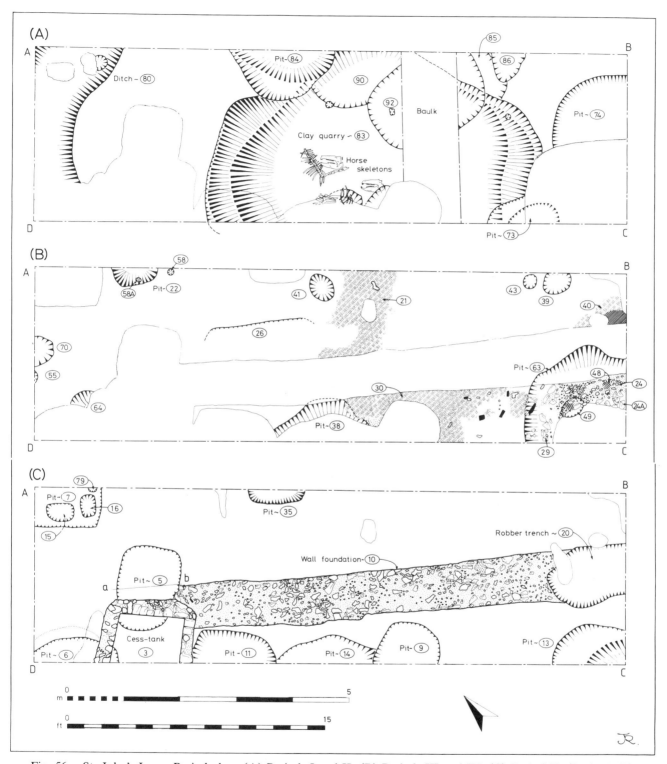

Fig. 56. St. John's Lane: Period plans (A) Periods I and II; (B) Periods III and IV; (C) Period V. (Scale: 1:67)

The excavation took place in three half-cellars belonging to a row of cottages fronting St. John's Lane. No direct evidence for the date of construction of these buildings was found, but it is likely that they were built with no. 3 Marlowe Avenue in the early 1830s. The masonry used in the construction of the cellars may have come originally from a boundary wall which surrounded the area from *c.* 1625 (see pp. 144 and 159).

Natural Deposits

The natural subsoil was head brickearth at an approximate level of +11.2 m. O.D. The natural gravel terrace underlying the brickearth was not exposed, but bands of sand and sandy brickearth were encountered at about +10.00 m. O.D.

Period I – First-century Features (Fig. 56A)

The earliest deposit excavated (76) overlaid the natural brickearth and consisted of pale browny-yellow clay, mottled with light grey clay (Fig. 57, Sections A–B, B–C, C–D). Few diagnostic objects were recovered from it.

A number of features cut layer 76. Most were only partially within the excavated area. The largest was a subrectangular pit or quarry nearly 6 m. across (83), which had removed most of the pre-Roman horizon in the central area of the site. The feature was about 2 m. deep, with irregular stepped sides (Fig. 57, Section C–D). The fill was mainly light grey-brown or orange-brown clays, with some flecking of carbon and daub, but quantities of redeposited brickearth around the edges and lenses of dark olive-grey clay were also evident. Pottery dating to the mid first century was recovered. Parts of two semi-articulated but badly preserved horse skeletons were also found in the feature. These had been thrown in after the pit had been half backfilled.

To the north, Pit 83 cut a smaller feature (85), which contained a homogeneous fill of light buff-brown clay. To the east 85 was cut by a shallow feature containing a similar fill 86 (Fig. 57, Section A–B). Very few datable objects were found in either feature.

At the far west end of the site, a short length of V-shaped ditch (80) was excavated. The ditch traversed the width of the trench, curving from a north–south to a north-east–south-west alignment. Because the ditch was bisected longitudinally by the west side of the trench, its width was not determined, but it was probably about 1.4 m. The feature contained a fill of mainly light buff and yellow-brown clays slightly flecked with charcoal and was virtually sterile, only a few sherds of mid first century or possibly earlier pottery being recovered.

Pit 74 was only partially within the excavated area at the west end of the site. This pit definitely cut layer 76, possibly from within the first few centimetres of a succeeding deposit ((71/72), Fig. 57, Section B–C). Much of the feature was cut away by a later pit dating to the mid to late second century (63). The earliest deposit within pit 74 consisted of dark grey-brown clay heavily flecked with carbon and containing pebbles and some Belgic chaff-tempered brick. Over this was a complex series of lenses of carbon and grey ash (74A). The fill of this pit had subsided considerably and it was capped by slumped later deposits (71/72). Pottery recovered from the feature ranged from pre- to early Flavian in date.[98]

---

98. Grog-tempered ware from (74) and (74A) included two lids, both with full profiles and one near-complete. Lids of this period are very rare (M.J. Green).

Other features were all situated in the centre of the trench and all cut the quarry (83). The most substantial of these was a roughly circular pit (84) which was cut from the top of layer 76. It contained various fills including buff-brown and orange-brown clays, lenses of carbon and dark grey-brown clay and yielded some pre- to early Flavian pottery and struck flints.

To the west Pit 84 cut feature 90 which was in turn cut by 92. Both these features were shallow and filled with a very dark brown clay heavily flecked and striated with charcoal. Quantities of slag and daub were also found. The features were covered by a deposit of dark olive-brown clay heavily flecked with charcoal, daub and shell (89), which may have been a dump of material capping subsidence into the pits. No useful datable material was recovered from these levels. All of these features and layer 76 were sealed by a later deposit (71/72).

Conclusion

The excavation indicates that considerable activity, mainly pit digging, was occurring in the immediate area from around the mid first century to the Flavian period. Dating evidence suggests that all these features were backfilled before the construction of the major Roman street, excavated on the Marlowe Avenue site.

The V-shaped ditch was probably the earliest feature on the site and may have been dug during the first half of the century, although the lack of silting up might suggest a date not long before the middle of the century. It may have been an enclosure ditch, but no precise definition is possible. No features relating to the Early Iron Age (such as found by Dr F. Jenkins about 100 m. to the west of the present excavation)[99] were discerned.

The large pit (83) was similar to other features of this period excavated in Canterbury and was almost certainly a clay quarry; it contained relatively little domestic refuse. The two horse skeletons were probably interred here for convenience, after the pit had been half filled in. The lower levels suggest that the backfilling occurred shortly after its excavation. Features 84 and 74, both probably early Flavian in date, were rubbish-pits. The same identification may hold for Pits 90 and 92, but the quantities of slag and burnt material incorporated in their fill may mean that they had some connection with industrial activity.

Period II – Late first- to early second-century Features and Deposits (Fig. 56A)

Overlying all of the earlier features and layer 76 was a deposit of light to medium grey loamy clay (71/72). The deposit was flecked with carbon, oyster shells and some daub and yielded pottery of the late first to early second century and a coin of A.D. 98–99 (S.F. No. 70).

Only one pit of this period was found (73). This was situated in the south-east corner of the site and cut the earlier clay-quarry (83), being sealed by a later deposit ((61); Fig. 57, Section C–D). Much of the pit was removed by a later pit (63) and consequently its shape could not be determined. The pit was filled with mid to dark olive-grey clay heavily flecked and mottled with carbon, shell, daub and pale yellow clay and contained pottery dating from the late first to the early second century.

---

99. *The Archaeological Newsletter*, March 1951, 145–7; *The Archaeological Newsletter*, August–December, 1952, 157–9.

Conclusion
Layer 71/72 was the first of a sequence of virtually identical deposits between layer 76 and the modern cellar floor, which truncated the Roman levels. The deposits originated in the late first to early second century and their nature suggests that they represent a gradual accumulation of soil possibly commencing with the construction of the Roman street (situated a few metres east) (Fig. 48). The absence of substantial pre-street deposits on the present site, unlike the *c.* 40 cm. of pre-street levels excavated in 1981, and the shallowness of some of the Flavian features, may mean that the immediate area to the west of the street was reduced and levelled before construction of the street.

Layer 71/72 and its successors were, however,different in nature to contemporary deposits on the east side of the road. The deposits were not silty enough to have derived from material washed from the street alone and were interspersed with fair quantities of charcoal, oyster shells and other domestic refuse. It is possible that much of this material accumulated from the digging of pits in the area, although only one rubbish-pit (73) of this period was found on site.

This pit's proximity to the Roman street and the absence of any structural remains imply that here no buildings fronted the street at this time.

Period III – Mid to late second-century Soil Build-up and Features (Fig. 56B)
Sealing layer 71/72 was a virtually identical but slightly loamier deposit (47/54). The junction between these layers (horizon 66) was faintly discernible in section as a line of oyster shells and small pebbles. This horizon was more clearly delineated at the eastern end of the trench, where a thin lens of mottled pale yellow clay 61 separated the two deposits (Fig. 57, Section A–B). Layer (61) was about 5–10 cm. thick at its maximum, but tapered away and eventually disappeared a few metres to the west of the trench edge. Layer 47/54 contained large quantities of mid- to late second-century pottery and other domestic refuse. The lens (61) contained similar pottery.

Layer 47/54 was sealed over most of the trench area by an identical deposit (23/45/59), which also contained pottery of the mid to late second century. This level was in turn truncated and sealed in places by the modern cellar backfill and to the south was considerably disturbed by later pits.

Only one major feature was associated with these levels. This was a large pit (63) in the extreme south-east corner. The pit cut layer 61 and removed much of the earlier pits 73 and 74 (Fig. 57, Sections B–C, C–D). Its upper fill appeared to be contiguous with the horizontal deposit (47/54) and it was almost certainly sealed by the later level (23/45/59), although this had considerably subsided into the pit. The fill consisted of a fairly homogeneous dark olive or greenish-grey glutinous clay, heavily flecked with carbon, daub and oyster shells and interspersed with tip-lines of flints and pebbles, oyster shells and Roman tile and brick. The pit also yielded plaster and *opus signinum*, *tesserae*, nails, daub and glass and large quantities of pottery most of which dated to the mid to late-second century.

A number of other small amorphous features and post-holes (64), (70), (55), (58), (58A) was also found relating to these deposits, but little could be inferred from them.

Conclusion
The close similarity of the horizontal deposits (23/45/59) and (47/54) to the earlier layer (71/72)

suggests that little change in land use occurred through the second century. No evidence for habitation was discovered and the continuing presence of large rubbish-pits close to the street frontage may mean that no buildings were situated here at this time. The levels themselves suggest open, unoccupied ground, maybe cultivated.

Period IV – Truncated Roman Deposits and Features (Fig. 56B)

All the remaining Roman features and layers were truncated by the construction of the post-medieval cellar. Most of the features were consequently very shallow; some were considerably disturbed by later pits and most yielded few diagnostic objects.

Pit 22 contained a mid olive-brown loam with oyster shells, pebbles and flecks of charcoal and mortar as well as some late second-century pottery (Fig. 57, Section A–B).

Very little remained of feature 38 but it was probably a pit. Feature 26 was only a few centimetres deep and only one side and two corners of it were found. Both features yielded second-century pottery. A number of other features, post-holes and shallow scoops, were also excavated ((39), (41), (43)).

In three areas the mid to late second-century deposits (23/45/59) were sealed by irregular spreads of redeposited brickearth ((21), (30) and (40); Fig. 57, Sections A–B, B–C, C–D).

These layers had been considerably disturbed by the post-medieval cellar and had formed part of its trodden earth floor. The deposits were never more than 10 cm. thick and may have been contiguous originally. The patch of clay (40) had been burnt on its upper surface.

These clay layers were obviously associated with a sequence of deposits excavated in the south-east corner (although only (30) could be related directly). This complex sequence of layers had been preserved from the destruction caused by the post-medieval cellar because they had slumped into the earlier pits (74 and 63). The layers were cut away in the extreme corner by a later pit (13) and to the north were partially removed by a wall-foundation (10). The deposits were numerous and mainly thin interconnecting lenses. The whole sequence sealed Pit 63 and the upper horizontal layer (23/45/49) and was in turn truncated and sealed by the modern cellar backfill (1) (Fig. 57, Sections B–C, C–D).

The deposits included lenses of crushed chalk and chalk lumps in a glutinous brown clay (24A) and (29), a thick deposit of orange river-gravel (24), a number of layers 2 cm. thick of possibly poured chalky mortar (28) and (29A), lenses of dark brown loam, one of which contained numerous small pebbles, pea-grit and horizontal Roman tiles (37) and other layers of variously coloured clays. One of these (53/56) was overlapped by the area of clay (30) mentioned above. The clay layer (40) must also have been closely related to these deposits, but any stratigraphical relationships had been removed by the wall foundation (10).

Few diagnostic objects were recovered from these levels, but some contained small quantities of second- or third-century pottery as well as painted plaster, nails and Roman glass.

Also cutting from within the sequence were two post-holes, one purely a void (48), the other a 'ghost' in a post-pit packed with tiles and flints (49). These features were in a stratigraphically similar position, being sealed by layer 36 and cutting layer 37.

Conclusion

It is conceivable that the isolated deposits described above were merely dump layers, levelling up subsidence into the earlier pits. Their variety and complex nature and the presence of the intervening post-holes, however, make this unlikely. The layers probably originally extended over a much wider area, but were removed elsewhere upon the construction of the cellar. Some of them may indeed be consecutive levellings up to counteract the slump, e.g. the gravel layer 24, but others, especially the mortar lenses, suggest building activity, if not in the immediate vicinity, certainly nearby. Layer 37 with its mass of horizontal tiles may have been a rough metalled surface, and the layers of redeposited brickearth possibly clay floors. Unfortunately, no definite structural components, apart from the two post-holes, were found and the layers extended over such a small area that no definite interpretations of their function can be drawn. However, it is possible that at some time towards the end of the second century structures may have been erected along the street frontage. This would explain the noticeable lack of any Roman pits later than the second century near the street.

Period V – Late-Roman Wall Foundation and Pit and post-Roman Features (Fig. 56C, Pl. XXXIV)
All of the remaining features were truncated by the construction of the post-medieval cellar.

1. *Late-Roman Wall Foundation and Pit* (Fig. 56C)
Extending approximately east–west across most of the trench (and cutting all of the latest remaining Roman deposits) was a wall sub-foundation (10) (Fig. 57, Section B–C). The foundation was about 0.90 m. wide and between 30–50 cm. of its depth survived under the cellar floor. The foundation was trench-built and constructed of flints, considerable amounts of chalk lumps and rammed river gravel. At its west end it was completely cut away by a later pit (5) and cess-tank (3). The wall did not extend beyond either of these features and therefore probably turned south at this point. About 1.40 m. of the west end of the foundation was partially cut away by a robber trench (20). This contained a fill of dark grey loamy clay and small pebbles, with quantities of white mortar and chalk, but no datable objects.

The wall-foundation (10) was completely removed at the eastern end of the trench by a pit (5). The pit, which was completely excavated, contained small quantities of organic silt in its base, but the main fills were a dark olive-grey clay and a mixture of mid brown loam, dark grey and orange clays (Fig. 57, Section A–B). Some fourth-century and residual first- to second-century pottery, a coin of the late third century and one dating to *c*. A.D. 355–65. (S.F. Nos. 13 and 14) were found. However, a Roman date for the pit is not totally secure since it also yielded fragments of a loom-weight (S.F. No. 17) which may have been of late Saxon provenance.

2. *Post-Roman Features* (Fig. 56C)
Seven post-Roman pits were excavated. Five of these spanned the south side of the trench, all bisected by the section. They appeared to respect the position of the wall-foundation.

Pit 13 was in the extreme south-east corner of the site and was not bottomed (Fig. 57, Sections B–C, C–D). The varied backfill included dark brown loams and lenses of carbon, very dark grey-brown clays and a very mixed deposit of orange gravel and brown clay. Roman and medieval tiles, and pottery dating to the early medieval period, possibly the twelfth century, were recovered.

Pit 9 (Fig. 57, Section C–D) contained layers of brown organic sediment, loose black loam banded with organic material, black clay, dark grey and brown loams containing numerous

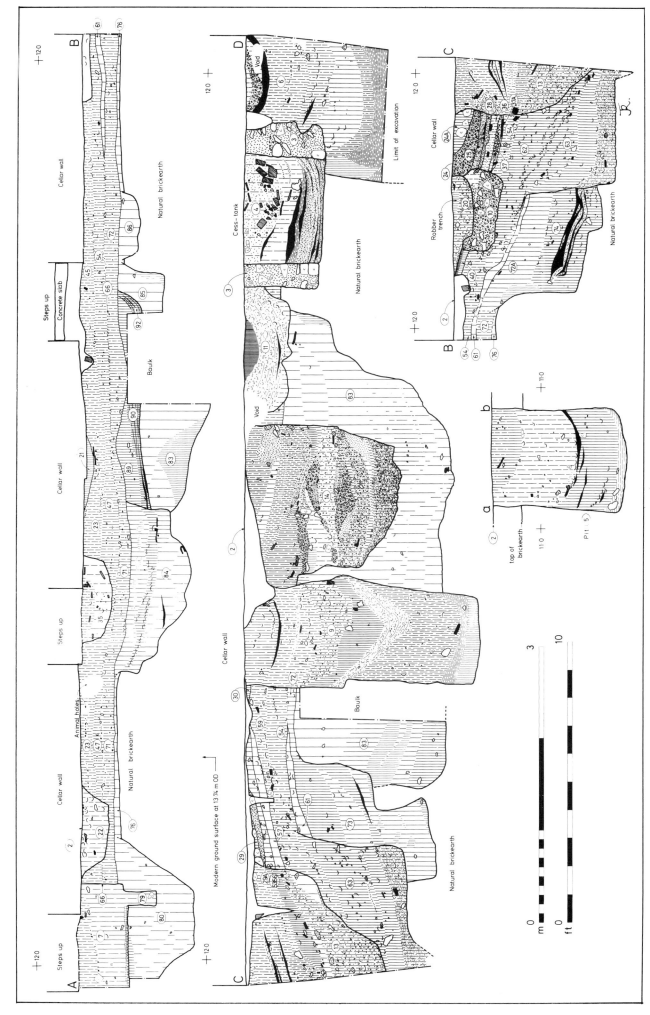

Fig. 57. St. John's Lane: Sections. (Scale: 1:40)

lenses of ash and charcoal and a dump of striated grey and dark brown ash. The pit yielded animal bone and some pottery including early medieval sherds.

To the west Pit 9 cut 14. Only a small portion of this feature was excavated and it was not bottomed. It contained a complex sequence of deposits including dark grey and brown loams, ash, yellow clay, crushed chalk and sand. Distributed throughout the fill, either as distinct layers or within the general matrix, was a large proportion of orange sandy gravel, similar to that in the make-up of the wall foundation (10). The pit also yielded animal bone and eleventh- to twelfth-century pottery. Pit (11) was immediately adjacent to Pit (14), but the exact relationship between them was removed by a modern disturbance. The pit was shallow and was backfilled with burnt clay and daub over a deposit of intricately banded ashes, varying in colour from bright orange to black, with some lenses of charcoal interspersed. A few sherds of possibly early medieval pottery were also found.

Pit 6 was in the extreme south-west corner and because of its proximity to the trench edge and the looseness of its fill, it was not completely excavated. The pit contained a variety of deposits, including banded dark brown organic material, dark grey and brown loams, carbon and gravel, incorporating animal bone and quantities of possibly eleventh- to twelfth-century pottery. Both this pit and Pit 11 were cut by a later cess-tank (3).

Feature 7 in the north-west corner of the site was flat-bottomed and contained a fill of mixed orange clay and dark grey loam flecked with chalk, mortar and carbon (Fig. 57, Section A–B). This deposit yielded pottery dating from Belgic to the fourth century. On the lower surface of the feature were thin layers of trodden clay and dark brown silty clay. Three post-holes (15), (16) and (79) were found around the edges of the pit in its base. These and the trodden clay layer suggested that the feature may have been a cellar and, consequently, the trench was extended north from the modern cellar at this point. Unfortunately, little extra information about its function was gained, but its upper fill was found to be a dark brown loam containing much oyster shell, animal bone and pottery which dated to c. 1050–1100.

Only a small portion of Pit 35 was within the trench and it was very shallow. The feature contained a fill of brown loam and orange-brown clay with numerous peg-tiles. Animal bone, medieval glazed floor-tiles and fourteenth-century pottery were found.

A truncated, stone-walled cess-tank (3) was excavated in the south-west corner of the trench. The feature cut Pits 5, 6 and 11 and wall-foundation 10 (Fig. 57, Section C–D). The tank was trench-built, with walls constructed of uncoursed flints and chalk-blocks bonded with a darkish yellow lime mortar. The inside faces were rendered with similar mortar, leaving an internal width of 1.20 m.

The backfill (4) of the tank included layers of light brown and grey silt banded with carbon and ash, orange brown cess-like material and loose brown loam and mortar. These deposits were capped with brick rubble in a mixture of light brown mortary loam and brickearth. The feature yielded peg-tiles, medieval glazed floor-tiles and pottery of the late fourteenth and fifteenth centuries.

Conclusion

No contemporary stratigraphy relating to any of the above features survived destruction by the post-medieval cellar and, consequently, their chronology depends almost entirely upon the dating of artefacts recovered from their fills.

Pits 6, 9, 11, 13 and 14 all contained small quantities of eleventh- to twelfth-century or early medieval material as well as residual Roman wares. Most of these features were rubbish- or cess-pits, although Pit 9 may have originally been a well. The fact that many contained material similar to the make-up of the wall sub-foundation 10 and that they appeared to respect its alignment and position suggests that they post-date it. Unfortunately, no conclusive evidence for the date of this wall survived; but, despite the sub-foundation being constructed with large amounts of chalk (unusual for Roman walls in Canterbury), it is likely that it is of late Roman origin. The wall is almost exactly perpendicular to the major Roman street, which certainly implies a Roman context.

Also, unless the position of the early medieval pits is coincidental, which is unlikely considering their number, the wall must pre-date the eleventh century.

The strongest evidence for a Roman origin of the wall, however, is given by Pit 5. This pit cut the wall and therefore supplies a *terminus ante quem*, at least for the period of use of the structure it represented. The preponderance of late Roman material in the fill, including two coins, and the absence of any later artefacts, apart from fragments of a possible loom-weight, suggest strongly that the pit is late fourth century in date.

In conclusion, it can be said that although no direct evidence disproving a post-Roman provenance of the wall was discovered, it seems likely that it was constructed in the late Roman period, probably prior to the late fourth century and represents a building fronting the major Roman street. If this is so, the fact that a number of early medieval pits appear to respect its position and alignment suggests that the wall may have still been standing in the eleventh century and may even have constituted a property boundary.

The date of the establishment of St. John's Lane is uncertain, but the position of the rubbish pits would imply that the road originated during or shortly after the twelfth century, perhaps as a result of the construction of the church of St. John at about this time.

Feature 7 dated to *c.* 1050–1100. The regular shape of this feature, the trodden clay layer on its lower surface and the post-holes around its edge may mean that it was a lined cellar and that the clay layer was a rough floor. Alternatively, the feature may have been a wood-lined tank or pit. The basal layers of the feature consisted of redeposited Roman soils, which also filled the post-holes, indicating that the lining was removed before the feature was backfilled. The upper levels contained large quantities of domestic refuse, so the feature, if not a rubbish-pit originally, was eventually utilized as such.

The remaining features dated to the fourteenth or fifteenth century. The cess-tank (3) probably belonged to properties along Watling Street and its position on the frontage of St. John's Lane suggests that there were no buildings here at this time.

Phase VI – Post-medieval Cellar (Fig. 48)

All of the later deposits on site were truncated by three half-cellars, once belonging to a row of cottages along St. John's Lane. The excavation produced no direct evidence for the exact date of construction of these buildings.

The cellar walls survived to a height of about 2 m. above the floor, were 20 cm. thick on average, and were composed mainly of limestone blocks and bricks which were probably seventeenth century in date. The construction of the walls was varied, being coursed in places but often irregular.

Each cellar had internal dimensions of about 3.45 m. × 3.05 m. (11 ft. 6 in. × 10 ft.) and small extensions to the north which had originally contained wooden steps. There were coal-shutes in the south wall, i.e. on the road frontage. The cellars were all earth-floored directly on the underlying Roman deposits. Post- and stake-holes had been dug in the floor and other disturbances included animal holes.

Conclusion

The cottages are not shown on the coloured map of Canterbury of *c.* 1640. Shortly before this date the area became a garden belonging to no. 16 Watling Street (see p. 144), with a large boundary wall separating it from Marlowe Avenue and St. John's Lane. A similar situation is also shown on Doidge's map of 1752, which suggests that the cottages must have been constructed after this date. Since the bricks appear to be seventeenth century, it is quite probable that they were re-used having originally come from the seventeenth-century boundary wall, which would have been demolished before the erection of the cottages.

In the early 1830s, no. 3 Marlowe Avenue was constructed on the corner of Marlowe Avenue and St. John's Lane. This building possesses cellars virtually identical to those excavated. The width of the cottage cellars shows (assuming that all the cottages were the same size, as is shown on the Ordnance Survey map of 1874) that the west wall of no. 3 Marlowe Avenue is constructed exactly on the position of the east wall of the adjacent cottage.

Since the plan of the cottages suggests a nineteenth-century date of construction, the above strongly implies that they were in fact erected at the same time as no. 3 Marlowe Avenue, probably in the same 'build'. These particular cottages were demolished in the late 1960s and the cellars backfilled with brick rubble (1), probably from the superstructure. The area has been a car park since then.

Marlowe Avenue and St. John's Lane – General Conclusions

The excavations at Marlowe Avenue and St. John's Lane, although limited in size, have produced some important evidence bearing on the nature of the area during the Roman period.

The main result was the location of the major Roman street which was probably constructed in the late first or early second century and remained in use up until the fifth century.[100] This road ties in with the Roman street-plan deduced from previous excavations in the city, and is a continuation south of Watling Street (20 m. north of the Marlowe Avenue excavation) of the road extensively excavated on the Marlowe Theatre site. This street was first located by Professor S.S. Frere, who did in fact extrapolate it south into the position proved by excavation. Unfortunately, the width of the road was not determined and it did not extend as far west as the St. John's Lane site, nor were any features (such as side-ditches) associated with it found here.

The land immediately to the east of the street was probably unoccupied open ground throughout most of the Roman period. The sequences of posts excavated on site probably represent a much-replaced fence-line; but it is possible, considering the small size of the

---

100. The evidence recovered does not supply a more precise date for the construction of the road. However, the roads excavated on the Marlowe sites appear to originate *c.* A.D. 110, and it is likely that the Marlowe Avenue street is contemporary with these (see *The Archaeology of Canterbury*, vol. v, forthcoming).

excavated area, that they may have been part of timber structures of which nothing else survived.

Because of the truncation of the Roman levels on the St. John's Lane site, the main deposits investigated dated from the early Roman period to the second century. However, even during this period, a lack of occupation on this side of the street is also evident. No definite Roman structures were encountered; it is possible that buildings were sandwiched in the unexcavated area between the site and the Roman street, but the smallness of the area and the presence of large pits in this position (63 and 73) make it unlikely.

The deposits on this site were substantially different to those encountered on the Marlowe Avenue excavation, and this may indicate a different use of the land. Certainly, clay-quarrying and pit-digging took place here from the mid first to the late second century, and there is little evidence for this on the Marlowe Avenue site during this period, although allowances must be made for the small area investigated.

The isolated deposits of clay, mortar and gravel which date possibly to the third century might represent occupation, but they were so disturbed that no firm conclusions can be drawn from them.

The main evidence for Roman occupation is the wall sub-foundation (10). The problems relating to the date of this wall are discussed above (p. 156), but it is almost certainly of Roman origin, possibly constructed at some time between the third and first half of the fourth centuries. If so, the feature is probably the foundation of the north wall of a late Roman building which fronted the street.[101]

East of the street, traces of metalling, possibly the forecourt of a Roman building dating to the very end of the Roman period, were encountered.

Post-Roman deposits, apart from truncated pits, were only excavated on the Marlowe Avenue excavation. These deposits included the ubiquitous 'dark earth'. No sunken featured buildings were found but, considering the small area sampled, it is still possible that sporadic Saxon occupation extended this far south from its nucleus in the Marlowe Theatre area. During this period the position of the Roman street was lost, a fate shared by all other Roman streets in the city.

The later levels suggest that the area remained open ground, probably gardens or fields, for much of the medieval and post-medieval periods. From the seventeenth century this situation is shown on successive maps of Canterbury.

At some time in the medieval period, St. John's Lane came into being. The exact date of this road is uncertain, but the early medieval pits excavated on the St. John's Lane site suggest that it was some time during or after the twelfth century, possibly when the church of St. John was constructed. More light may be thrown on this subject when the church is excavated on the forthcoming Watling Street excavation.

From c. 1625 the area of land bounded on the east and south sides by Marlowe Avenue and St. John's Lane, respectively, became a garden belonging to no. 16 Watling Street (see above p.

101.   The wall may be related to a number of possible Roman walls found in 1868; see J. Pilbrow, 'Discoveries made during Excavations at Canterbury in 1868', *Archaeologia*, xliii, 1871 (see also Fig. 48).

144). This garden was surrounded by a boundary wall much of which was probably still extant in the early 1830s when no. 3 Marlowe Avenue was constructed.[102]

The cottages, in the cellars of which the St. John's Lane excavation took place, appear to have been contemporary with no. 3 Marlowe Avenue. It is likely that the cellar walls were constructed out of re-used seventeenth-century masonry, probably from the garden boundary wall itself.

102. Parts of this wall can still be seen incorporated into present boundary walls in the area.

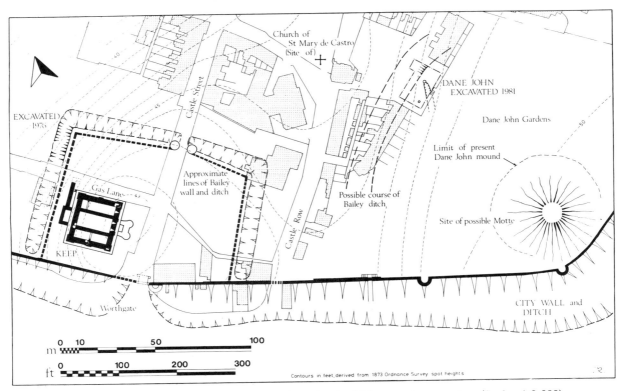

Fig. 58.   No. 15A Dane John: Site location plan and Norman topography. (Scale: 1:2,000)

XXIX. No. 15A DANE JOHN

INTRODUCTION

Between Easter and July 1981, excavations prior to redevelopment were undertaken on the site of the old City Council offices at 15A Dane John. These excavations were financed by the developers, D.J. Developments Ltd.

The site was situated immediately adjacent to the west side of the Dane John Gardens, about 100 m. north of the Dane John mound (Fig. 58). Unusual aspects of the site included an almost complete absence of Roman levels and a deposit *c.* 2 m. thick of post-eighteenth-century material that was largely removed mechanically.

SUMMARY

Period I

Although the excavation proved to be one of the deepest ever undertaken by the Trust and extended over an area of about three hundred square metres, virtually no pre-Norman stratigraphy was found. This was mainly the result of later extensive disturbances. Only a few possible Roman features were excavated, all truncated by later terracing.

Period II

The most important discovery was of a large flat-bottomed ditch running approximately north-east to south-west across the north side of the excavated area (Fig. 59B). The ditch, at least 17 m. wide and over 3 m. deep, was almost certainly late eleventh-century in date. This is probably part of the outer bailey ditch for the early Norman motte and bailey castle (the present Dane John Mound probably being the site of the motte), which would have been constructed by William the Conqueror just after the Conquest. The military life of this castle would perhaps have ended with the completion in the early twelfth century of the later Norman castle (and keep) to the west (Fig. 58). During this period the rest of the excavated area was probably covered by a bailey rampart.

Period III

In the late twelfth or thirteenth century, the bailey defences were probably razed and the ditch partially backfilled. A number of features, including pits, wells and small ditches, was then dug in the area. The features were later truncated and disturbed. No definite signs of occupation were found. The partially backfilled bailey ditch was re-cut at this time with a channel at the sump. This new ditch, which may have been an open running sewer, might be the predecessor of the 'Black Ditch' or 'Black Dyke', which documentary sources describe as being an open sewer, extant in this vicinity until the eighteenth century. The re-cut bailey ditch was progressively backfilled and virtually levelled by the sixteenth century.

Period IV

Few deposits of the later medieval period survived a reduction of the ground level that occurred in the early sixteenth century. After this the area became a garden (large quantities of soil being imported) and remained so up to and throughout the seventeenth century.

Period VA

Towards the end of the seventeenth century the gradual south-east to north-west downwards slope of the area was terraced. This terrace removed most of the stratigraphy in the south-eastern part of the site (Fig. 59D). Probably post-dating this terracing, but possibly associated with the garden, which was still in use nearby, was a number of rubbish-pits and a heavily-rutted cart-track, which probably ran south-east from an entrance on Castle Row next to the present White Hart public house.

Period VB

In the eighteenth century levelling up occurred and a road or courtyard, made mainly of crushed brick fragments, was laid within the terraced area and also partially across the top of the garden deposits. Adjacent to the road was a wooden post-supported structure with an oval pit to the east of it. These obviously associated features can be dated to a period between *c.* 1737 and *c.* 1790 (though at present no definite use can be ascribed to them). This building was eventually demolished and the pit and courtyard area used for the dumping of rubbish, including large amounts of eighteenth-century pottery and quantities of butchered bone.

Period VC/D

In 1790 the 'Dane John land', of which the area covered by the site was part, was leased by the City to Alderman James Simmons, who undertook to level the site and landscape the entire gardens. This landscaping was still in progress in the early nineteenth century.

From around this time a large amount of dumping occurred on site, raising the level by about one metre. It is possible that some of this material was derived from the landscaping works, but the dating of the levels suggests that most of the dumping occurred slightly later, possibly when cellared buildings to the south-west (Dane John Grove) were erected in 1822.

The dump deposits were cut by the foundations of Shakespeare's Terrace (nos. 12–15 Dane John), constructed at some time in the 1840s, and by a boundary wall and brick-lined well (Fig. 61).

Sealing all of these features was a thick layer of twentieth-century dump deposits, over which lay the shallow foundations of the recent City Council offices.

THE EXCAVATION

Natural Deposits

The local natural subsoil consisted of a layer of Pleistocene brickearth, occasionally containing irregular lenses of gravel, at least 2.40 m. thick, overlying sandy gravel of unknown depth. Because of extensive disturbances over the excavated area, it was impossible to determine the original level of the surface of the pre-Roman natural deposits with any certainty, but a gradual slope downwards from the east to the west remained. This may indicate the nature of the original pre-Roman topography. The existing levels of the top of the natural brickearth were +12.30 m. O.D. in the east corner of the site and +10.70 m. O.D. in the west corner.

Period I – Roman Features (Fig. 59A)

Only three features could be definitely ascribed to the Roman period and these were completely truncated by later disturbances and features. They consisted of two pits (178) and (156) and a small feature (114). Pit 178 was cut by 156; it was about 1.10 m. deep and contained a mainly sterile fill of greenish-yellow clay and redeposited brickearth. The fill and the surrounding brickearth were stained bright green. Pit 156 was 0.90 m. deep and contained a fill of almost completely sterile redeposited brickearth and a few lenses of dark olive-grey silt which yielded some pottery, animal bones and Roman building material (Fig. 64, Section D–K). Feature 114 was shallow (Fig. 62, Section B–E) and yielded early Roman pottery. One other feature that may belong to this phase was a shallow depression (184), but this contained no finds. Pit (178) has been dated to the late first to early second century by the pottery, and Feature 156 to the second century. No other stratigraphy of the Roman period survived later reduction of the ground level, so that it was impossible to say what sort of activity, if any, took place.

No signs of any other occupation occur until the eleventh century. However, the fact that only two pits were found over quite a wide area may indicate that no substantial occupation occurred, despite the presence of Roman building-materials in later pits.

In conclusion, it can be said that it is quite possible that the area in the immediate vicinity of the site was open ground for at least a millenium.

Period II and Period IIIA – Norman Bailey Ditch and twelfth- to thirteenth-century Features (Fig. 59B)

1. *Norman Bailey Ditch* (Pl. XXXVI)

The largest and most important feature discovered during the excavation was a flat-bottomed ditch running north-east to south-west across the north-west side of the trench. Because of time restraints and the large size of this feature, only a 5.75 m. length of it was totally excavated (this entirely by hand). The complete profile of the ditch was not examined; but, if it was symmetrical, it would have been at least 17 m. across at the top. The existing depth of the ditch was over 3 m., but because of later reductions of the ground level it may originally have been deeper (Fig. 62, Section A–B).

The primary fills of the ditch, which were below the water table, were firstly a lens of light grey sandy silt containing grit and gravel (145). Overlying this was a complex of layers, mainly bluish-grey organic clays (130). These waterlogged organic deposits yielded large amounts of preserved branches and twigs as well as a fair amount of pottery dating to the twelfth century and probably confined to the first half. Sealing these primary deposits was a complex sequence of lenses, layers 121, 124 and 129. These consisted mainly of redeposited brickearth, yellow, orange and grey clays and lenses of dark brown silty loams as well as one of washed yellow silt containing gravel. These layers contained large amounts of residual Roman material and a few sherds of pottery ranging in date from the eleventh to the thirteenth century.

2. *Twelfth- to thirteenth-century Features* (Fig. 59B)

Several features and deposits were excavated to the south of the great ditch, but most of these were truncated and heavily disturbed by later reductions of the ground level. Stratified levels of this period only existed in the western area of the site, mostly sealed by a sixteenth-century horizon (141). Towards the east all the layers were increasingly sheared off and eventually

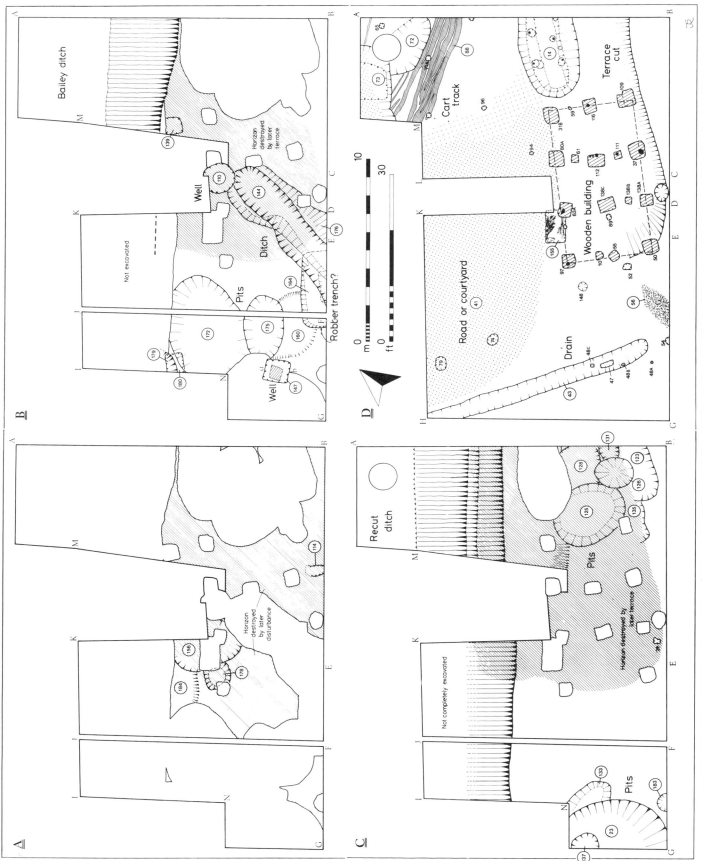

A

M

K

Horizon destroyed by later disturbance

156

184   178

I   N   E   G

B

Bailey ditch

M

139

Well   110   144

Horizon destroyed by later terrace

Not excavated

Ditch   176

'Robber trench?'   164   160

Pits

172   175

179   147

180   Well   N

C

Recut ditch

M

K

Pits   125   135   126   123   128   131

Horizon destroyed by later terrace

Not completely excavated

I   E

133   Pits   23   183

137   N

D

65   72   88   73

14

Terrace cut

Cart track   96   109

59   116   31B

D94   80A   111

80A   61   37

112

138C   138B   138A

Wooden building   63A

89   155   65   50

97   10

52

148   56

Road or courtyard   41

79   74   48C

Drain   54

43   47   48B   48A

m 0 ——— 10

ft 0 ——— 30

Fig. 59.   No. 15A Dane John: Plans (A) period I, (B) periods II and IIIA, (C) period IIIB, (D) periods IV, VA and VB. (Scale: 1:200)

completely removed by a post-medieval terrace. None of the deposits or features could be related to the ditch because of the terracing and a later recutting of the ditch itself. The stratigraphy was shallow and consisted of a complex series of deposits (154, 158, 159, 160, 168, 170 and 173) Fig. 64, Section F–J) which directly overlaid the natural subsoil. In one area the layers seemed to be deposited into a shallow depression ((160) Fig. 59B). The layers generally consisted of bands of very thin silt or lenses of redeposited clay and gravel and one of dark brown loam containing much carbon. They incorporated large amounts of residual Roman material, animal bone, some sherds of pottery dating to c. 1080–1150 and others that could have been early medieval or medieval.

The deposits sealed four pits (172, 175, 179 and 180), Fig. 59 B; see also Fig. 63, Sections G–H, N–I). Pit 172 appeared to be sealed by material spilling out from Pit 175 (layer (167), which also cut it. Pit 172 cut Pit 179 and contained a variety of fills, including gravel and flints in a matrix of light brown sandy silt, redeposited brickearth and a very dark brown, almost black, glutinous clay-loam. Most of the datable artefacts recovered from it were residual, including quantities of Roman roofing- and flue-tiles, but two thirteenth-century pot sherds were also found. Pit 175 contained lenses of redeposited brickearth, mortar and gravel and very mixed olive-brown and grey clays as well as a layer of dark grey-brown loamy clay that also spilled out over Pit 172. Unfortunately, very little datable material was recovered from this pit, but amongst the residual Roman pottery present were three early medieval sherds. Very little remained of Pit 179 and it was only partially excavated. It cut Pit 180, was itself cut by Pit 172 and contained a fill of clay which varied from light orange to brown. Animal bones and a few sherds of pottery dating to c. 1080–1150 were recovered from the fill. Pit 180 was cut by 179 and contained a fill of very dark olive-grey clay which had stained the surrounding brickearth bright green. It yielded large quantities of animal bone and some pottery of a date-range similar to those found in (179).

Most of the other features excavated cut the horizontal layers (154), etc., and were in turn sealed by later medieval or post-medieval deposits. Cutting the deposits in the area of depression 160, was a flat-bottomed gully (164). The feature was filled with redeposited brickearth which contained very little pottery or bone, but a fair amount of Roman building debris. Since 164 was heavily disturbed by later features and because only a small portion of it extended into the excavated trench, no definite conclusions as to its function can be formed. However, because of its profile and course, it is possible that it was a robber trench.

Another major feature was a U-shaped ditch (176) which ran south from a terminal end situated 3 m. from the edge of the large ditch (Fig. 59B). This feature was nearly 3 m. across and 1.50 m. deep, and was almost entirely filled with sterile natural clay with very fine lenses of grey-brown loam down one edge (the other edge was almost entirely removed by a recutting; Fig. 62, Sections B–E, E–G). There was little rapid silt and no signs of turf-line in its base. Although a length of nearly 7 m. of this ditch was excavated, the only datable material it contained was a small amount of residual Roman pottery. After the ditch had been backfilled, it was recut on an axis slightly to the west and aligned in a more south-westerly direction, although the terminal ends of both ditches coincided. The recut (feature 144) cut robber trench 164 and was more flat-bottomed than the earlier ditch. It contained an extremely complex series of deposits with few signs of silting on its edges. These deposits comprised very mixed yellow and brown clays, redeposited brickearth, gravel, mortar and black loams, amongst others. Incorporated in the backfill was a large amount of residual Roman material, nails, slag and clinker together with a few sherds of pottery which could date to the twelfth century.

Two possible wells were also excavated. One of these (feature 110) was sunk to at least 0.50 m. below the water-table. Because of this it was not completely excavated. The well cut ditch 144, but was completely truncated by a post-medieval terrace and, therefore, could not be related to any other contemporary deposits. The upper fill of 110 was fairly homogeneous grey clay flecked with yellow clays and carbon (Fig. 64, Section C–L); the lower fill was organic. Pottery from these deposits indicated that the feature was backfilled after the eleventh or twelfth century, possibly after a period of use as a cess-pit.

Feature 147, also probably a well, consisted of a shuttered 'well pipe' set in a backfilled construction-pit. Although no sign of any shuttering remained, its original presence and position could be deduced from the section (Fig. 62, Section A–B). Both the well pipe itself and the construction-pit surrounding it were roughly square and about 0.70 m. and 1.20 m. across respectively. The feature was 2.60 m. deep from the horizon sealing it, but did not extend below the present day water-table. The construction-pit for the well (147) contained a packing of clays, gravel and brickearth with some pottery dating to c. 1080–1150. When the well went out of use any wooden shuttering may have been robbed since no sign remained of the original wood. The resulting void was then filled with a mixture of material including grey clay with large flints and pebbles, which yielded some pottery dating to the late twelfth century.

One other pit (139) was excavated, but only a small portion of this feature had survived. It contained a fill of dark loamy clay heavily stained green and flecked with large quantities of carbon. Animal bone and pottery dating to the twelfth or early thirteenth century was recovered from the fill.

Discussion and Conclusion

1. The Motte and Bailey

In the past many historians have suggested that the Dane John mound (Pl. XXXV), situated about 100 m. south of the excavation, might be the site of a Norman motte constructed just after the Conquest (the name Dane John must be a corruption of the Norman French *donjon*). The existence of a castle situated by St. Mildred's Church (established there certainly by 1086 at the latest) and of a fine stone Norman keep erected at the turn of the eleventh to the twelfth century (Fig. 58) has often been used in the argument against a motte and bailey in the Dane John area.

However, the evidence from the excavation, in particular the presence and position of the large, almost certainly eleventh-century defensive ditch (the size of this feature must indicate its defensive function), strongly suggests a motte and bailey in the Dane John area, presumably pre-dating the Norman castle to the west. Further still, it is argued below that two motte and bailey castles, one in the Dane John area and one by St. Mildred's Church, may have existed in the immediate post-Conquest period.

The Dane John would have been a good position for a motte and bailey castle because the area was probably unoccupied open ground and to the south and east was protected by the remains of the Roman city wall and rampart. It is also possible that the motte was raised over an already existing, earlier mound; at least eight mounds that might be pre-Norman are known to have existed in the vicinity. Most Norman baileys were protected by a large rampart surmounted by a palisade as well as by means of a ditch. The absence of any definitely Norman features apart from the ditch suggests that this was the case here. Therefore, most if not all of the site area south of the ditch would have been underneath the rampart.

Unfortunately, because of later disturbance, very little intact contemporary stratigraphy survived in this area and even what remained could not be dated with any certainty.

Levels probably deposited after the Norman Conquest were directly superimposed on natural brickearth. It is quite likely that the construction of the motte and bailey castle required not only a general clearance of the area, but probably the digging and removal of material to erect the motte, or perhaps to increase the height of the earlier mound on which it was located. This may explain the complete absence of any Roman stratigraphy. Alternatively, the removal of all earlier deposits may have occurred when the defences were totally reduced. No definite remains of a rampart were found *in situ*, or any signs of a palisade, probably because if any rampart did survive into the late medieval period it would have been destroyed when terracing took place (see below). However, there is other evidence to suggest that there was a rampart which may have been dismantled or partially reduced before this time. The numerous features that were dug in this area appeared to be cut from a level just above natural brickearth. These features and the shallow levels that were associated with them all contained large amounts of residual Roman material and very little pottery of Norman or medieval date. Overlying the primary organic fills in the large ditch was an extensive dump of similar nature to many of these deposits. It is quite likely that much of this material was produced from the levelled rampart, which would have been largely composed of pre-Norman or natural material. Once the rampart was demolished, features (described above in section 2 and discussed below p. 168) were dug in the vicinity. Pottery recovered from these features and from the dump in the ditch suggests that the rampart may have been wholly or partially dismantled in the late twelfth or thirteenth century.

The long period between the original construction of the motte and bailey castle and the possible reduction of the rampart and partial backfilling of the ditch are also suggested by the primary fills in the ditch. It is likely that the ditch originally contained water, at least at certain times of the year. The flat-bottomed nature of the ditch implies this, since Norman defensive ditches were usually V-shaped when dry.[103] The primary fills also suggested originally waterlogged conditions, because of the preserved wood and branches that they contained. These mainly organic deposits were probably the result of a natural accumulation of humic material from the decomposition of weeds and other plants growing in and around the ditch. (These conditions were similar to those existing in the ditch of the later Norman castle).[104] The quantity of the organic layers suggests a fairly long period of deposition.

The excavations at no. 15A Dane John have almost certainly proved the existence of an early Norman motte and bailey castle probably centred on the present Dane John mound.[105]

The possible existence of a second motte and bailey castle contemporary with the Dane John

103.   D.F. Renn, *Norman Castles in Britain*, 14.
104.   Excavated 1976–77, Bennett *et al.*, *Excavations at Canterbury Castle, The Archaeology of Canterbury*, vol. i (1982), 51.
105.   This mound is in fact called Donjon in a rental of *c.* 1200 ('*vicum qui ducit uersus Danjun*' – Chapter archives, Register H).

earthwork,[106] on the site of the later Royal Castle, is suggested by a document of 1089.[107] This document describes an incident when rebellious monks, refusing to accept Lanfranc's nominee after the death of Abbot Scotland in September 1087, picketed the castle, near St. Mildred's Church (*sat castor secus aecclesiam Sanctae Miltrudae consedisse*).

It is not reasonable to assume that the Dane John mound, situated *c.* 300 m. west of St. Mildred's, is the castle referred to in this document. The building of the castle keep was not begun until the last decade of the eleventh century at the earliest.[108]

The existence of a second mound is also tentatively supported by the present topography of the castle area, with rising ground at the south-west end of Castle Street and at the south-east end of Gas Lane. This rising ground is also shown on the 1st edition Ordnance Survey for 1873.[109]

The military life of the Dane John earthwork would have been short, probably ending upon the completion of the castle keep before 1130, but the earthwork itself may have remained virtually intact for a fairly long period of time. Its final reduction and the backfilling of the bailey ditch may have occurred as late as the thirteenth century.

2. *Twelfth- to thirteenth-century Activity* (Fig. 59B)

Probably after a period of abandonment of the bailey area and after the levelling of any rampart, activity continued with the digging of pits and other features.

The dating of these features is extremely uncertain. Most of them contained large quantities of residual material with only a few contemporary artefacts. However, the stratigraphy suggests that most were cut from just above the level of natural brickearth, i.e. after the removal of any rampart in the twelfth or thirteenth century. Some of the features, however, especially the very shallow truncated pits, could have been cut at an earlier date from a higher level and through a slighted rampart.

The earliest pits (179 and 180) were very shallow and were sealed and truncated by the shallow stratigraphy (layers 154, 158, etc.; see above p. 165). These contained pottery not later than early medieval and could have been cut from higher up through a slighted rampart.

The later pits (172 and 175), were of a different nature and their backfill was closely related, even contemporary, with the deposits of shallow stratigraphy. Their shallowness and large area suggest that they may have been clay-extraction quarries, which were rapidly backfilled with material that was also used to build up the surrounding level. These pits contained mainly

---

106. The presence of two contemporary motte and bailey castles close to one another is not unknown, e.g. at Lewes and York.

107. Corpus Christi College Cambridge MS 173. See also W. Urry, *Canterbury under the Angevin Kings* (London, 1967), 208.

108. See D.F. Renn, 'Canterbury Castle in the Early Middle Ages', in *The Archaeology of Canterbury*, vol. i, *Excavations at Canterbury Castle* (1982), 70–77, 'The Decoration of Canterbury Castle and Keep' in *Medieval Art and Architecture at Canterbury* (British Archaeological Association 1982), 125–28, and T.W.T. Tatton-Brown, 'The Use of Quarr Stone in London and East Kent', in *Med. Arch.*, xxiv (1980), 00.

109. A thick black deposit of 'made ground' pre-dating the keep construction, located in the castle area during excavations in 1955 and interpreted as 'occupation deposits', may well have been part of a slighted mound for an early motte. See S.S. Frere and Sally Stow, 'Excavations at the Castle Keep' in *Excavations at Canterbury Castle, The Archaeology of Canterbury*, vol. i, 61.

redeposited Roman material with some early medieval, twelfth- and thirteenth-century pottery. It is possible, therefore, that much of this material came from the bailey rampart possibly still extant in other areas at this time.

Very little can be said about Feature 164 except that it was almost certainly a robber trench. No evidence for the type of wall it represented was found, and because of this and the small amount it extended into the trench area, nothing can be deduced about the building it may have represented.

No firm conclusions about the nature or function of the smaller ditch and its recut can be made. The original ditch (176) was obviously open for a very short period, and was rapidly backfilled with completely homogeneous sterile material. The recut (144) may have been dug shortly afterwards, on a diverging alignment. This feature cut the robber trench (164) and was probably backfilled in the late twelfth or possibly thirteenth century. This suggests that the building represented by the robber trench may have had a short life.

The two wells were truncated by later reduced horizons and, therefore, cannot be related directly with any of the preceding layers or features, but pottery recovered from their fills suggests that they were broadly contemporary. Well 147 may have been related to the possible building represented by the robber trench, but Well 110 was sunk after the destruction of the building, since it cut through the small ditches.

No firm conclusions can be made about the activity occurring in this area because of the disturbed nature of the stratigraphy and the paucity of datable material. However, it seems likely that the features and deposits date to the twelfth or thirteenth century, certainly after the military abandonment of the motte and bailey castle, and probably after the partial or complete destruction of the Norman defences in the immediate area.

No definite evidence for occupation was found, although the possible robber trench, the two wells and the few rubbish pits may indicate that occupation took place nearby.

Period IIIB – Late-medieval Deposits (Fig. 59C)

Very few features and virtually no stratigraphy of the later medieval period were discovered on the excavation. This was mainly because of later terracing of the area.

After the partial backfilling of the bailey ditch with possible rampart material in the thirteenth century, the feature was recut. In the western part of the site the recut had removed all traces of the earlier bailey ditch, as far as was excavated. To the east all the upper levels, as well as the edge of the earlier ditch, were cut away. The recut was of different profile than the original ditch, with what appeared to be a sump or channel at the base (Fig. 62, Section A–B). The sump was filled with black organic clay (120) which was waterlogged but only partially under the level of the water table. The layer contained animal bones and some pottery dating to the twelfth and thirteenth centuries. Few preserved artefacts were found, only two pieces of leather and a few wooden objects being recovered. Down the edge of the ditch and partially mixed with the organic deposits was a dump of gravel and flints (113). This layer contained animal bone and some pottery of the fourteenth century and appeared to run the whole length of the ditch.

Above these primary deposits was a complex sequence of large dumps, generally very similar in composition. These remained to a height of about 1.60 m. above the top of the organic layer and consisted mainly of homogeneous olive-brown to greenish-brown, sometimes glutinous, loamy clays containing flints and pebbles as well as animal bones, shells, medieval roof- and floor-tiles, fair quantities of residual Roman material and pottery ranging in date from the late thirteenth to the sixteenth century. Although all these deposits were similar, the backfilling may have occurred in two phases. The earlier levels (107 and 105) contained pottery of the late thirteenth and fourteenth centuries while the upper layers (100, 101, 102 and 105A) contained pottery ranging in date from the late fourteenth to the sixteenth century with a predominance of pottery of the latter date.

In the western part of the site, the upper deposits were of slightly different composition but of similar date and also gave the impression of rapid backfilling. The layers included clays ranging from very dark grey and black to orange in colour (layers 132, 132A, 136, 136A, 150, Fig. 63, Section N–I; Fig. 64, Sections D–K, J–F).

Over most of the length of the ditch, the original top edge had been removed by late and post-medieval terracing and the upper fills consequently sealed by post-medieval layers. However, at the west end of the site an upper edge of the ditch may have survived. Here the ditch cut the only other medieval stratigraphy (layers 146 and 166, Fig. 64, Section F–J). These layers partially sealed the earlier shallow twelfth- and thirteenth-centuries deposits and consisted of very mixed yellow and grey clays and lenses of light brown silt. Pottery dating to the twelfth and thirteenth centuries was found in the deposits.

Nine pits dating to this period were excavated, all being truncated by later disturbances (Fig. 59C). Three of these 23, 133 and 137 were in the south-west corner of the site (Fig. 63, Sections G–H, N–I). Pit 137 was completely sealed and almost removed by Pit 23. It contained a fill of redeposited brickearth and a mixture of light grey and brown clays with medieval roofing-tiles. Pit 133 was also cut by 23 and cut in turn Pits 172, 175 and well 147. This pit contained a fill of brown clay loam heavily flecked with yellow clay. Material dating to the late thirteenth to fourteenth century was found in the fill. The latest and largest of the pits was 23, but only about half of it extended into the excavated area. Tip layers within it included yellow and orange clays, redeposited brickearth, dark grey-brown loamy clay and a mixture of brown and yellow clays flecked with mortar and daub and interspersed with small pebbles and a lens of oysters. This pit also contained medieval roofing-tiles, animal bone and pottery dating to the twelfth or thirteenth and possibly fourteenth centuries.

In the eastern corner of the site six intercutting pits (123, 125, 126, 128, 131 and 135) were excavated, all of which had been disturbed by a post-medieval terrace (Fig. 59C). These pits were generally circular and covered a large area. Their fills were complex (apart from pit 123) but very similar, mainly consisting of redeposited brickearth and gravel striated with lenses of light yellow and orange clays (Fig. 62, Section B–E–G). Pit 126 also contained dark grey and black clay loams flecked with charcoal, mortar and daub. Pit 123 was almost completely full of redeposited natural brickearth, much of which seemed to have slumped into the pit from the edges. The top of both Pits 123 and 135 was heavily disturbed by roots. The majority of the features contained little or no medieval pottery, but probably post-dated the fourteenth century since pottery dating to the mid- to late fourteenth century was recovered from one of the earliest of the group (Pit 128).

The small quantities of contemporary rubbish and the complete absence of cess in the backfill of any of the pits mentioned above suggest that their function was not connected with any domestic activity, and because of the large area of most of them it is possible that they were clay-extraction pits, the group in the east backfilled in the late fourteenth or fifteenth century, the group in the west probably late thirteenth or fourteenth century in date. This function is compatible with the area being open ground during this period, an assumption indicated by the absence of any structural remains or pits of a domestic nature on the site.

After the recutting of the Norman bailey ditch possibly in the fourteenth century, the side of the new ditch may have been stabilized by the deposition of gravel layer (113). The primary deposits in the sump of the feature were very similar to those excavated in the base of the bailey ditch and may have originated under the same conditions. The profile of the recut, with a channel at the bottom, may indicate that it was a running sewer at this time and was dug specifically for this purpose. It is possible that further to the east it diverged from the original bailey ditch and ran into the city ditch outside the walls, although no direct evidence to suggest this exists.

That the recut ditch was used as a drain or dyke is also suggested by the eventual establishment of the documented 'Black Ditch' or 'Black Dyke', an open sewer which skirted the Dane John gardens until the first quarter of the eighteenth century.[110] This feature was almost certainly not the ditch excavated on the present site, since the 'Black Dyke' may have originated in 1644, when there 'was made by the Corporation a certain official hole or pit into which the refuse of the city was ordered to be cast'.[111] It is possible, however, that the recut bailey ditch was the predecessor of the new dyke, and the dating of the backfill of the earlier ditch suggests that it may have been levelled with upcast from the new channel. Also the ditch contained little domestic rubbish, which would certainly have been present, if the two channels were the same. The exact position of the 'Black Dyke' remains unknown, but it may have been just north-west of the excavation, parallel to the recut bailey ditch and running behind lavatories belonging to early nineteenth-century properties fronting Castle Row, and thence into the city ditch somewhere in the vicinity of Wincheap Gate. This position is indicated by Brent, who says the 'Black Dyke' abutted 'almost onto the precinct of the church of St. Mary de Castro'[112] (Fig. 58).

Period IV – Sixteenth- to seventeenth-century Garden (Fig. 59D)
In the sixteenth century the whole area in the immediate vicinity of the site was terraced. This reduction removed much of the earlier stratigraphy and produced an horizon across the trench (horizon 141, Fig. 62, Section B–E–G; Fig. 63, Section G–H/N–I; Fig. 64, Section J–F). Large quantities of garden soil were then imported and laid across the area levelling any depressions or slump remaining over the virtually backfilled recut bailey ditch. These deposits of garden soil almost certainly originally covered the entire area of the excavation, but to the north they were increasingly graded off and eventually were entirely removed by another post-medieval terrace. The garden soils consisted of homogeneous grey-brown clayey loams flecked with oyster shells, mortar and charcoal, ranging from between 0.50 m. and 1.20 m. in thickness. They contained large amounts of small stones and pebbles, oyster shells and medieval roofing-tiles as well as some brick, slate, animal bones and nails. Tip-lines were evident in the matrix and a lens of

110. D. Gardiner, *The Story of Canterbury Castle and the Dane John and its Manor* (1951), 37.
111. J. Brent, *Canterbury in the Olden Time* (1879), 141. This volume provides a general history of the Dane John area, 139–147.
112. *Ibid.*, 144.

oyster shells, tiles, charcoal and small pebbles divided the garden soils into two distinct phases. The earlier phase (13, 13A, 13B, 17 and 106) contained large amounts of medieval pottery, but also some dating to the fifteenth or sixteenth century, as well as a silver penny of Edward I, *c.* 1302–1310 (S.F. No. 255). The upper phase (layers 7, 7A, 7B, 42, 51 and 51A) contained pottery of the sixteenth and early seventeenth centuries.

The garden deposits were partially sealed by a thin lens of dark brown loam, heavily impregnated with carbon, charcoal, coal and ash which also contained roofing peg-tiles, brick, animal bone and oyster shells (layer (49/49A); see also Fig. 63, Section H–M). This deposit yielded large amounts of pottery dating from the mid sixteenth to early seventeenth century, clay pipes of the early seventeenth century, a seventeenth-century knife (S.F. No. 312), a James I farthing of 1614–1625 (S.F. No. 184), and a Nüremberg jetton of *c.* 1580–1610 (S.F. No. 129), as well as large numbers of other post-medieval bronze and iron objects including pins and boot-lace tags. Overlying this deposit to the extreme south-east of the site was a disturbed layer of yet more garden soil (45), this in turn sealed by eighteenth- or nineteenth-century material.

Few features belonging to the period were encountered; most were post-holes cut from within the garden soils. The fills of these were almost identical to the garden soil that they were cut through. Most contained no finds whatsoever, but they were placed within the phase of the garden by their stratigraphical position. Two groups were noted, one a line of post-holes running approximately east to west (79, 74, 148, 52), and the other aligned north-west to south-east (48A, 48B, 47, 48C). Included amongst these was Feature 54 which was slightly off the line of this latter group. The only other context that was identified was a small irregular patch of metalling (56) that lay over horizon 141, but was sealed by the garden-soil deposits.

The use of the area for horticultural purposes is indicated by numerous maps, the earliest of which is the coloured map of Canterbury dating to *c.* 1640.[113] The levels within the garden soil itself suggested that it was deposited in two main phases, the first in the sixteenth century and the second probably in the seventeenth although, because of possible ploughing and 'turning over', these deposits were mixed in some areas. Although the area to the north of the site possibly remained as a garden into the eighteenth century, the garden deposits mentioned above were sealed by a layer that can be well dated to the second quarter of the seventeenth century. This layer (49/49A) contained large quantities of domestic refuse, was relatively undisturbed and may have represented a temporary abandonment of cultivation of the garden, or a complete termination of the immediate area's use for horticulture. The layer of garden soil (45) might have been (if this latter assumption is correct) the result of the garden soil in the east of the site being dumped to the west upon the excavation of a slightly later terrace (see below).

Period VA – Seventeenth-century Terrace and other Features (Fig. 59D)
In the seventeenth century a terrace was cut into the gradual slope existing in the gardens. The terrace was along the south-east side of the site in the eastern half of it. The area within the terrace was levelled down by about 0.50 m. at the most, increasingly removing the earlier stratigraphy towards the east, so that in the eastern half of the site all that survived were the truncated remains of earlier features, including the recut bailey ditch (Fig. 62, Section A–B; Fig.

---

113. Map 123 in the Cathedral Archive and Library, Canterbury.

64, Sections C–L, D–K). It is possible that the spoil produced by these earthworks was dumped to the west (layer 45).

A number of features was found within the levelled area of the terrace; these were almost certainly later than the cutting of the terrace itself. The earliest of these was a heavily rutted cart-track (88) that ran approximately east–west across the northern corner of the site. The ruts of this trackway were impressed into the top fills of the recut bailey ditch. Because of later disturbance and the position of the excavation, the full width of this trackway could not be discerned. The ruts themselves, at most 0.25 m. deep, were filled with grey brown silty loam containing quantities of building rubble and pottery dating to the seventeenth century (layer 82/86/91).

After the decline of the trackway and the levelling of its rutted surface two pits were dug in the vicinity. The earliest of these, Pit 72, cut through the trackway and the levelling up over it. It was about 1 m. deep at the most and contained a variety of fills which spilled out over its shallow northern side. These fills included a lens of yellow clay heavily flecked with grey clay, carbon, mortar and tile, a lens of greenish yellow clay also flecked with carbon and tile, a dump of brick, tile and mortar rubble, lenses of ash, carbon and loose brown silt. The pit also contained animal bone, building rubble, glass and clay pipes and pottery dating to the seventeenth century. To the west this pit was cut by Pit 73 which was 1.80 m. deep and contained a variety of fills including lenses of building rubble in a dark olive-grey glutinous clay. Also recovered were animal bones, clay pipes, window glass, bottles and quantities of post-medieval pottery.

One other pit (155) was excavated, this in the centre of the site. The feature may have been dug before the terrace and truncated by it, but this was not certain. Very little datable material was recovered apart from one post-medieval sherd and some residual pottery. The pit contained a fairly uniform fill of mixed grey and yellow clays. Lying on its side in the base was the almost completely articulated skeleton of a horse or donkey with its head to the south-west. The legs of the animal had been removed prior to burial and then laid along the southern edge of the pit.

After the cutting of the terrace, quantities of material accumulated within the terraced area, and also down its edge. These deposits (9, 36, 67, 69, 70 and 80) were mainly thin interconnecting lenses of widely different compositions and included washed and redeposited brickearth, yellow and grey clays, grey and brown loams, oyster shells and heavily burnt clay, many incorporating rubble of bricks, tiles, mortar, chalk and flints (see also Fig. 63, Section H–M). The deposits also yielded large quantities of post-medieval pottery including Delftware, stoneware and 'china' most of which dated to the seventeenth century as well as animal bones, coal and slate. In the area of the terrace cut, the layers and the brickearth under them were heavily mottled with root disturbance.

Since the terracing cut through most of the garden soil deposits, and probably succeeded the well-dated layer (49/49A), it is likely that it occurred around the middle of the seventeenth century. It is possible that the terrace is represented on the c. 1640 coloured map of Canterbury (and also on Doidge's map of 1752, Fig. 60) in which case its inception may have occurred shortly after the deposition of layer 49/49A in the second quarter of the century. The heavy root disturbance along the top edge of the terrace cut suggests that it was planted with trees or bushes, a situation also shown on Doidge's map.

Although the garden soil in the area of the terrace had been completely removed, and the fact that horticultural activity may have ceased to the south-west of the site (see p. 172), it is likely

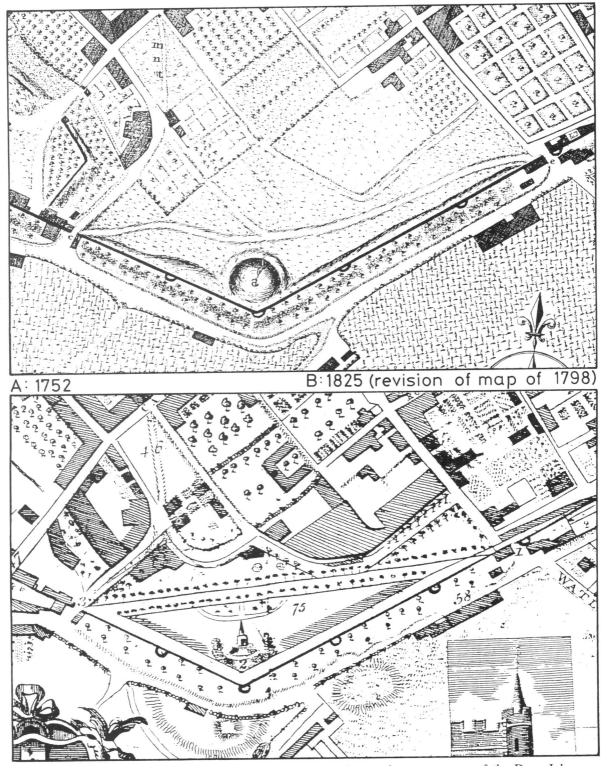

A: 1752

B: 1825 (revision of map of 1798)

Fig. 60. No. 15A Dane John: Details from eighteenth- and nineteenth-century maps of the Dane John area.

that the land to the north and north-east of the site remained as gardens throughout this period and at least up to the mid eighteenth century (a formalized garden is shown in the area on Doidge's map). The rutted, unpaved track found during the excavation was, therefore, almost certainly connected with this garden activity and probably ran south from an entrance onto Castle Row (that still exists adjacent to the present public house (Fig. 61)), and then west to east across the northern corner of the site. Although a number of tracks is shown in the formalized gardens represented on Doidge's map, the trackway found during the excavation had almost certainly gone out of use by the end of the seventeenth century.

Pits 72 and 73 served as a dumping ground for building-rubble and other rubbish and were either associated with the nearby gardens or with domestic buildings in the neighbourhood. Pit 73 was almost certainly late seventeenth- or early eighteenth-century. Pit 155 was unusual and could not be dated with any certainty. The fact that this pit contained virtually nothing apart from an almost sterile backfill and a semi-articulated but complete horse skeleton, suggests strongly that the pit was excavated purely for the burial of the horse. This theory is enhanced by the fact that the skeleton (apart from its legs) fitted the pit void almost exactly. Presumably the torso was dismembered to enable it to be buried more easily in a smaller pit.

Although the terraced area was later utilized (see below, p. 176), there was no indication of its original function, but documentary sources indicate that the area was first used as a garden and then a timber yard at some period in the seventeenth or eighteenth century.[114] It is possible that the abandonment of the garden and the cutting of the terrace had some connection with this latter activity.

Period VB – Eighteenth-century Road and wooden Structure (Figs. 59D and 61)

In the eighteenth century after the backfilling of the pits, a courtyard or road was laid across part of the terraced area and partially across the garden soils to the east of the site. Before this a certain amount of levelling up for the road occurred. Then a wooden structure was erected between the edge of the road and the terrace cut, and a large oval pit probably associated with the structure was dug, as well as a drainage ditch which served the site.

The levelling deposits (layers 22 and 41A) existed only in the central area of the site. These deposits sealed all the earlier dumps of material within the terrace area (Fig. 63, Section H–M; Fig. 64, Sections C–L, D–K) and were mainly interconnecting lenses of different composition, including a heavy dark grey clay containing many small pebbles and lenses of light grey silt containing small flints, tile, oyster shells and brick. These layers yielded quantities of clay pipes and pottery dating to the first half of the eighteenth century.

Over this levelled area was laid a road or courtyard (41) composed mainly of crushed and rammed brick fragments with pebbles, flints and tile. The deposit varied in thickness from between a few centimetres at its edges to over 0.30 m. and contained two distinct phases of deposition in some areas. The road curved from a south-west to north-east to a northerly direction, and was gradually disturbed and eventually completely eroded to the north of the site. The surface of the road was heavily worn and very uneven. Large quantities of pottery mostly

114. D. Gardiner, *The Story of Canterbury Castle and the Dane John and its Manor* (1951), 38.

dating to between the late seventeenth and mid eighteenth centuries were recovered from the matrix.

Partially adjacent to the western edge of the road, but extending further to the south-east of it, was a U-shaped gully or drainage ditch (43). The feature cut all the previous garden-soil deposits and contained a fill of dark brown silty loam (Fig. 63, Sections G–H, N–I). Material dating to the late seventeenth to mid eighteenth century, including a William III halfpenny of 1698–1699 (S.F. No. 2), was recovered from it.

Possibly immediately after the laying of the road a rectangular post-supported structure was erected inside the terraced area, sandwiched between the terrace cut and the edge of the road. The position of the building exactly coincided with the end of the terrace. Eighteen post-pits, some with post-voids, were all that remained of this structure. The posts in the outer circuit of the building were obviously the main structural supports, since their post-pits were deeper (on average about 1 m. deep) than any of the post-holes or pits inside it. The posts within the structure were set in transverse lines.

The post-pits contained fills of redeposited brickearth or mixed yellow and grey clays containing bricks and tiles and some datable material was recovered from them including a George II farthing of 1737 (S.F. No. 130) from post-pit 50. The features all cut the earlier dump deposits within the terraced area and most were vertical-sided and flat-bottomed in profile.

Feature 14 was an oval-shaped pit situated to the north-east of, and immediately adjacent to, the post-supported building, with a similar alignment of its longest axis. The feature cut some of the earlier dump material within the terraced area and also some of the levelling deposits for the road, but no stratigraphical evidence to show whether its inception pre- or post-dated the building was obtained. Seven post-pits, some with post-voids were found in its sump. The post-pits contained fills of gravel and redeposited brickearth. The voids, which were rectangular or square, extended up through the later backfill of the feature by between 0.50 m. and 1.50 m. and some contained fragments of rotted posts. The basal deposits in the pit were mainly washes of rapid silt, but at the south-west end the decayed remains of five planks were encountered.

The primary silts and the planks were sealed by a mass of redeposited brickearth and gravelly yellow and grey clays which had slumped down the edge of the pit (layer 33, Fig. 62, Section A–B).

Various factors indicate that all the features mentioned above were broadly contemporary. The dating evidence obtained is not incompatible with this assumption. The similar alignments, just within the terrace, of both the post-supported building and Pit 14, their proximity with each other and their identical stratigraphical position imply that not only were they contemporary, but that their respective functions were in some way connected. That the building was erected after the deposition of the Road 41 is suggested from the stratigraphy. The stratigraphy also indicated that no material had built up over the road before the post-pits for the building were first dug. Since both the building and Pit 14 respected the position of the edge of the road, it is probable that the road was extant upon their construction and that it served as access.

Datable material from the road and its levelling deposits indicated that it was laid at some time during or just after the first half of the eighteenth century. To the west the road swung around to the north-west. It is reasonable to assume, therefore, that it ran to an entrance onto Castle Row, adjacent to the present-day public house (Fig. 61). This gateway (which still exists)

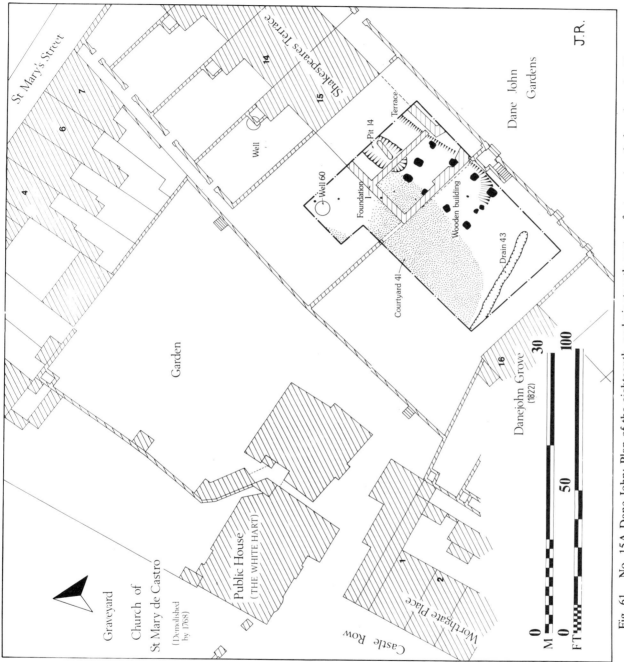

Fig. 61. No. 15A Dane John: Plan of the eighteenth- and nineteenth-century features (partly based on the First Edition Ordnance Survey, 1874). (Scale: 1:400)

is shown on Doidge's map of 1752, and was probably the same as that utilized by the earlier cart-track (see p. 173).[115]

The gully (43) was obviously an open drain and its termination, some 4.50 m. to the south-west of the building, implies that its primary function was to conduct surface water away from the particular area around the structure and from the road. No evidence to explain why the gully did not exactly follow the edge of the road was discovered, but it is possible that originally the road extended into the area between the end of the building and the drain.

Very little about the structure or appearance of the building could be deduced. The exact size of the structure could not be proved because post-voids were not evident in all the post-pits; but it was probably about 4.55 m. × 8.40 m. (15 ft. × 27 ft. 6 ins.). The topography of the site suggests that any entrance into the building must have been on the north-west or south-west sides. The two smaller posts in the outer circuit (10) and (55) may indicate that the entrance was at the south-west end. The presence of an arrangement of post-holes within the building may mean that the floor was supported above the ground level on transverse lines of posts; alternatively they could represent internal partitions, but this is unlikely because of the restriction of space within the building that this would impose. A *terminus post quem* of 1737 for the construction of the building is supplied by the coin of George II. Because of the probable contemporaneity of all the features mentioned above, it is likely that the whole sequence commenced after this date. However, neither the building nor the road is shown on Doidge's map of 1752 (Fig. 60). On the second edition of this map dating to 1798, however, a road in a position exactly corresponding with the road is shown, although no sign of any structure similar to the building is evident. It is quite likely that Road 41 is the same as that shown on the 1798 map, and this may indicate that the whole phase began between 1752 and 1798.

The post-holes found in the sump of Feature 14 may indicate that originally it contained some form of wooden framework, or that it was planked over. The planks found in the sump possibly belonged to this structure.

At present the function of the building remains unknown.

Other features found relating to this phase were a number of post-holes and two stake-holes some of which cut the courtyard. Some of these (65, 71A, 81, 96, 94) ranged in a line north from the south-west side of the building and may have been fence-posts.

Period VC/D – Late eighteenth to early nineteenth-century Abandonment and Landscaping and modern Features

In the late eighteenth century the area was temporarily abandoned and used for the deposition of rubbish. Eventually, the post-supported building was demolished, material was dumped over the road and finally the whole region was levelled. Since many of these deposits were removed by machine (apart from those within Pit 14) not all the stratigraphic relationships were preserved. However, enough information was gained, both from the sections and by the hand excavation of the remaining deposits, to enable a logical sequence of events to be deduced. First, the wooden structure within Feature 14 was partially dismantled. Some of its posts, however, were left *in situ* upon the eventual backfilling of the pit, since post-voids were seen at

115.   The area is also shown on a print of 1704 (The south prospect of ye Citie of Canterbury drawn from Dungeon Hill) in the Royal Museum.

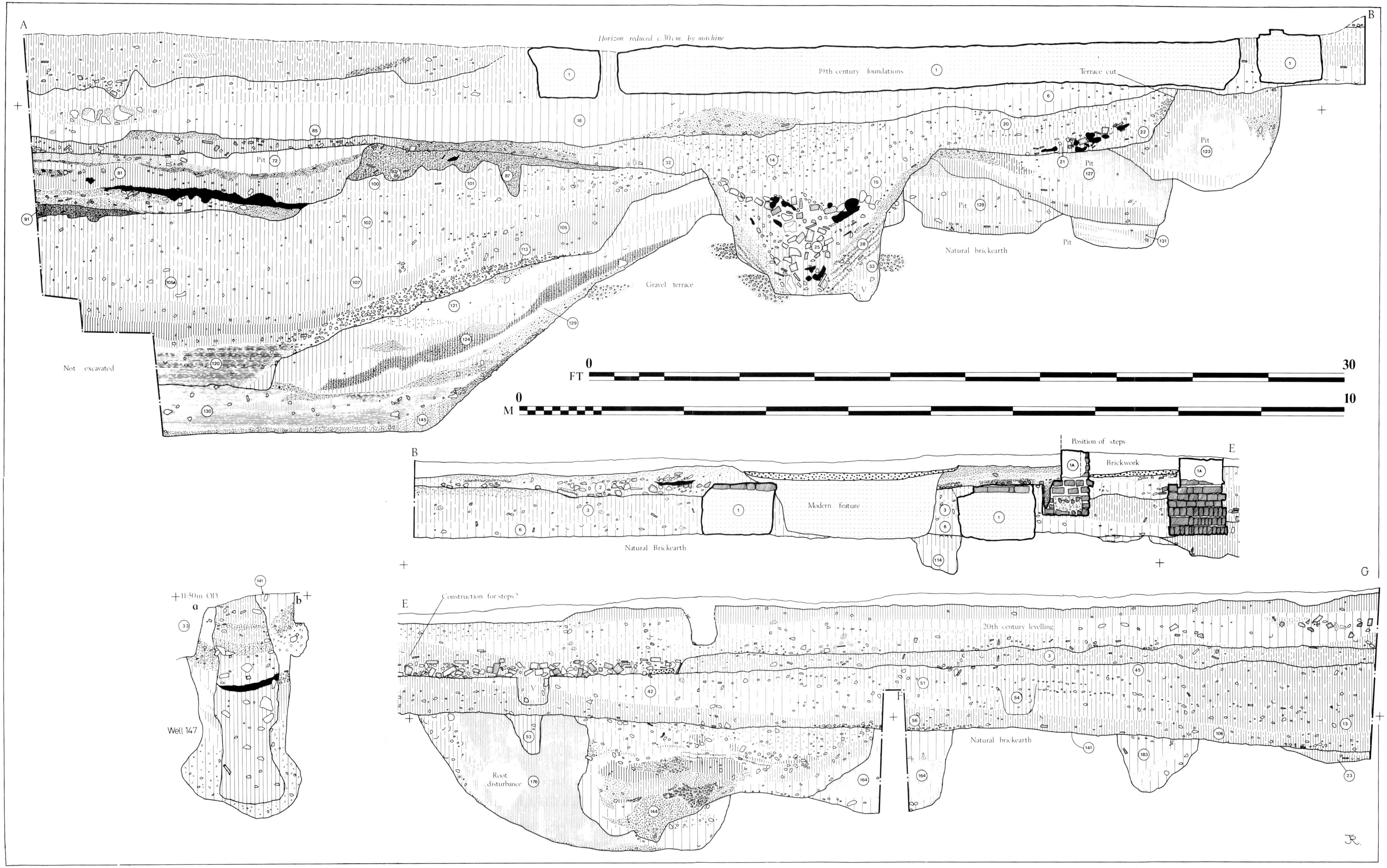

Fig. 62. No. 15A Dane John: Sections A–B, B–E, E–G and a–b. (Scale: 1:40)

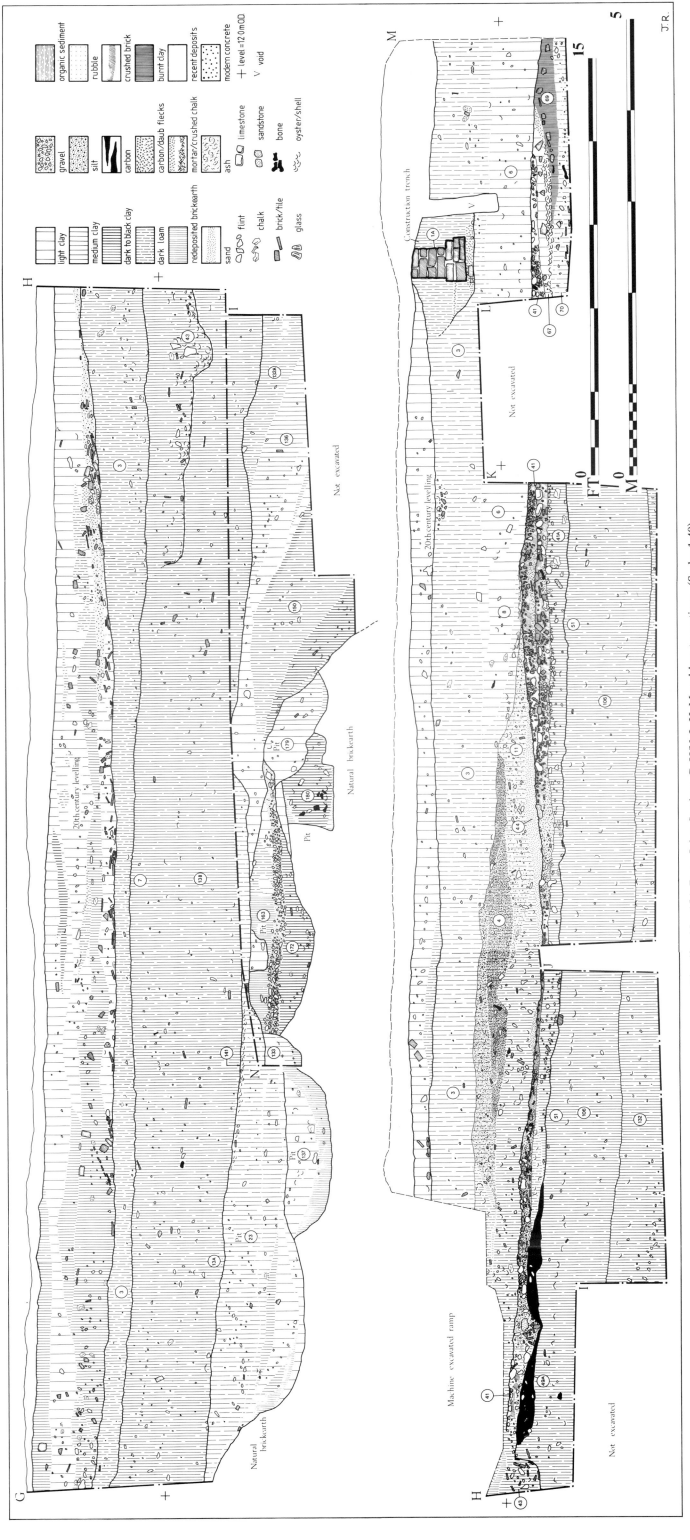

Fig. 63.   No. 15A Dane John: Sections G–H/N–I, H–M and key to sections. (Scale: 1:40)

high levels within the backfill, and some also contained portions of decayed timber from the posts themselves. The pit and area within the terrace was then backfilled. These dump layers (14, 15, 20, 21, 25, 28, 32, 44, 85) were of widely differing nature, but mainly consisted of thick lenses of pale yellow clay heavily mixed with grey clay, brick, tile and flint rubble (Fig. 63, Section H–M; Fig. 64, Section C–L, D–K). Most of this material had been dumped down the edge of the terrace, at the extreme south-east corner of the site, as if it had been specifically intended to fill Feature 14 (Fig. 62, Section A–B). All these layers yielded quantities of building-rubble, massive amounts of butchered bone (mainly from horses), quantities of bronze and iron objects of all sorts and a large assemblage of mainly eighteenth-century pottery which included over 1,000 sherds of post-medieval earthenware, over 500 sherds of 'china', 175 sherds of Delftware and about 360 sherds of post-medieval stoneware. The main concentrations of the bone and artefacts occurred within the backfill of Feature 14 (layers 14, 15, 25 and 28). The deposits dumped over the road (4, 11, 19) could not be stratigraphically related to the dumps mentioned above, but the dating evidence suggests that they were later. They consisted of a complex sequence of lenses of sand, carbon and coke and browny and pinkish brown silty dumps containing large quantities of building rubble, clay pipes and nearly 1,000 sherds of late eighteenth- to early nineteenth-century pottery. Also recovered were coins dating to 1746–1754 and 1773 (S.F. Nos 61 and 121).

Probably during the deposition of this material the wooden building was demolished. The lower levels of the dump deposits sealed some post-pits of the structure and were cut by Pits 31 and (63) dug to extract the posts of the building.

The entire north-east three quarters of the site was then covered with a thick layer which completely sealed all the deposits mentioned above. This homogeneous deposit (6/6A/6B/18, 8, 16, 27) appeared to have been dumped from the south and completely levelled the area within the eastern half of the trench (see also Fig. 62, Section B–E–G). The deposit consisted of a mixture of brickearth and grey-brown clay containing pottery dating to the first half of the nineteenth century as well as significant quantities of residual material of all periods. This deposit was capped by a layer of brown loam (3), which extended across the whole site. These two phases of dumping raised the ground surface by about 1 m.

Documentary evidence relating to the area may explain the later deposits investigated during the excavation. In 1790, the 'Dane John land' was made over to Alderman James Simmons for two and a half years for a peppercorn rent.[116] He undertook to 'level the land called Dane John except for the great hill there. . . .' Before this time most of the land had either been waste or allotments, but Simmons set about landscaping the entire area, during which process the Dane John mound was enlarged to its present dimensions (Pl. XXXV). This work, which cost £1,500, was still incomplete on 22 May, 1792. Simmons later surrendered his lease after an argument and, by the 1800s, the works were abandoned and the area left 'prey to petty theft and wanton destruction'. The landscaping works were later taken up by Alderman Cyprian Bunce, the gardens being restored in the 1800s. When the work was finally completed is not documented, but it was certainly well before 1822 when the Dane John Grove buildings were erected to the south-west of the site (see Fig. 61).

116. D. Gardiner, *op. cit.* (note 114), 38–39.

No precise *terminus ante quem* for the demolition of the wooden building was obtained, but the presence of the two separate dumps, one filling the terrace and Pit 14 and the other over the road, may suggest that the abandonment of the building and its final demolition were separated by a considerable period of time. The first dump, which probably dates to the late eighteenth century, filled Pit (14) and may therefore indicate the abandonment of the building and immediate area. Many of these deposits may originate from the clearance and landscaping of the gardens as well as from rubbish disposal. The dump over the courtyard contained pottery dating to a period between 1810 and 1830, and since this deposit was cut by demolition disturbance for the wooden structure, final demolition may have occurred at some time in the first few decades of the century, possibly before 1822 (see below). The later extensive dump deposits (6/6A/6B/18, 8, 16, 27) post-date this activity. They may relate to landscaping work carried out on the Dane John gardens but, since the gardens are shown in a reasonable state of completion on the map of 1798, this is unlikely.

A more probable explanation is that these deposits were the result of the construction of the cellared Dane John Grove buildings in 1822. After this, the area became a garden with the deposition of the garden soil (3). The whole sequence is given a *terminus ante quem* by later foundations (1) which probably date to the 1840s. These substantial footings belonged to a range of buildings (Shakespeare's Terrace, now nos. 12–15 Dane John), most of which still stands to the north-east of the excavation (Fig. 61). The foundations consisted of large trench-built footings of mortared brick and limestone rubble (1). They were sealed by modern deposits.

The construction of the foundations had probably completely destroyed a length of brick wall which may have originally spanned the trench from north-west to south-east (1A). Only a few courses and the foundations of this wall survived, at the sides of the trench, but it may have originally butted the south-west end of Shakespeare's Terrace, a situation shown on the 1st Edition Ordnance Survey map. In the area of the site it appears that only the foundations of the block were completed, since this end of the building is only shown dotted on the Ordnance Survey map. Alternatively, this end of the building may have been demolished during alterations before 1873.

In the extreme northern corner of the site a brick-lined well (60) was excavated. The internal diameter of the lining was 1.24 m. (4 ft.), and it was supported on two circular hoops of wood each 2.50 cm. (1 in.) thick, nailed together. The well was sunk to a depth of over 5.50 m. below the modern ground surface. The exact stratigraphical position of the well was not determined, but it was almost certainly related to the Shakespeare's Terrace buildings. Another possibly similar well was found 13 m. to the north-west in the 1960s. This well was sealed by lavatories built onto the back of Shakespeare's Terrace before 1872, suggesting that both wells went out of use then, which accords with the dating of material recovered from Well 60. At this time, the brick lining was robbed to the water table and the void backfilled with rubble and other rubbish.

Sealing all the nineteenth-century features mentioned above was a thick layer of twentieth-century dump deposits. These were probably laid after the Second World War before the construction of the City Council offices and adjacent car-park.

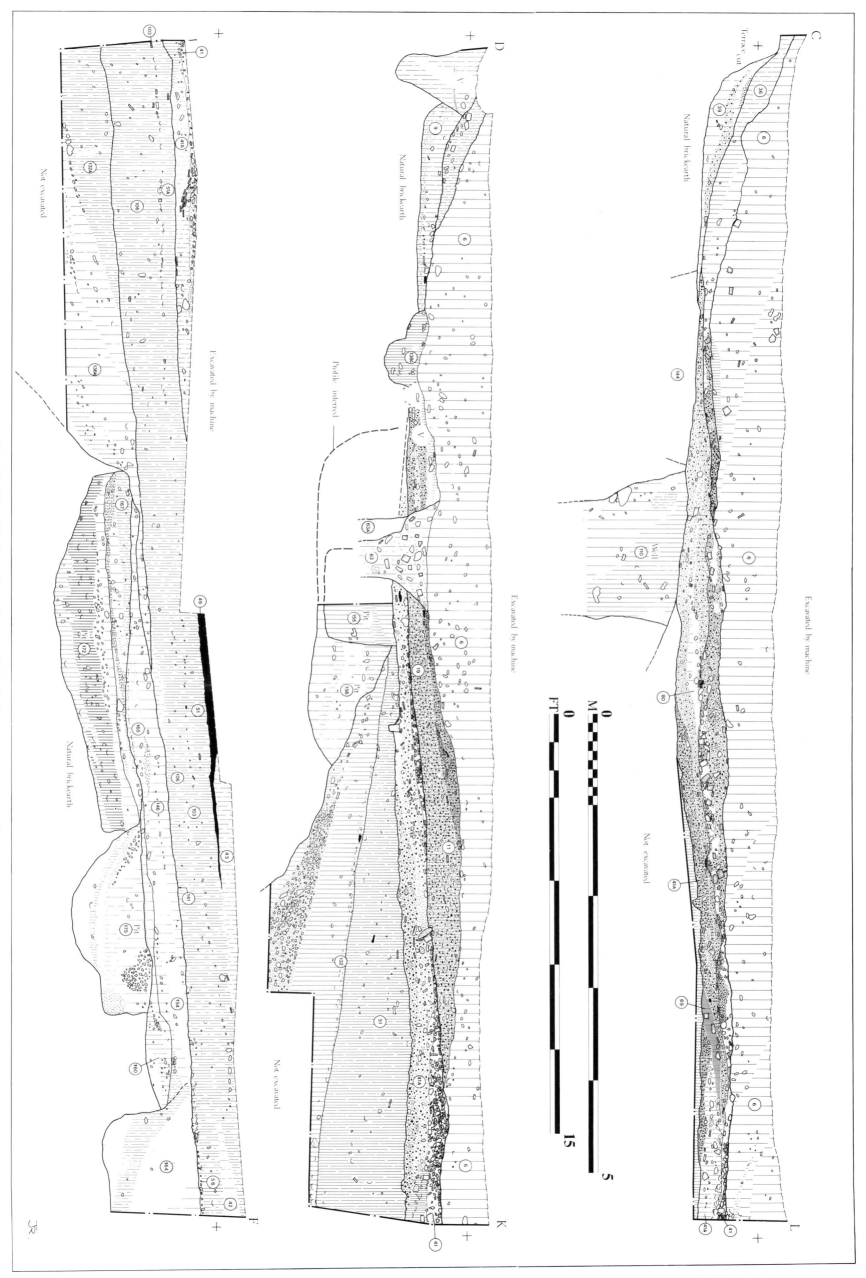

Fig. 64. No. 15A Dane John: Sections C–L, D–K and J–F. (Scale: 1:40)

PART III: THE FINDS AND POTTERY FROM THE CANTERBURY EXCAVATION COMMITTEE SITES 1946–60

IIIA: THE FINDS by Sally Stow

(i) THE COINS[117]

1. THE COINS FROM THE WHITEHALL ROAD SITE (Site W)

1.   Dubnovellaunus. *Mack* 290. 31.675 grains
        C XXVII W V 38, Pit 36. Belgic pit pre-dating hut.
2–3.   Cunobelin (two). *Mack* 222 (two). 32.669 and 32.978 grains
        C XXVII W V 35 (2). Roman.
        C XXVII W V 39, Pit 20. Roman.
4.   Agrippa, *As. RIC* (Tiberius) 32
        C XXVI W V 36, Pit 14. Second century.
5.   Hadrian, *As. Rev.* illegible
        C XXVI W V 16 (1). Plough soil.
6.   Radiate. *Rev.* illegible
        C XXVI W V 16 (1). Plough soil.
7.   Constantine I. *Rev.* illegible
        C XXIV W II. Above south edge of road.
8–9   Constantius II (two). *Rev.* illegible
        C XXVI W V 31 (1). Plough soil.
        C XXVI W V 35, Pit 20. Roman.
10.   *Urbs Roma*
        C XXVII W V. Unstratified.
11.   *Constantinopolis*
        C XXIV W II. Unstratified.
12–13. Constans (two). *Rev. Fel. Temp. Reparatio*
        C XXVI W V 22 (2). Plough soil.
        C XXVI W V 20, Pit 2. Roman.
14.   *Fel. Temp. Reparatio*. Barbarous copy
        C XXVII W V 38 (1). Plough soil.

117.   The coins were identified by the late B.H. St. J. O'Neil, C.M. Kraay and R. Reece.

15.   ?Henry IV or V, English silver penny. Illegible
        C XXV W IV (1). Plough soil.

16.   Henry V, English silver penny. Possibly *Brooke* type B, p. 144
        C XXV W IV (1). Plough soil.

17.   Henry VI, silver penny of Calais mint. *Brooke* type II.
        'Rosette-maxle' issue *c.* 1425–28
        C XXV W IV (1). Plough soil.

18.   German counter; probably Hans Krauwinckel *c.* 1580–1600
        C XXIV W II East ext. (1). Plough soil.

19.   Charles II, copper farthing, 1675; edges hammered
        C XXVI W V 3 (1). Plough soil.

20.   William III, copper halfpenny
        C XXV W IV base of (1). Plough soil.

2. THE COINS FROM CHURCH STREET (ST. PAUL'S)

1.   Gallienus, *antoninianus*. *RIC* 255. C XX A I Pit 7. Late Roman pit.
2.   Tetricus I, *antoninianus*. *RIC* 127. C XX A I Pit 3. Thirteenth-century pit.
3.   Tetricus I, *antoninianus*. *Rev.* illegible. C XX A II Pit 4. Medieval pit.
4.   Tetricus II, *antoninianus*. *RIC* 272. C XX A I Pit 3. As No. 2.
5.   Carausius. *Rev. Pax Aug.*, transverse sceptre. C XX A II 3a. Fourteenth-century make-up.
6.   Crispus. As *RIC* VII p. 191, no. 321. Mint Trier. C XX A II Pit 3. Post-Roman north–south gully.
7.   Constantine I. *CHK* i, 352. Mint Arles. C XX A II Pit 4. Medieval pit.
8.   Constantine II. *Rev. Gloria Exercitus*. Mint illegible. C XX A II 7. Late Roman dark earth (= 6 B).
9.   Constans. *CHK* i, 454. Mint Arles. C XX A II 6. Late Roman dark earth.
10.   Barbarous *Fel. Temp. Rep.* (fallen horseman). C XX A I Pit 4. Saxon pit.
11.   Valens. As *CHK* ii, 276. Mint ?Lugdunum. C XX A II 6. Late Roman dark earth.
12.   House of Theodosius. *Rev. Salus Reipublicae*. Mint illegible. C XX A II Pit 4. Medieval pit.
13.   Jetton *c.* 1360–80. C XX A I Pit 8. Recent pit.
14.   Seventeenth-century trade token. *Obv.* Thomas Jenings, Grocer. *Rev.* Canterbury, Grocer. *Williamson* I 351. C XX A I 1. Seventeenth-century chalk floor below modern brick floor of cellar.
15.   Seventeenth-century trade token. *Obv.* Thomas Peirson, Tallow chandler. *Rev.* The Minories 1654 (London). *Williamson* I 675. C XX A I 1. (See No. 14).
16.   Seventeenth-century trade token. *Obv.* James Cheener. *Rev.* Canterbury 1657. *Williamson* I 350. C XX A I 1. (See No. 14).
17–19.   Three illegible seventeenth- to nineteenth-century tokens. C XX A I 1 (two), (see No. 14) and C XX A I Pit 2, recent pit.

3. THE COINS FROM THE FLEUR-DE-LIS YARD

1.   Postumus, *antoninianus*. *RIC* 89
        C XXVIII B II (1). Medieval black soil.

2.   Diocletian, *antoninianus*. *RIC* 162
        C XXVIII B III (2). Roman mortar debris.

3.   House of Constantine. *CHK* i, as 48
        C XXVIII B I (6). Medieval pit.

4.   French. Fifteenth century. *Barnard*, p. 118, No. 43
        C XXVIII B III (1). Pit.

5.   Nüremberg counter, Hans Schultes (*c.* 1550–74). *Barnard*, p. 222, as No. 85 but HANS SCHULTES N. WEHR
        C XXVIII B I (1). Dark soil. Eighteenth or nineteenth century.

6.   Nüremberg counter, Hans Krauwinckel (*c.* 1580–1610). *Barnard*, p. 222, No. 85
        C XXVIII B II (2). Cess-pit.

7–8.   Charles I, two Rose farthings (1625–49)
        C XXVIII B I (2). Cess-pit. Eighteenth century.
        C XXVIII B I (8). *Opus signinum* above Roman tessellated floor (coin intrusive).

4. THE COINS FROM NO. 53 KING STREET (C XXII K), NO. 3 PALACE STREET (C XXII J) AND ST. PETER'S LANE (C XXII H)

1.   Gallienus, *antoninianus. Rev.* illegible
        C XXII H II (21). Medieval pit.
2.   Tetricus I, *antoninianus. Rev.* illegible.
        C XXII H II (17). Fourteenth-century occupation layer.
3–5.   Barbarous radiates. *Rev.* illegible.
        C XXII H II (21). Medieval pit.
        C XXII K I (5A). Dark soil. Third or fourth century.
        C XXII J I. Unstratified.
6.   Constantine I. *Rev.* (?)*Providentia*
        C XXII H II (20). Medieval loam floor.
7.   *Constantinopolis.* cf. *CHK* i, 383
        C XXII H II (17A). Black earth. Fourth century
8.   *Urbs Roma. CHK* i, 190
        C XXII H II (17). Fourteenth-century occupation layer.
9.   Constantinian. *Rev.* two Victories
        C XXII K Pit 2. Medieval.
10.   Barbarous *Fel. Temp.* (fallen horseman)
        C XXII H II (21). Medieval pit.
11.   Magnentius. *Rev.* illegible. Fragment cut into a rough circle cf. Lydney Hoard.
        C XXII J I (2). Gritty silt *c.* A.D. 120–220 (intrusive).
12.   Valens. *RIC* 21A
        C XXII H II 17. Fourteenth-century occupation layer.
13.   Valens. *Rev.* illegible
        C XXII K (3). Black earth. Probably medieval.
14.   Gaucher de Châtillon, Count of Porcieu 1303–29. Mint Yves. Silver sterling imitating English penny of
        Edward I–II.
        C XXII H II (10). Fourteenth-century earth and plaster.

(ii) THE GOLD PIN

(Pl. XXVII, F–H). Solid gold pin,[118] probably of the late seventh century. Length, 3.9 cm. Around the head two twists of beaded wire are soldered to surround plain gold flanges. Each individual bead has a cut across it at its maximum diameter, *äquatorschnitt*; this technique is Hellenistic in origin but became common in the goldsmiths' work of the eighth century and Carolingian period; it is found on goldwork at Sutton Hoo and on the Sarre brooch.[119] The gold flanges are battered for the original reception of convex or *cabochon* garnets of the type familiar from the Sarre and Dover brooches. The present stones are probably secondary; one is sub-rectangular and clearly not cut for this pin, and both have heavy surface scratches and signs of wear which they are unlikely to have sustained in their present position.[120] Shortly after discovery the pin was returned at the request of the Warden of St. Augustine's

118.   Thanks are due to Dr Rupert Bruce-Mitford and Mrs. Sonia Hawkes for commenting on this pin.
119.   *Antiq. Journ.*, xxx (1950), 173.
120.   The stones may be red glass rather than garnet – a hard stone which seldom shows signs of wear. This could not be established save by removing the stones; but removal was not undertaken because this would have damaged the battering of the gold flange.

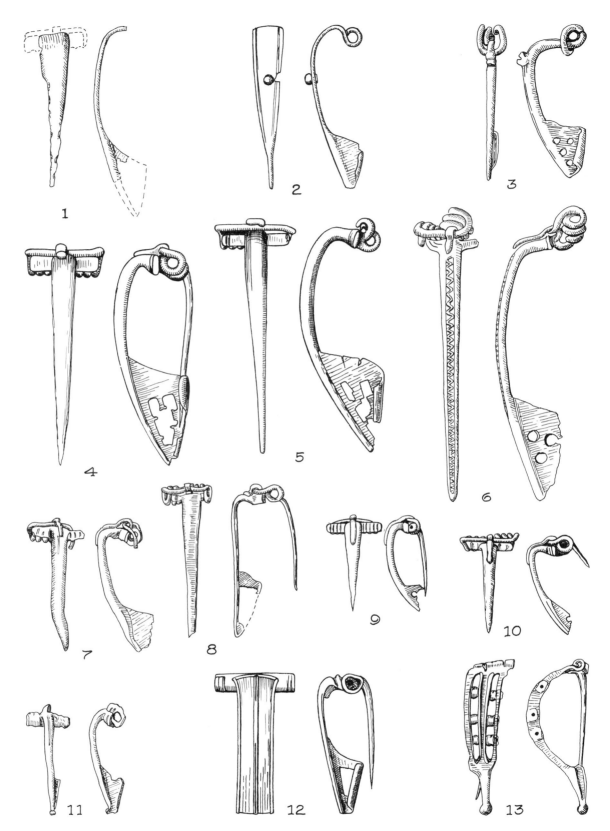

Fig. 65. Copper alloy brooches from Whitehall Road (Site W). (Scale: ½)

College, representing the land-owner, for display in the College's museum. C XX B IV 16, Lady Wootton's Green. Residual in twelfth-century layer.

(iii) OBJECTS OF COPPER ALLOY

(a) THE BROOCHES[121] (Fig. 65)

1. 'Nauheim' derivative (*Camulodunum* Type VII),[122] bow only; foot open and broken. C XXVI W V 36, Pit 14. Second century.

2. 'Nauheim' derivative as No. 1, bow and catch-plate. The small stud in the centre of the bow is an unusual feature. C XXVI W V 27, Pit 9, Belgic drainage ditch.
    Another fragment, sharply angular bow only, closely resembling *Camulodunum*, Pl. XCII, No. 60, came from C XXIV W II N–W extension, layer 5.

3. One-piece brooch of La Tène II type (*Camulodunum* Type I).[123] There are two small lobes on the bow which is oval in section; the catch-plate is perforated by four circular holes. C XXVI W V 35, layer 4. Claudian, latest floor of hut.

4. 'Colchester' type (*Camulodunum* Type III),[124] fine example with 8–turn spring and elaborately-perforated catch-plate. C XXVI W V 27, Pit 11, probably Belgic.

5. 'Colchester' type as No. 4. C XXVI W V 35, Pit 6. Fourth-century pit.

6. 'Colchester' type as No. 4, large example with 6-turn spring and plain side-wings. A groove with zig-zag decoration runs along the length of the bow. The catch-plate is pierced by three holes. C XXVI W V 35, layer 4. Claudian, latest floor of hut.

7. 'Colchester' type as No. 4, small example with 8-turn spring and side-wings decorated with vertical grooves. C XXIV W II, south extension, layer 1A. A.D. 150–200, loam below Roman house floor.

8. Brooch similar to *Camulodunum* Type III but with flat, straight bow and pierced catch-plate.[125] C XXVII W V 38, layer 10. Primary occupation of Belgic hut.

9. 'Colchester' type (*Camulodunum* Type IIIa),[126] 8-turn spring, small straight side-wings with vertical grooves and perforated catch-plate. C XXVI W V 39, layer 2. Neronian, hut ruins.

10. 'Colchester' type as No. 9. C XXVI W V 35, Pit 6. Fourth-century pit.

11. Derivative of *Camulodunum* Type IV,[127] small example, D-shaped bow with central groove along half its length, and toe slightly turned up. C XXIV W II, west extension, layer 1A. A.D. 150–200, loam below Roman house floor.

12. 'Langton Down' type (*Camulodunum* Type XII),[128] small example; it has an unusually plain bow and a pierced catch-plate. C XXVI W V 39, layer 9. Primary occupation of Belgic hut.

13. Hinged brooch related to Aucissa type.[129] It has a double bow pierced transversely three times by iron bars carrying bronze knobs. C XXVII W V 38, layer 2. Neronian, hut ruins.

121. The brooches were examined and commented on by the late M.R. Hull.

122. C.F.C. Hawkes and M.R. Hull, *Camulodunum, First Report on the Excavations at Colchester 1930–1939* (Oxford, 1947), 312–3; Pl. XCII, 55–64.

123. *Ibid.*, 308; Pl. LXXXIX, 1–3.

124. *Ibid.*, 308–310; Pls. LXXXIX–XC, 6–25.

125. Cf. E. Ettlinger, *Die römischen Fibeln in der Schweiz* (Bonn, 1973), 55–6, Taf. 4, 13.

126. *Hawkes and Hull, op. cit.* (note 122), 310; Pls. XC–XCI, 26–30.

127. *Ibid.*, 310–11; Pl. XCI, 36–46.

128. *Ibid.*, 317–8; Pl. XCIV, 85–100.

129. Cf. Ettlinger, *op. cit.* (note 125), 95, Taf. 9, 11; R.E.M. Wheeler, *Maiden Castle, Dorset* (Oxford, 1943), 262, Fig. 85, 30; E.M. Clifford, *Bagendon, A Belgic Oppidum* (Cambridge, 1961), 177, no. 46, Fig. 33, 1.

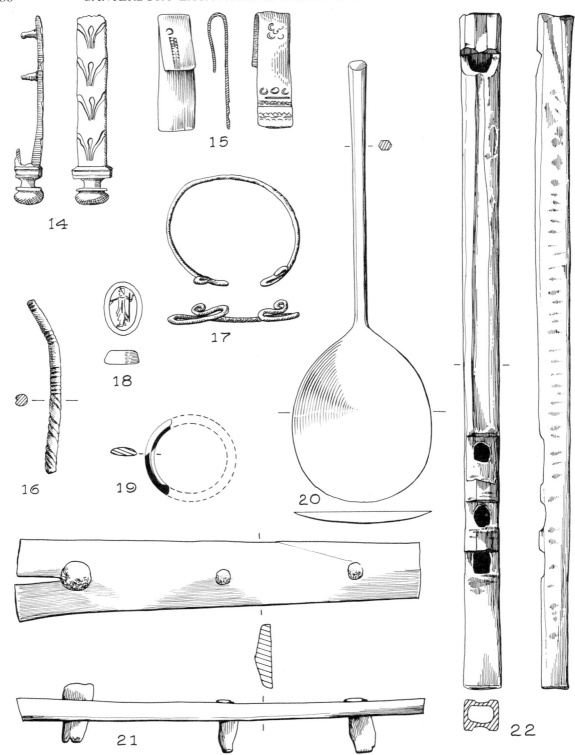

Fig. 66.   Objects of copper alloy (Nos. 14–17), nicolo (No. 18), jet (No. 19), silver (No. 20) and bone (Nos. 21–22). (Scale: ⅓)

(b) OTHER OBJECTS OF COPPER ALLOY (Fig. 66)

14.   Rectangular strap-end with knobbed terminal and two rivets for attachment to military leather belt or apron, decorated and silvered.
        C XXVI W V 40, Pit 34. Second-century pit.

15.   Flat strip with end folded over; there are two horizontal grooves near the bottom edge with herringbone decoration and above this a line of incised concentric circles. C XXIV W I A, east extension, layer 2. Plough soil.

16.   Pin decorated with horizontal and diagonal grooves; the head is bent and the shank incomplete. C XXVI W V 20, Pit 2, c. A.D. 200, Ditch B.

17.   Small penannular bracelet. C XXVI W V 35, Pit 23, undated.

(iv) OTHER MISCELLANEOUS FINDS

INTAGLIO (Fig. 66)

18.   Dr Martin Henig writes: 'Intaglio depicting a draped female figure holding a sceptre in her right hand and (?) a patera in her left hand. Dimensions 15 × 10 × 3 mm. I have only been able to examine a drawing, but the subject is almost certainly the goddess Juno.[130] It is very like representations of Juno on gems from Thistleton (Rutland), Chesterholm (Northumberland) and Bredon Hill (Gloucestershire),[131] and may be regarded as the female equivalent of the type of Jupiter standing with sceptre and patera.'[132] C XXIII K I 7, St. Mildred's. Medieval gravel. The object was stolen.

PIPE-CLAY FIGURINE (Pl. XXVII E)
Lower portion of a pipe-clay figurine of Venus. The fragment shows a broken part of the hemispherical base on which the goddess stands and a portion of the left leg and drapery. See F. Jenkins, 'The Cult of the Pseudo-Venus in Kent', *Arch. Cant.*, lxxii (1958), 60–76 with Pl. II B. C XXII K I (p. 78). King Street, on surface of third-century gravel floor.

OBJECT OF JET (Fig. 66)
19.   Ring fragment. C XXVIII B I 5, Forum area. Black post-Roman soil above arch of hypocaust.

OBJECT OF SILVER (Fig. 66)
20.   Eighteenth-century spoon. C XXVIII B I 2. Forum area, filling of eighteenth-century cess-pits.

OBJECTS OF BONE (Fig. 66)
21.   Part of knife-handle perforated by three iron rivets. C XXVIII B I Pit 3. Forum area, eleventh-century pit.

22.   End-blown flute (Pl. XXVIID) 18.7 cm. in length, made from the leg bone of a crane or similar large bird. Three carefully-recessed finger-holes and the voicing lip remain intact.[133] C XX B III 5, Lady Wootton's Green, occupation earth containing a twelfth- to thirteenth-century Andenne jar (Fig. 80, No. 149).

OBJECTS OF IRON (Fig. 67)
23.   Knife fragment with broken blade and tang, much corroded. C XXVI W V 34, Pit 17, Whitehall Road. The pit contained Belgic pottery with the addition of one Roman sherd.

24.   Clenched Belgic nail 12.5 cm. long. C XXIV W II 6, Whitehall Road. Occupation material associated with rectangular building, c. A.D. 15–43.

130.   As suggested by M. Henig in *A Corpus of Roman engraved Gemstones from British Sites* (*BAR* 8, ed. 2, Oxford, 1978), 213, No. 225.

131.   *Ibid.*, Nos. 222–4.

132.   *Ibid.*, 188, No. 15, and 297, No. App. 91 (Fenny Stratford (Buckinghamshire), and Cramond (Midlothian)).

133.   For a full discussion of this flute and parallels, see J.V.S. Megaw, *Med. Arch.*, xii (1969), 149, where, however, the wrong context is given.

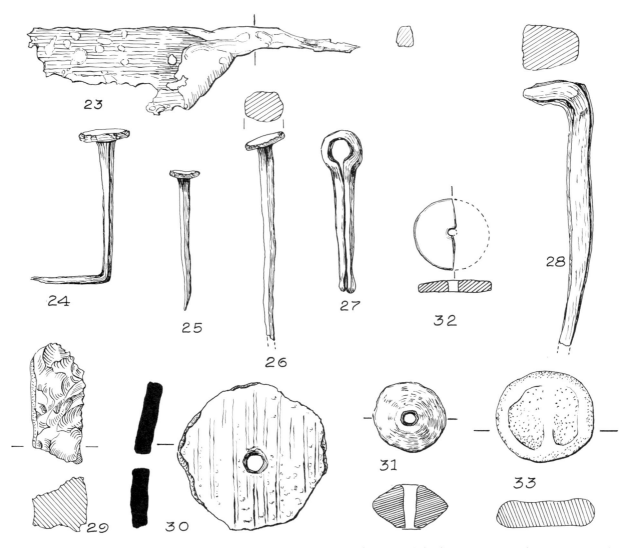

Fig. 67.   Objects of iron (Nos. 23–28), flint (No. 29) and clay (Nos. 30–33). (Scale: No. 23, $\frac{1}{1}$; Nos. 24–33, $\frac{1}{2}$)

25–26.   Belgic nails, 7.6 cm. and over 11 cm. long. *Ibid*.
27.   Belgic split pin. Find-spot as No. 24.
28.   Belgic iron wall-cramp fragment, broken at either end. Find-spot as No. 24.

OBJECT OF FLINT (Fig. 67)
29.   Struck flint showing two bulbs of percussion on one face: either a strike-a-light or a flint core. Find-spot as No. 24.

OBJECTS OF CLAY (Figs. 67, 68)
30.   Belgic spindle-whorl made from a wall sherd of a storage jar. Also a smaller one, diameter 5 cm. (not figured). Find-spot as No. 24.

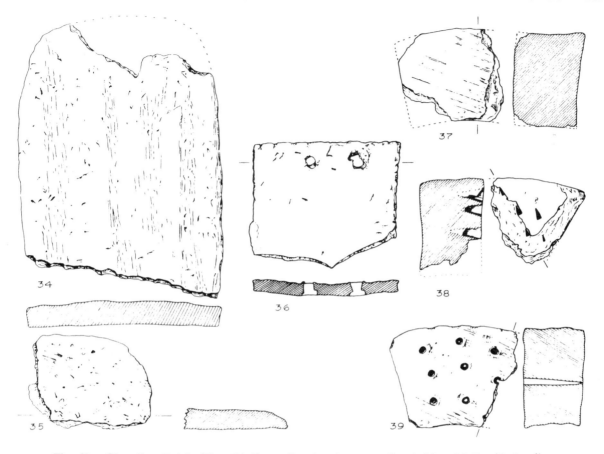

Fig. 68.   Clay tiles: Belgic (Nos. 34–5), medieval and post-medieval (Nos. 36–9). (Scale: ¼)

31.   Belgic bi-conical spindle-whorl in smooth grey-buff clay. Findspot as No. 24.

32.   Roman spindle-whorl fragment made from a flagon sherd in orange ware with cream slip. C XXIV W II 8, Whitehall Road. Pebble floor on south edge of Watling Street, A.D. 50–90.

33.   Counter made from an amphora sherd in finely granular orange-buff ware, with two worn depressions on top. C XXVI W V 16, Pit 24, Belgic or Roman.

34.   Belgic tile fragment with flat lower surface, vertical sides and one oval end (the other broken), roughly made in coarse reddish clay tempered with chaff and grass, with very little sand. Compared with a Roman tile, it is less well fired and breaks very easily. These tiles formed the floor of all the pre-Conquest hearths in the sunken hut in W V, where they were fused together in the centre into an amorphous mass by the heat. Apart from one stray fragment, they were not used in the wattle-and-daub hut walls. C XXIV W II 6. Occupation material associated with rectangular building, c. A.D. 15–43.

35.   Belgic tile fragment as No. 34 but with rounded edges. *Ibid.*

36.   Roof-tile fragment in hard reddish clay with a little mortar adhering, and two slightly splayed circular peg-holes. Tiles with circular peg-holes have been found in fourteenth-century contexts. C XXII OP I 1, Old Park. Seventeenth- or eighteenth-century gravel.

37–39.   Bricks, roughly shaped in red clay incorporating coarse sand, blue core, with slightly curved upper and lower edges, made in a sand mould. No. 38 has knife-perforations; in No. 39 these are circular and go right through. The coarseness of the brick suggests an industrial use, such as flooring or roofing a kiln:[134] No. 39 especially shows some signs of burning on upper and lower surfaces. C XXII OP I 5, Old Park. Loam floor above fourteenth-century gravel layer 6.

(v) SMALL FINDS FROM THE WATLING STREET SITES

NOTE: The small finds from the Watling Street sites are described separately from the rest of the finds from the Canterbury Excavation Committee sites. This is due to a change in publication plans following the postponement of new excavations in the Watling Street area in 1982. It had previously been intended to publish Professor Frere's excavations in a future Trust monograph dealing with the Watling Street area.

(1) COINS[135]

1.   Cunobelin. *Mack* 225. 30.293 grains
        C XVI B II (1). First-century pit.
2.   Meldi. *De la Tour* 7617. 40.123 grains
        C XXIV L III (15). First-century occupation layer.
3.   Trajan (?). *Rev*. illegible
        C XXIV L III. Above Street 5.
4–5.   Gallienus (two). *Rev*. illegible
        C XXVI M II (4). Medieval.
        C XXII F V Pit 1. Saxon.
6.   Claudius II. *RIC* 26
        C XXVI M II (7). Late Roman dark earth. Coin sealed by floor (6).
7.   Tetricus I. *RIC* 126
        C XXVI M II (7). Late Roman dark earth.
8.   Radiate. *Rev*. illegible
        C XXVI M II (7). Late Roman dark earth.
9.   Barbarous radiate. *Rev*. illegible
        C XXVI M II (7). Late Roman dark earth.
10.   Helena. *Rev*. illegible
        C XXVI M II (7). Late Roman dark earth.
11.   *Urbs Roma. Rev*. illegible
        C XXII F V (4). Medieval.
12.   *Constantinopolis. Rev*. illegible
        C XXIV L III (2A). Late Roman dark earth.
13.   Constans. *CHK* i, as 158
        C XXIV L III (2A). Late Roman dark earth.
14.   Constans. *CHK* i, as 90
        C XXVI M II (7). Late Roman dark earth.
15.   Constantius II. *CHK* i, as 89
        C XXIV L III (2A). Late Roman dark earth.
16.   Constantius II. *CHK* i, as 256
        C XXVI M I (9). Saxon or medieval.
17–18. Barbarous *Fel. Temp. Reparatio* (fallen horseman type) (two)
        C XXVI M II (5) (two). On floor (6). Later than A.D. 379.

134. Cf. E. Eames, 'A thirteenth-century Tile Kiln at North Grange, Meaux, Beverley, Yorkshire', *Med. Arch.*, v (1961), Pl. 25.
135. The coins have been identified by the late C.M. Kraay, R. Reece and the late B.H. St. J. O'Neil.

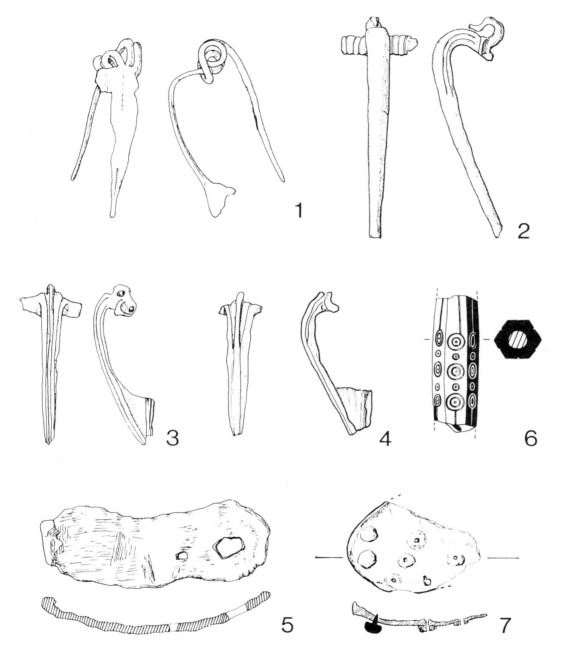

Fig. 69.   Copper alloy brooches (Nos. 1–4), lead object (No. 5), jet object (No. 6) and leather object (No. 7). (Scale: all ¼, except No. 7, ½) (Drawn by M.G. Wilson.)

19.   Magnentius. *CHK* ii, as 56
        C XXIV L III (2A). Late Roman dark earth.
20.   Valentinian I. *RIC* ix, p. 64, No. 9a
        C XXVI M II (5). On floor (6). Later than A.D. 379.
21.   Valens. *RIC* ix, p. 64, No. 9b
        C XXIV L III (2B). Late Roman dark earth.
22.   Gratian. *RIC* ix, p. 46, No. 21b
        C XXII F II Pit 2. Fourth century.
23.   Theodosius I. *Rev.* illegible
        C XXVI M II (5). On floor (6). Later than A.D. 379.
24.   Arcadius. *CHK* ii, as 2900
        C XXIV L III (2A). Late Roman dark earth.
25–26. House of Theodosius (two). *Rev.* illegible
        C XXVI M II (7) (two). Late Roman dark earth. One coin sealed by floor (6).
27–28. Late fourth century (two). Illegible
        C XXVI M II (5) (two). On cobble floor (6). Later than A.D. 379.
29.   Alfred (871–99). Silver. Cf. *BMC* A II, p. 58, No. 180 but different die
        C XXII F V Pit 2. Late ninth to early tenth century.

References in the list are to:
R.P. Mack, *The Coinage of ancient Britain (Mack)*;
H. de la Tour, *Atlas des Monnaies gauloises (De la Tour)*;
Roman Imperial Coinage. (Eds.) Mattingly, Sydenham, Sutherland and Carson *(RIC)*;
Late Roman Bronze Coinage; parts i and ii, Carson, Hill and Kent *(CHK)*; and
A Catalogue of English Coins in the British Museum. Anglo-Saxon Series. Volume ii (*BMC* A II).

(2) COPPER ALLOY BROOCHES[136] (Fig. 69)

'Nauheim' derivative: Camulodunum VII
1.   Damaged example with four-turn spring and plain flat bow tapering towards the foot. Dated by M.R. Hull to the mid first century. C XVI B II (1). First-century pit.

The 'Colchester' type: Camulodunum III
2.   Plain bow, oval in section; the side-wings are flat and decorated with vertical grooves and ridges. Pin and catch-plate missing. Dated by M.R. Hull to the first half of the first century. C XXIV L III (15). First-century occupation-layer.

Type Camulodunum IV
3.   The bow has a bold central rib and flat back; the side-wings are semi-cylindrical and undecorated. Spring and pin missing. C XXIV L III (4). Late Roman occupation material.
4.   Similar to No. 2 but bow has wider central rib. The perforated lug projecting from the head is broken; spring and pin missing. C XXIV L III below late Roman occupation-material (4) above (5).

136. The brooches were examined by the late M.R. Hull.

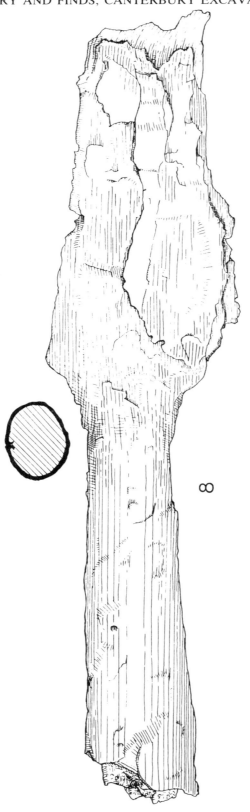

8

Fig. 70.   Iron spearhead (Scale: ⅓)

(3)   OBJECT OF LEAD (Fig. 69)

5.   Fragment of strap with square perforation near rounded end.
            C XXIV L III Pit 8. Roman.

(4)   OBJECT OF JET (Fig. 69)

6.   Part of a handle, hexagonal in section, decorated with double concentric-circle and central-dot motif.
            C XXIV L III (1). Medieval and post-medieval dark earth.

(5)   OBJECT OF LEATHER (Fig. 69)

7.   Part of a shoe. C XVI A I (8). Mid or late second-century pit.

(6)   IRON OBJECT (Fig. 70)

8.   Spear-head; badly corroded. C XXII F II Pit 2. Fourth century.

IIIB: THE POTTERY
by M.G. Wilson

(i) THE WHITEHALL ROAD AREA

A. NEOLITHIC

1.   Neolithic B Ebbsfleet ware; medium hard sandy buff-red ware with medium and large flint grit; deep finger-impressions at base of neck, and decorated with rows of angular incisions. The surface skin tends to flake off, suggesting a slip. Two or three other sherds with a black surface may have come from a separate bowl. W IV 8 and 9. Shallow scoops in natural brickearth. (Drawing and description by Isobel Smith).

B. BELGIC

Nos. 2–3: Pottery from W II 6A. Trampled surface below 6 occupation, *c.* A.D. 15–20.

2.   Rather coarse granular grey ware, unevenly burnished.

3.   Rather finely granular dark grey-brown ware, burnished above carination.

Nos. 4–53: Pottery from W II 6. Dark occupation material associated with rectangular building, *c.* A.D. 15–43

4.   Amphora (Dressel form 25) in hard finely granular buff ware; also sherds in hard orange-buff ware with cream slip. Perhaps Spanish.

5, 6.   Smooth white ware: No. 6 is probably two-handled (second handle found).

7.   Fine reddish paste, grey core, with finely micaceous cream slip. Cf. *Camulodunum* Form 165, native rendering of a Gallo-Belgic type.

8, 9.   Girth beakers decorated with fine incised lines in TR 3, cf. *Camulodunum* Form 82.

10.   Butt beaker sherd in TR 3, cross-hatched with double incised lines, from the upper half of a beaker, cf. *Camulodunum* Form 112.

11.   Sherds in fine cream ware with fine rouletting, from the lower half of a butt beaker, cf. *Camulodunum* Forms 112, 113.

12, 13.   Fine hard cream to grey-buff burnished ware with rouletted decoration, cf. *Camulodunum* Form 113.

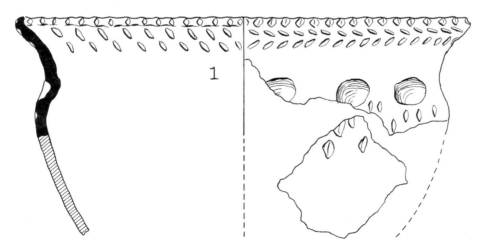

Fig. 71. Neolithic (Ebbsfleet ware) vessel from Whitehall Road (Site W). (Scale: ½)

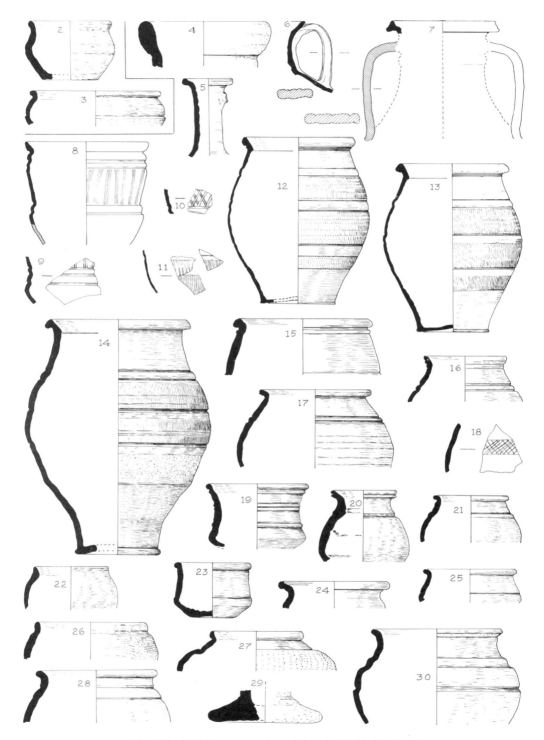

Fig. 72. Belgic pottery from Trench W II. (Scale: ¼)

14.   Rather finely granular grey-brown ware with combed decoration, surface partly burnished; three, and several other beakers in similar ware resembling this type. Locally-made butt beakers. There was also a plain sherd with a graffito (Fig. 79, No. 3).

15.   Ware as No. 14; twelve.

16.   Finely granular grey ware, smoothly burnished; three.

17.   Ware as No. 14, red-brown, with fine horizontal burnished lines on body; two.

18.   Beaker sherd with fine incised lattice, in finely granular grey ware, smoothly burnished; two. Cf. *Camulodunum* Form 92b.

19.   Rather finely granular grey-brown ware, smoothly burnished.

20.   Ware as No. 19, grey-buff, roughly finished inside.

21.   Ware as No. 19, red-buff.

22.   Finely granular brown ware, smoothly burnished.

23.   Rather finely granular dark grey ware, smoothly burnished black surface; twelve. The colour varies from dark to brown-grey and buff. Two others had graffiti (Fig. 79, Nos. 4–5).

24.   Ware as No. 23, grey-buff; two.

25.   Slightly granular light grey ware, unevenly burnished.

26.   Coarse granular grey-brown ware with uneven surface, burnished rim and neck; six other small inturned rims.

27.   Finely granular grey-brown ware, the rim and neck burnished black, and the body decorated with small irregular punched holes.

28.   Rather finely granular grey-buff ware, smoothly burnished; three, and another in black ware.

29.   Pedestal jar base in rather coarse hard granular light grey ware; three others in softer burnished grey and brown ware.

30.   Rather finely granular grey ware, smoothly burnished dark grey to buff surface; six other rims, and body sherds of three more. There were also sherds of six cordoned jars with bead rims of the same type as Rose Hotel Yard (fig. 86, No. 59.)[137]

31.   Rather hard granular dark grey ware, and five other rims of this type.

32.   Rather coarse grey-brown ware, unevenly burnished rim and neck, rilled body.

33.   Coarse granular grey-brown ware, unevenly burnished rim and neck, decorated with finger impressions on shoulder above finely furrowed body; five others, undecorated, with furrowed bodies, one coloured buff.

34.   Rather hard granular dark grey ware with horizontal lines of burnishing on body; six similar rims.

35.   Rather finely granular grey ware, smoothly burnished from rim to shoulder.

36, 37. Coarse granular red to dark grey ware, unevenly burnished rim and neck, with deeply impressed circles on shoulder.

38.   Rather finely granular burnished buff ware tinged with grey, fine grooves on shoulder.
        Also present in this layer was Fig. 79, No. 2, a vessel of the type represented by No. 89.

39.   Coarse granular grey-buff ware, burnished above furrowed body, with two perforations on shoulder; seventeen (unperforated).

40.   Storage jar sherd in coarse granular grey to brown ware, with roughly-stamped circles on furrowed shoulder.

41(three), Hard granular dark grey ware.
and 42. Hard granular dark grey ware.

43.   Rather finely granular burnished grey-brown ware.

44.   Storage-jar sherd in ware similar to No. 40, with roughly incised cross within a circle.

45.   Slightly granular rather soft reddish ware with irregular burnished surface.

46.   *Terra Rubra* 1(B), cf. *Camulodunum* Form 7, Skeleton Green Type 11.

47.   *Terra Nigra* 1; two. Cf. *Camulodunum* Form 2B, Skeleton Green Type 1A.

48.   *Terra Nigra* 1; two. Cf. *Camulodunum* Form 7, Skeleton Green Type 9.

49.   *Terra Nigra* 1, cf. *Camulodunum* Form 13, Skeleton Green Type 7.

137.   Report forthcoming in *The Archaeology of Canterbury*, vol. v.

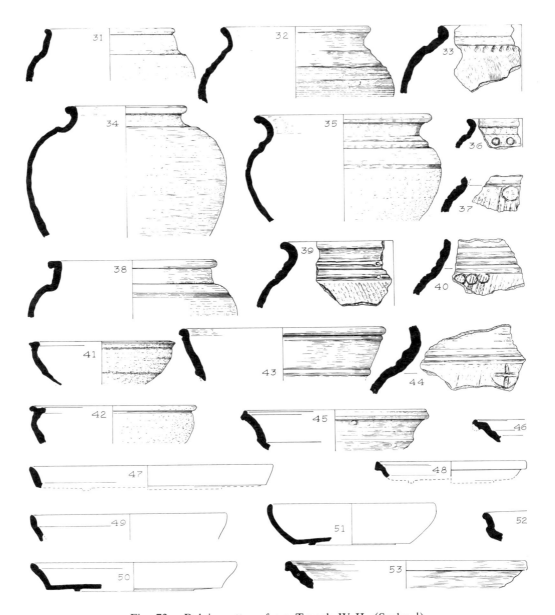

Fig. 73.   Belgic pottery from Trench W II. (Scale: ¼)

50.   *Terra Nigra* 1, of *Camulodunum* Form 14.

51.   *Terra Nigra*, of *Camulodunum* Form 16A, cf. Skeleton Green Type 2. There was also a base sherd with two bordered rouletted wreaths, cf. Skeleton Green Type 1a, and a base sherd of a large dish in mica-dusted *Terra Nigra* (unfigured).

52–3.   Native copies of Gallo-Belgic plates in rather finely granular burnished grey-brown ware. There were also fifteen as No. 71 copying *Camulodunum* Form 1, and one as No. 76.

54.   Gallo-Belgic butt-beaker sherd in very fine yellow-buff ware with notched-scroll decoration, cf. Skeleton Green Type 39 (in TR). W V 39 (10). Primary yellow loam floor of hut. Cf. No. 85 (cream).

Nos. 55–73: Pottery from W V 39 (9). Primary occupation of hut.

55.   Rather finely granular grey-buff ware, smoothly burnished rim to shoulder, with fine burnished lines on body.

56.   Darker grey-brown ware with shallow vertical combing under fine burnished lines.

57.   Rather finely granular grey-buff ware, buff surface, smoothly burnished on upper and lower part, perforation on neck; two.

58.   Ware as No. 55 with fine burnished lines on roughened body.

59.   Granular yellow-brown ware with grey core, smoothly burnished.

60.   Pedestal jar base in rather finely granular burnished grey-buff ware.

61.   Finely granular grey-buff ware, smooth surface with traces of silver mica-dusting. Cf. *Camulodunum* Form 102, Skeleton Green Fig. 51: import probably from Central Gaul.

62.   Rather coarse granular dark grey to brown ware, burnished rim and shoulder with perforation, body roughened below furrowing.

63.   Rather finely granular grey-brown ware, burnished from rim to shoulder, finely rilled body with burnished diagonal-line decoration.

64.   Rather coarse granular dark grey ware, upper part unevenly burnished.

65.   Coarse granular burnished light grey ware.

66.   Rather hard granular dark grey-brown ware, reddish core, with fine rilling on upper part of body, lower half smoothed; four perforations in base (half missing).

67.   Coarse granular grey-brown ware, unevenly burnished above furrowed body.

68.   Coarser ware than No. 67 with red-grey surface.

69–72.   Native copies of Gallo-Belgic plates in finely granular grey-brown burnished ware: Nos. 71–72 copy *Camulodunum* Form 1.

73.   Rather hard granular reddish grey ware.

There were also some imported amphora sherds in hard finely granular buff ware.

Nos. 74–78: Pottery from W V 35 (7). Primary occupation of hut.

74.   (Fig. 79, No. 1). Imitation Arretine cup (Loeschke 7) in *Terra Nigra* 1 with black coating, stamped **ANDECOVILOS** on base. Cf. *Camulodunum* Form 54, Skeleton Green Type 26 (both in *Terra Rubra*).

75, 76.   Native copies of Gallo-Belgic plates in smooth finely granular dark grey, and grey-brown burnished ware.

77.   Pedestal jar base in rather finely granular grey ware with reddish surface.

78.   Rather finely granular grey ware, unevenly burnished grey-buff surface.

Nos. 79–83: Pottery from W V 38 (7). Primary occupation of hut.

79.   Rather finely granular red-buff ware, burnished surface tinged with grey.

80.   Rather finely granular dark grey-buff ware, burnished from rim to shoulder with perforation on neck, and burnished decoration on body; two. Cf. No. 128.

81.   Ware as No. 80, the whole surface burnished.

82.   Rather soft granular red-brown ware, grey core, smoothly burnished surface.

83.   Coarse granular dark grey-buff ware, burnished rim, furrowed body; seven similar rims.

There were also a *Terra Rubra* plate as No. 46, a native copy of a Gallo-Belgic plate as No. 71 and imported amphora sherds in hard granular buff ware.

Nos. 84–91: Pottery from W V 5 (35 (6), 39 (7), 38 (5)). Occupation on secondary floor of hut.

84.   *Terra Rubra* 1(A), with red coating on upper surface, cf. *Camulodunum* Form 5.

85.   Gallo-Belgic butt-beaker sherd in *Terra Rubra* 3(B), with notched-scroll decoration, cf. No. 54 (cream). Cf. Skeleton Green Type 39.

86.   *Terra Nigra* 1, from 35 (6).

87.   Smooth hard cream-buff ware, with rouletted body sherds (unfigured) as Nos. 11, 12. Cf. *Camulodunum* Form 113.

88.   Rather soft and granular grey-buff ware, smoothly burnished.

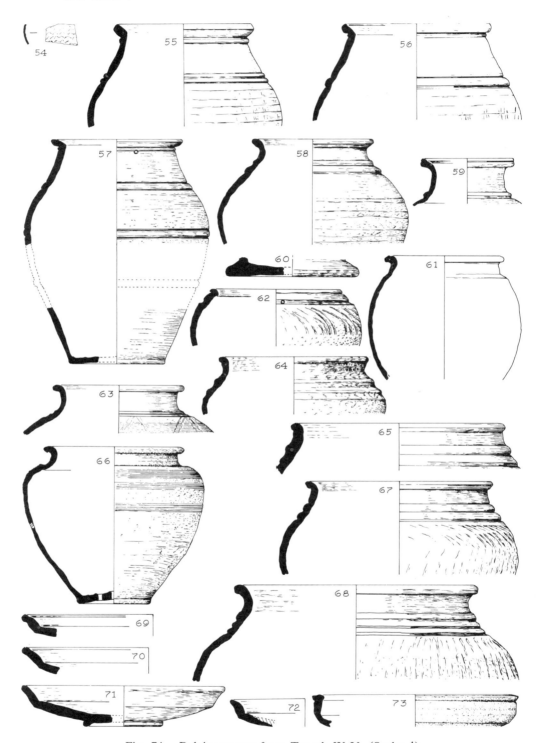

Fig. 74.   Belgic pottery from Trench W V. (Scale: ¼)

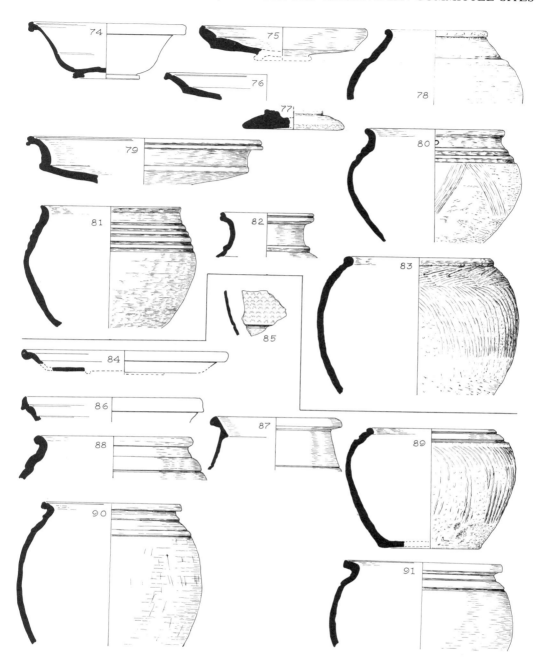

Fig. 75.   Belgic pottery from Trench W V. (Scale: ¼)

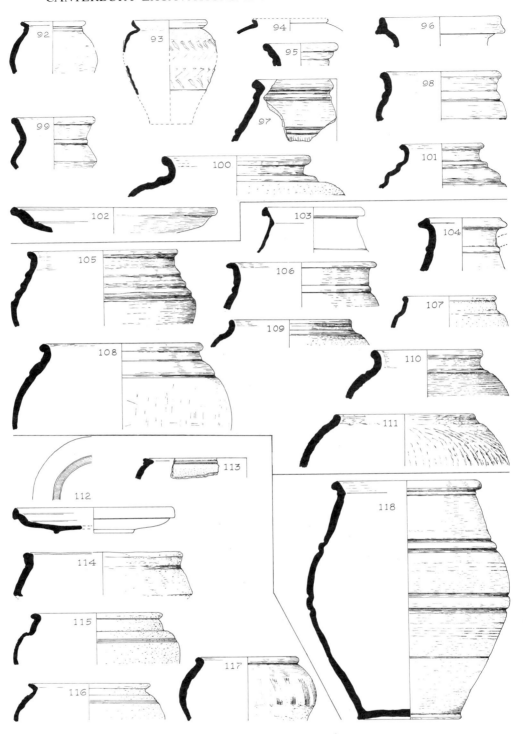

Fig. 76.   Belgic pottery from Trench W V and (No. 118) from cremation 2. (Scale: ¼)

89.   Coarse granular dark grey ware, burnished rim and neck, furrowed body. Cf. Fig. 79, No. 2 for a graffito on this type of jar.

90.   Rather finely granular grey-brown ware, smoothly burnished surface with slight vertical tooling on body, from 39 (7).

91.   Ware as No. 90, grey-buff.
      There were also amphora sherds in finely granular orange-buff and coarser and harder buff ware.

92.   Finely granular dark grey to buff ware, smoothly burnished, W V 38 (4). Third loam floor of hut.

Nos. 93–102: Pottery from W V 39 (5) and 38 (3). Occupation on third floor.

93.   Gallo-Belgic beaker with barbotine herringbone decoration, in very fine white ware with mica-coated orange slip on rim and shoulder above the decoration. Cf. *Verulamium* 1936, Pl. LV, No. 1 from Prae Wood. Coarser examples are *Camulodunum* Form 114, Skeleton Green Type 49.

94.   Smooth hard white ware.

95.   Flagon in finely granular smooth red-brown ware, burnished.

96.   As No. 95, red-buff with grey core, from 38 (3).

97.   Butt beaker in ware similar to No. 95 with shallow rouletting on body.

98, 99.   Finely granular dark grey ware, smoothly burnished.

100. Granular grey-brown ware, burnished from rim to cordon.

101. Smooth rather finely granular grey-brown burnished ware.

102. Smooth finely granular brown burnished ware.

Nos. 103–111: Pottery from W V 39 (4) and 35 (5). Fourth loam floor of hut.

103. Butt beaker in fine hard cream ware with grey-brown burnished surface, and sherd (unfigured) with fine rouletting as Nos. 12, 13. Cf. *Camulodunum* Form 113.

104. Flagon in rather finely granular grey ware, black inside, smoothly burnished brick-red outside; three-ribbed flat handle (unfigured) in similar ware.

105. Rather coarse red-grey burnished ware.

106. Rather finely granular grey-brown ware, smooth dark burnished surface.

107. Hard granular dark grey ware, with more grit and better fired than Belgic wares, from 35 (5).

108. Granular grey-brown burnished ware with lightly scratched combing on body.

109. Finely granular grey-brown ware with darker surface, burnished from rim to shoulder, roughened body.

110. Rather coarse granular grey-brown ware with dark burnished rim and neck, and finely rilled body.

111. Coarse granular dark grey to reddish ware, burnished rim and neck, furrowed body; two.

Nos. 112–117: Pottery from W V 38 (2) and 39 (3). Final occupation and ruins of hut.

112. *Terra Nigra* 1 with internal wreath. Cf. *Camulodunum* Form 7, Skeleton Green Type 10.

113. Granular red-buff ware.

114. Coarse granular grey-brown ware with some fine shell grit, irregular surface.

115, 116. Granular light and dark grey ware.

117. Coarse rather granular red-buff ware, burnished rim and shoulder; furrowing on body, smoothed below this.

118. Butt beaker used as cremation urn. Rather finely granular red-brown ware, smoothly burnished, with burnished horizontal lines on body. The beaker contained a token quantity of cremated bones of a youth of either sex, aged about twenty years or less.[138] It was accompanied by part of a small cordoned jar of the same type as Rose Hotel Yard,[139] fig. 86, No. 59: six of these were found also in W II 6 rectangular building. Whitehall Field Cremation 2.

138. Information from Dr I.W. Cornwall.
139. See p. 197, note 137.

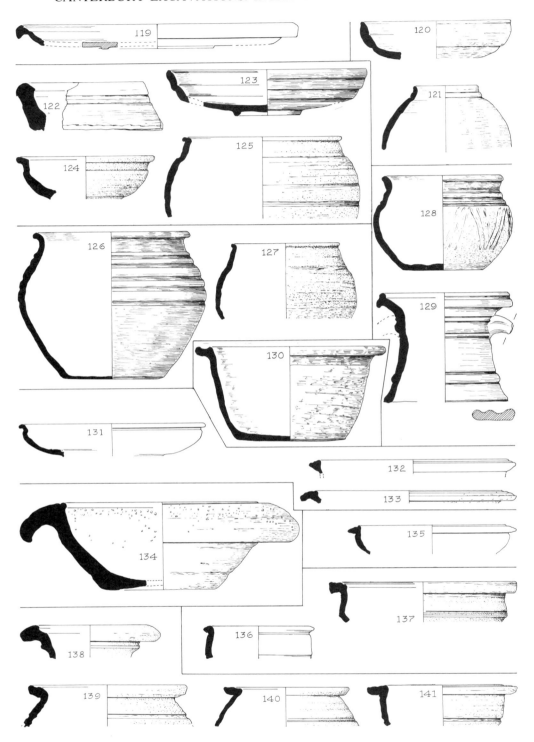

Fig. 77. Belgic and Roman pottery from Site W. (Scale: $\frac{1}{4}$)

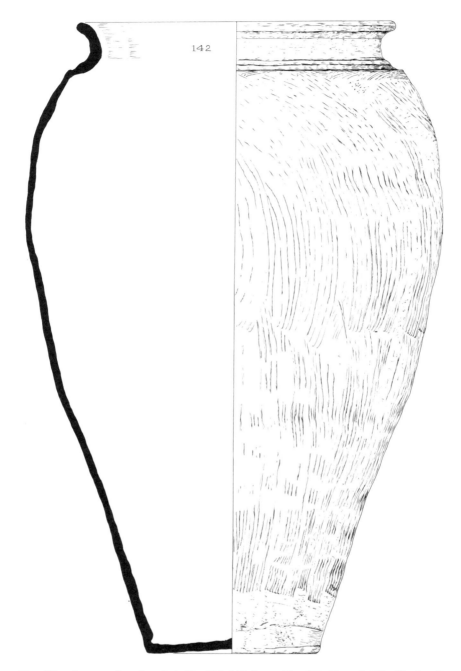

142

Fig. 78.   Storage jar dated A.D. 125–160 from Site W, Trench IB. (Scale: ¼)

Cremation 1 contained the base of a similar butt beaker, with bones of a youth aged about twenty years. This was accompanied by part of a smaller beaker in the same ware.

119. *Terra Nigra* 1, reconstructed with base sherd from 38 (2). *Camulodunum* Form 3, normally pre-Conquest. W V 4 Pit 34, residual with samian forms 27, Flavian-Trajanic, and 45, late Antonine.

Nos. 120–121: Pottery from W V 35 Pit 8.
120–121. Rather finely granular grey-brown Belgic ware, smoothly burnished.

Nos. 122–125: Pottery from W V 29 Pit 10.
122. Mortarium in hard cream-buff ware (pre-Claudian or Claudian, Gaulish) cf. *Camulodunum* Form 191B.
123. Grey-brown smoothly burnished Belgic ware; two.
124. Hard granular grey Romano-British ware.
125. Granular grey to reddish Belgic ware.

Nos. 126–127: Pottery from W V 27, Belgic drainage-ditch
126. Smoothly burnished grey-brown Belgic ware.
127. Granular grey-brown Belgic ware, smoothed near base. There were also two jars as No. 34 from this pit in soft grey sandy ware; this ware approaches a Romano-British fabric, but can be distinguished from it and is found in pre-Roman contexts; also present was a scrap of pre-Flavian Arretine or samian.

Nos. 128–129: Pottery from W V 21 (4). Belgic pit.
128. Coarse granular dark grey-brown ware, burnished from rim to shoulder, with diagonal burnished decoration on body, smoothed near base. Cf. No. 80.
129. Smooth burnished orange to grey-buff ware.

130. Coarse granular grey-brown hand-finished ware, unevenly burnished inside and to below flange outside, slightly burnished body. Second half of the fourth century. W V 35 Pit 20, upper filling.

Nos. 131–133: Pottery from W I 7. Occupation-layer pre-dating floor of first building. c. A.D. 80–115.
131. Fine burnished buff ware, grey core.
132. Mica-coated grey-buff ware.
133. Hard finely granular grey-buff ware.
There was also a carinated bowl in fine dark grey burnished ware, similar to Rose Hotel Yard,[140] fig. 148, No. 102.

134. Hard whitish ware, white and grey grits (A.D. 50–80, probably north-east France).[141] W IB 4B. Pit cut through floor of first building, A.D. 125–160. The pit also contained a very large storage jar No. 142.
135. Hard burnished grey ware. W IA 4. Floor of second building. There was also a flagon of the same type as Fig. 82, No. 15.

Nos. 136–137: Pottery from W II 5. Second surface of Watling Street. A.D. 120–160.
136. Burnished orange-red ware.
137. Hard granular grey ware.

Nos. 138–141: Pottery from W II 10. Drain bordering Watling Street.
138. Flagon in hard finely granular buff ware with a few large grits.
139–141. Hard granular grey ware.

140. p. 197, note 137.
141. See K.F. Hartley's Group I in (Eds.) J. Dore and K. Greene, *Roman Pottery Studies in Britain and Beyond* (*BAR* Supplementary Series No. 30 (Oxford, 1977)) 10 and Fig. 2.1.

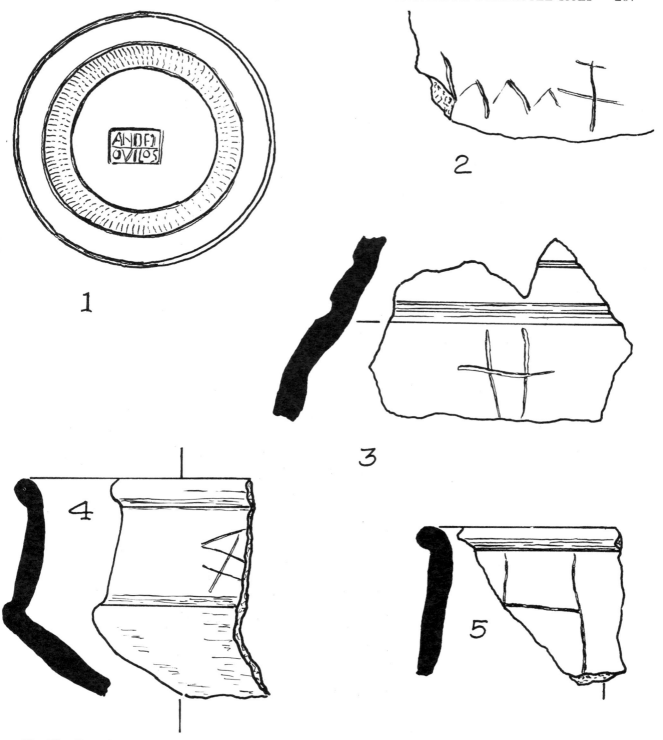

Fig. 79.   Potter's stamp on *Terra Nigra* (No. 1) and graffiti on Belgic pottery (Nos. 2–5) all from Site W. (Scale: ¼)

142.   Very coarse granular red to light grey ware, burnished rim and neck, furrowed body. W IB 4B. Pit cut through floor of first building, A.D. 125–160. See also No. 134.

(ii) POTTER'S STAMP AND GRAFFITI, WHITEHALL ROAD (Fig. 79)

1.   Stamp on base of TN 1 cup No. 74. **ANDEC/OVILOS** (C reversed). A stamp from the same die has been identified at Camulodunum (No. 21) unstratified. The dating evidence is provided by another die of Andecovilos, examples of which occur in a Tiberian pit at Colchester 1970; Cemetery S at Nijmegen c. A.D. 30–37; Paris c. A.D. 15–40.[142] From W V 35 (7).
     The stratigraphical position of this vessel suggests a date of c. A.D. 10–20 (pp. 50–2).

Graffiti on Belgic Pottery from W II 6, A.D. 15–43
2.   NVX; N is reversed, X has an extra cut. Placed vertically on the body of a jar similar to No. 89.
3.   H on butt beaker of the same general type as No. 57.
4.   XXI vertically on a cup of the same type as No. 23.
5.   H on a cup as No. 23.

(iii) POTTERY FROM LADY WOOTTON'S GREEN (Fig. 80)

Nos. 143–146: Pottery from B I 18. Gravel-pit filling cut by inhumation graves. Late first or early second century.
143.   Fine burnished grey ware, rouletted below neck cordon.
144.   Rather soft burnished red-buff ware.
145.   Coarse granular grey-brown ware, unevenly burnished neck and lip.
146.   Hard granular light grey ware.

Nos. 147–148: Pottery from cremation-burial inserted into grave of second inhumation in B I
147.   Fine hard burnished light grey ware, c. A.D. 120–200, filled with cremated bones below burnt flints.
148.   Coarse granular light buff to grey ware, accompanying No. 147.

149.   (Pl. XXX). Belgian import. Andenne jar in finely granular buff ware with tubular spout, and handle fragment attached to the rim (two handles have been reconstructed in Pl. XXX); decorated with applied thumbed strips and nearly covered with glassy golden-yellow glaze. These jars were made in the twelfth century and continued into the thirteenth.[143] B II 5. Black occupation material below medieval gravel floor.

(iv) POTTERY FROM NOS. 7 AND 8 CHURCH STREET (ST. PAUL'S) (Fig. 81)

150.   Fine hard burnished dark grey ware; another rim, light grey, and a dark cordoned body sherd. C XX A II 8A. Charcoal layer on primary gravel floor, with early Flavian samian.

Nos. 151–162: Pottery from A II 8 (ashy occupation on primary gravel floor). c. A.D. 80–110.
151.   Fine light grey burnished ware.
152.   Fine hard burnished grey ware, with incised wavy line on shoulder.
153.   Ware as No. 152.
154.   Rather granular dark grey ware, partly burnished.

142.   Information kindly provided by Valery Rigby.
143.   Borremans et Lassance, *Céramique d'Andenne au Moyen Age*, Pl. L, 1–5.

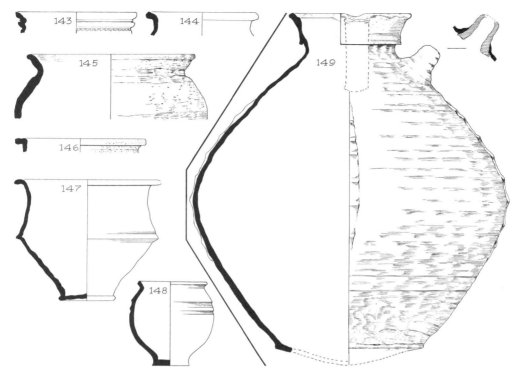

Fig. 80.   Pottery from Lady Wootton's Green: Nos. 143–8 Roman; No. 149 imported jar of Andenne Ware.
(Scale: ¼)

155.   Ware as No. 152.
156.   Hard rather finely granular grey-brown ware, dark grey to buff surface, partly burnished.
157–158. Coarse granular grey ware, burnished rim and neck, finger-nail decoration on shoulder.
159.   Ware as No. 157, with furrowed body.
160.   Hard granular light grey ware.
161.   Finely granular dark grey-brown ware, rather unevenly burnished.
162.   Very coarse granular dark grey ware, burnished rim and neck, with irregular shoulder grooves and furrowed body; some burnishing on body.

Nos. 163–167: Pottery from A II 6B and 7. Dark earth on possible secondary floor. Late fourth century.
163.   Orange-red colour-coated Oxfordshire ware, with stamped demi-rosettes, cf. Young's Type C 83.5 dated mid to late fourth century.
164.   Ware as No. 163, with demi-rosettes between rouletted bands, cf. Young's Type C 84, of the same date.
165–166. Coarse granular dark grey hand-made ware, unevenly burnished. Jars in this ware are not found before *c.* A.D. 360 in Canterbury.

167.   Similar ware to No. 165, grey to buff. Dishes of this type are dated A.D. 320–410.
168.   Hard reddish Oxfordshire ware with red-brown colour-coating, rouletted, of Young's Type C 75, dated A.D. 320–400. A II 'Pit 3'. Gully cut into layer 6B.
169.   Saxon cooking-pot in hard rather finely granular light grey ware with darker faceted surface, partly burnished; probably wheel-turned. Ninth to tenth century. A I Pit 4.

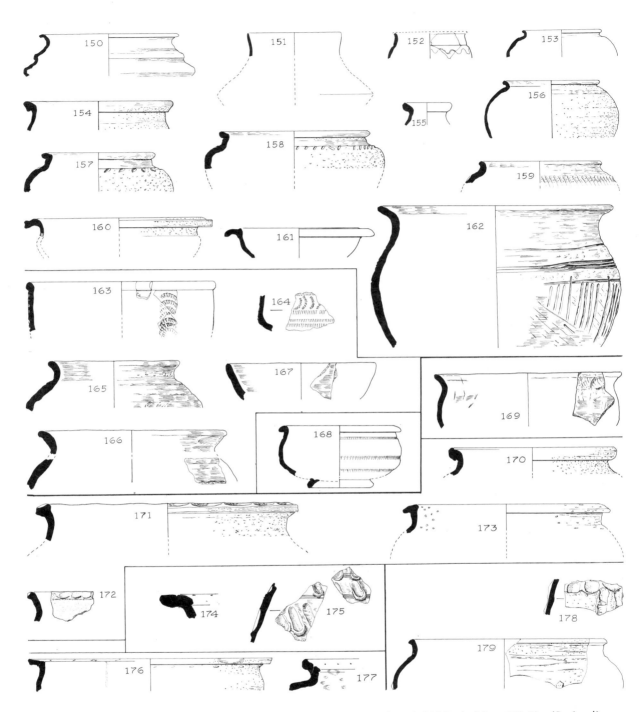

Fig. 81.   Pottery from Church Street (St. Paul's) (Nos. 150–177) and Old Park (Nos. 178–9).   (Scale: ¼)

Nos. 170–173: Pottery from A II 4. Thick deposit of dark medieval soil. Twelfth to early thirteenth century.
170.   Hard rather finely granular grey ware, probably second half of the twelfth-century.
171.   Cooking-pot with wide thumb-impressions on rim, in hard rather finely granular reddish ware, grey core. Twelfth century, perhaps second half.
172.   Similar ware to No. 171.
173.   Red-brown shell-tempered ware, probably second half of the twelfth century. There was also a reddish jug sherd with thin, patchy glaze similar to thirteenth-century ware.

Nos. 174–175: Pottery from A II 3A. Dirty loam below floor (2). Fourteenth century.
174.   Pierced rim of large dish or bowl in hard rather finely granular reddish ware, grey core.
175.   Jug sherds with plain shoulder (not figured) and thumb-impressed decoration on body, in hard granular grey ware partly covered with thin glaze, dark green. A whole jug of this type was found in the fourteenth-century well in Canterbury Lane (vol. vii, no. 401).

Nos. 176–177: Pottery from A II 2. Loam floor. Fourteenth century.
176.   Bowl in hard rather finely granular reddish ware with a drop of thin glaze, orange, on the pierced rim.
177.   Cooking-pot with pierced rim, in rather coarse hard red-buff ware, grey core, with splashes of thin glaze, orange-green, inside.

(v) POTTERY FROM OLD PARK, STURRY ROAD (Fig. 81)

178.   Cooking-pot sherd with vertical and horizontal applied thumbed strips in low relief, in hard rather finely granular red-buff ware, grey core, as fourteenth-century. C XXII O P 5. Loam floor.
179.   Hard rather finely granular bright reddish ware, partly grey core, smoked grey outside, with fragment perhaps of a vertical applied strip. Fourteenth century. O P 6. Gravel below loam floor (5).

(vi) POTTERY FROM NO. 53, KING STREET (C XXII K) (Fig. 82)

1.   (Unfigured) Dish of the same type as No. 18. K 10. Primary gravel floor.
2.   (Unfigured) Dish as No. 18. K 7. Occupation earth above (10) floor.
3.   Colour-coated beaker sherd with applied scale-pattern, in fine hard white paste, grey-brown 'metallic' coating. K 7A. Secondary gravel floor. Cf. Gillam Type 93, A.D. 180–250.

Nos. 4–8: Pottery from K Pit 7, sealed by occupation layer 5 on Phase 2 floor. First quarter of third century.
4.   Bowl inspired by Dr. 37 in hard rather granular grey ware with burnished decoration; the surface is burnished between the decorated zones. Probably second century.
5.   Light grey-buff rather granular ware with burnished buff surface.
6.   Burnished grey-buff ware with panel of applied dots.
7.   Fine hard light grey ware, burnished above rouletted body. Local copy of colour-coated beaker.
8.   Hard granular grey ware, reddish inside.

Nos. 9–10: Pottery from K Pit 1, cut through black soil above occupation-layer 5 of Phase 2. First half of the seventeenth century.
9.   Hard finely granular pale buff ware, covered inside with rather thin glaze, yellow.
10.   Hard finely granular reddish ware, grey core, with rather uneven surface; covered inside with glaze, orange to green, thin in places.

(vii) POTTERY FROM NO. 3 PALACE STREET. C XXII J (Fig. 82)

11.   Finely granular brown Belgic ware with grey-black burnished surface. J II 4. Burnt layer sealing first Belgic house.

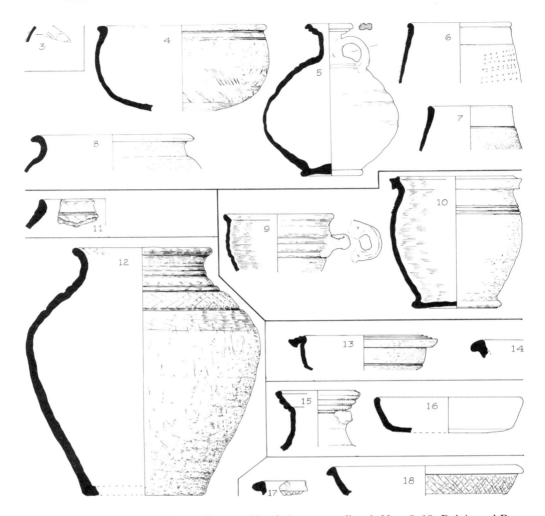

Fig. 82.   Pottery from No. 53 King Street: Roman, Nos.3–8; post-medieval, Nos. 9–10; Belgic and Roman pottery from No. 3 Palace Street (Nos. 11–16), and Roman pottery (Nos. 17–18) from St. Peter's Lane, Trench II.   (Scale: ¼)

12.   Coarse granular grey-brown Belgic ware with burnished lattice, and unevenly burnished surface above and below this. J II. Post-hole 2 of first Belgic house.

Nos. 13–14: Pottery from J I 4. Occupation-earth above third house, A.D. 50–170.
13.   Hard finely granular grey ware; two.
14.   Dish in hard mottled grey-buff burnished ware.

Nos. 15–16: Pottery from J II Pit 3. Post-hole of possible colonnade, *c.* A.D. 200–240.
15.   Hard finely granular buff ware, orange core.
16.   Hard finely granular light grey burnished ware; and a dish with burnished lattice of the same type as No. 18. Pit 2 contained a dish similar to Gillam's Type 222, dated A.D. 150–210, and another comparable to Type 319, dated A.D. 200–350.

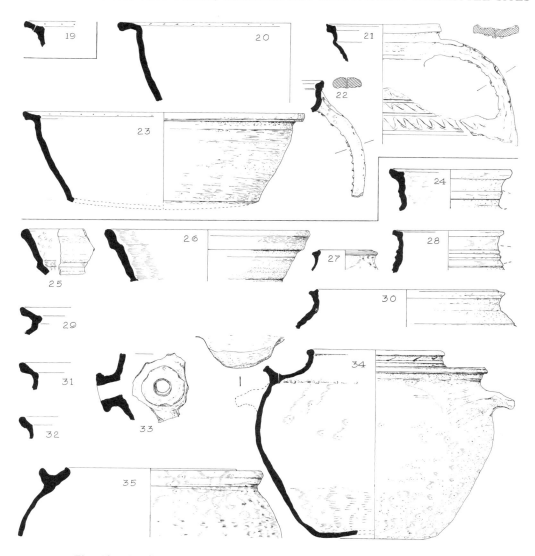

Fig. 83.   Medieval pottery from St. Peter's Lane, Trench II. (Scale: ¼)

(viii) POTTERY FROM ST. PETER'S LANE. C XXII H (Fig. 82)

Nos. 17–18: Pottery from H II 22. Latest Roman earth below medieval layers.
17.   Black-burnished 2 ware with lattice, cf. Gillam's Type 223 dated A.D. 150–210.
18.   Hard burnished grey-buff ware.

MEDIEVAL (Fig. 83)
19.   Hard rather finely granular reddish ware, grey core. H II 13. Occupation layer sealing Phase 2 building.
         Fourteenth century.

Nos. 20–23: Pottery from H II Pit 4, sealed by Phase 3 secondary floor. Fourteenth century

20.   Hard rather finely granular reddish ware, with stab-marks on rim.
21.   Hard granular reddish to grey ware with a little transparent glaze over scored shoulder decoration; thumb impressions on both edges of pierced handle (position of decorated sherd conjectural).
22.   Hard granular red-buff ware, decorated with stripes of buff slip, horizontal below rim, vertical on handle which is pierced in three lines.
23.   Hard rather finely granular red-brown ware, smoothed outside, smoked.

Nos. 24–35: Pottery from H II 3. Earth and tiles outside Phase 4 wall. Fourteenth century.

24.   Hard granular dark grey ware, partly red core, with some transparent glaze, green, on rim and inside neck.
25.   Hard rather light grey ware with smooth surface and some transparent glaze, green, inside.
26.   Hard rather finely granular grey-buff ware with some glaze inside.
27.   Finely granular yellow-buff ware with some glaze, mottled light green, outside.
28.   Hard rather finely granular reddish ware, grey core, with traces of glaze.
29.   Hard granular grey ware.
30.   Hard rather finely granular brown-grey ware, partly red core.
31.   Coarser ware than No. 30.
32.   Ware as No. 30, red-grey.
33.   Spigot-hole made evenly with a stick. Ware similar to No. 34; another in reddish ware.
34.   Hard granular dark grey ware, partly red core, with transparent glaze, green-brown, on base inside and splashes elsewhere, stabbed on neck and flange.
35.   Hard finely granular orange-buff ware, with patchy glaze, orange-green, outside; two.

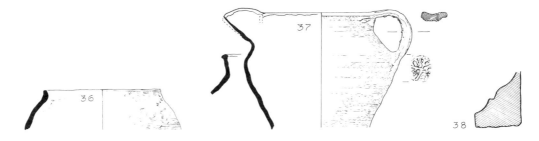

Fig. 84.   Pottery and a marble moulding from the Fleur-de-Lis Yard. (Scale: ¼)

(ix) POTTERY FROM THE FLEUR-DE-LIS YARD C XXVIII B (Fig. 84)

36.   Saxon cooking-pot, hand-made in grass-tempered grey-black ware with uneven burnished surface, grey-brown outside. Sixth to seventh century. B III 1. Medieval pit.
37.   Jug with bridged parrot-beaked spout (broken) and stamp at base of pierced handle, in hard finely granular yellow-buff ware tinged with brown. Import from western France, end of twelfth to thirteenth century. B I Pit 1, with fourteenth-century sherds.
38.   Section of coarse white marble moulding, broken at the top (Pl. XXVIII, No. 9).

(x) POTTERY FROM THE WATLING STREET SITES (Figs. 85–87)

Nos. 1–9: Pottery from C XVI A, layers 2–7. Mid or late second-century pit

1.   Hard burnished dark grey ware (7).
2.   Black-burnished 2 ware (7).

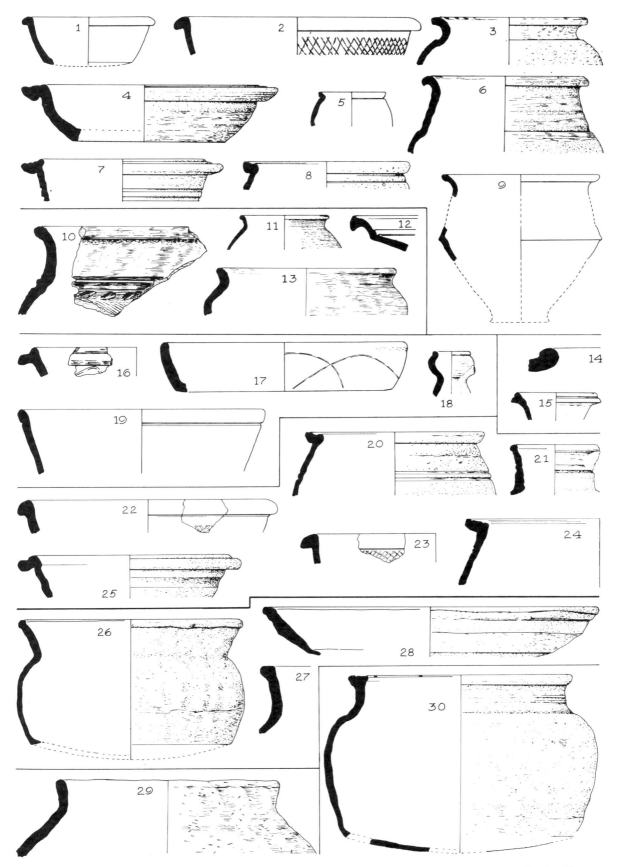

Fig. 85. Pottery vessels. Roman Nos. 1–25; Saxon No. 29; medieval Nos. 26–28 and 30. (Scale: ¼)
(Drawn by M.G. Wilson).

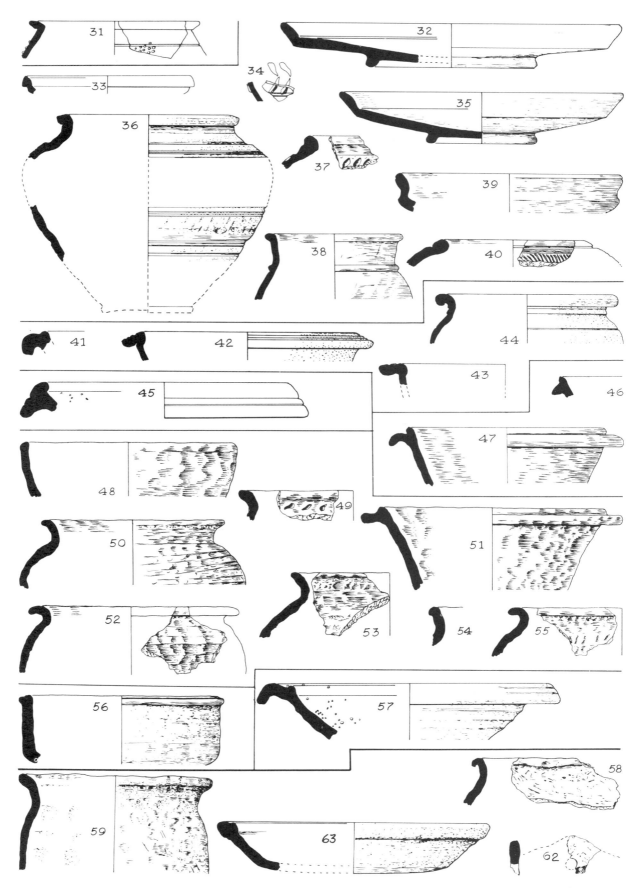

Fig. 86.   Pottery vessels. Roman Nos. 31–57; Saxon Nos. 58–62; medieval No. 63. (Scale: ¼)

3.   Coarse granular light grey ware, unevenly burnished rim and neck (7).

4.   Granular grey ware, partly smoothed (7).

5.   Fine hard burnished grey ware (4).

6.   Hard granular light grey ware with lines of burnishing (4).

7.   Hard rather finely granular dark grey ware (3).

8.   Ware as No. 7, with some white grits, smoked (2).

9.   Fine hard burnished grey ware (2).

Nos. 10–13: Pottery from C XVI B II Pit 1, layers 2, 1. First century

10.   Storage jar in coarse granular grey ware, unevenly burnished rim and neck, furrowed shoulder with incised decoration. Also a bead-rim jar with similar decoration (2).

11.   Hard finely-granular light grey ware, partly smoothed (2).

12.   *Terra Nigra* plate in fine hard whitish ware, worn grey coating (2).

13.   Rather soft dark grey-buff Belgic ware, unevenly burnished (1).

Nos. 14–15: Pottery from B III Pit 3. First century

14.   Bead-rim jar in coarse granular light red-grey ware.

15.   Flagon in fine orange-buff mica-coated ware; also a *Terra Nigra* plate (sherd).

Nos. 16–19: Pottery from B II Pit 2. Third to fourth century

16.   Flanged bowl with burnished arcading in Black-burnished 1 ware. Cf. Gillam No. 228, A.D. 290–370.

17.   Black-burnished 1 ware. Cf. Gillam No. 329, A.D. 190–340.

18.   Flagon in hard finely granular orange-buff ware.

19.   Hard burnished light grey ware; two.

Nos. 20–25: Pottery from B III Pit 1. Late second century

20.   Hard granular grey ware, smoked; two.

21.   Flagon in hard granular grey ware.

22.   Smooth hard light grey burnished ware, lighter core.

23.   Black-burnished 2 ware. ?Cf. Gillam No. 222, A.D. 170–210.

24.   Hard rather granular dark grey ware; two.

25.   Hard granular grey ware.

Nos. 26–28: Pottery from C XVI A, Pit 2. Second half of eleventh century

26–27.   Medieval cooking-pots in hard granular light red-grey ware with uneven surface, partly smoothed near base; also six other Group II cooking-pot rims.

28.   Medieval dish in hard rather finely granular red-brown ware. Sooted.

29.   Hand-made Saxon cooking-pot in coarse dark grey grass-tempered ware, uneven lighter surface. C XVI B I Pit 1. Saxon.

30.   Medieval cooking-pot with lightly-pierced rim in hard granular grey ware, uneven grey-brown surface, smoothed near base. B II Pit 4. Thirteenth century.

31.   Fine hard smoothly-burnished grey ware, with panel of raised dots. C XVI C I. Occupation-material on loam floor. *c.* A.D. 70–100.

Nos. 32–38: Pottery from C XXIV L III 15. Mid first-century occupation layer

32.   *Terra Rubra* plate in micaceous brick red paste and coating (TR 2), burnt.

33.   *Terra Nigra* plate, burnt.

34.   Imported Gallo-Belgic beaker sherd in very fine hard white ware, barbotine herring-bone decoration. Cf. *Verulamium* 1936, Pl. LV, No. 1; *Camulodunum* No. 114.

35.   Hard slightly granular ware, burnt, burnished buff internal surface remaining: a good copy of a *Terra Rubra* plate.

64   65

Fig. 87.   Pottery vessels. Roman No. 64, Amphora Stamp; No. 65 Rosette stamped. (Scale: ½)

36.   Fairly hard and finely granular grey ware, smoked, lighter grey and red core; two.
37.   Bead-rim jar in coarse granular grey ware, burnished rim and neck, incised shoulder-decoration.
38.   Rather granular burnished buff ware with fine mica, grey core.

39.   Rather soft and granular grey-buff ware, smoothly burnished. C XXIII L I 12. First-century building debris.
40.   Coarse granular grey-buff ware, burnished rim, furrowed shoulder; and another with plain shoulder. L I 11.
         First-century building debris.

Nos. 41–44: Pottery from C XXIV L III 32. Street 3
41.   Mortarium in hard cream ware (second century, perhaps *c.* A.D. 140–200, Colchester or Kent).
42–43.   Hard granular light grey ware.
44.   Hard finely granular rather light grey ware, smoked.

45.   Smooth red-buff ware, grey core, white and grey grits (third century, Kent). L III 28. On surface of Street 6.
46.   Flanged bowl in smooth hard burnished light grey ware. L III 27. Street 7.
47.   Coarse burnished dark grey ware. L III 26A. Street 8.

Nos. 48–55: Pottery from C XXIV L III 2A, 2. Late Roman dark earth
48.   Coarse granular dark grey ware, unevenly burnished, hand-made (2A).
49.   Jar with incised shoulder-decoration similar to No. 36 (Belgic), in ware as No. 47 (2A).
50–55.   Coarse granular dark grey to brown ware, unevenly burnished, hand-made (2).

56.   Coarse granular dark grey-brown Belgic ware, partly burnished uneven surface. C XXVI M II 10.
         First-century occupation-layer.
57.   Hard finely granular red-buff ware, white grits (second century, probably not later than A.D. 170, Kent). C
         XXVI M II 9. Collapsed loam wall. Second century.
58.   Saxon hand-made cooking-pot in grey-black grass-tempered ware, very irregular burnished surfaces. C
         XXVI M I 9. Saxon or medieval occupation-earth.
59.   Saxon cooking-pot in hard rather finely granular grey-black ware, uneven surface with patchy burnishing.
         This lacks the knife-trimming characteristic of Group I (?early eleventh century) or the sharply everted rim
         of ninth- to early tenth-century cooking-pots such as Nos. 60–61, and may provisionally be attributed to the
         later tenth century. M I Pit 2. Second half of tenth century.

Nos 60–61: Pottery from C XXII F V Pit 2. Late ninth century, associated with coin of Alfred (not illustrated)
60.   Rim in hard rather finely granular dark grey ware, brown core, with vertical knife-trimming on neck,
         unevenly burnished, cf. Vol. vii, No. 342; several sherds of this cooking-pot, and also of others in this ware.
61.   Rim in ware as No. 60, cf. Vol. vii, No. 330.
62.   Hand-made Saxon cooking-pot sherd with perforated lug handle as Vol. v, No. 40, in coarse grey
         grass-tempered ware, sixth century. C XXII F V Pit 1. Saxon.

63.   Medieval dish in hard granular grey-buff ware, uneven body-surface, smoothed on base, similar to Group II ware. M II Pit 2. Eleventh century.

64.   Amphora-stamp on handle]BAR/COLSICETASI. Callender No. 179. C XXIV L III 1 (residual).

65.   Saxon cooking-pot in hard finely granular reddish ware, with finger impressions on rim and deeply stamped rosettes on neck. C XXVI M II Pit 1 (residual in Medieval Group II pit).

IIIC: THE ROMAN AND SAXON GLASS

By D. Charlesworth and A.J. Price[144]

This chapter describes all that is worth publishing of the Roman glass found in the excavations of 1946–60 by the former Canterbury Excavation Committee. The great majority of pieces found were extremely fragmentary and were consequently unidentifiable. Some, however, are of considerable interest, for a few examples of very fine table-ware are represented; but most of the publishable pieces come from everyday household forms and from bottles. The glass ranges in date from the mid first to the late fourth century. The heavy flaking iridescence on a number of fragments is somewhat unusual in Britain, where most Roman glass is only dulled, and much is entirely unweathered. Weathering of the type described usually occurs where there is deep stratification, and so is found most frequently on glass from town sites. In Canterbury the preservation of both glass and metal objects has been affected most adversely by the seepage from ubiquitous medieval pits with their organic content.

In the catalogue below 'vol. vii', etc., refers to the numbered volumes of *The Archaeology of Canterbury* series. The dates given are those of the contexts.

Nos. 1–3: Polychrome and coloured cast glass (Fig. 88)
1. C XXII C I 35, *c.* A.D. 150–200. Canterbury Lane, Building I (ii) floor and occupation (vol. vii, p. 83). Rim fragment of pillar-moulded bowl; dark blue ground with amber patches, flecked with opaque white and opaque yellow chips. The inside and shoulder outside are ground, the ribs fire-polished; some iridescence.

    These bowls (Isings[145] Form 3) were made in the first century A.D., and the polychrome examples probably went out of production soon after A.D. 50–60. They are not very common in Britain, though a number are known at early sites such as Camulodunum,[146] and a few pieces have been found on Flavian sites in northern Britain.
2. C XXXI S I Pit 4, *c.* A.D. 130–160. Simon Langton Yard, well filling (vol. v, forthcoming). Pillar-moulded bowl fragment in deep blue, probably not later than the Flavian period. Coloured metals seem to lose their popularity in the 70s and the later examples are in natural green or blue-green glass.
3. C XX C I 9A, A.D. 390–450. Accumulated dark soil above Roman building in Canterbury Lane (vol. vii, p. 87). Fragment of everted-rim bowl with truncated conical upper body; dark green, both surfaces polished. Rim-edge rounded, deep groove cut in upper surface.

    The exact date of production of these bowls is uncertain, though the technique and colour suggest the first half of the first century A.D. A colourless version of the same form is found in later first- and second-century contexts, and a few polychrome specimens are known (see Fishbourne[147] Nos. 2, 4 for profiles of these bowls).

Nos. 4–13: Colourless glass bowl and beaker fragments (Fig. 88)
4. C X L I 2, A.D. 260–300. South side of Burgate Street, in Period III building (vol. vii, p. 111). Base of bowl in good-quality colourless glass, probably cast in a mould, both surfaces polished and small base-ring formed by cutting. Shape unknown, but metal and technique suggest a first-century date.
5. C XIII RY V A 4. Rose Yard, fifth-century robbing of Roman Building (vol. v, forthcoming). Beaker with slightly everted polished rim, with cut line below and another on the shoulder; milky weathering.

---

144. This chapter is mainly compiled from notes left by the late Dorothy Charlesworth; the advice of Dr Jennifer Price is gratefully acknowledged, in particular over Nos. 13 and 14. See *The Archaeology of Canterbury*, vol. v, forthcoming, for further discussion of chariot cups found in Canterbury.
145. C. Isings, *Roman Glass from Dated Finds* (Gröningen, 1957).
146. D.B. Harden, in C.F.C. Hawkes and M.R. Hull, *Camulodunum* (Oxford, 1947), 287–307.
147. D.B. Harden and J. Price, in B. Cunliffe, *Excavations at Fishbourne 1961–69* (London, 1971), 317–68.

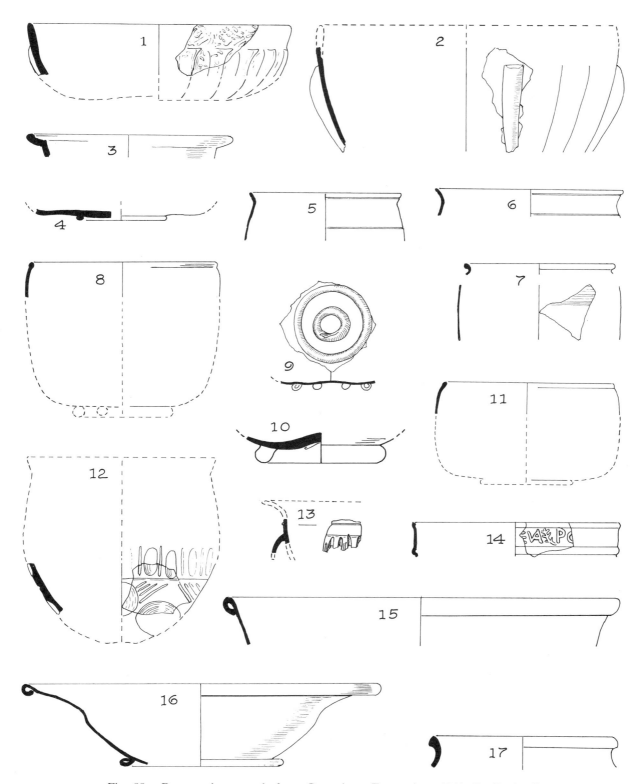

Fig. 88.   Roman glass vessels from Canterbury Excavations 1946–60. (Scale: ½)

6. C XVII E V 16, A.D. 220–260. South of Marlowe Theatre, occupation on floor of Period I Building (vol. v, forthcoming). Similar to No. 5 but less weathered.

   Fishbourne 56 is the same sort of beaker, but its rim is more sharply everted. There exists a number of beakers all varying in detail, some bulbous, some straight-sided and curving sharply to the base, decorated with a few cut lines, which date mainly to the Hadrianic-Antonine period.[148]

7. C XXXI S III 30, A.D. 160–220. Simon Langton Yard, timber slot of Building II (vol. v, forthcoming). Straight-sided vessel, probably a beaker, decorated with faint wheel-cut lines, in good colourless glass. A rounded rim-fragment seems to belong to the same vessel residual in S III 31, A.D. 300–400.

8. C XV R I Ext. 1, 2 (= I 27), A.D. 220–250. North of St. George's Street, loam floor of Building (vol. vii, p. 71). Rim rounded and slightly thickened, straight side; iridescent. Probably Isings Form 85b, A.D. 160–250.

9. C XIV M III 4, A.D. 280–320. North-west corner of Iron Bar Lane – Burgate Street junction, occupation on loam floor (vol. vii, p. 117). Base with double base-ring, the outer tubular and the inner trailed on, with pontil scar; flaking silver weathering. Isings Form 85b; see Fishbourne 74, 75.

10. C XIV M III 4, A.D. 280–320. *Ibid.* Base and applied base-ring of bowl. Slightly curved base with central 'kick' and pontil scar; dull, some silver weathering. Shape uncertain, but the presence of the pontil mark indicates that the rim was fire-finished. Probably second or third century.

11. C XXXI S IV 10 (= 6), A.D. 290–320. Simon Langton Yard, loam layer, probably demolished wall material (vol. v, forthcoming). Rim of cylindrical bowl as Nos. 8–9; made in the middle Rhineland *c.* A.D. 160–250, and found on most sites of that period in this country. The type is best known from the complete example found outside the Roman province at Airlie.[149] Rim rounded in the flame and thickened, straight sides and two concentric coil base-rings.

12. C XXIX E XX D 9, A.D. 290–320. Rose Lane, occupation on Period II floor (vol. v, forthcoming). Part of a hemispherical bowl with linear and facet-cut decoration consisting of alternate vertical oval facets and fine lines, separated by a horizontal band of abraded lines from a design of circular facets and diagonal fine lines. Good colourless glass with flaking silver weathering, and strain cracks. These bowls were common in the Rhineland in the third century, and are quite frequently found in Britain. Six with similar designs are known from Verulamium (Nos. 48–53).[150]

13. C XXVIII C XX 39, late Saxon pit. Canterbury Lane (vol. vii, p. 102). *Diatretum* or cage-cup: part of vertical side with fine raised horizontal ridge and projecting openwork flange of ovolo pattern (edges missing but wheel cuts visible). Some silver weathering, especially in cutting.

   Diatreta were vessels of very great luxury, produced in the late third and early fourth centuries,[151] and only two other fragments have been identified in Britain – one from Silchester which has an openwork flange similar to the Canterbury piece,[152] and a small fragment of one mesh of network from Great Staughton, Huntingdon.[153] These vessels were blown, and the outside surface cut away to produce an openwork decoration consisting of one or more of the following: figures, an inscription frieze, a horizontal flange of ovolo pattern, a network cage of circular meshes. Apart from the Silchester fragment, several other fragments of deep bell-shaped colourless cups and a complete shallow bowl have features like this piece; these are known from Trier[154] and Tác-Fövenypuszta, Hungary,[155] and in the Constable-Maxwell collection.[156]

148. D. Charlesworth, *Journal of Glass Studies*, xiii (1971).
149. W.A. Thorpe, *English Glass* (London, 1949), Pl. VI b.
150. D. Charlesworth, in S.S. Frere, *Verulamium Excavations*, i (Oxford, 1972), 196–215.
151. The principal works on *diatreta* are (a) D.B. Harden and J.M.C. Toynbee, 'The Rothschild Lycurgus Cup', *Archaeologia*, xcvii (1959), 179–212; (b) O. Doppelfeld, 'Das Kölner Diatretglas', *Germania*, xxxviii (1960), 403–17; (c) D.B. Harden, *Journal of Glass Studies*, v (1963), 9–17.
152. For the Silchester cup, see Harden and Toynbee (*op. cit.*, note 151(a)), A 13.
153. For the Great Staughton fragment, see Harden (*op. cit.*, note 151(c)), B 13.
154. Harden and Toynbee (*op. cit.*, note 151(a)), A 12.
155. Harden (*op. cit.*, note 151(c)), B 17.
156. *The Constable-Maxwell Collection of Ancient Glass*: Sotheby's sale catalogue (London, June 1979), No. 41.

Mould-blown sports cup (Fig. 88)

14. C XV S II Pit 4, A.D. 110–130. South side of St. George's Street, pre-dating timber building below Apsed Building (vol. vii, p. 41). Rim fragment of cylindrical cup in mid-blue. Small curved rim, edge cracked off and ground smooth with inward bevel, vertical side with part of inscription in raised letters]EV̂A ⋋ PO[, with raised moulding below. Dull.

  Mould-blown cylindrical cups showing circus scenes are found in the western provinces of the Roman empire, and are most common at the military sites along the Rhine frontier and in Britain, where they often occur in Neronian to early Flavian contexts. They usually show chariots racing or gladiators fighting, and bear an inscription frieze, and either one or two main decorative friezes.[157]

  This fragment comes from a chariot cup with one main decorative frieze, and is closely comparable with one in greenish glass from Vindonissa (No. 6826)[158] which bears the inscription]EV̂A ⋋ POEN̦[and shows part of two horses approaching an obelisk from the left, and a charioteer with wreath in his right hand, driving a chariot with four-spoked wheels, and one horse together with the hind legs of three others, drawing away from the obelisk. It is virtually certain that the two pieces were produced from the same mould. Both pieces come from cups with an inscription similar to the nearly complete brown specimen from Mainz, formerly in the Sangiorgi collection,[159] and now in the Corning Museum of Glass (66.1.34), which reads OLYMPEVA FOENIXVA EVTYCH EVA M[, though this cup does not have a palm frond dividing OLYMPUS and FOENIX, the second charioteer's name begins with F, not P and the chariots have six-spoked wheels.

Nos. 15–35: Natural green glass (first and second century)

A. Bowls (Fig. 88)

15. C XVII E IV 18, A.D. 80–110. South of Marlowe Theatre, upper filling of pit (vol. v, forthcoming). Hollow tubular rim, iridescent. This is a long-lived type found throughout the Empire in the first and second centuries, and often surviving later. Complete examples include several in the British Museum,[160] and fragments occur at Verulamium.[161]

16. C X J I Ext. 2 (1), undated. South of St. George's Street, topsoil (vol. vii, p. 53). Hollow tubular rim, carinated body, tubular pushed-in base ring, convex base of shallow bowl or plate. Similar to No. 15, though shallow examples have not often been found in Britain.

17. C XXII K I Pit 7. King Street, Roman pit, *c.* A.D. 200–225 (this volume, p. 78). Rounded rim and shoulder of bowl or jar; cloudy weathering.

B. Bottles (Fig. 89)

These fragments are more easily identified because the thicker glass tends to survive in larger fragments, so the listed bottles reflect no true proportion in relation to other glass. In only a few examples can the shape of the body be identified. All are mould-blown unless otherwise noted.[162]

18. C XVII Y II 4 Pit 4, fourth century or later. Area Y south of Burgate Street (vol. vii, p. 121). Flattened in-folded rim.

19. C XVII E V 13B, medieval earth. South of Marlowe Theatre (vol. v, forthcoming). Flattened in-folded rim.

20. C XVII Y II 4 (14A), post-Roman earth. Area Y, south of Burgate Street (vol. vii, p. 123). Handle fragment.

157. See J. Price, 'Trade in Glass', in (Eds.) J. du Plat Taylor and H. Cleere, *Roman Shipping and Trade: Britain and the Rhine Provinces* (C.B.A., London, 1978), esp. pp. 73–4 and Figs. 54–5 for the distribution, and illustration of the main features of chariot- and gladiator-cups.

158. This fragment was not published in L. Berger, *Römische Gläser aus Vindonissa* (Basel, 1960). Dr Price is indebted to Dr D.B. Harden for information of its existence and for the loan of his plaster cast of the piece.

159. G. Sangiorgi, *Collezione di Vetri antichi* (Rome, 1914), No. 105.

160. D.B. Harden, K.S. Painter *et al., Masterpieces of Glass* (British Museum, 1968), No. 110.

161. *Op. cit.* (note 150), Nos. 6–10.

162. D. Charlesworth, 'Roman Square Bottles', *Journal of Glass Studies*, viii (1966), 26–40.

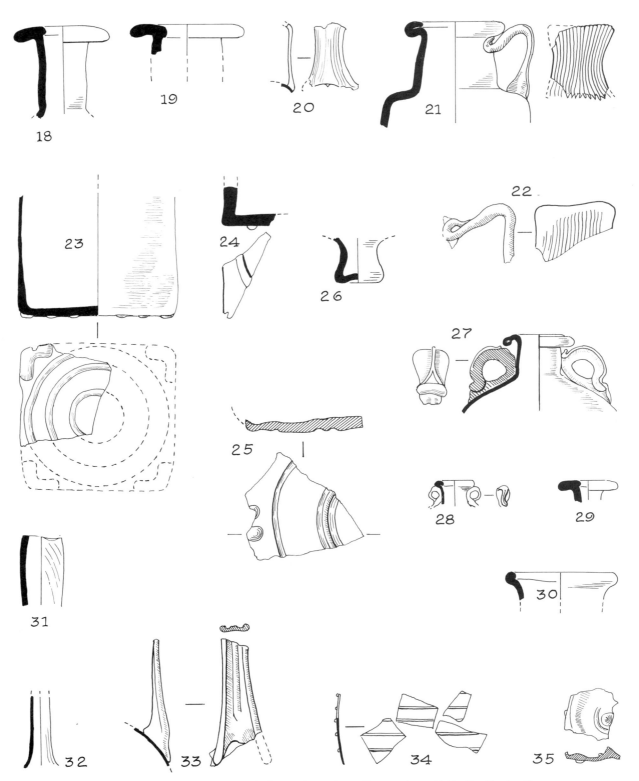

Fig. 89. Roman glass vessels from Canterbury Excavations 1946–60. (Scale: ½)

Six more fragments (not figured) come from:

(a) C XVII Y III 2 (28 = 40), A.D. 140–170. *Ibid.* Building east of Roman lane, occupation on gravel floor (vol. vii, p. 121).

(b) C XVII Y II 4 (19), second or third century. *Ibid.* Building west of lane, occupation on mortar floor.

(c) C XVII E IV 9, A.D. 310–340. South of Marlowe Theatre, rubble-filled trench in Period II house (vol. v, forthcoming).

(d) C XX E XII 2, A.D. 200–250. *Ibid,* road silt.

(e) C XXII C II 21, late Saxon cobbled floor in Canterbury Lane (vol. vii, p. 88).

(f) C XXIV Castle III 4, A.D. 270–290. Roman city bank (vol. ii, p. 54).

21. C XXVIII C XX 62, A.D. 180–220. Canterbury Lane, loam and chalk floor (vol. vii, p. 101). Square bottle with in-folded rim.

22. C XXVIII B I 9. Forum area, Period I demolition of hypocaust arch prior to rebuilding in second half of fourth century (this volume, p. 96). Handle of bottle, free-blown and flattened; another from C XVII E IV 14, A.D. 250–270. South of Marlowe Theatre, mortar floor of Period II building (vol. v, forthcoming).

23. C XII R I 24, A.D. 70–110. Building south of St. Margaret's Street Baths, pit cut by Period II wall-footings (vol. v, forthcoming). Square bottle with angular corner supports and parts of three concentric circles on base.

24. C XV S II Pit 4, A.D. 110–130. St. George's Street, below primary floor of timber building preceding Apsed Building (vol. vii, p. 41). Base fragment of square bottle showing part of one circle. Four more square bottle fragments (not figured) came from:

(a) C XXVII R IX 13, A.D. 150–200. Building south of St. Margaret's Street Baths, collapsed clay walling in eastern part of structure.

(b) C XV V I 3, second half of second century. South of St. George's Street, pit filling (vol. vii, p. 46).

(c) C XIV N I 4, *c.* A.D. 270–300. North-east corner of Iron Bar Lane – Burgate junction, pit (vol. vii, p. 117).

(d) C XV X III 19, fourth century. St. George's Lane, make-up (vol. vii, p. 135).

25. C XXVII R IX 13, A.D. 150–200 (as No. 24a). Part of base with sunk markings of two concentric circles, plain band and another circle, with possibly the remains of a letter in the outer zone. This may be barrel-shaped, rather than the normal first- to second-century square or cylindrical bottle. A cylindrical fragment came from C XV S II 34, A.D. 190–220. St. George's Street, occupation on floor of Period I timber building preceding Apsed Building (vol. vii, p. 41).

C. Miscellaneous (Fig. 89)

26. C IX A IV 2, A.D. 170–220. St. George's Street Baths, gully outside the building (vol. vii, p. 29). Half base of small unguent jar; some iridescence (Isings Form 68).

27. C X H 13, A.D. 100–140. West side of Canterbury Lane, black soil sealed by primary street-metalling (vol. vii, p. 76). Bath-flask or bottle with wide tubular rim rolled up and inward, short narrow neck, broad ring-handles applied to sloping shoulder and bent up, round and down to form circular opening, then trailed back along outside surface.

This probably comes from a large globular bath-flask (Isings Form 61, Fishbourne 82)[163] though it may belong to short-necked cylindrical bottle with ring-handles, both produced in the first to the third century A.D. Two similar handles come from:

(a) C XXVII R IX 13, A.D. 150–200. Building south of St. Margaret's Street Baths, collapsed clay walling in eastern part of structure (vol. v, forthcoming).

(b) C XXIV Castle III 13, fourth century. Accumulation on back of Roman city bank (vol. ii, pp. 55–6). Handle with part of rim and attached shoulder in blue-green glass.

28. C XVII Y I 1 (4), medieval. Area Y south of Burgate Street (vol. vii, p. 123). Small bath-flask with rim edge rolled inwards, cylindrical neck, thin ring-handle applied to shoulder and bent up to underside of rim, then down to shoulder to form circular opening (Isings Form 61). Fragments are quite often found in Britain, especially in drains and other deposits connected with bath-houses. They were used to carry the oil employed in

---

163. For these references, see notes 145 and 147.

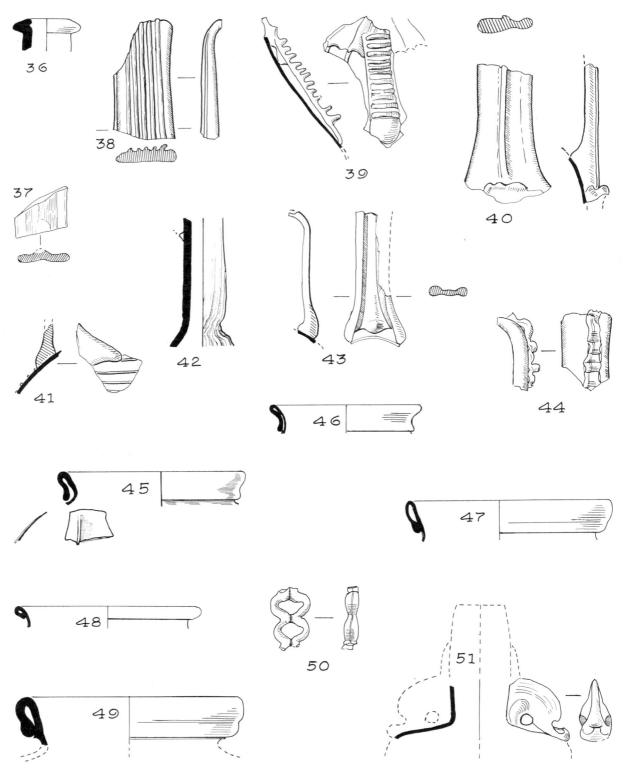

Fig. 90. Roman glass vessels from Canterbury Excavations 1946–60. (Scale: $\frac{1}{2}$)

the bath-house for massage after bathing. They were manufactured from the mid first until late in the third century, when decorated as well as plain examples were made.

29. C IX A IV 4, A.D. 170–220. St. George's Street Baths, gully outside the building (vol. vii, p. 29). In-folded, flattened rim of flask.

30. C XV X I 23, late fourth to fifth century. St. George's Lane, earth below Saxon layers (vol. vii, p. 135). In-folded rim of flask.

31. C X K I Pit 2, c. A.D. 80–140. North of St. George's Street (vol. vii, p. 62). Neck fragment in poor-quality bubbly glass; original rim apparently broken and the rough edges smoothed.

32. C XV T I 3, probably fourth century. St. George's Street, pit outside Apsed Building (vol. vii, p. 44). Small neck, narrowing upwards; iridescent.

33. C XXIV Castle III 23, A.D. 270–290. Tip in Roman City Bank (vol. ii, pp. 54–5). Handle, flat and thickened at edge. Clouded and slightly iridescent, with black impurities and yellow streaks.

34. C IX RY I 21, Flavian. Rose Yard, gravel floor beneath main Building (vol. v, forthcoming). Small fragment of bulbous vessel with horizontal trailing.

35. C XXIX E XX C 6, A.D. 320–330. Rose Lane, destruction of stone Building (vol. v, forthcoming). Four melted fragments of pushed-in tubular base-ring and concave (?) base with pontil mark.

Nos. 36–44: Flagons, c. A.D. 60–150 (Fig. 90)
The fragments are mainly from the handles of distinctive flagons made in the Seine/Rhine area.[164] There are two main divisions, those with globular and those with conical bodies. The deep blue flagons are probably Flavian.[165]

36. C XV X V Pit 8, late Saxon pit in St. George's Lane (vol. vii, p. 142). Deep blue rim, iridescent.

37. C X J I 2, A.D. 200–300. South of St. George's Street, Roman earth (vol. vii, p. 53). Flat handle fragment with central rib which has been knocked off; deep blue; iridescent.
     Also a deep blue neck-fragment from C XVII Y II 3 (22), early third century. Area Y south of Burgate Street, north–south Roman lane (vol. vii, p. 121).

38. C XX A I Pit 7, A.D. 270–300. Church Street, St. Paul's (this volume, p. 39). Reeded handle fragment, amber.

39. C XII Y II 2 (4), medieval earth. Area Y south of Burgate Street (vol. vii, p. 124). Lower sticking part, horizontally ridged, from handle of conical-bodied ribbed green flagon, iridescent. The long ridged tail is normal on the conical flagons.

40. C XXIV Castle III 24, A.D. 270–290. Tip in Roman City Bank (vol. ii, pp. 54–5). Part of handle with central rib, green, iridescent.

41. C XXVIII Castle XI 1, *ibid.* (vol. ii, pp. 56–8). Part of handle and body with twisted ribbing, yellow-green.

42. C XXX E XXI C 18, A.D. 110–140. Rose Lane, floor of Period I Building (vol. v, forthcoming). Part of neck and top of ribbed conical body, yellow-green. Also a neck fragment in yellow-green from C XVII Y III 3 (23), c. A.D. 180–210. Area Y south of Burgate Street, secondary metalling of north–south Roman lane (vol. vii, p. 121); and ribbed greenish body fragments from C XV X III 20, A.D. 270–350. St. George's Lane, occupation earth (vol. vii, p. 135).

43. C XXIV Castle II 8, late or post-Roman soil in Castle keep (vol. i, pp. 61–2). Lower part of amber handle.

44. C XXII F V 6, second-century earth. Marlowe Avenue Car Park. Part of flat handle with ridged trail along it, blue-green. (This volume, p. 125).

Nos. 45–49: Globular-bodied Jars, c. A.D. 70–150 (Fig. 90); see Isings Form 67c and Verulamium *i, Nos. 25–6.*

45. C IX RY I 21, Flavian. Rose Yard, gravel floor beneath main Building (vol. v, forthcoming). Fragments of 'collar' rim and ribbed side in deep blue, probably Flavian.

46. C XXVIII Castle XI 1, A.D. 270–290. Tip in Roman City Bank (vol. ii, pp. 56–8). Blue-green.

47. C XV X I 18, medieval earth. St. George's Lane (vol. vii, p. 137). Blue-green.

48. C XVII Y III Pit 4, post-Roman. Area Y south of Burgate Street (vol. vii, Fig. 49). Blue-green.

164. G. Faider-Feytmans, 'Les Verreries du Tumulus de Frizet' in *Études d'Histoire et d'Archéologie namuroises dédiées à Ferdinand Courtoy* (1952), 71–81.

165. D.B. Harden, *Antiq. Journ.*, xlvii (1967), 238–40.

49. C XXVII R XI 2, fourth-century floor of Portico south of St. Margaret's Street Baths (vol. v, forthcoming). Similar to No. 46 but thicker, highly iridescent.

Nos. 50–51: Flasks and Jugs, (Fig. 90) third to fourth century
50. C XXIX E XX D 9, A.D. 290–320. Rose Lane, occupation on Period II floor (vol. v, forthcoming). Chain handle fragment, slightly curved, formed from two vertical rods pinched together at intervals; greenish colourless glass, iridescent. Chain handles were applied to several second- to early fourth-century jug-forms found in the Rhineland, northern Gaul and Britain.[166] Some complete vessels occur in burials at Colchester[167] and Verulamium, but most pieces are very fragmentary, and the vessel-form cannot be identified.
51. C XVII E VI Pit 2, medieval. South of Marlowe Theatre (vol. v, forthcoming). Eyelet (dolphin) handle, greenish. One of a pair from the shoulder of a cylindrical or angular-bodied flask (Isings form 100). A similar handle was found at Verulamium (vol. iii, No. 275 (Fig. 68, No. 128)).

Nos. 52–56: Late fourth-century Beakers and Bowls (Fig. 91)
52. C X C II 7, A.D. 360–390. St. George's Street Baths, building debris in Room 7 (vol. vii, p. 35). Slightly everted knocked-off rim, faintly scratched line below and line on side. Yellow-green, iridescent.
53. C XXVIII C XX 33, medieval. Canterbury Lane (vol. vii, p. 102). Rim and body fragment of segmental bowl with faintly scratched line below rim; yellow-green, iridescent.
54. C XXXII S VII 15A, A.D. 300–400. Simon Langton Yard, Roman rubble (vol. v, forthcoming). Rounded rim of beaker, yellowish-green, clouded.
55. C XXVIII C XX 33, (as No. 53). Fire-rounded beaker rim fragment; greenish, iridescent.
56. C XXVI M I 11, late Saxon layer. Garden of 3 Watling Street. Beaker (?) rim, edge fire-rounded; amber, bubbly glass. (This volume, p. 120).

These beakers and bowls are common late fourth-century types.[168] The cracked-off and unworked rim occurs at an earlier date than the fire-rounded rim, but both are found in the last quarter of the fourth century.[169] The rounded rim, however, outlives the unworked type, and may be found on early fifth-century glass as well as on the typical Frankish or Saxon vessels.

Nos. 57–58: Flasks (Fig. 91), late fourth century
57. C XXI E XV III 3, late Saxon layer. East of Marlowe Theatre (vol. v, forthcoming). Outsplayed, almost flat rim fragment, rounded at the tip. Blue-green, an uncommon colour in the late fourth to early fifth century, when most glass was either yellow-green or greenish, and usually very bubbly.[170]
58. C XXXII S V 9, seventh-century Saxon hut 1. Simon Langton Yard (vol. v, forthcoming). Curved rod handle, greenish. The vessel's form is not certain, but the handle may come from a small flask found in late Roman contexts, as at Lankhills, Winchester[171] and Burgh Castle.[172]

166. C. Isings, *Roman Glass in Limburg* (Maastricht, 1971), Nos. 117–18, listing many complete and fragmentary examples.
167. *Masterpieces* (*op. cit.,* note 160), No. 111.
168. M. Vanderhoeven, *Verres romains tardifs et mérovingiens du Musée Curtius* (1958), Pl. XVIII 62–4 (conical beakers), Pl. X 45–6 (less common form with foot). Isings Form 116.
169. A group of late fourth- to early fifth-century vessels from Burgh Castle contains both rim forms. See D.B. Harden, 'Anglo-Saxon and later medieval Glass in Britain: some recent Developments', *Med. Arch.,* xxii (1978), Pl. IA: *idem* in S. Johnson, *Burgh Castle: Excavations by Charles Green 1958–61,* E. Anglian Archaeology Report No. 20 (Norfolk Archaeological Unit), 1983, 81–9.
170. *Vanderhoeven* (*op. cit.,* note 168), Pl. VIII 39 and Pl. IX 42 (from an inhumation at Celles) probably illustrate the complete vessel, both bluish glass, as more possibly does one with a cylindrical body from Andernach, O. Doppelfeld, *Römisches und frankisches Glas in Köln* (1966), No. 174.
171. G. Clarke, *The Roman Cemetery at Lankhills* (Oxford, 1978), Fig. 27 VI.
172. See note 169.

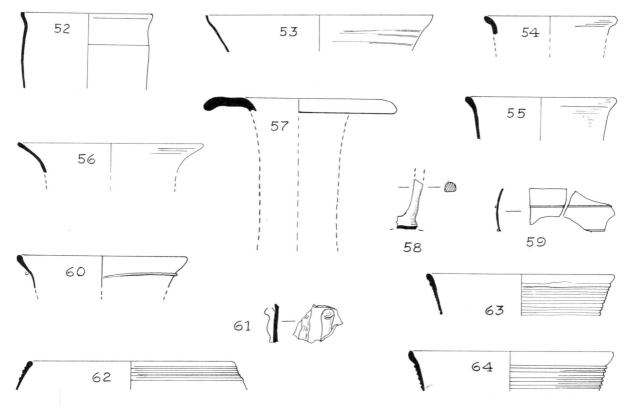

Fig. 91.   Roman glass vessels from Canterbury Excavations 1946–60. (Scale: ½)

Nos. 59–64: Miscellaneous coloured fragments (Fig. 91), mainly fifth-century; Nos. 59 and 60 were found in third-century contexts.

59.   C XV S II 20, A.D. 250–300. St. George's Street, Apsed Building, occupation on primary concrete floor (vol. vii, p. 44). Thin amber glass with tooled trails, striated; iridescent.

59a.   (not figured) C XV X I Pit 6, sixth century. St. George's Lane, Saxon pit (vol. vii, p. 141). Body fragment in deep green with opaque white marvered trails.[173]

60.   C X L I 11, A.D. 240–280. South side of Burgate Street, occupation in Period III Building (vol. vii, p. 112). Rim fire-rounded; olive green with pale blue trail, heavy flaking iridescence.[174]

61.   C XVII E IV 4c, early to middle Saxon layer. South of Marlowe Theatre (vol. v, forthcoming). Body fragment of cone or bag-beaker with tooled trails, yellow-green.[175]

173.   This metal is used, for example, for a flask and a bowl from St. Severin, Cologne (O. Doppelfeld, *Römisches und frankisches Glas in Köln* (1966), Nos. 170, 171, and, for a flask from Follais, Vanderhoeven (*op. cit.*, note 168), Pl. XVI 57.

174.   Brown or white trails are more common, but blue are used for instance on the Castle Eden claw-beaker (*Masterpieces* (*op. cit.*, note 160), 126) and on a flagon from Koninksem in the Musée Curtius (Vanderhoeven, *op. cit.*, note 168, Pl. XIII 52); also on late Roman vessels, Doppelfeld, *op. cit.* (note 170), 137, 139.

175.   D.B. Harden, 'Glass Vessels in Britain and Ireland A.D. 400–1000' in *idem* (Ed.), *Dark Age Britain* (London, 1956), 132–67, Type III or VI. Tooled trails on a funnel/cone beaker from Alfriston thought to be late Roman (Pl. XV a), and on bag beaker from Faversham (Pl. XVIII d).

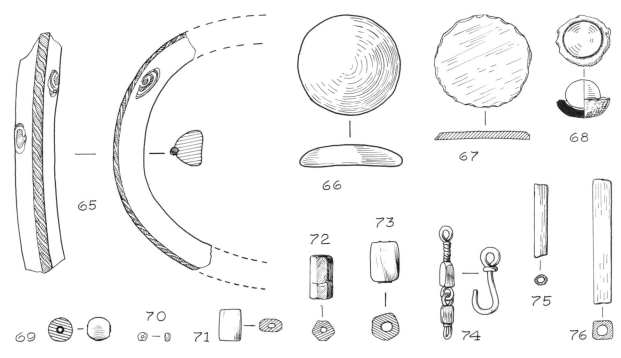

Fig. 92.   Roman glass objects from Canterbury Excavations 1946–60. (Scale: ½)

ITEM 63 ✓
62. C XV X I 22, mid fifth to sixth century. St. George's Lane, early Saxon occupation earth (vol. vii, p. 137). Fire-rounded rim and body fragment of convex curving bowl or jar. Pale greenish, with opaque white marvered trails; bubbly. The form has not been recognised, though the quality and decoration of the glass indicate a fifth-century date.

ITEM 62 ✓
63. *Ibid*. Fire-rounded rim and nearly cylindrical upper body with closely wound spiral trail, amber. Anglo-Saxon, most likely from claw-beaker, produced in the fifth to sixth century.[176]

ITEM 61 ✓
64. C XXIX E XX C Pit 2, post-Roman. Rose Lane (vol. v, forthcoming). Similar beaker to No. 63.

Nos. 65–76: Glass objects (Fig. 92)

65. C XIII CW 36, A.D. 100–180. Defences south of Riding Gate, pre-bank occupation material (vol. ii, p. 41).Bangle-fragment with D-shaped section. Blue-green, with blue and opaque white twisted-cord moulding at centre, and two oval blobs with blue and opaque white spirals.

This comes from a bangle of Kilbride-Jones type 2.[177] Many have been found at military sites in northern Britain in Flavian and later contexts. Fragments are also known from several sites in southern Britain; two from

176.   For Anglo-Saxon vessel forms see Fig. 25 in Harden, *op. cit.* (note 175); see also V.I. Evison, 'Anglo-Saxon Glass Claw-beakers', *Archaeologia*, cvii (1982), 43–76.

177.   These objects were studied by H.E. Kilbride-Jones, 'Glass Armlets in Britain', *Proc. Soc. Antiq. Scotland*, lxxii (1938), 366–95. See also R.B.K. Stevenson, 'Native Bangles and Roman Glass', *ibid.*, lxxxviii (1956), 208–21 and 'Romano-British Glass Bangles', *Glasgow Archaeological Journal*, iv (1976), 45–54, for additional information, especially relating to the evidence from northern Britain.

Fishbourne and others from Usk, as well as one from Valkenburg, Holland, come from pre- or very early Flavian contexts.[178]

66. C XIV M II 7, late third century. West side of Canterbury Lane, loam floor (vol. vii, p. 117). Gaming counter in turquoise glass. Others (not figured) were found on different sites, in green, blue and dark glass.

67. C XIV P I 4, undated Roman pit. South of St. George's Street (vol. vii, p. 62). Flat gaming counter with roughly cut edges in highly iridescent blue/purple glass, apparently re-used from the base of a vessel.

68. C XIII T I 2, post-Roman earth, south of Burgate Street (vol. vii, p. 130). Imitation jewel in natural greenish glass, set in a circular bronze bezel, perhaps from a bracelet.

69. C VII RY I 9, A.D. 340–360. Rose Yard, rubble from destruction of main Building (vol. v, forthcoming). Globular bead.
       Another from C XXIV Castle II 6, medieval layer in the keep, above Roman earth (vol. i, pp. 61–2). Diameter 0.5 cm.

70. C XVII Y III 3 (7), undated. Area Y south of Burgate Street, Roman earth (vol. vii, p. 129). Small annular green bead.
       Another from C XVI E I 2, A.D. 360–420. East of Marlowe Theatre, late Roman earth (vol. v, forthcoming). Diameter 0.35 cm.

71. C XXI E XV 1 (1), medieval. East of Marlowe Theatre, black soil (vol. v, forthcoming). Bead with rectangular section.

72. C XIV M II 4, A.D. 315–330. North-west corner of Iron Bar Lane – Burgate Street junction, chalk floor (vol. vii, p. 117). Long hexagonal bead in opaque pale green glass, threaded on bronze wire.
       Another (without wire) from C XXVII R XI 7, A.D. 180–240. Building south of St. Margaret's Street Baths, make-up for *opus signinum* floor (vol. v, forthcoming).

73. C X H 13, A.D. 100–140. West side of Canterbury Lane, dark soil below street surface 1 (vol. vii, p. 76). Hexagonal bead in opaque bright green glass, resembling an emerald.

74. C VII RY IB 9, A.D. 320–370. Rose Yard, collapsed building debris (vol. v, forthcoming). Bronze chain with loop terminal and separate hook for fastening, from a necklace or bracelet set with (two) polygonal glass beads. A gold chain necklace set with green glass beads was found in the St. Margaret Street Baths (publication in vol. v, forthcoming).

75. C XIII T III Pit 1, medieval. South side of Burgate Street (vol. vii, p. 133). Cylindrical bead in pale green opaque glass.

76. C XXIII C V A 7, A.D. 360–fifth-century. Canterbury Lane, black soil above destruction of Period III Building (vol. vii, p. 87). Long square-sectioned bead in bright blue opaque glass, dated by M. Guido to the third and fourth centuries.[179]

There was also a number of melon beads (not figured) in turquoise frit, dated by M. Guido to the first and second centuries A.D.[180]

178. For Fishbourne see *op. cit.* (note 147), Nos. 108–9. Usk, at present unpublished, from W.H. Manning's excavations. Valkenburg: S.M.E. van Lith, 'A Romano-British Glass Bangle from Valkenburg, ZH' in (Eds.) B.L. van Beck *et al.*, *Ex Horreo* (Amsterdam, 1977) (= *Cingula* iv), 130–4.
179. M. Guido, *The Glass Beads of the Prehistoric and Roman Periods in Britain and Ireland* (London, 1978), 96.
180. *Op. cit.* (note 179), 100.

IIID: THE POST-MEDIEVAL GLASS (Figs. 93–99)
(Sixteenth to Eighteenth Century)
by R.J. Charleston

The glass excavated at Canterbury shows a good average cross-section of the types found on English sites from the late sixteenth century until about 1800.[181] There is no material of clearly medieval date, and very little that can be definitely dated in the nineteenth century rather than the late eighteenth.

It is convenient to begin this survey with the Venetian or Venetian-style glass which dominated the upper end of the market from late medieval times until about 1675. Its distinctive characteristic was the use of a crystalline material fluxed with soda (from the salt-bearing plants which flourished round the Mediterranean littoral), which at its best was brilliant in surface-quality, capable of being worked into the thinnest and most fanciful forms, and often virtually colourless, although almost always having a faint greyish or brownish cast, usually more clearly discernible in the fracture. From as early as the opening years of the sixteenth-century Venetian glassmakers had migrated from their home base of Murano to a number of centres in Austria, France, etc., drawn – despite the heavy penalties imposed by the Venetian State on its defecting workers – by the rich rewards offered by European princes anxious to add this sought-after industry as a jewel in the crown of their countries' artistic achievements. Unfortunately, probably owing to differences in the raw materials available, *'façon de Venise'* glass did not always match up to the standards achieved in Murano. The Venetians were often obliged to take on natives as co-workers, and the results tended to be heavy-handed, and the material thicker and inferior to the Venetian. To distinguish between Venetian and *'façon de Venise'* is one of the most testing, and as yet unresolved, problems in the study of glass history.[182]

The dilemma faces one immediately with what are probably the earliest of the Canterbury glasses in this tradition (Fig. 93, No. 1). The art of Venetian glass-making had been brought to England already in the reign of Edward VI, but this apparently ephemeral episode was overtaken in significance during Queen Elizabeth I's reign by the establishment of a furnace in London by Jean Carré, an entrepreneur from the Low Countries. Arriving in 1567, he seems to have aspired to monopolize the whole glass industry in England, setting up or taking over simultaneously furnaces in the Weald of Surrey/Sussex for exploitation by the teams of Norman and Lorraine workers whom he had also introduced. These men, however, made mainly window-glass in the 'natural' green potash-glass of the 'forest' tradition. Carré died in 1572, and his London furnace for crystal-glass in the Venetian manner was ultimately taken over by Giacomo Verzelini, a Venetian by birth who had come to London by way of Antwerp, the most important centre of *'façon de Venise'* glass-making in northern Europe. In 1574, Verzelini obtained a monopoly of Venetian-style glass-making in England, and he continued in effective enjoyment of it until his retirement, probably in 1592. The fruits of his monopoly were then wrested from him and his sons by Sir Jerome Bowes, a courtier, and from Bowes in 1615 by a company which had obtained a monopoly of the use of coal for glass-making. Their control of the industry was assured by a proclamation of the same year banning wood as fuel, on grounds of timber-conservation. This company was finally taken over by one of its members, Sir Robert Mansell, who controlled the industry, with varying degrees of success, until the Civil War.[183]

A dozen or so of Verzelini's glasses, whole or fragmentary, have been identified, mainly by reason of their diamond-engraved English inscriptions or subject-matter. They seem to form a reasonably coherent group. Only one glass, however, seems to have survived from the time of Sir Jerome Bowes's patent (Barbara Potter's glass, dated 1603), and not a single example with decoration fixing it within the time-span of Sir Robert Mansell's reign has yet come to light. Some evidence, however, has been gleaned from archaeological sources, the best coming from the excavation of what must have been a glass-seller's store-room in Gracechurch Street, London.[184] The 'cut-off' date

181. R.J. Charleston, '16th-17th century English Glass', *Bulletin de l'Association internationale pour l'Histoire du Verre* (Liège, 1980), 77–95.
182. R.J. Charleston, 'Venetian Glass in the 17th-century', *Apollo* (Nov. 1979), 400–7.
183. See E.S. Godfrey, *The Development of English Glassmaking, 1560–1640* (Oxford, 1975), *passim*.
184. A. Oswald and H. Phillips, 'A Restoration Glass Hoard from Gracechurch Street, London', *The Connoisseur* (Sept. 1949), 30–6.

for this cache may have been the Great Fire (1666), but a number of the glasses found go back to the early years of the century, and this is probably true of the tall tapering 'cigar-stemmed' goblets which, by analogy with silver forms, may be dated to the period before the Civil War. Also in the Gracechurch Street hoard were found drinking-glass stems which had a ribbed hollow-blown 'knop' as a central feature,[185] an element which recurs frequently in the Verzelini *œuvre*, but which here has been reduced in size as one element in a tall stem answering the fashion for height exemplified in the 'cigar-stem' glasses. That the type had a longish life, however, seems demonstrated by the fact that a very similar glass occurs among the 'Greene drawings' (see below, p. 235) datable probably to 1667, although it was by this time evidently an outmoded shape (only a few dozen were commissioned, as against the hundreds of dozens of short-stemmed glasses ordered at the same time). Secondly, a glass of the same general stem-type survives with the date 1663 (the 'Royal Oak' goblet).[186] Both this and the Greene glasses, however, had flat-based 'bucket bowls', whereas the Canterbury stems (Fig. 93, Nos. 1–1a) were found with fragments of round-funnel bowls (No. 1b), a feature also of the Gracechurch Street 'cigar-stem' goblets. As to quality, the Greene glasses were Venetian-made, and the 'Royal Oak' goblet may perhaps have been so. The relatively heavy-handed nature of English-found fragments suggests that they were probably home-made.

A constantly recurring feature of Venetian glasses throughout the sixteenth and seventeenth centuries was the use of opaque-white (*lattimo*) threading as a means of decoration. A rim fragment, apparently of a wine-glass bowl, shows this feature (Fig. 93, No. 2), with a number of turns of mainly thin thread occurring in a band a little way below the rim. A wall fragment (No. 2a), of greyish-colourless crystal, shows a fine horizontal trail of eight turns. It may be supposed that horizontal trailing left proud of the surface was the first stage, and threading marvered in flush with the surface the second. No chronological indications, however, can be drawn from this, and the fragments Nos. 2b and 4, with threading incorporated in the base glass, are unlikely to be of a very different date from those already mentioned. They represent, however, a simple form of the more advanced techniques by which threads and twists were incorporated into the glasses they decorated, forming a virtual sheath of decoration over the whole surface, a system probably established well before the middle of the sixteenth century.[187] No examples of these more complex glasses were discovered, however, at Canterbury.

Another decorative technique, already referred to, was in use in Venice probably before 1540 and certainly continued in use there and elsewhere well into the seventeenth century. This was the use of the diamond-point for scratching designs on the glass, a technique perhaps taken over from the glazier, who was using diamonds to cut glass already in the fifteenth century. Only one fragment was found at Canterbury (No. 5), and that not in a style which can with any certainty be referred to the engraver of the Verzelini glasses (probably one Anthony de Lisle, a Frenchman). It seems to come from a flat glass, perhaps a *tazza*, of which one example probably referable to Verzelini has been found in the City of London.[188] The formal character of the engraving, with its simple hatching, suggests that, if not executed before 1600, it was made not long after.[189]

A well-recognized family of glasses with a distinctive type of decoration faces us with the question of origin in its most intractable form. The decoration was executed by wrapping a spiral ribbon of glass round the body of the vessel (usually starting below what was to become the pushed-in foot) then blowing the '*paraison*' (the glass vesica) into a mould with projecting ribbing which made vertical furrows across the trail.[190] This 'broken spiral trail' form of decoration varied in accordance with the thickness of the trail, the intervals at which the spiral turns occurred, and the spacing of the ribs in the mould. The technique appears to have been at home at least in Germany/Bohemia and the South Netherlands, but was probably even more widespread, for it appears in a simple form among the green glasses

185. *Ibid.*, No. 6; R.J. Charleston, 'Some Aspects of 17th-century Glass found in England', *Annales de l'Association internationale pour l'Histoire du Verre* (Liège) 7 (1978), 283–97, Fig. 3c.

186. Charleston, *op. cit.* (note 185), Fig. 6.

187. A. Polak, 'Venetian Renaissance Glass: the Problems of dating *vetro a filigrana*', *The Connoisseur* (Aug. 1976), 270–7.

188. I. Noël Hume, 'Tudor and early Stuart Glasses found in London', *The Connoisseur* (Aug. 1962), 272, Nos. 9–11.

189. W. Buckley, *Diamond Engraved Glasses of the 16th Century* (London, 1929), 7–8.

190. H. Tait, 'Glass with Chequered Spiral-Trail Decoration', *Journ. of Glass Studies*, ix (1967), 94–112.

made on a number of English 'forest' glasshouse sites dating from about 1600.[191] The examples found in excavations of English town-sites, therefore, may be of English origin, although they may equally be imports from the Netherlands, where their prevalence is attested by their frequent occurrence in still-life paintings of the middle years of the seventeenth century. They may well be considerably earlier,[192] however, as the English examples in green glass suggest. Two types frequently occur, and both are represented in the Canterbury excavations. The first is a cylindrical two-piece glass on which the trail occupies only the upper half of the beaker, the foot being a second '*paraison*' 'backed on' and left undecorated. It is represented at Canterbury by (Fig. 93) Nos. 6, 6a and probably 6b. It is not possible to say how many different glasses are represented by these fragments.

The second type of 'broken spiral trail' beaker has normally a greater diameter than the first type and is made in one piece standing on its own base, the centre of which is pushed in to form a low 'kick': this foot-rim is then strengthened and embellished by a thick thread of glass lapped round the basal angle, flattened underneath and then decorated by milling, usually with a 'rigaree', an instrument resembling a pastry-cook's wheel. The type is represented here by Nos. 7–9b.[193] The first four of these are rim-fragments and show not only the characteristic out-turned lip of this shape, but also the variation in the spiral threading already referred to.

Somewhat akin to this type of beaker is one which is virtually certainly of Continental origin. This is a beaker of hexagonal or octagonal bowl-section, immortalized in Rembrandt's famous self-portrait with Saskia (1638), now in the Gemäldegalerie at Dresden. These beakers are made of a single '*paraison*' with pushed-in foot, giving a pedestal base of double thickness, the 'kick' protruding into the base of the bowl.[194] They are often mould-blown with close diagonally 'wrythen' ribbing, and were long supposed to have been blown into polygonal moulds. It has recently, however, been shown that they were more probably made by thrusting into the tall cylindrical bowl a tapering tool of refractory material which in cross-section resembled an eight-point star, these points producing the angles of the polygon.[195] Fragments of such tools have been found on glass-making sites in Denmark (where beakers of this sort were made in green glass) and in the Hessian glass-making area of Germany. Similar glasses were made in Sweden, and since the glass-makers working in these Scandinavian glasshouses were themselves mainly of Hessian and Thuringian origin, the home of these technically distinct glasses is probably to be looked for in that area. The great predominance of this glass in the Netherlands, as indicated by its frequent appearance in Dutch *genre* and still-life paintings of the seventeenth century, is easily accounted for by the fact that the natural export route for the glasses produced in the southern parts of Germany was down the Rhine. It is established that the Dutch traders went to such entrepots as Cologne to purchase their glass supplies.[196] The Hessian glass-makers included 'English beer-glasses' among their stock lines, so it seems likely that they also aimed at the English market, although the beaker-type here dealt with is in fact fairly rare in England, and can hardly be identified with the 'English beer-glass'. The Canterbury fragment (Fig. 93, No. 10) is decorated with a blue milled thread, a feature which is by no means uncommon on these glasses.

Of a simpler character are beakers which have the applied milled foot-ring of the second 'broken spiral thread' type. An unusual example is to be seen in No. 11, which has not only mould-blown twisted ('wrythen') ribbing, but two horizontal milled bands laid round the glass at about a third of its height. This also diverges from the normal cylindrical shape of these beakers by expanding somewhat from base to rim. Further examples with mould-blown designs are Nos. 12–12c. One base fragment (No. 12a) had the applied foot-ring diagonally notched and flattened beneath to give the glass stability; and showed on the base a symmetrical design of four trident *motifs* together forming a rosette,[197] a common feature on such beakers when decorated by a diaper of raised blobs, one of which is

191. Charleston, *op. cit.* (note 181), 88–9.
192. Tait, *op. cit.* (note 190), 101.
193. Cf. Oswald and Phillips, *op. cit.* (note 184), 36, Nos. XV–XVI.
194. Cf. Tait, *op. cit.* (note 190), Fig. 2.
195. M. Schlüter, 'The Reproduction of octagonal Passglas found at Danish glasshouses from about 1660', *Annales du 8ᵉ Congrès de l'Association internationale pour l'Histoire du Verre* (Liège, 1981), 235–41.
196. Solms, Ernstotto Graf zu, *Geschichte der Glashütten des Laubacher Waldes* (Frankfurt a.M., 1956), 3–26.
197. Cf. R. Chambon, 'La Verrerie dans le Brabant Wallon au Début de la Renaissance', *Journ. of Glass Studies*, iii (1961), 39–49, Figs. 3–4.

preserved at the bottom of the wall of this fragment. The diaper is clearly observable in three framents from the same site (No. 12b); one a base-angle with a neat plain thread laid round it, the other two being a rim fragment showing a slightly out-turned lip, and a wall fragment, both decorated with a diaper of raised ovals. Another fragment (No. 12) came from a domed base with a large rough pontil-mark and was decorated with an applied notched thread and mould-blowing which appeared in the form of the rosette of four trefoils already referred to; here, however, the wall-decoration appears to have continued as vertical ribbing. A further variety of mould-blowing is exemplified in two small but joining fragments giving the shape of a slightly flaring rim (No. 12c). They are decorated with a clearly discernible raised mesh-pattern. A plain unpatterned example, but with milled foot-rim, is No. 12d. The colours of these fragments vary considerably, ranging from a brownish-colourless (No. 12b) to a markedly greenish tone (Nos. 12, 12a, c). The characteristics of all these pieces are matched by fragments from at least two glass-making sites in the Netherlands,[198] and the considerable number found at Plymouth, an obvious point of entry for imported goods, suggests that they may have been made on the Continent. There is nothing, however, to have stopped them being made in England, and examples found on English glass-making sites prove that at least the plain beaker with milled foot was made here in green glass, if not in a crystalline metal.[199] The very green tone of No. 12a may mark it out as an English 'forest-glass' production. The Netherlands factory-sites probably date from the late sixteenth century, and the English 'forest-glass' sites referred to probably span the turn of the sixteenth/seventeenth century. These glasses, therefore, are probably to be placed within this period.

A rim fragment of reasonably pure *cristallo* glass appears to derive from a small shallow dish (No. 13) of which a number have been identified on English sites in recent years.[200] It seems likely that these dishes were used for the service of fruits and sweetmeats at desserts.

The Civil War seems to mark in the glass-industry a watershed as pronounced as it did in politics. It is not really known what happened, but when the Restoration is reached it is evident not only that taste had changed but that there was a substantial import of 'crystal' glass from Venice. This situation is mirrored in the correspondence between the London glass seller John Greene and his supplier in Venice, Allesio (Alvise) Morelli, between the years 1667 and 1672 (British Library, Sloane Ms. 857).[201] Not only does this reveal the scale of the commerce, but, being accompanied by drawings,[202] it provides us with an exact notion of what glasses were fashionable about 1670. Apart from a few forms, intended no doubt to meet the demands of more old-fashioned customers (see p. 233 above), the Ms. reveals that the fashionable glasses of the time were funnel- or bucket-bowl goblets with short stems usually in the form of plain or ribbed spherical bulbs, with one or two discs interposed between bowl and stem, and stem and foot. Examples of such glasses are numerous in English excavations, and variations in quality suggest that if Greene got his supplies from Venice, others may have obtained them from the English glasshouses. Canterbury, too, provides its own quota of these glasses.

No. 14 is the base of a tapering bucket-bowl with a plain thread laid round the basal angle, with a plain hollow-blown spherical knop between 'mereses'. The shape may be reasonably confidently reconstructed. From the same general context came Nos. 15 and 16, the former having a vertically ribbed knop and a milled thread laid round the base, the latter being a ribbed knop with insufficient remaining above and below it to authorize a reconstruction of the bowl and foot forms.

An apparently new shape included in the Greene correspondence is a low tumbler, about as high as it is wide, apparently used for the consumption of brandy, and occasionally supplied in 'nests'. They are variously decorated, and a fragmentary example at Canterbury decorated with horizontal mould-blown ribbing (No. 17) seems to fit into

198. *Ibid.*, 41–3.
199. Rosedale (D.W. Crossley and F.A. Åberg, 'Sixteenth-century Glass-making in Yorkshire', *Post-medieval Archaeology*, vi (1972), 107–59, Figs. 60, 18–19). Hutton (*Ibid.*, Figs. 67, 111–2). A.G. Vince, *Newent Glasshouse* (Bristol, 1977), 15–16, Figs. 14–15.
200. S. Moorhouse, 'Finds from Basing House . . . Part ii', *Post-medieval Archaeology*, v (1971), 65–6, Fig. 27, No. 18; P.J. Huggins, 'Excavations . . . at Waltham Abbey, Essex, 1969–71', *Med. Arch.*, xx (1976), 86, 88, Fig. 31, No. 2; Nonsuch Palace (unpublished).
201. Transcribed in A. Hartshorne, *Old English Glasses* (London and New York, 1897), 440–51.
202. See *Ibid.*, Pls. 30–32; W.A. Thorpe, *History of English and Irish Glass* (London, 1929), 113–5; Thorpe, *English Glass* (London, third ed., 1961), 172–3.

this category. Comparable beakers are occasionally found in Netherlands *genre* paintings, and examples have been found at Nottingham from suitably dated contexts.[203]

A number of the more decorative items among Greene's commissions to Morelli were to be made in 'enamel' (or opaque-white) glass; and an example of this type of glass, if not made in one of the Greene shapes, is to be found at Canterbury (No. 18, a neck fragment with out-turned lip). In the same general category, much employed at Venice although not specified in Greene's orders, is the opalescent glass called by the Venetians *'girasol'* in the eighteenth century. Of this material is a base fragment probably of a cylindrical beaker (No. 19) with a low domed 'kick' and a plain thread applied round the base: this piece was probably decorated with mould-blown ribbing.

Of a decorative type of glass popular at the end of the seventeenth century is the handsome amethyst flask No. 20; it is also of a shape found in other coloured glasses excavated in a late seventeenth-century context (Hereford).

Not easily classifiable are a curved fragment, apparently from the neck of a flask, of a brownish glass decorated with several turns of horizontal trailed thread (No. 21a), and an enigmatic colourless fragment (No. 21b), with a raised oval formation, to which no parallel seems to be known, and a series of 'hatched' lines which may possibly be inscribed with a diamond-point (cf. p. 235).

If Venice was the main supplier of imported glasswares into England, there was also a steady trickle of green glasses from Germany, very probably from the Hessian glasshouses to which allusion has already been made. From an early date (fifteenth century) the prunted drinking-glasses generally called *'Nuppenbecher'* had been reaching England, to be replaced in the late sixteenth or seventeenth century by the similarly decorated *'Roemer'*, a goblet with flaring (later ovoid) bowl giving into a hollow cylindrical stem decorated with prunts and standing on a conical foot normally made from a single spiral thread.[204] At Canterbury No. 22 (Fig. 94) represents the type, being the bottom of the stem, with part of a moulded 'raspberry prunt' still adhering, and a trace of what was probably the normal 'spun' foot showing at the bottom of the fragment. Three fragments (No. 23) of a far less normal type come from two intersecting pits on the Roman Theatre site. Although they do not fit together, they seem to belong to the same vessel, which would have had a cylindrical upper portion of approximately 9 cm. diameter, encircled by several turns of applied threading. The uppermost turn, lying along the rim, has been pinched up into a series of projections along the tops of which another substantial thread has been run to form an openwork top. Below the threaded zone there was an area with prunted decoration, two of the small prunts still surviving. There seem to be no obvious Continental parallels for this configuration – indeed, it is difficult to imagine why a rim should be decorated in this way unless the vessel was some kind of puzzle-glass – but the technique is to be seen used for decorative purposes on the body of several surviving German beakers datable to the early years of the sixteenth century;[205] and for the openwork foot of another type of drinking-glass dated to the second quarter of the sixteenth century.[206]

Most of the green glass used in this period (sixteenth to seventeenth century), however, apart from these sophisticated import types, was made in the country itself,[207] as it had been since medieval times – thinnish glass bottles with globular body, tapering neck and funnel-mouth, often cut off aslant; urinals with rounded base showing the pontil-mark underneath, and having either a globular body and straight neck or a piriform body with tapering neck, but in either case a wide flat rim sometimes turned up at the edge; lamps (not represented at Canterbury); and smaller vials.

The old-fashioned thin-walled bottle, often with mould-blown vertical ribbing, usually most evident on the neck, continued in use (it seems) well into the seventeenth century. At Canterbury the type is represented by several characteristic examples of both necks and bases (Nos. 24–28), showing the enamel-like brownish weathering which normally occurs on this class of glasses, and occasionally 'wrythen' mould-blown ribbing (Nos. 29–30). A variant is

203. R.C. Alvey, 'A Cess-pit Excavation at . . . Nottingham', *Trans. Thoroton Soc. of Nottinghamshire*, lxxvii (1973), 58–70, Nos. 16–19, especially No. 19.
204. A-E. Theuerkauf-Liederwald, 'Der Römer, Studien zu einer Glasform', *Journ. of Glass Studies*, x (1968), 114–55; *Ibid.*, xi (1969), 43–69.
205. F. Rademacher, *Die Deutschen Gläser des Mittelalters* (Berlin 1933), Pls. 44 a, b; 48 a, b; 49 a.
206. *Ibid.*, Pl. 57 c–d.
207. Charleston, *op. cit.* (note 181), 84–9.

presented by No. 31, which is probably the neck belonging to the base fragment No. 31a (not illustrated). The 'cut-out' construction of this base, producing a foot-ring from the same single *paraison* of glass, copies a technique first seen in this country (as far as bottles are concerned) in imported Venetian *cristallo* flasks of *c.* 1500 and later. Not to be anticipated before the latter part of the sixteenth century, and continuing probably throughout the seventeenth century, is the short-necked bottle normally blown in a mould to produce a square or polygonal container. When square on plan, the flask was probably intended for putting up in a wooden container of four or more compartments – a 'case' bottle – for the transport of spirits, etc., especially by sea. In the absence of enough wall or base fragments, however, it is impossible to say whether one of these short necks derives from a case-bottle or a more than ordinarily large 'apothecary's vial' (Nos. 32–32b). Canterbury did, however, produce one hexagonal flask with slightly indented sides (No. 33), of a general type known to have been produced in the English 'forest-glass' furnaces (intact example from the Woodchester glasshouse site, dating from the years about 1600).[208]

More commonly found on sixteenth- to seventeenth-century sites, and represented at Canterbury by one or two intact examples, are the small vials for apothecaries' use, but certainly more generally used for a variety of purposes. By the end of the sixteenth century, they had probably already attained the cylindrical shape which they were to keep for at least a further three centuries, but their rounded shoulder (e.g. No. 34) tended in the seventeenth century to straighten out to give the workaday form which they kept into the present century (e.g. No. 38).[209]

In the apothecary's shop such flasks, in a great range of sizes, were used for liquid medicaments. For more solid preparations, such as ointments, the old pottery form of the *albarello* was translated into glass, often reproducing faithfully the waisted shape of the ceramic original, but often translating it into a plain cylinder (matching the 'vial') with rounded shoulder and wide out-turned neck, round which the customary paper or vellum cover could be secured with twine. At Canterbury the form occurs in a mesh-moulded fragment (No. 40), the shape of which can be matched in an intact London example in the Victoria and Albert Museum. In due course this form, like the vial, was translated into clear colourless glass, the making of which, for Excise purposes (after 1745/6), was restricted to the 'flint-glass' houses (p. 240 below). An undecorated example occurs at Canterbury (No. 41).

Of urinals, contrary to the general rule, the Canterbury excavations seem only to have produced a single rim fragment (No. 42) rather than the thicker and more durable base which usually survives.

If all these types of home-produced glass are in varying degrees direct descendants of medieval types, one sort of green glass not apparently found much before the middle of the sixteenth century is the drinking-glass. William Harrison in his *Description of England* (1577), in a well-known passage, wrote: '. . . The poorest also will have glass if they may; but sith the Venetian is somewhat to deere for them they content themselves with such as are made at home of ferne and burned stone.' This seems to correspond with the known archaeological facts, for no fragments of such glasses appear to occur on glasshouse sites dating from before the mid-sixteenth century, whereas thereafter they are a standard production, their pushed-in bases, made in a single piece with the body of the glass, being almost the type-fossil for sites of the late sixteenth to early seventeenth century. Canterbury examples may be seen in Nos. 43–46 (Fig. 98). Most display the customary vertical mould-blown ribbing (sometimes spirally 'wrythen' – Nos. 47–49), but one has the less usual embellishment of a diaper of mould-blown ovals (No. 50). Most seem to follow the usual pattern of a cylindrical body very slightly drawn in towards the rim (Nos. 48–50). The 'broken spiral trail' type of beaker (pp. 234–5 above) in green glass seems not to be represented at Canterbury.

By far the most important innovation in English green glass manufacture, however, was the invention, possibly in the 1630s, of the thick glass beer- or wine-bottle for both storage and transport. To this quality of relative indestructibility it added a second of being also relatively impervious to light, a factor which encouraged its use in the laying-down of wine. This development, however, could not take place before a convenient instrument for removing corks had been discovered. The corkscrew ('bottle screw') is mentioned in 1681, and may have existed some time before this date. The qualities mentioned above ensured the English wine-bottle a vast market on the Continent, and it was probably for long the most important type of glass, in economic terms, made in England. Starting as a globular-bodied, long-necked vessel with a diminutive 'kick' in the base, it underwent in the course of the eighteenth century a number of changes until with the cylindrical bottle, capable of being binned on its side, and having a deep

208. Godfrey, *op. cit.* (note 183), Pl. IV c.
209. I. Noël Hume, 'A Century of London Glasses', *Connoisseur Year Book*, (London, 1956), 100 ff.

kick or 'punt', the ideal shape was attained.[210] This evolution can be approximately followed in the Canterbury examples (taken in date order, Nos. 52–59, Fig. 97).

If by and large the English bottle captured the Continental market, there were still a number of Continental bottles which reached England during the eighteenth century. These came in for the sake of their contents. Two of the main types, both found at Canterbury, were the Pyrmont water-bottle (No. 63), usually distinguished by a seal (No. 64) stamped with the arms of the Prince of Waldeck, in whose territory the Pyrmont spring was; and the 'betty' (a corruption of 'bottiglia') in which 'Florence wine' (from the Chianti area) was imported (Nos. 65, 65a, b). These last were probably usually covered and protected by a rush jacket which has normally disappeared, although traces of it may be discernible. Like its modern jacketed counterpart, the 'betty' was unstable without the support of its covering.[211]

In the last quarter of the seventeenth century a profound change came over European glass-making, undermining the dominance which Venice had exercised since the fifteenth century. Instead of the lightness of touch and thinness of material on which the Venetians had relied for their pre-eminence, absolute clarity of material (Venetian *cristallo* was seldom completely colourless) and a solidity recalling rock-crystal became the desired qualities. In Central Europe this aspiration was realised by a refinement of the potash-lime glass current there by the addition of a quota of chalk or other calcium: this provided the ideal glass for the wheel-engraving and wheel-cutting which were perfected there (exemplified at Canterbury by No. 66). In England, the same end was achieved by the development of 'flint glass', a misnomer for a glass partially fluxed by oxide of lead. This 'discovery' is credited to George Ravenscroft, who had worked out the formula by about 1676 and perfected it by 1677–78. He signalised his improved metal by the addition to his glasses of a small seal stamped with a raven's head, from his family arms. This habit was followed by others making the new 'crystalline' glasses (Ravenscroft's patent lapsed in 1681), and the Canterbury finds include one wine-glass stem (No. 67) stamped with an S, variously interpreted as that of the Salisbury Court glasshouse, the Southwark glass-house, or possibly the Savoy glass-house when not actually in use by Ravenscroft.[212] Its date is probably between 1676 and 1680. A second Canterbury fragment (No. 68) comes from a similar wine-glass with the lobed inverted-baluster stem common to most glasses of this period: its improved metal, free from the defect of 'crizzling' (internal cracking) afflicting No. 67, suggests a date about 1680–85. By 1690, the English 'glass of lead', made by adding increasing quantities of lead to the batch, was fully developed, and a small number of wine-glass stems (Nos. 69–71) reflect the favoured forms of this – the 'baluster' – period in English glass-making (late seventeenth to early eighteenth century). One 'drawn-stem' fragment with enclosed air-bubble probably belongs to the first, or at latest the second, quarter of the eighteenth century (No. 72).

In the course of the eighteenth century the use of the new lead 'metal' (perhaps slightly modified) was extended to the cylindrical apothecaries' phials (Nos. 73–73c), the manufacture of which in colourless glass was restricted to the 'flint' glasshouses.

Of the coloured glasses made in the eighteenth century Canterbury produced one example – the ribbed foot No. 74, in blue metal, no doubt from a small bowl.

CATALOGUE OF POST-MEDIEVAL GLASS

H. = Height; D = Diameter, W. = Width.
The volume nos. cited are those of *The Archaeology of Canterbury* in which the sites are published.

1. Wine-glass stem, greyish-colourless glass with slight surface weathering, consisting of central hollow-blown ribbed knop (16 ribs), above which is a small baluster and below which is a tall thin capstan joining it to the foot

210. I. Noël Hume, 'The Glass Wine Bottle in colonial Virginia', *Journ. of Glass Studies*, iii (1961), 91–117.
211. *Ibid.*, 109–10.
212. R.J. Charleston, 'George Ravenscroft: New Light on the Development of his "Christalline Glasses"', *Journ. of Glass Studies*, x (1968), 161. D.C. Watts, 'How did George Ravenscroft discover Lead Chrystal?', *The Glass Circle*, ii (1975), 75–6.

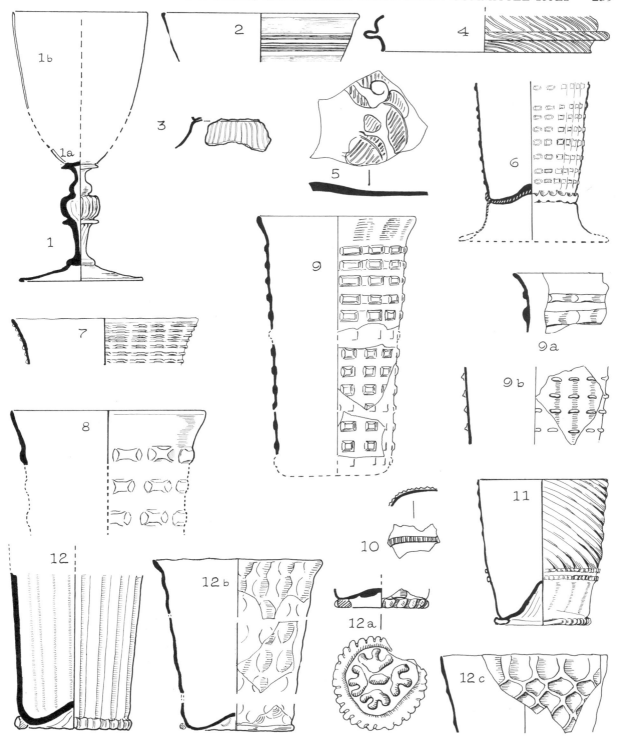

Fig. 93. Post-medieval glass vessels from Canterbury Excavations 1946–60. (Scale: ½)

which has a folded edge. H. 6.5 cm. D. of foot 6.6 cm. Probably second quarter of seventeenth century. Vol. v: C VII RY I 4. Rose Hotel Yard. Late seventeenth-century black earth.

1a. Stem similar to No. 1 though with incomplete foot; the baluster can be seen joining the knop to a fragment of bowl (added to No. 1). *Ibid.*

1b. Fragments of a bowl which may belong to Nos. 1 or 1a (added to No. 1). *Ibid.*

2. Rim-fragment of beaker, greenish-colourless glass decorated with eight applied thick and thin threads of opaque-white glass partially marvered into the surface. H. 3 cm. D. 9 cm. (approx.). Sixteenth to seventeenth century. Vol. v: C XII RY IV 2. Rose Hotel Yard. Clay layer, first half of seventeenth century.

   (a) (not figured). Fragment of greyish-colourless glass with beige enamel-like weathering, and fine horizontal trail of opaque-white threading (8 turns). H. 3.5 cm. Sixteenth to seventeenth century. vol. v: C XXVIII A I 1. St. Margaret's Street, Conservative Club Garden soil.

   (b) (not figured). Two curved wall fragments of thin (approx. 1 mm.) greyish *cristallo* with spaced-out embedded *lattimo* stripes. D. approx. 7.5 cm. Vol. v: C XII RY IV Pit 3. Rose Hotel Yard. Seventeenth-century pit.

3. Fragment of base of a beaker, colourless glass with decoration of vertical opaque-white (*lattimo*) stripes, with flaky silvery/iridescent weathering. Probably cylindrical beaker of approx. D. 6.5 cm. H. 2.3 cm. Sixteenth to seventeenth century. Vol. v: C VII RY I 2. Rose Hotel Yard. Eighteenth-century black earth.

4. Three fragments of a cover from a goblet, greyish *cristallo* with opaque-white thread decoration of plain stripes. D. approx. 9 cm. Probably first half of seventeenth century. This volume: C XXVI W V Square 20 (1). Whitehall Road, topsoil.

5. Cream/iridescent enamel-like weathering on fragment tapering in thickness (perhaps centre of a *tazza*?). Diamond-point engraved with hatched leaves. *c.* 1580–1620. *Britannia*, i (1970): C XVI D I Pit 1. Roman Theatre. Seventeenth-century wall-lined pit.

6. Foot/body fragment of beaker, dark greenish-grey *cristallo*, with iridescent weathering and 'broken spiral trail decoration' (24 ribs, 8 turns of trail). H. 8 cm. D. approx. 6 cm. *c.* 1600–50. Vol. v: C XII RY IV Pit 3. Rose Hotel Yard. Seventeenth-century pit.

   (a) (not figured). Fragment of similar beaker with thinner trail. Approx. internal D. 6.5 cm. *c.* 1600–50. Vol. vii: C XVII Y II 2 (1). Area Y. Mid seventeenth-century yard metalling.

   (b) (not figured). Rim fragment of cylindrical beaker of apparently colourless glass with creamy/iridescent weathering, with 'broken spiral trail' decoration. Approx. D. 6.5 cm. *Britannia*, i (1970): C XVII D IV 3. Roman Theatre site.

7. Rim fragment of beaker, greenish-colourless glass, with thin brown weathering and 'broken spiral trail' decoration. H. 2.5 cm. D. 9 cm. Vol. vii: C XXVIII C XX Pit 2. Canterbury Lane. Pit with late sixteenth-century pottery.

8. Rim fragment of beaker, greyish-colourless glass with overall iridescent weathering and 'broken spiral trail' decoration. H. 3 cm. D. of rim 10 cm. (approx.). *c.* 1600–50. Vol. v: C XII RY IV 2. Rose Hotel Yard. Clay layer, first half of seventeenth century.

9. Lip and body fragments of beaker, slightly greenish *cristallo* with patchy beige weathering and overall iridescent film, with 'broken spiral trail' decoration. Rim D. approx. 9 cm. *c.* 1600–50. Vol. vii: C XVII Y II 2 (1). Area Y. Mid seventeenth-century yard metalling.

9a. Lip fragment of greyish-colourless *cristallo*, with 'broken spiral trail' decoration. D. approx. 8.6 cm. *Ibid.*

9b. 'Broken spiral trail' wall-fragment of beaker, yellowish-colourless (?) covered with overall beige/iridescent weathering. *c.* 1600–50. *Britannia*, i (1970): C XVII D IV 7. Roman Theatre site: loam floor of seventeenth-century building corresponding to *ibid.*, Fig. 4, Section A–B, layer 44.

10. Wall fragment of polygonal *Passglas*, with applied milled blue thread. *c.* 1600–50. This volume: C XXVIII B I 2. Fleur de Lis Yard. Dark soil below modern yard metalling.

11. Fragmentary beaker, greyish-colourless glass, with mould-blown ribbing and applied milled bands. H. 7.9 cm. Probably first half of seventeenth century. Vol. v: C XII RY IV Pit 1. Rose Hotel Yard. Seventeenth-century pit.

12. Two fragments of mould-blown cylindrical beaker, greenish-grey glass, with notched applied thread round base, rosette pattern on base and vertical ribbing. D. approx. 7 cm. Late sixteenth/seventeenth century. Vol. vii: C XVII Y II 2(1). Area Y. Mid seventeenth-century yard metalling.

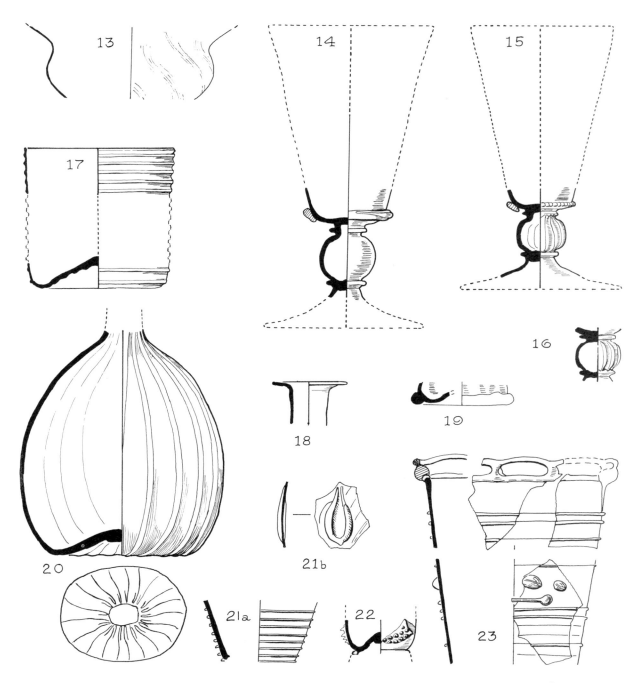

Fig. 94.   Post-medieval glass vessels from Canterbury Excavations 1946–60. (Scale: $\frac{1}{2}$)

12a. Base of mould-blown cylindrical beaker, greenish glass, with one raised blob showing on the wall, and an applied trail at basal angle, flattened underneath and diagonally notched; rosette pattern on base. D. 5 cm. Late sixteenth/seventeenth century. *Ibid.*

12b. Base fragment of mould-blown cylindrical beaker, with neat plain thread applied round base, brownish-colourless glass with some iridescent weathering. Mould-blown with diaper of raised dots. Approx. D. 5 cm. *Ibid.*

Two further fragments, apparently from same beaker, brownish, unweathered. One a rim fragment. Rim D. approx. 9 cm. Late sixteenth/seventeeth century. *Ibid.*

   (c)   Two small wall fragments of cylindrical beaker (?), one apparently a rim fragment, slightly greenish with beige/iridescent weathering and mould-blown mesh design. D. approx. 9 cm. *Ibid.*

   (d)   (not figured) Foot fragment of a cylindrical beaker, probably originally colourless glass, now with overall iridescent weathering; low 'kick', with an applied 'rigaree' band round the foot. D. 6.5 cm. (approx.). H. 1.2 cm. Vol. v: C XII RY IV 1A. Rose Hotel Yard. Dark soil, late seventeenth to early eighteenth century.

13. Rim fragment of a (?)dish, greyish-colourless glass with pronounced striations, thin patchy brown weathering and iridescence overall. D. of *cavetto* approx. 9 cm. Sixteenth/seventeenth century. Vol. v: C VII RY I 4. Rose Hotel Yard. Late seventeenth-century black earth.

14. Fragment of a (?)beer-glass, greyish-colourless unweathered glass. Flat-based conical bucket-bowl with plain thread round the base; hollow-blown spherical knop above conical foot. H.6 cm. *c.* 1670. *Ibid.*

15. Fragment of a (?)wine-glass, greyish-colourless glass with slight surface iridescence. Flat-based conical bucket-bowl with 'rigaree' band round base; hollow-blown stem made in a ribbed mould (11 ribs). H. 4.8 cm. *c.* 1670. *Ibid.*

16. Knop from the stem of a wine-glass, greyish-colourless glass, hollow-blown in a ribbed mould (11 ribs), and connected by mereses to the bowl above and the foot below. The foot shows traces of a pontil-scar. H. 3 cm. *c.* 1670. *Ibid.*

17. Rim and base fragments of a beaker, colourless glass with thin iridescent weathering, decorated with horizontal mould-blown ribbing. Cylindrical form of undetermined height, the base with low 'kick'. D. of base 8 cm. H. of rim fragment 2.7 cm, of base 1.7 cm. (to top of 'kick'). *c.* 1670. Vol. vii: C XIX Z II 1. South side of St. George's Street. Seventeenth-century building rubble.

18. One opaque-white neck. D. approx. 4 cm. H. 2.5 cm. Sixteenth to seventeenth century. *Britannia*, i (1970) and vol. vii, Appendix 1: C XVII D III Pit 2. Roman Theatre site. Eighteenth century.

19. Base-fragment of (?)beaker, opaline glass with bluish iridescent weathering. Slightly 'kicked' base, probably of a cylindrical beaker, with a plain applied thread round the angle of base with side. Probably blown in a ribbed mould. D. 5.5 cm. approx. (to edge of thread). Seventeenth century. Vol. v: C VII RY I 4. Rose Hotel Yard. Late seventeenth-century black earth.

20. Fragmentary flask of purple glass, blown in a ribbed mould (20 ribs) and flattened; slightly 'kicked' base. W. of base (point of contact) 5.5 cm. Second half of seventeenth century. Vol. v: C VII RY I 5. Rose Hotel Yard. Eighteenth-century pit.

21a Light-brown, thickish (1.5/2 mm.) (?)neck-fragment with self-coloured trail (7 turns). H. 3.5 cm. Uncertain origin and date. Vol. vii: C XV X VI 6. Bus Station site.

21b Wall fragment of colourless glass with applied dragged oval, applied threads and hatched lines, possibly by diamond-point. H. 3.5 cm. Uncertain origin and date. Vol. v: C XIII R IV 1. Fountain Hotel site, St. Margaret Street. Black garden soil.

22. Fragment of *Roemer* stem, pale green, with fragment of raspberry prunt. D. of 'foot-rim' approx. 3.5 cm. Second half of seventeenth century. Vol. v: C XII RY IV Pit 1. Rose Hotel Yard. Seventeenth-century pit(?).

23. (i)   Bluish-green fragment with iridescent weathering. Rim-thread. See No. 23 (ii). *Britannia*, i (1970), and vol. vii, Appendix 1: C XVI D I Pit 1. Roman Theatre site. Seventeenth-century wall-lined pit.

23. (ii)   Bluish-green fragment with iridescent weathering. Perhaps belongs to previous fragment. The rim-thread has been pinched up into two points, on top of which has been laid a thread. See No. 23 (iii). *Britannia*, i (1970), and Vol. vii, Appendix 1: C XVI D I Pit 2, cut by Pit 1; with pre-seventeenth-century pottery.

23. (iii)   Bluish-green fragment, almost unweathered, perhaps belonging to previous two, but from lower down. Being unweathered, this glass looks bluer than the previous two fragments. Perhaps sixteenth century. C XVI D I Pit 2. *Ibid.*

24. Rim fragment of bottle, green glass with thick encrusted brown weathering. H. 4.3 cm. D. approx. 6.5 cm. Sixteenth to seventeenth century. Vol. v: C XII RY IV 2. Rose Hotel Yard. Clay layer, first half of seventeenth century.

25. Neck-fragment of bottle, light green glass with thick layer of brown weathering (or adherent earth). H. 4.2 cm. D. 5.3 cm. Sixteenth to seventeenth century. Vol. v: C XII RY IV 1. Rose Hotel Yard. Dark soil, first half of seventeenth century.

26. Bottle-neck, pale green glass with spotty brown weathering. D. 5 cm. Sixteenth to seventeenth century. Vol. v: C XII RY IV Pit 3. Seventeenth-century pit.

27. Bottle-neck of pale green glass with silvery iridescent weathering, black in patches. H. 10.7 cm. D. 4.3 cm. Sixteenth to seventeenth century. Vol. v: C XII RY IV 1. Rose Hotel Yard. First half of seventeenth century.

28. Bottle-neck, pale green with patchy brown weathering. H. 9.5 cm. D. 2.5 cm. Sixteenth/seventeenth century. Vol. vii: C XVII Y II 2 (1). Area Y. Mid seventeenth-century yard metalling.
    (a) (not illustrated). Rim fragment of bottle, brownish glass with heavy grey-brown weathering. H. 2.5 cm. D. approx. 2.5 cm. Sixteenth to seventeenth century. Vol. v: C XII RY IV 2. Rose Hotel Yard. Clay layer, first half of seventeenth century.
    (b) (not illustrated). Base fragment of bottle, brownish almost colourless glass with thick brown weathering. Domed base of irregular profile. W. 6 cm. Sixteenth to seventeenth century. *Ibid.*
    (c) (not illustrated). Base fragment of bottle, pale-green glass with grey-green mottled enamel-like weathering. Domed 'kick' of irregular profile, with traces of ring-pontil in dome. W. 8 cm. Sixteenth to seventeenth century. *Ibid.*

29. Bottle-neck, very pale green with beige enamel-like weathering and 'wrythen' mould-blown ribbing. D. approx. 5 cm. Sixteenth to seventeenth century. Vol. v: C XII RY IV Pit 3. Rose Hotel Yard. Seventeenth-century pit.
    (a) (not illustrated). Neck fragment of bottle, yellowish glass with thick black enamel-like weathering. Cylindrical neck with irregular 'wrythen' mould-blown ribbing. H. 7 cm. Sixteenth to seventeenth century. Vol. v: C XII RY IV 1. Rose Hotel Yard. First half of seventeenth century.
    (b) (not illustrated). (?)Neck fragment of large 'wrythen' ribbed bottle, pale green almost unweathered glass. W. at base of neck approx. 5 cm. Sixteenth to seventeenth century. Vol. v: C XII RY IV Pit 3. Rose Hotel Yard. Seventeenth-century pit.
    (c) (not illustrated). Base of neck, vertical ribbing, blue-green with patchy white/silvery weathering. D. approx. 2.5 cm. Rose Hotel Yard (unstratified).
    (d) (not illustrated). Base fragment of No. 29. Faint wide ring-pontil. W. 5 cm. Sixteenth to seventeenth century. C XII RY IV Pit 3. *Ibid.*
    (e) (not illustrated). Bottle-base, yellowish-green unweathered glass with ribbing visible inside foot and broken ribbing or diaper on body. W. 8 cm. Sixteenth to seventeenth century. *Ibid.*

30. Rim fragment of (?)bottle, milky pale green with spotty beige weathering. D. approx. 6.5 cm. Sixteenth to seventeenth century. Vol. v: C XII RY IV Pit 3. *Ibid.*

31. Neck of very large bottle, bluish-green (thickness ± 2 mm) with some patchy beige weathering. H. 14.5 cm. Sixteenth to seventeenth century. Vol. v: Rose Hotel Yard (unstratified).
    (a) (not illustrated). Large base fragment, with folded edge, almost certainly belonging to No. 31. D. approx. 15 cm. Rose Hotel Yard (unstratified).

32. Neck and shoulder of case-bottle(?), roughly finished rim of pale green glass with silvery/beige enamel-like weathering. W. approx. 10 cm. H. 6 cm. Probably first half of seventeenth century. C XVII D III Pit 1. Roman Theatre site (*Britannia*, i (1970) Fig. 4). Eighteenth-century pit.
    (a) (not illustrated). Base, possibly of No. 32, but with patchy brown weathering. D. approx. 8.5 cm.
    (b) (not illustrated). Short neck of (?)case-bottle, pale-green. H. 7.5 cm. Rose Hotel Yard (unstratified).

33. Hexagonal bottle, green glass. H. 10.5 cm. Late sixteenth century to *c.* 1650. C XVII D 1 Ext. Cellar. Seventeenth-century cellar over outer wall of Roman Theatre.

34. Vial, light bluish-green glass. H. 9 cm. Seventeenth century. C XVII D III Pit 1 (See No. 32).

35. Neck and shoulder of vial, light bluish-green glass; two. Seventeenth century. C XVII D III Pit 1. *Ibid.*

36. Similar vial. *Ibid.*

37. Vial, dark grey-green glass, with some patchy brown encrustation. H. 6.3 cm. D. 3.5 cm. Seventeenth century. C XVII D III Pit 1. *Ibid.* (See No. 32).

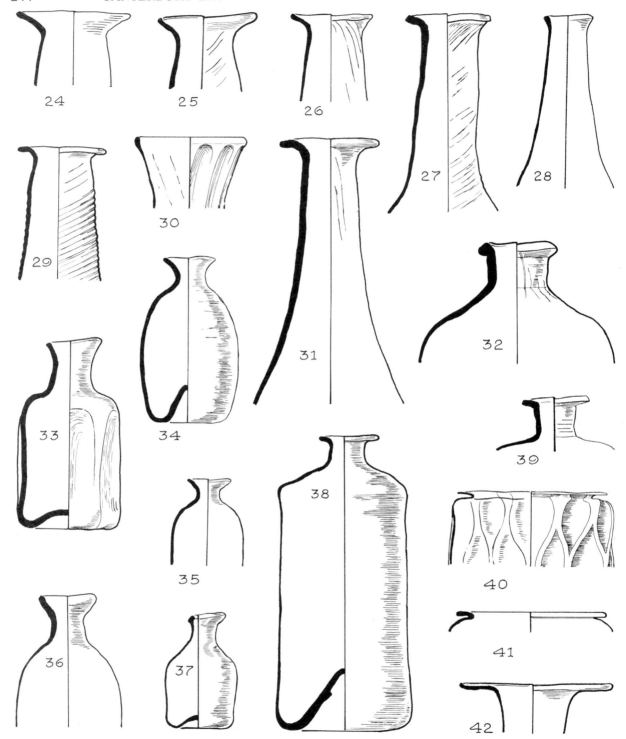

Fig. 95.   Post-medieval glass vessels from Canterbury Excavations 1946–60. (Scale: ½)

38. Large vial, light green glass. H. 16 cm. Probably late seventeenth century. *Britannia*, i (1970), and Vol. vii, Appendix 1: C XVII D III Pit 2. Roman Theatre site, eighteenth-century pit with earlier residual material.
39. Neck and shoulder fragment of vial, light green glass. D. 3.6 cm. Probably late seventeenth century. C XVII D III Pit 2 (See No. 38).
    (a) (not illustrated). Fragmentary slender waisted vial in bright blue-green glass with long vertical bubbles. H. 10 cm. *Ibid.* An accompanying slender neck fragment of similar glass perhaps does not belong. H. 4.5 cm. Seventeenth or eighteenth century.
    (b) (not illustrated). Numerous fragments of similar vials occurred in C XVII D III Pit 2 (see No. 38); C VII RY I 5 and Ia 2 (Rose Hotel Yard, eighteenth-century pit) and C XXVIII A II Pit 1 (Vol. v: St. Margaret's Street, Conservative Club garden, eighteenth-century pit).
40. Fragment of an *albarello*, green glass, with mould-blown mesh-design. D. 8 cm. Seventeenth to eighteenth century. C XVII D III Pit 2. *Ibid.*
41. Rim fragment of jar, colourless glass. D. 8 cm. Eighteenth century. C XVII D III Pit 2. *Ibid.*
42. Rim of a urinal, pale green glass, with spotty brown weathering. W. 7.8 cm. Sixteenth to seventeenth century. C XII RY IV Pit 3. Rose Hotel Yard. Seventeenth-century pit.
43. Beaker-base, greenish-colourless glass with silver/iridescent weathering and black patches. D. 6.3 cm. H. 3.7 cm. Late sixteenth century to *c.* 1650. C XII RY IV 1. Rose Hotel Yard. Dark soil, first half of seventeenth century.
44. Beaker-base, pale green glass with patchy silvery weathering, mould-blown with faint vertical ribbing. D. approx. 10 cm. Late sixteenth century to *c.* 1650. Vol. vii: C XVII Y II 2 (1). Area Y. Mid seventeenth-century yard metalling.
45. Beaker-base, green glass with patchy buff weathering. D. approx. 7 cm. H. to apex of 'kick' approx. 4 cm. Late sixteenth century to *c.* 1650. *Ibid.*
    The following pieces (unillustrated) are of the same date:
    (a) Fragment of beaker-base, unweathered very pale green and thin glass. D. of foot 5 cm. C XII RY IV Pit 3. Rose Hotel Yard. Seventeenth-century pit.
    (b) Beaker-base, pale green glass with beige enamel-like weathering. D. approx. 9 cm. C XVII D III Pit 2 (see No. 38).
    (c) Beaker-base, pale green glass with beige enamel-like weathering. D. approx. 6.5 cm. *Ibid.*
    (d) Fragment of beaker-base, light green glass with flaky silvery weathering. D. 7.5 cm. (approx.). C XII RY IV 1. Rose Hotel Yard. Dark soil, first half of seventeenth century.
46. Beaker-base, pale green glass with patchy brown weathering, mould-blown with faint 'wrythen' ribbing running from lower right to upper left. D. of foot approx. 9 cm. Vol. vii: C XVII Y II 2 (1). (See No. 44.)
47. Rim-fragments of beaker, light blue-grey brilliant glass, decorated with mould-blown ribbing 'wrythen' from lower left to upper right. D. approx. 9 cm. C XII RY IV Pit 3. Rose Hotel Yard. Seventeenth-century pit.
    (a) (not illustrated).(?)Beaker-wall fragment with vertical mould-blown ribbing. D. approx. 7.5 cm. Late sixteenth century to *c.* 1650. *Ibid.*
48. Rim of a beaker, pale green glass, with thickened rim, the body decorated with mould-blown ribbing 'wrythen' from lower left to upper right. H. 3.8 cm. D. 9 cm. approx. Late sixteenth century to *c.* 1650. C XII RY IV 2. Rose Hotel Yard. Clay, first half seventeenth century.
    (a) (not illustrated). Two fragments of beaker-rim, blue-green glass, mould-blown 'wrythen' ribbing from lower left to upper right. D. approx. 7.5 cm. Late sixteenth century to *c.* 1650. Vol. vii: C XVII Y II 1 (1). Area Y. Mid seventeenth-century occupation layer.
    (b) (not illustrated). Five wall fragments of beakers, pale green glass, mould-blown with ribbing 'wrythen' from bottom right to top left. Late sixteenth century to *c.* 1650. C XVII Y II 2 (1). Mid seventeenth-century yard metalling.
49. Rim fragment of beaker, pale green glass, mould-blown ribbing 'wrythen' from lower right to upper left. Late sixteenth century to *c.* 1650. *Ibid.*
50. Rim fragment of a beaker, virtually colourless glass with heavy black/iridescent weathering. Mould-blown apparently with a diaper of raised (?)ovals. H. 2.8 cm. D. 9 cm. (approx.) Late sixteenth century to *c.* 1650. Vol. vii: C XIX Z II Pit 2. South side of St. George's Street. Seventeenth-century pit.
51. Rim of a beaker, pale green glass, with thickened rim. H. 3.3 cm. D. 7.5 cm. (approx.) Late sixteenth century to

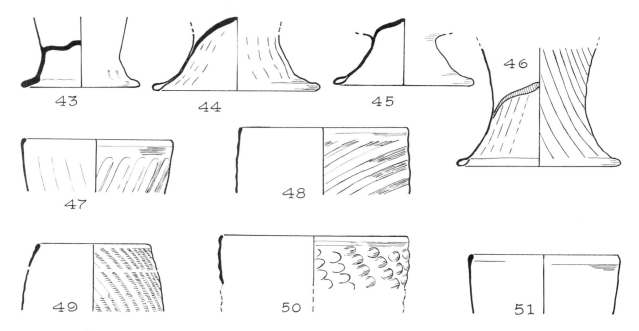

Fig. 96.   Post-medieval glass vessels from Canterbury Excavations 1946–60. (Scale: ½)

c. 1650. C XII RY IV 2. Rose Hotel Yard. Clay, first half of seventeenth century.

52. Wine-bottle, green glass. H. 19.2 cm. ?*c*. 1670–90. C VII RY I 4. Rose Hotel Yard. Late seventeenth-century black earth.

53. Fragmentary bottle, thick green glass with thin beige weathering. H. 12.5 cm. *c*. 1685–1715. *Britannia*, i (1970), and Vol. vii, Appendix 1: C XVII D III Pit 2. Roman Theatre site. Eighteenth-century pit.

54. Bottle, dark green glass. H. 15.2 cm. *c*. 1690–1710. Rose Hotel Yard (unstratified).

55. Bottle-neck fragment, dark green glass. *c*. 1700. Vol. vii: C XV R II 2. Seventeenth-century cess pit fill.

56–57. Bottle-neck fragments, dark green glass. *c*. 1700. Vol. v: C VIII RY IIB 1. Rose Hotel Yard. Eighteenth-century soil.

58. Fragmentary bottle, dark green glass. H. 17.6 cm. *c*. 1720–40. C XVII D III Pit 2 (as No. 53).

59. Fragmentary bottle, pale green glass with silvery/iridescent (mainly peacock-blue) weathering. H. 21 cm. *c*. 1750–70. Vol. v: C XXVIII A II Pit 1. St. Margaret's Street, Conservative Club. Eighteenth-century pit.

60. Bottle-neck with string-rim and base with low domed 'kick', pale green glass with silvery weathering. H. of neck 12.5 cm. Uncertain date. C XXVIII A II Pit 1. *Ibid*.

61. Bottle-neck, clear green glass. Probably *c*. 1660. Vol. v: C VII RY I 4. Rose Hotel Yard. Late seventeenth-century black earth.

62. Bottle-neck, dark green glass. Indeterminate date. C XVII D III Pit 2 (as No. 53).

63. Bottle-neck, pale green, perhaps a Pyrmont water bottle. Mid eighteenth century. Vol. vii: C XIII T II 2. Burgate Street. Mid eighteenth-century demolition layer.

64. Seal, green glass stamped with the arms of Pyrmont. D. 3.5 cm. Mid eighteenth century. Vol. vii: C XI N I 5. North side of St. George's Street. Fill of eighteenth-century cellar.

65. Flattened flask ('Betty'), pale yellowish-brown glass with slight dimpled 'kick', without pontil-mark. Reconstructed with rim of No. 65a. Eighteenth century. Vol. v: C XXVIII A II Pit 1. St. Margaret's Street, Conservative Club garden, eighteenth-century pit.

   (a) Neck of 'Betty', green glass. H. 12.5 cm. Not illustrated separately, but rim added to No. 65. *Britannia*, i (1970), Fig. 4: C XVII D III Pit 1. Roman Theatre site, eighteenth-century pit.

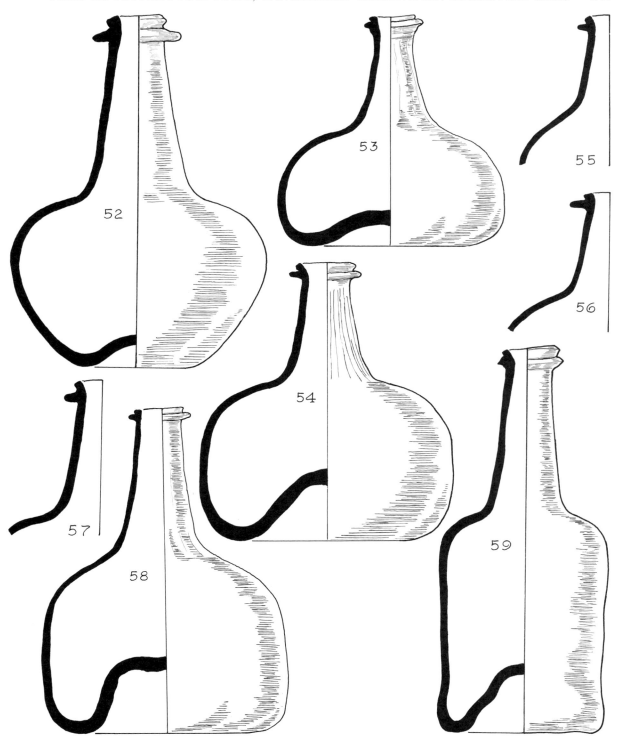

Fig. 97.   Post-medieval glass vessels from Canterbury Excavations 1946–60. (Scale: $\frac{1}{2}$)

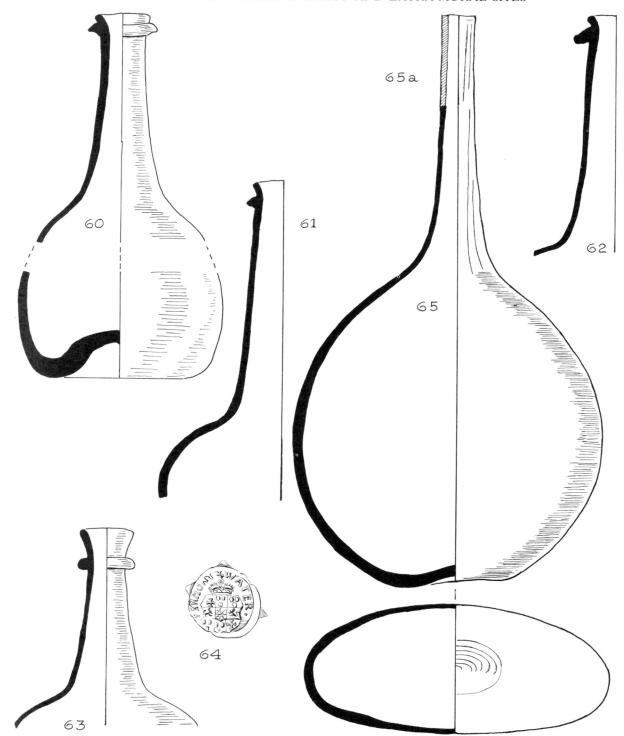

Fig. 98.   Post-medieval glass vessels from Canterbury Excavations 1946–60. (Scale: ½)

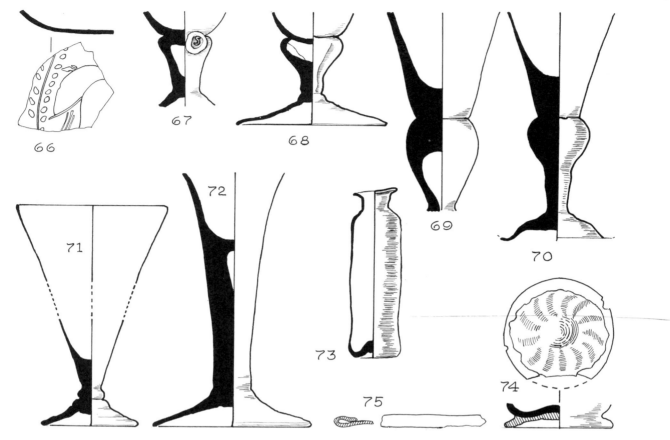

Fig. 99.   Post-medieval glass vessels from Canterbury Excavations 1946–60. (Scale: ½)

(b)   (not illustrated). Flattened flask ('Betty'), dark green glass. Eighteenth century. C XVII D III Pit 2 (as No. 53).

66.   Fragment of crystal, thickish (*c.* 2 mm.) with rough superficial engraving of tulip and rows of dots. L. 5.5 cm. Probably Bohemian; late eighteenth century. This volume: C XXVIII B I 1. Fleur de Lis Yard. Dark soil below modern yard metalling.

67.   Stem fragment of a wine-glass, heavily 'crizzled' colourless glass. Fragmentary round-based bowl set directly into a shouldered conical stem, itself set on a rising conical foot. On this shoulder is an applied pad bearing the letter S impressed in relief. H. 5.5 cm. English (London); about 1676–80. Vol v: C VII RY I 4. Rose Hotel Yard. Late seventeenth-century black earth.

68.   Stem and foot fragment of a wine-glass, bluish-colourless glass with patchy thin brown weathering and iridescence. The shouldered stem is four-lobed, the lobing being smoothed out in the lower part of the stem, which is clumsily joined to the high conical foot. The base of a round funnel bowl is set directly on the stem. H. 6 cm. D. of foot 7.5 cm. About 1680–85. Vol. v: C VII RY I 4. Rose Hotel Yard, black earth.

69.   Base of bowl and top of inverted baluster stem, enclosing tear; heavy lead glass with thin film of beige weathering. H. 11.5 cm. Late seventeenth century. C XVII D III Pit 2. Roman Theatre site (See No. 53).

70.   Fragmentary wine-glass, heavy lead glass, flaky beige weathering on inside: solid inverted baluster stem. H. 12.5 cm. Late seventeenth century. *Ibid.*

71.   Fragmentary wine-glass or 'dram', thin lead glass, patchy thin beige weathering. H. 5.8 cm. Probably early eighteenth century. *Ibid.*

72. Fragmentary wine-glass, lead crystal. Drawn-stem glass with elongated pear-shaped tear in the stem and plain conical foot. H.15 cm. D. of foot 8.5 cm. (approx.). Probably first quarter of eighteenth century. Vol. v: C XXVIII A II Pit 1. St. Margaret's Street, Conservative Club. Eighteenth-century pit.

73. Apothecary's phial, colourless glass. H. 9 cm. approx. Eighteenth century. Vol. v: C XII RY IV Pit 3. Rose Hotel Yard. Intrusive in seventeenth-century pit.

Other phials (not illustrated) are:

    (a) Base, greyish-colourless glass with opalescent sheen. D. 5.1 cm. (approx.). Eighteenth century. Vol. v: C VII RY I 4. Rose Hotel Yard. Black earth.

    (b) Base and two neck fragments of cylindrical apothecary's flasks, colourless glass with slight iridescent weathering. D. of base fragment approx. 2.5 cm. Eighteenth century. C VII RY IA 2. Rose Hotel Yard. Eighteenth-century pit.

    (c) Base fragment of colourless glass. D. approx. 4.5 cm. Eighteenth century. C XVII D III Pit 2. Roman Theatre site. Eighteenth-century pit (See No. 53).

74. Foot fragment of a blue (?)bowl, with patchy iridescent weathering. Heavy pad foot applied to a body mould-blown with apparently 13 ribs. D. 6 cm. Eighteenth century. C VII RY I 5. Rose Hotel Yard. Eighteenth-century pit.

75. Folded edge fragment, probably from the circumference of a window 'crown', pale blue-green glass. Vol. vii: C XVII Y I 4. Area Y. Mortary layer sealing lower chalk drain.

APPENDIX 1

REPORT ON THE MARBLE FROM C XXVIII B (p. 95)

by Miss H.A.H. Macdonald (Geological Survey and Museum)
(Pl. XXVIII, Nos. 1–11, Pl. XXIX, Nos. 12–29)

1, 2, 7.	Cream-coloured marble, finely veined with purple. Giallo Antico (*marmor Numidicum*) from Algeria or Numidia.
3.	Pink breccia. Probably *Breccia Corallina minuta nuvolata*.
4, 8.	Cyrena limestone similar to specimens from Weald Clay, Wealden Series, Lower Cretaceous from Staplehurst, Kent.
5, 12.	Cream-coloured marble with purple fragments and veins similar to some specimens of Pavonazzetto or *Marmor Synnadicum* from Phrygia.
6.	Glauconitic sandstone similar to a specimen from Hythe Beds, Lower Greensand, from Sandgate, Kent.
9, 10, 11.	Coarse white marble, possibly to be compared with coarse varieties of Carrara marble (*Marmor lunense*) from Carrara, Italy. Perhaps painted.
13.	A pink and cream breccia similar to specimens of Pavonazzetto cupo from Phrygia.
14, 15, 19.	Hornblende-diorite.
16, 17, 18.	Red marble similar to specimens of *Marmor Chium* from Island of Chios, Greece.
20, 24, 25, 26.	Green porphyry similar to specimens of Porfido Verde Antico from Marathonisi, Greece.
21, 27.	A green breccia similar to some specimens of Verde Antico from Larissa, Thessaly, Greece.
22, 23.	White marble similar to specimens of Carrara marble, Italy.
28, 29.	Red porphyry similar to specimens of Porfido Rosso Antico from Djebel Dokhan, Egypt.

APPENDIX 2

REPORT ON THE BONES FROM
C XXVIII B, Trench I, layers 9 and 3 (Late Roman layers: p. 97)

by Anne Brocklebank

Species identified, and the number of recognizable specimens of each, were as follows:

Ox	Pig	Sheep or Pig	Dog	
28	1	2	1	Total 32

A horn-core of a size too large to have belonged to the Celtic ox suggests the presence of an improved breed of oxen, probably imported. Only one really young individual was identified, but in three or four cases the remains were of animals not more than three years old. Pig was clearly represented only by a tusk and perhaps some ribs. A single femur of a dog was the only find of this species.

Of the ox-bones a great many were scapulae and vertebrae, some with marks of cutting or chopping. Sirloin and fore-quarter seem to have been the favoured joints.

APPENDIX 3

MORTARIUM STAMPS FROM CANTERBURY

By K.F. Hartley

1. **(Fig. 101, No. 12)** C X L I 15. Vol. vii, No. 586. Diameter 34 cm. About one-third of a very heavily worn mortarium in hard fine-textured pink-brown fabric with few inclusions, including very occasional calcareous material; cream surface in places, perhaps the remains of a slip; only two white quartz trituration-grits survive. The fabric is typical of some of the mortaria made in Kent and it could well be from a workshop in Canterbury. Other stamps probably from the same herringbone die are known from Balmuildy, Cadder, Camelon, Old Kilpatrick and Rough Castle in Scotland; and from Canvey Island, Essex; Harrietsham, Kent; London; Richborough; and an unknown site in Kent. A.D. 130–170.

2. **(Fig. 100, No. 4)** C XX E XIII 5. Vol. v. South-east of Marlowe Theatre. A flange fragment in pinkish-brown fabric with greyish core and abundant tiny inclusions of flint, transparent and pinkish quartz and black ?quartz. The incompletely-impressed two-line stamp is from the single die of Iuvenalis. His mortaria have now been noted from Box, Wilts.; Canterbury (five); Richborough; Worth; an unknown provenance; and from Boulogne. The handle of a kind of amphora with the same stamp is recorded from Richborough (Bushe-Fox, *Richborough*, iv (1949), 244, No. 43), from a pit filled *c*. A.D. 90. The fabric and distribution point to production in Kent, those from Wiltshire and Boulogne being casual carries from the area, the latter no doubt by the *Classis Britannica*. A date of *c*. A.D. 80–130 may cover his activity.

3. **(Fig. 100, No. 3)** C XX C I 8. Vol. vii: Canterbury Lane, residual in occupation on ninth-century Saxon floor. This is a different mortarium from No. 2 but has a stamp of the same potter, Iuvenalis. The fabric is similar but is of a finer texture and includes some calcareous material.

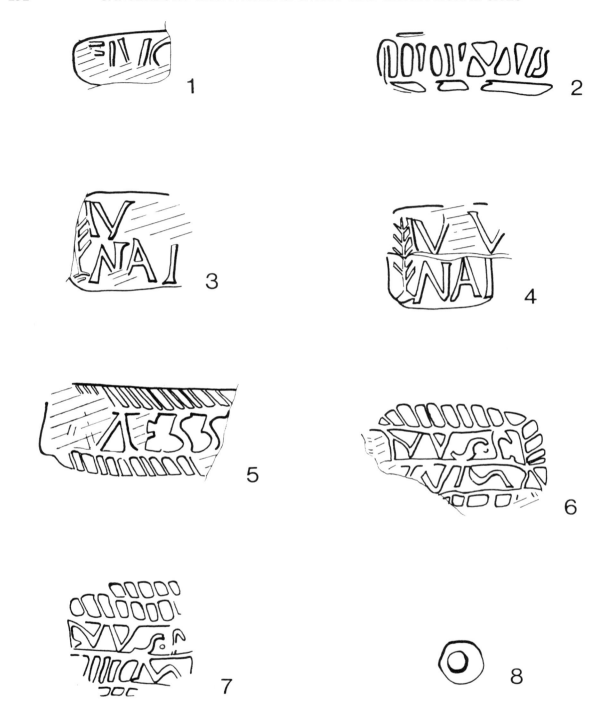

Fig. 100. Mortarium stamps from Canterbury. (Scale: ½)

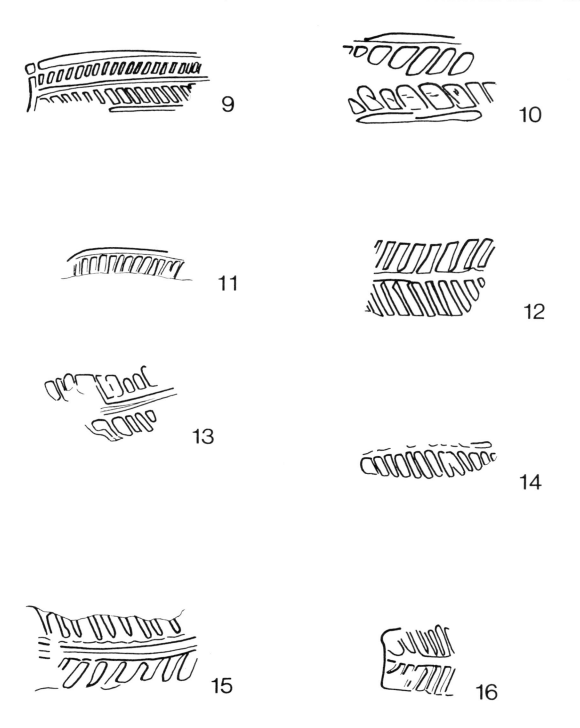

Fig. 101.   Mortarium stamps from Canterbury. (Scale: ½)

4. (**Fig. 100, No. 6**) C XX E XII 2. Vol. v. Garden of No. 18 Watling Street. Diameter *c*. 30 cm. Fine-textured brown fabric with pinkish-brown surface; a good amount of quartz and red-brown and occasional calcareous inclusions; no slip visible. For comment see No. 5.

5. (**Fig. 100, No. 7**) C XXIV Castle III 7. Vol. ii, 136, No. 27. Diameter *c*. 29 cm. Hard, orange-brown fabric with thin drab core and probably with thin buff slip; a good amount of quartz, red-brown and occasional black inclusions; trituration included white quartz. The potter's stamp has been impressed above an earlier attempt.

   Two mortaria (Nos. 4, 5) in slightly differing fabrics, with stamps from the same die. The upper line reads N (or V) VS.F (for F) but only clearer examples will elucidate the lower line, which may read from left or right or be inverted. Another stamp from the same die is noted from Richborough (unpublished). There are several characteristics of the stamps, fabric and rim-forms used, which link these mortaria with the work of Valentinus. If the unread line is inverted, it is just possible that it may be from a die of Valentinus; but one may at least accept that the potter was active in the same workshop as Valentinus, at the time when he was working in Kent. The rim-forms point to a date within the period A.D. 110–160. Valentinus was probably not working in Kent before *c*. A.D. 120, so that a date of A.D. 120–160 is most likely.

6. (**Fig. 100, No. 8**) C XV X II 13. Vol. ii, 64, Section F–G. Hard fine-textured orange-brown fabric with dark grey core and very fine quartz and red-brown tempering; cream slip; trituration includes quartz. The potter's mark has been made by impressing a tube, probably of metal, into the clay. The fabric indicates production in Kent and a stamped mortarium with this profile must have been produced in the Antonine period.

7. (**Fig. 101, No. 16**) C XXVI RG III 10. Vol. ii, 45. Rampart at Riding Gate. Diameter 27 cm. Hard, fine-textured, orange-brown fabric with thick dark grey core and mostly fine tempering; thick cream slip; trituration consists mostly of flint with a little red-brown material. The partial impression of a herringbone stamp is from the same die as a single stamp apparently found in the excavation of the Dane John kiln at Canterbury, but not published in the report (*Arch. Cant.*, liii (1940), 109–16). The rim-forms clearly point to a date in the period A.D. 130–170, and although they cannot be attributed to this kiln they were certainly made in Kent and could have been made in the vicinity.

8. (**Fig. 101, No. 10**) Butchery Lane 1945, Building 1. Mixed layers over wall (*Arch. Cant.*, lxi (1948), 20, Fig. 9, No. 5a). Diameter *c*. 30 cm. A worn and burnt mortarium in fine-textured pink-brown fabric with very fine tempering (generally similar to the fabric of No. 1); trituration consists of transparent and white quartz, flint and occasional red-brown material; there may have been a thin light slip. The herringbone stamp is recorded only from Kent (Canterbury (six) and Eccles). Three of the Canterbury stamps are from the Dane John kiln (*Arch. Cant.*, liii (1940), 121, Nos. 8–10) and this potter can confidently be attributed to a workshop in the immediate vicinity, although the recorded evidence is not sufficient to prove use of this particular kiln. The rimforms indicate production in the mid second century and are, incidentally, very different from those used by the maker of No. 7.

9. (**Fig. 101, No. 13**) C XXIII C V A 13A. Vol. vii, 86. Canterbury Lane. Diameter 36 cm. A heavily-worn mortarium in fine-textured drab cream fabric with brownish-pink core; a fair amount of tiny quartz inclusions with occasional calcareous material; the trituration grit is mostly worn away but a few quartz and red-brown fragments survive. For comment, see No. 10.

10. (**Fig. 101, No. 14**) C XV V I 3. Vol. vii. East of Apsed Building, Section P–Q. Flange fragment differing slightly in colour from No. 9 because only the surface is fired to cream; otherwise it is so close that it might be from the same vessel. But the two sites are 80 m. apart.

   The herringbone stamps on these fragments (Nos. 9, 10) are from the same die; stamps attributed to this die are recorded from Canterbury (three, including these); East Cliff villa, Folkestone; London (two); Rochester; Springhead; Worthing Museum (unknown provenance), and Old Kilpatrick. Some of the impressions are, like No. 9, damaged or incomplete; but there seems to be no reason to doubt that all are from the same die, which is so far unique in having the spines on both sides of the stamp lined up in the same direction. The distribution points to manufacture in Kent and the fabric would be in keeping with a workshop at Canterbury. The rim-profiles suggest activity *c*. A.D. 130–170.

11. (**Fig. 101, No. 15**) C XVII E IV 14B. Vol. v. Roman building south of Marlowe Theatre. Diameter *c*. 27 cm. Granular greyish-cream fabric filled with quartz inclusions; surface orangy in parts. The fabric is typical of mortaria made in workshops near Watling Street in the Verulamium region, such as those at Brockley Hill and Radlett. The only other stamp from the same herringbone die is from Mumrills (*Proc. Soc. Ant. Scotland*, xciv

(1960–61), 86–132, fig. 9, No. 6). The latter must be of Antonine date and, as the practice of stamping mortaria ceased in the Verulamium region in the mid-second century, a date of *c.* A.D. 120/130–155 is probable. For further comments on such stamps see K.F. Hartley, in S.S. Frere, *Verulamium Excavations*, iii (1984), No. 117.

12. (**Fig. 100, No. 5**) C XVII Y III 3 19. Vol. vii, 121. Diameter 33 cm. A well-worn mortarium in fine-textured cream fabric with a few quartz, red-brown and probably flint inclusions. The smeared stamp ᴍESS[is from one of the three dies of Messor who worked at Colchester (M.R. Hull, *The Roman Potters' Kilns at Colchester* (1963), 111, Fig. 60, Nos. 19–20). His other stamps, excluding those from the kiln-site, are known from Cambridge; Caistor St. Edmund's, Norfolk; Chignall St. James, Essex; Hockwold-cum-Wilton (Norfolk); and London in England, and Cadder and Camelon in Scotland. On one of his mortaria from the kiln this stamp is associated with a herringbone stamp (*ibid.*, fig. 60, No. 27, not represented in Scotland), which has been recorded in the Corbridge destruction-deposit of *c.* A.D. 180. Activity within the period A.D. 140–180 is highly probable.

13. (**Fig. 100, No.2**) C XXII K I Pit 10. This volume, Fig. 26, No. 53 King Street. Diameter 36 cm. A well-worn mortarium in granular greyish cream fabric, packed with quartz inclusions and fired to brownish-orange at parts of the surface; such trituration as is not worn away consists mainly of flint. This is an incompletely-impressed stamp from one of the four dies Doinus of Brockley Hill (*Arch. Journ.*, cxxix (1972), 84). Over a hundred of his stamps are known from Britain; stamps from Flavian forts in Scotland (Loudon Hill, Newstead (two) and Dalswinton II) show that he was at work in the period A.D. 70–110. This die is associated only with rims which are certainly earlier than A.D. 100.

14. (**Fig. 100, No. 1**) C XXIV L III 3A. Watling Street road-silt. A flange fragment in fabric of the same type as No. 13 but with thick brownish-orange core. The fragmentary stamp F. LVGVDV is from a counterstamp of Albinus. See S.S. Frere, *Verulamium Excavations*, i (1972), Fig. 145, No. 8 for a counterstamp probably from the same die; *ibid.*, Nos. 2–11 and Frere, *Verulamium Excavations*, iii (1984), No. 61; and Saunders and Havercroft, *Hertfordshire Archaeology*, v (1977), 109–56, for a detailed discussion of this most important potter and for the use of such counterstamps. (This volume, p. 117.)

   More than three hundred stamps of Albinus are known, all from Britain, far more than for any other Romano-British potter. None of his kilns is known, but his mortaria are certainly products of the important workshops in the Verulamium region. Kilns are known to have existed at Brockley Hill, Radlett, and Verulamium; but the only kiln excavated where comparable counterstamps, incorporating the place-name Lugdunum or Lugudunum, have been found is at Bricket Wood, Herts. (Saunders and Havercroft, *op. cit.*). Albinus's work is well represented in Flavian deposits in Scotland and one of his counterstamps is recorded from Verulamium in a deposit dated A.D. 55–61 (Richardson, *Archaeologia*, xc (1944), 123, No. 4). His work should probably be dated A.D. 60–90.

15. (**Fig. 101, No. 11**) C XXIV Castle III 27. Vol. ii, 53. Building below Roman defences. The fragmentary herringbone stamp is probably from the same die as two others from Canterbury and an unpublished stamp from Richborough. The fabric and distribution indicate manufacture in Kent, probably in Canterbury. A date of A.D. 140–170 would fit the rim-profiles.

16. (**Fig. 101, No. 9**) C VII H I Pit 1. Rose Lane, *Arch. Cant.*, lxviii (1954), 102, Pit M 9. Stamp type as Hull, *Roman Potters' Kilns at Colchester* (1963), Fig. 60, No. 33.

17. (not illustrated). From Burgate Street. Stamp type as Hull, *op. cit.* (1963), Fig. 60, No. 29.

   These two stamps are from herringbone dies used at the Colchester workshops probably within the period A.D. 130–170. The Colchester potters who used herringbone stamps sold large quantities of their mortaria in Antonine Scotland; twelve of Hull type 33 are recorded from Scotland, none of Hull type 29 (for discussion of this trade, see *ibid.*, 114–6 and *Proc. Soc. Ant. Scotland*, cx (1978–80), 261–4).

APPENDIX 4

CHRONOLOGICAL LIST OF CANTERBURY EXCAVATION COMMITTEE SEASONS DIRECTED BY S.S. FRERE
compiled by Marion Wilson

Note: C stands for Canterbury, followed by a Roman numeral for the season. Letters A, B, C etc., denote sites (as shown in Appendix 5), followed by further Roman numerals for trenches. Seasons I–V were carried out by Mrs. Audrey Williams in 1944–45.

CODE	SEASON	YEAR
C VI	April	1946
C VII	Summer	
C VIII	December	
C IX	April	1947
C X	Summer	
C XI	December	
C XII	April	1948
C XIII	Summer	
C XIV	April	1949
C XV	Summer	
C XVI	April	1950
C XVII	Summer	
(no C XVIII)		
C XIX	April	1951
C XX	Summer	
C XXI	April	1952
C XXII	Summer	
C XXIII	April	1953
C XXIV	Summer	
C XXV	April	1954
C XXVI	Summer	
C XXVII	April	1955
C XXVIII	Summer	
C XXVIII	April	1956
C XXX	April	1957
C XXXI	April	1960 directed by J. Wacher
C XXXII	June–July	1960 directed by M.G. Wilson.

APPENDIX 5

LIST OF CANTERBURY EXCAVATION COMMITTEE SITES
compiled by Marion Wilson

A	C IX–X A,C,D,E; C XV D	St. George's Street Baths.
	C XVI A	South side of Watling Street, deep Roman loam pit.
	C XX A	Church Street (St. Paul's), outside (east of) walls, second-century Roman floors.
	C XXVIII A	Garden west of Conservative Club in St. Margaret's Street, south-west of St. Margaret's Church, Roman building with tessellated pavement.
B	C XV B	Whitefriars Entry, south of St. George's Street, late medieval burials.
	C XVI B	North side of Watling Street, west of Rose Lane, Roman and medieval pits.
	C XX B	Lady Wootton's Green, outside walls, Roman inhumations.
	C XXVIII B	Fleur-de-Lis Yard in White Horse Lane, Forum area: walls, arch, tessellated pavement.
C	C XX, XXII, XXIII–IV C + C XXVIII	Canterbury Lane, east side Roman building, late Saxon floor, etc., medieval well.
	C XXIV Castle I–V	Medieval floors inside keep.
	III	Roman City wall outside
	C XXVIII Castle	Extreme south east corner of Castle grounds, adjoining Worthgate.

CW	C X CW	in Cattle Market	
	C XIII CW	near Riding Gate	City Wall
	C XXI CW	in Westgate Gardens	
	C XXVI CW	in Burgate Lane	

D	C XVI–XIX D	Theatre
DJ	C XXV DJ	Wall tower adjoining Dane John.
E	C XX E XXIII	Public Analyst's Garden to south of Marlowe Theatre, in Watling Street, Roman street.

Area E in Fountain/Corporation Car Park
South of Marlowe Theatre
C XVI E II, C XVII E III–VI, Roman building with tessellated pavement.
and C XIX E IX
East of (behind) Marlowe Theatre
C XVI E I, C XIX E VIII,   Saxon area with hut, etc., fragmentary Roman floors and wall footings.
C XXI E XV, C XXV E XVI
North-east corner of Car Park
just south of Rose Yard
C XXX E XXI, with   On site of temporary Barclay's Bank, south of Wellworthy's. Both are a
C XXIX E XX to east   continuation of the buildings in Rose Yard (RY).
of E XXI.

F	C XXII F	Marlowe Avenue Car Park (north of Dane John), pits, one with ninth-century pottery and Alfred coin.
G	C X G	North side of St. George's Street, part of apsed building extending from south side (C XV S,T,V).
	C XXII G	No. 7 St. George's Place outside the eastern defences.
H	C VII H	Roman drain and early ditch, Rose Lane, west side.
	C X H	West side of Canterbury Lane, Roman street; floor, timber wall.
	C XXII H	St. Peter's Lane I on east side, adjoining School of Architecture; II on west side, on St. Peter's Church Hall site, medieval hearth and walls (no Roman).
	C VII J	Rose Lane, east side.
J	C X J	Cellar south of St. George's Street, Roman timber wall, floor.
	C XXII J	No. 3 Palace Street, N–S Roman street, robbed wall and earlier floors, Belgic hut.
	C VII K	The Parade, south side.
K	C X K	North of St. George's Street, medieval walls.
	C XXII K	King's Street
	C XXIII K	St. Mildred's, some Roman and later medieval.
L	C VII L	The Parade, south side: Belgic ditch.
	C X L	Cellar in Burgate Street west of C XIV M, sequence of Roman floors, some post-holes.
	C XXIII–XXIV L	Cellar of No. 44 or 5 Watling Street, on south side, opposite Lady Huntingdon's Chapel, Roman street, *opus signinum* floor, timber wall.
M	C VIII M	East side of Rose Lane.
	C X M	West side of Canterbury Lane, further north than C X H. Roman timber wall, floors.
	C XIV M	North-west corner of Iron Bar Lane with Burgate Street (east of C X L). Roman timber walls, floors, good medieval ovens and walls.
	C XXVI M	Garden of No. 3 Watling Street, two 'hut' floors, first century and late Roman.
N	C XI N	North side of St. George's Street, between two Banks, early Roman post-holes and gully (or sleeper trench).
	C XIV N	North-east corner of Iron Bar Lane with Burgate Street.
	C XV N	East side of Canterbury Lane, north of Loyn's Bakery, continuation of main Canterbury Lane site (C XXVIII C, etc.), Roman floor, timber wall; Saxon floors and post-holes.
O	C XI O	Cellar south of St. George's Street nearly opposite Iron Bar Lane. Saxon and medieval pits.
OP	C XXII OP	Old Park, north-east of Canterbury along Sturry Road, medieval and later.
P	C XI P	South side of St. George's Street. Pits: Roman, Saxon, medieval.

	C XIV P	South-west corner of Iron Bar Lane with St. George's Street, 'very little useful information'.
Q	C XIV Q	South-east corner of Iron Bar Lane with St. George's Street, medieval walls.
R	C XII–XIII Q	St. Margaret's Street, Fountain Hotel Site.
	C XII–XIII R	St. Margaret's Street, Fountain Hotel Site.
	C XXVII R	In car park behind (east of) St. Margaret's Street, Roman baths. See also C XII–C XIII S.
	C XV R	Area north of St. George's Street cellars, between Iron Bar and Canterbury Lanes. Interesting Roman streets, floors, late fourth- or fifth-century hut.
RG	C XXIV, XXVI RG	Riding Gate, Roman gate.
RY	C VII, VIII, XII, XIII RY	Rose Yard (north-west end of Rose Lane behind Lyons). Same Roman building as C XXIX–XXX E. Note: drain outside (east of) building in C VII H.
S	C XII–XIII S	South of C XII–XIII R, east side of St. Margaret's Street (Fountain Hotel Baths).
	C XV S	South side of St. George's Street, part of apsed building with C XV T,V and C X G.
	C XXXI–XXXII S	Simon Langton School site. Roman building, Saxon huts.
T	C XV T	South side of St. George's Street. Same building as C XV S, V and C X G.
	C XIII T	Cellar in Burgate Street.
V	C XV V	South side of St. George's Street. Same building as C XV S, T and C X G.
W	C XXIV–XXVII W	Whitehall Road. Watling Street, Roman timber building, gully; Belgic timber building and hut.
X	C XV X	Between St. George's Lane and City wall, site of new Bus Station.
Y	C XVI–XVII Y	An area south of Burgate Street, east of Longmarket.
Z	C XIX Z	South side of St. George's Street, between Kentish Gazette and Marks and Spencer, medieval walls.

APPENDIX 6

LIST OF CANTERBURY EXCAVATION COMMITTEE SITES
(C I–V directed by Audrey Williams, 1944–45)

Note: References to Volume iii, Volume vii, etc., are to volumes in *The Archaeology of Canterbury* series.

C I		Burgate Lane	*Arch. Cant.*, lix (1946), 64–81
C II		Burgate Street	*ibid.*
C III		Burgate Street	*Arch. Cant..* lx (1947), 68–87
C IV		Watling Street, Huntingdon Chapel	*ibid.*
C V–C VI	A–G	Butchery Lane	*Arch. Cant.*, lxi (1948), 1–45
C VII	H,J,K,L	Rose Lane/The Parade	*Arch. Cant.*, lxviii (1954) 101–43
	RY	Rose Hotel Yard, Rose Lane	Volume v, forthcoming
C VIII	M	Rose Lane, east side	Volume v, forthcoming
	RY	Rose Hotel Yard, Rose Lane	Volume v, forthcoming
C IX–C X	A,C,D,E	St. George's Street Baths	Volume vii, 27–40
C IX	B	St. George's Street, south side	Volume vii, 51
	RY	Rose Hotel Yard, Rose Lane	Volume v, forthcoming
C X	CW	City Wall, Old Cattle Market	Volume ii, 62
	G	St. George's Street, Apsed Building	Volume vii, 41–8
	H	Canterbury Lane, west side	Volume vii, 76–8
	J	St. George's Street, south side	Volume vii, 53
	K	St. George's Street, north side	Volume vii, 62
	L	Burgate Street, south side	Volume vii, 109–13
	M	Canterbury Lane, west side	Volume vii, 78–80
C XI	N	St. George's Street, north side	Volume vii, 64–7
	O,P	St. George's Street, south side	Volume vii, 54–6
C XII–C XIII	Q,R,S	St. Margaret's Street Baths	Volume v, forthcoming
C XII	RY	Rose Hotel Yard, Rose Lane	Volume v, forthcoming
C XIII	CW	City Wall near Riding Gate	Volume ii, 40–43
	RY	Rose Hotel Yard, Rose Lane	Volume v, forthcoming
	T	Burgate Street, north side	Volume vii, 130–33
C XIV	M I–II	Burgate Street, south side	Volume vii, 113–17
	N	Burgate Street, south side	Volume vii, 117–20
	P	St. George's Street, north side	Volume vii, 62–4
	Q	St. George's Street, north side	Volume vii, 58–62
	RY	Rose Hotel Yard, Rose Lane	Volume v, forthcoming

C XV	B	St. George's Street, south side	Volume vii, 53
	D	St. George's Street Baths	Volume vii, 27–40
	M III	Burgate Street, south side	Volume vii, 113–17
	N	Canterbury Lane, east side	Volume vii, 81–100
	R	Area north of St. George's Street	Volume vii, 69–76
	S,T,V	St. George's Street, Apsed Building	Volume vii, 41–9
	X	Bus Station Site, St. George's Lane	Volume vii, 135–43
C XVI	A	Watling Street, south side	This volume
	B,C	Watling Street, north side	This volume
	D	Roman Theatre	*Britannia*, i (1970), 83–113
	E I	East of Marlowe Theatre	Volume v, forthcoming
	E II	South of Marlowe Theatre	Volume v, forthcoming
	Y	Area south of Burgate Street	Volume vii, 120–30
C XVII	D	Roman Theatre	*Britannia*, i (1970), 83–113
	E III–VII	South of Marlowe Theatre	Volume v, forthcoming
	Y	Area south of Burgate Street	Volume vii, 120–30
C XVIII		Not used	
C XIX	E VIII	East of Marlowe Theatre	Volume v, forthcoming
	E IX	South of Marlowe Theatre	Volume v, forthcoming
	Z	St. George's Street, south side	Volume vii, 57–8
C XX	A	Church Street (St. Paul's)	This volume
	B	Lady Wootton's Green	This volume
	C	Canterbury Lane, east side	Volume vii, 81–100
	D	Roman Theatre	*Britannia*, i (1970), 83–113
	E XII	Watling Street, Public Analyst's garden, Roman street	Volume v, forthcoming
	E XIII	Trench SE of Marlowe Theatre	Volume v, forthcoming
C XXI	C	Canterbury Lane, east side	Volume vii, 81–100
	CW	City Wall, Westgate Gardens	Volume ii, 24–30
	E XV	East of Marlowe Theatre	Volume v, forthcoming
C XXII	C	Canterbury Lane, east side	Volume vii, 81–100
	F	Marlowe Avenue Car Park	This volume
	G	No. 7, St. George's Place	No finds
	H	St. Peter's Lane	This volume
	J	No. 3, Palace Street	This volume
	K	King Street	This volume
	OP	Old Park	This volume
C XXIII	C	Canterbury Lane, east side	Volume vii, 83–100
	K	St. Mildred's	This volume
	L	Watling Street, south side	This volume
C XXIV	C	Canterbury Lane, east side	Volume vii, 83–100
	Castle I–II, IV–V	Inside Castle Keep	Volume i, 60–659

	Castle III	City Wall at Castle	Volume ii, 51–6
	L	Watling Street, south side	This volume
	RG	Riding Gate	Volume ii, 43–51
	St. Peter's Street	Roman Street	This volume
	W	Whitehall Street	This volume
C XXV	E XVI	East of Marlowe Theatre	Volume v, forthcoming
	LD	Lanfranc's Dormitory	Volume iii, forthcoming
	W	Whitehall Road	This volume
C XXVI	CW	City Wall, Burgate Lane	Volume ii, 34–40
	DJ	Wall tower at Dane John	Volume ii, 59–61
	M	No. 3 Watling Street	This volume
	RG	Riding Gate	Volume ii, 43–53
	W	Whitehall Road	This volume
C XXVII	Bus Station	Roman wall tower	Volume ii, 61–2
	R	St. Margaret's Street Baths	Volume v, forthcoming
	WG	Westgate Gardens, London Gate	Volume ii, 30–4
	W	Whitehall Road	This volume
C XXVIII	A	Conservative Club Garden, St. Margaret's Street	Volume v, forthcoming
	B	Forum area, Fleur-de-Lis yard	This volume
	C XX, XXI	Canterbury Lane, north end	Volume vii, 101–8
	Castle	Defences near Worth Gate	Volume ii, 56–8
C XXIX	E XX	Rose Lane – Marlowe area	Volume v, forthcoming
C XXX	D	Roman Theatre (west side of St. Margaret's Street)	*Britannia*, i (1970), 83–113
	E XXI	Rose Lane – Marlowe area	Volume v, forthcoming
C XXXI–C XXXII	S	Simon Langton School Yard	Volume v, forthcoming

PART IV: THE FINDS AND POTTERY FROM THE CANTERBURY ARCHAEOLOGICAL TRUST SITES 1980–84

1. CRANMER HOUSE, LONDON ROAD

A. THE HUMAN BONES by P.H. Garrard

Burial 1 Weight: 1.675 kg.
Fragments of long bone, mostly 40–60 mm. long, show distortion and cracking.
Identifiable bones:
Head of one femur; lower end of tibia.
Eight pieces of the vault of the skull, inner and outer tables intact.
Head of one humerus.
Conclusions:
Adult, sex not determined.
Long bones exposed to high temperature cremation, skull to a moderate temperature.

Burial 2 Weight: 3.200 kg.
The fragments of long bone show whitening and scoring, and one fragment shows distortion. The pieces are large and crushing is incomplete.
Identifiable bones:
Nine bodies of vertebrae, with the epiphiseal plates detached, presumably by heat, but suggesting incomplete fusion. Head and neck of one femur, and part of the head of the other. One calcaneus. These bones have been hardly affected by heat.
A piece of the shaft of a femur, 50 cm. long.
Ten pieces of the vault of the skull, the sutures separated, suggesting a low temperature cremation in this area.
Conclusions:
Young adult male.
The application of heat has been irregular, the hips and spine being less exposed than the shafts of the long bones.

Burial 3 Weight: 1.370 kg.
Some distortion of the long bones; longest fragment of bone 70 mm., other fragments were well crushed.
Identifiable bones:
Part of head and neck of femur. Part of shaft of femur.
Four pieces of the vault of the skull, sutures ununited, inner table detached in one fragment.
Conclusions:
Adult, probably male.
Moderate temperature cremation.

263

Burial 4 Weight: 1.750 kg.
Preservation good; largest bone fragment 60 mm. long.
Most of the bones have been crushed into small pieces.
The long bones show superficial cracking, but no distortion.
Identifiable bones:
Parts of the heads of both femora.
Part of an acetabulum; 50 mm. long piece of the shaft of a femur.
Parts of the heads of the humeri; the upper end of one radius.
One patella. A phalanx from the hand.
Parts of seven vertebrae.
Fifteen pieces of the vault of the skull.
One adult molar tooth.
Conclusions:
Adult, probably male.
Cremation at a moderate temperature.

Burials 5 and 6 No cremated bones recovered.

Burial 7 Weight: 150 gm.
Preservation good; no distortion. Largest fragment 40 mm. long.
Identifiable bones:
Skull; ten fragments, nine from the vault and one from the base. They are fairly thick and show no signs of fusion of the sutures.
Fragment of ilium.
Pieces of two vertebrae including the second cervical which is very small.
Upper end of one radius, the epiphysis not fused.
Some fragments of long bones.
Conclusions:
Adolescent, age 13–16 years. Sex not determined.
Cremation at moderate temperature.

Burial 8 No cremated bones recovered.

Burial 9 Weight: 75 gm.
Bone crushed into small fragments. None were identified.

Burial 10 Weight: 300 gm.
All the bones have been crushed to a small size; the longest fragment was 25 mm.
Some pieces showed calcination, with grooving and scoring but no distortion.
Identifiable bones:
Four pieces of the vault of the skull, rather thin.
Pieces of long bone of small diameter.
One small incisor tooth; four fragments of tooth and one root.
Conclusions:
An adult probably of small stature, sex not determined.
Cremation of moderate temperature.

Burial 11 Weight: 1.125 kg.
Many large fragments suggesting incomplete crushing after cremation. No distortion or calcination of the bones, but some scoring and splitting.
Identifiable bones:
Bodies of eleven vertebrae from lumbar, thoracic and cervical regions. No lipping. Detached epiphyseal plate of one vertebra.
Part of head of femur and humerus.
Part of iliac bone.
Pieces of the vault of the skull, some of the outer and some of the inner table, some are complete.
Sutures of the skull are not united.

Conclusions:
  Young adult male.
  Cremation at low temperature.

Burial 12   No cremated bones recovered.

Burial 13   Weight: 860 gm.
  Pieces of long bone distortion and scored.
  Skull and lower vertebral column almost unaffected by cremation.
Identifiable bones:
  Six pieces of vault of the skull, with inner and outer tables intact; a piece of the base of the skull; sutures not united.
  Four lumbar vertebrae, epiphyseal plates of vertebrae detached.
  Part of the sacrum.
Conclusions:
  Young adult male.
  High temperature cremation uneven, the skull and lower vertebral column almost unaffected by heat.

Burial 14   Weight: 640 gm.
  Very well crushed bone, the largest piece 20 mm. long.
  Some calcination, superficial cracks and scoring.
  No distortion.
Identifiable bones:
  Fragments from the upper end of one humerus.
  Six to eight pieces of skull.
Conclusions:
  Adult, sex not determined.
  Cremation at medium or low temperature.

Burial 15A   Weight: 1.800 kg.
  Largest bone fragment 70 mm. (part of pelvis).
  Preservation is good. Bones well crushed, pale, many showing calcination, especially those of the skull, with superficial cracks and fissures. None show distortion.
Identifiable bones:
  Skull; the bones of the vault are thin; pieces from the base of the skull, and one temporal bone. None of the sutures have fused.
  One canine tooth and one incisor and fragments of several other teeth.
  Vertrebral column; seventeen vertebrae including the second cervical. There is no osteoarthritic lipping of the bodies.
  Lower limb; the head of one femur. Part of the acetabulum of the pelvis.
  Lower end of fibula.
  Upper limb; heads of both humeri.
  Lower end of both ulnae and one radius.
  One proximal phalanx.
Conclusions:
  Young adult, sex not determined.
  Moderate temperature cremation.

Burial 15B   Weight: 1.320 kg.
  Most of the bones have been well crushed, the largest 45 mm. long (long bone).
  Preservation good; the bones show cracks and scoring, some show calcination, a few show blue discolouration. None are distorted.
Identifiable bones:
  Upper ends of both humeri.
  Many fragments of long bones.
  Seventeen pieces of the vault of the skull; part of the right temporal bone.

Seven teeth, all mature but very small.

Parts of two vertebrae.

Conclusions:

Adult, sex not determined.

Uneven cremation at moderate temperature.

Burial 16   No cremated bones recovered.

Burial 17   Weight: 525 gm.

A high proportion of pieces of long bones, 40–60 mm. long. The bones are calcined, some distorted with cracking and scoring; some are blackened.

Identifiable bones:

Pieces of femur, humerus and smaller long bones.

Pieces of skull, outer table.

Conclusions:

Adult male.

High temperature cremation.

Burial 18   Weight: 725 gm.

Most of the bones have been well crushed, the largest fragment about 50 mm. long. Some distortion and cracking of the long bones.

Identifiable bones:

Four pieces of the vault of the skull, the sutures not united.

Parts of the heads of both femora.

Pieces of the smaller long bones.

Pieces of left and right talus.

Conclusions:

Adult, probably male.

High temperature cremation.

Burial 19   Weight: 150 gm.

Bones crushed to small fragments, the largest 25 mm. long.

Identifiable bones:

Pieces of four vertebrae of small size with the epiphyseal plates unfused.

One scaphoid bone of the wrist.

Detached crown of one deciduous molar tooth, unworn.

Conclusions:

Adolescent about twelve years, sex not determined.

Burials 20 and 23   (accidentally mixed during examination)

Weight: 1.100 kg.

Some pieces of long bone are approximately 80 mm. long; most of the bone is finely crushed. Some of the long bones show calcination and superficial cracking; some are blue in colour.

Identifiable bones:

There are two skeletons:

(i)   Sixteen pieces of the vault of the skull, all rather thin, sutures fused, probably from the temporo-parietal area.

(ii) Six pieces of the heads of two humeri, all separated at the epiphyseal line.

One fragment of femur.

Pieces of several long bones of upper and lower limbs.

Conclusions:

Adult, probably male.

Young adult, probably male.

Cremation from evidence of the condition of the long bones of moderate temperature, or exposure to uneven temperatures, as few pieces are distorted.

Burial 21   No cremated bones recovered.

Burial 22   Weight: 135 gm.
  Largest pieces of bone, long bone, 15–20 mm.
  Whitened, scored and distorted.
Identifiable bones:
  A fragment of the inner table of the skull.
  Some pieces of long bones.
Conclusions:
  Adult, sex not determined.
  High temperature cremation.

Burial 23   See above.

Burial 24   Weight: 250 gm.
  Largest bone fragment 15 mm. long. No distortion.
Identifiable bones:
  A fragment of tibia.
Conclusions:
  Adult male.
  Moderate temperature cremation.

Burial 25   Weight: 300 gm.
  Finely crushed bone, but one larger recognisable fragment of long bone scored and cracked,
  no fragments show distortion.
Identifiable bones:
  Fragment of humerus.
  Two fragments of the vault of the skull showing separation of inner and outer tables.
Conclusions:
  Adult, sex not determined.
  Moderate temperature cremation.

Burial 26   Weight: 100 gm.
  Longest piece of bone 30 mm. long. Most of the fragments show distortion.
Identifiable bones:
  About twelve pieces of the vault of the skull, inner and outer tables separated. Sutures not
  fused.
  Body of thoracic vertebra.
  Some heavy pieces of bone, probably from the pelvis.
Conclusions:
  Adult, sex not determined.
  High temperature cremation.

Burial 27   Weight: 600 gm.
  Fragments of long bone approximately 50 mm. long.
  Most of the remaining bone 10 mm. or less. Fragments whitened and scored, but no
  distortion.
Identifiable bones:
  Two small pieces of the vault of the skull, which are thin, the inner and outer tables intact.
Conclusions:
  Adult, sex not determined.
  Moderate temperature cremation.

Burial 28   Weight: 1.435 kg.
  Longest fragment, long bone, 80 mm; most of the fragments are well crushed to 2–3 mm.
  Larger fragments distorted and several burnt to blue colour.
Identifiable bones:
  Fragments of the vault of the skull, the inner and outer tables separated. Sutures not united.
  Upper end of one radius.
  Part of the head of a femur.

Conclusions:
  Adult, probably young male.
  High temperature cremation.

Burial 29 Weight: 110 gm.
  Well crushed bones, largest piece 35 mm. long; bone shows calcination and scoring.
Identifiable bones:
  Probable adult humerus.
Conclusions:
  Adult, probably male.
  Cremation at moderate temperature.

Burial 30 Weight: 950 gm.
  Well crushed bone, fragments range from 90 mm. to fine fragments. Preservation good.
  Bones show calcination with transverse grooves and cracks.
Identifiable bones:
  Part of the right scapula.
  Fragments of the heads of both femora and part of the shaft of one. The epiphyses have united.
  Fragments of pelvic bone.
  One bone from the foot.
  Long bone fragments.
  Thirteen pieces of the vault of the skull.
Conclusions:
  Adult male.
  Cremation at moderate temperature.

Burial 31 Weight: 425 gm.
  Several fragments of long bone 50–80 mm. long, the other bone well crushed. Some calcination of the bones.
Identifiable bones:
  Four thick pieces of the vault of the skull.
  Manubrium sterni.
Conclusions:
  Adult male.
  Cremation at medium or low temperature.

Burial 32 No cremated bones recovered.

Burial 33 Weight: 375 gm.
  Long bone fragments whitened and scored. No distortion.
Identifiable bones:
  Fragments of the skull, one showing separation of the inner table.
  Part of the head of femur or humerus of small size.
  Body of small vertebra, with the epiphysis fused.
  Double root of a small tooth.
Conclusions:
  Adult, probably small female.
  Cremation at moderate temperature.

Burial 34 No cremated bones recovered.

Burial 35 Weight: 650 gm.
  Some large pieces of bone amongst the rest of the well crushed bone.
Identifiable bones:
  Five pieces of the vault of the skull, inner and outer tables not separated. Sutures not fused.
  Upper ends of both femora, separated epiphyses.
Conclusions:
  Probably young male adult, eighteen to twenty years.

Burial 36

Low temperature cremation.
Weight: 75 gm.
  Finely crushed bone.
Identifiable bones:
  Two small pieces of skull, one very thin.
Conclusions:
  Probably child, under nine years.

Burial 37

Weight: 225 gm.
  Finely crushed bone. Little cracking or whitening of the bone; no distortion.
Identifiable bones:
  Fragment of humerus.
Conclusions:
  Adult, sex not determined.
  Low temperature cremation.

Burial 38

Weight: 215 gm.
  Bone well crushed, largest pieces about 5–6 cm.
  Some calcination and cracking of pelvic bone fragments.
Identifiable bones:
  Head of one femur, the epiphyseal line fused; part of the head of the other femur.
  Pelvic bone fragments.
  Long bone fragment.
  No sign of arthritis.
Conclusions:
  Adult male, aged twenty-five to thirty years.
  Moderate temperature cremation with uneven exposure to heat.

Burial 39

Weight: 400 gm.
  Well crushed bone, largest piece, long bone, 5 cm. Cracking and calcination and distortion of long bone fragments. Some fragments show blue discolouration.
Identifiable bones:
  Skull fragment, outer table.
  Adult tooth.
  Long bone fragments.
Conclusions:
  Adult, sex not determined.
  Cremation uneven.

Burial 40

Weight: 550 gm.
  Finely crushed bone, largest fragment 5 cm.
  Pieces of long bone calcined, cracked and distorted.
Identifiable bones:
  Two pieces of vault of skull, the inner and outer tables separated.
Conclusions:
  Adult, sex not determined.
  High temperature cremation.

Burial 41

Weight: 1.075 kg.
  About twenty pieces of long bone, the longest 6 cm. The other bones are crushed to a small size. All show calcination and some distortion.
Identifiable bones:
  Pieces of thick long bones.
  Two vertebrae with the epiphyses detached.
  Some skull bones including part of the mandible with seven tempty tooth sockets.

Conclusions:
  Young adult male.
  High temperature cremation.

Burial 42   Weight: 125 gm.
  Heavily fragmented bones, the largest 3 cm. across.
Identifiable bones:
  Most pieces are from the vault of the skull. The inner and outer tables are not separated, sutures not fused. Fragments of long bones of small diameter.
Conclusions:
  Adult, sex not determined.
  Moderate temperature cremation.

Burial 43   Weight: 775 gm.
  The bones are well crushed. Longest piece of pelvic bone 4 cm; longest piece of long bone 6 cm. No distortion of long bones.
Identifiable bones:
  Body of vertebrae (?thoracic) showing fusion of epiphyseal plate.
  Pieces of vault of skull showing separation of inner and outer tables. Part of petrous part of one temporal bone. Sutures not fused. One premolar tooth, the crown missing.
Conclusions:
  Adult, sex not determined.
  The skull may have been subjected to a higher temperature than the rest of the skeleton.

Burial 44   Weight: 975 gm
    Specimen well crushed after cremation. Largest fragment 6 cm.
Identifiable bones:
  Pieces of long bones including part of tibia.
  Two pieces of vault of skull with inner and outer tables not separated.
Conclusions:
  Adult, sex not determined.
  Moderate temperature cremation.

Burial 45   Weight: 35 gm.
  A few pieces of bone, some calcined but not distorted, some showing blue discolouration.
Identifiable bones:
  A piece of tibia 2.5 cm. long.
  Part of the arch of a vertebra.
Conclusions:
  Adult, sex not determined.
  Moderate temperature cremation.

Burial 46   Weight: 5.975 kg.
  Two skeletons. Longest bone 8 cm.
Identifiable bones:
  Two adult vertebrae.
  Pieces of skull.
  Part of tibia.
Conclusions:
  Two adults, one male.
  High temperature cremation.

Burial 47   No cremated bones recovered.

Burial 48   Weight: 200 gm.
  Fourteen fragments of long bone 1–1.5 cm. long. The bones are whitened, pitted and scored, but not distorted.
Identifiable bones:
  Pieces of adult bone, probably from upper limbs.

Conclusions:

Adult, sex not determined.

Moderate temperature cremation.

Burial 49   No cremated bones recovered.

Burial 50   Weight: 600 gm.

Longest piece of bone is 6 cm. with twenty pieces about the same size. Long bones show calcination, scoring and distortion.

Identifiable bones:

Part of the head of the humerus.

Parts of some long adult bones.

Fifteen pieces of the vault of the skull of moderate thickness.

Conclusions:

Adult, sex not determined.

High temperature cremation.

Burial 51   No cremated bones recovered.

Burial 52   Weight: 80 gm.

Bones show calcination and scoring. Longest piece 3 cm. Other bones finely crushed.

Identifiable bones:

Parts of some juvenile long bones.

Conclusions:

Pieces of long bones suggest a child of seven to ten years.

Burial 53   Weight: 25 gm.

A few pieces of cremated bone.

Identifiable bones:

A piece of radius or ulna 1.5 cm. long.

Conclusions:

Adult, sex not determined.

Burial 71   Inhumation burial.

The post-cranial skeleton consists of a number of short pieces of badly deteriorated bone and pieces of tibia the longest 7 cm. There was also a piece of probably adult humerus and possibly a piece of rib.

Pieces of the vault of the skull were present, including both temporal bones which were heavy and thick. The front part of the maxilla was present; five teeth left and four right. The enamel was brittle but the teeth were generally not worn. Gingivitis was evident. The mandible was largely intact; six front teeth left, and five right.

Conclusions:

Male, aged thirty to thirty-five years.

B. THE SMALL FINDS AND GLASS by P. Garrard

Burial 2 S.F. 46.   One iron nail,[213] complete and uncorroded: square shaft, flat head. (Not illustrated.)

Burial 3 S.F. 4.   **Fig. 102, No. 3A**, Circular mirror of *speculum* with detached handle. Dr G. Lloyd-Morgan writes: 'Although this mirror was found in approximately thirty fragments, the edge with its characteristic wide border, defined by an engraved circle, on the non-reflecting side, identified it immediately as belonging to Group X. No other trace of applied decoration was noted. The

213.   The iron objects from Cranmer House were reported by Paul Barford and the notes here are extracted from that archive report.

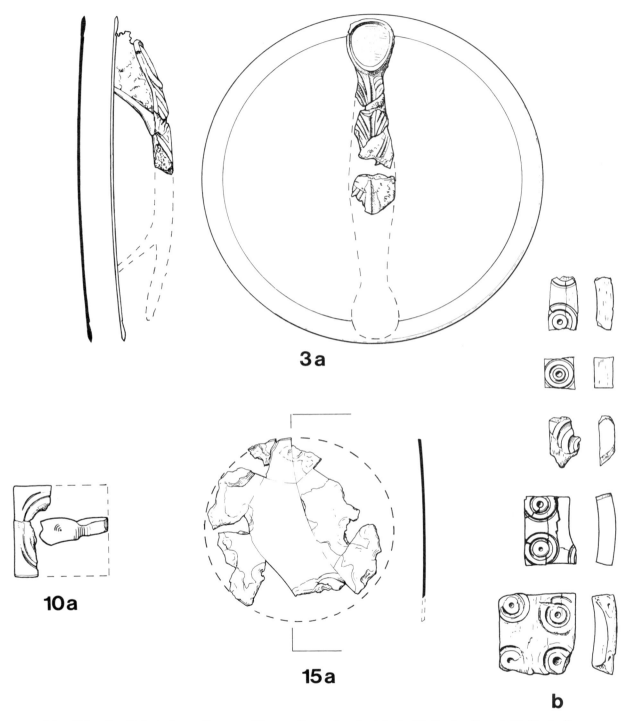

Fig. 102. Small finds from Cranmer House: Cremation burials 3, 10 (Scale: $\frac{1}{1}$) and 15 (Scale:$\frac{1}{2}$)

piece can be paralleled by an earlier find from Canterbury, diameter: 93 mm., now in the Museum.[214] That piece, also undecorated, is without its handle which would have been soldered on at two points across the back of the disc. The new piece was found with most of the handle, one foot and part of the grip extending across it.

Very few mirrors of Group X, either plain or decorated, have ever been found with their handles, though traces of the solder or outline of the feet seen as a difference in colouration of the patina of the metal are not uncommon. An incomplete mirror with compass-drawn decoration on the back, from Siscia now in the Archeolóskog Muzej, Zagreb, No. 4514, has only the feet of the handle still *in situ*. A second piece complete with a plain disc and handle was found with a cremation group at St. Albans by Dr Ian Stead in 1966–8, SUAD burial 4, D.O.E. Lab. no. 670277. That handle is a sturdy item with stylised leaf-shaped solder plates projecting outwards from an angular flattened C-shaped handle, reminiscent of those on some of our older saucepan lids. In the middle of the grip, as part of the cast decoration, are stylised acanthus leaves emerging from either side of a ring.

The Canterbury handle can be paralleled amongst some of the mirrors of the related Group W, also with handles across the back of the disc. Although some of the handles may be similar in shape to that on the St. Albans mirror, others like the Canterbury piece have a more complex form with the grip extending across the feet giving an elongated 'π' shape when seen in side view. The grip may have a very plain outline when seen from above, relieved only by a few lines of hatching, as in Allard Pierson Museum, Amsterdam, No. 1687, or have the more elaborate outline with moulded and engraved detail as in R.G. Museum, Cologne, No. 1024, or the two mirrors now in Leiden, No. 1. 1930/128 from the celebrated Simpelveld sarcophagus, and No. NH b .8 and .10 also numbered V370 from a cremation group found in Nijmegen in 1840, cf. *Catalogue of Roman Mirrors*, Nijmegen 1981, Group W No. 6 and 7, pp. 91–2, Pl. 23, 24.'

A report on the microstructure and an analysis of this mirror fragment, by Dr David A. Scott, of the Department of Conservation and Material Science, Institute of Archaeology, London, is housed in the excavation archive.

	S.F. 50.	Two iron nails, curved, with void corrosion: calcined bone attached to one nail: also a fragmentary nail. (Not illustrated.)
Burial 4	S.F. 12.	Corroded iron lump containing a nail shank, two possible pin shanks and a domed stud. (Not illustrated).
	S.F. 33.	Iron nail, bent and corroded, with calcined bone attached. (Not illustrated).
Burial 7	S.F. 1.	Approximately thirty corroded iron hobnails: (no replaced leather attached to them). (Not illustrated.)
Burial 8	S.F. 15.	Two incomplete corroded iron nails. (Not illustrated.)
Burial 9	S.F. 17.	Iron corroded nail shank; sixteen corroded iron hobnails. (Not illustrated.)
Burial 10	S.F. 47.	**(Fig. 102, No. 10a)** Burnt antler fragments. Dr Stephen Greep writes: 'Three small fragments of burnt ?antler. These are probably from the same object, which appears to have been a small square with an oval raised central boss.'
Burial 11	S.F. 20.	Approximately twenty corroded iron hobnails, some have replaced leather attached to them. (Not illustrated.)
Burial 14	S.F. 19.	One complete corroded iron nail; one iron corrosion lump with calcined bone attached. (Not illustrated.)
Burial 15	S.F. 5.	**(Fig. 102, No. 15a)** Circular *speculum* mirror, fragmented and incomplete. Dr G. Lloyd-Morgan writes: 'Fourteen large fragments and other tiny pieces of a disc mirror of Group F. Two adjoining edge pieces and one other survive, with a slight bevel on the convex reflecting side, and it can be estimated that the complete piece may have had a diameter of some 10 cm.

214. G. Lloyd-Morgan 'Some Mirrors from Roman Canterbury', *Arch. Cant.*, xcix (1983), 231–6. Cf. p. 233 and Fig. 2.

As might be gathered from the notes above, finds of mirrors in a funerary context are not rare. What is less common are detailed accounts of the layout and relationship between the various items in the graves. Our mirror is described as having been found as a lid over the vessel containing the cremation. It can be paralleled by another cremation with a mirror as a cover found in the summer of 1982 in Monson Street, Lincoln.[215] This was the disc of a hand mirror of Group Hc, dated to the first century A.D. Another hand mirror of Group Gc, which may have been contained in its own wooden box though only a few fragments of wood survived, was placed above a shallow bowl containing the cremation found in Burial 1, 17 Stanley Avenue, Norwich, in 1950.[216] A similar arrangement may have obtained in Grave 195 St. Pancras Cemetery, Chichester.[217] The same arrangement with a mirror disc acting as lid to the glass jar holding the cremation was found in the unique Roman burial from Stoneyford, Co. Kilkenny, Ireland.[218] An even more elaborate arrangement was noted in Grave 21, Cologne Eigelstein. The grave was filled with a veritable nest of containers, with the mirror carefully placed over the pot holding the ashes.[219] Unfortunately, the mirror has since been lost and cannot be classified from the illustration.

It should be noted that a silver mirror disc was used as a lid over the *patera* containing the hoard of coins and jewellery found at Backworth, Northumbria in 1812 and now in the British Museum.[220]

The discovery of another disc mirror covering a cremation at Canterbury is, therefore, a useful addition to the record of burial practice during the earlier years of the Roman period in Britain and north-west Europe.'

S.F. 22.   **(Fig. 102, No. 15b)** Burnt antler fragments. Dr Greep writes: 'A number of burnt antler fragments consisting of at least five squares decorated with ring-and-dot in each corner. Similarly decorated antler squares, triangles and circles, usually described as inlay for boxes, have been recovered from a number of sites. The only comparable grave find is from Owslebury associated with a second-century cremation and where such squares formed only one element amongst a number of similarly decorated antler objects.[221] Several fragments including a single ring-and-dot decorated small antler triangle were recovered from a ?third-century cremation at Usk (unpublished excavations Dr W.H. Manning). Such antler objects occur throughout the Roman period, the earliest being a small triangle from Winchester from a context of *c*. A.D. 60.'[222]

Burial 18 S.F. 58.   One heavily corroded iron hobnail. (Not illustrated).
Burial 19 S.F. 18.   **(Fig. 103, No. 19a)** Ring fitting of copper alloy, broken, of D-section. Lying *in situ* against corrosion lump at the fracture was a half polished bone bead.

215.   Monson Street, Lincoln, No. M82 (128) 83. Information kindly supplied in advance of publication by members of the Lincoln Archaeological Trust.

216.   *The Archaeological Newsletter*, iii, No. 4 (1950), 72; *JRS*, xli (1951), 132.

217.   A. Down and M. Rule, *Chichester Excavations I*, (Chichester, 1970), 110.

218.   G. Lloyd-Morgan, 'Roman Mirrors and Pictish Symbols, A Note on Trade and Contact', in W.S. Hanson and L.J.F. Keppie, *Roman Frontier Studies 1979, Papers Presented to the 12th International Congress of Roman Frontier Studies*, *BAR* International Series (Supplementary) No. 71 (i) (1980), 97–106. Cf. Appendix No. 11, 104 for bibliography.

219.   W. Haberey, 'Ein Früh-römisches Brandgrab mit Spenderohe aus Köln', *Festschrift* A. Oxé (Darmstadt 1938), 197–204, cf. Abb. 1, No. 8. R.G. Mus. Cologne, No. 34.368.

220.   Department of Prehistoric and Roman Britain, No. 50, 6–1.2, Walters *British Museum Catalogue of Plate*, 1921, No. 184, 46–8 Fig. 48.

221.   J. Collis, 'Owslebury (Hants.) and the Problems of Burials on Rural Settlements' in (Ed.) R. Reece, *Burial in the Roman World*, C.B.A. Research Report 22, 1977, 26 and 35, Fig. 11.

222.   B. Cunliffe, *Winchester Excavations 1949–60*, Vol. I (Winchester, 1964), Fig. 25, 4.

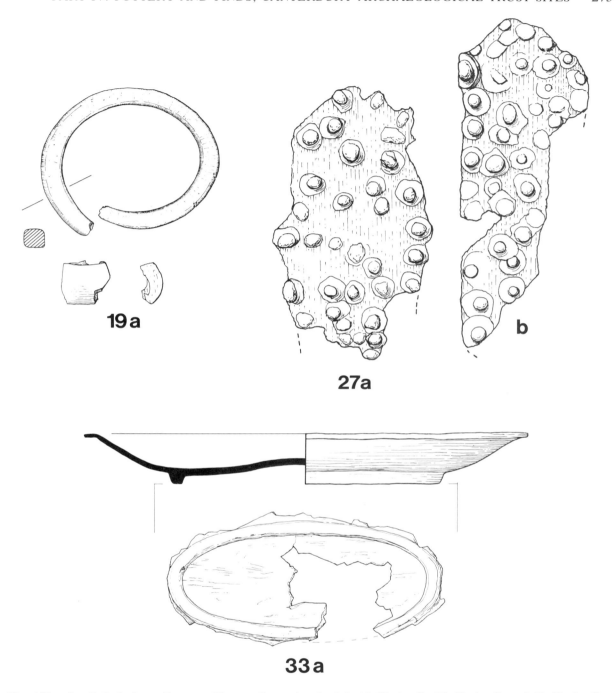

Fig. 103.   Small finds from Cranmer House: Cremation burials 19 (Scale: $\frac{1}{1}$), 27 (Scale: $\frac{1}{2}$) and 33 (Scale: $\frac{1}{4}$)

	S.F. 16.	Two incomplete, corroded iron nails. (Not illustrated).
Burial 27	S.F. 57.	**(Fig. 103, No. 27a)** Two shoe or sandal soles of replaced leather, studded with iron hobnails.
Burial 28	S.F. 55.	Fragment of replaced leather, studded with three to four iron corroded hobnails. (Not illustrated.)
Burial 30	S.F. 2.	Two corroded fragmentary iron nails. (Not illustrated.)
Burial 33	S.F. 10.	**(Fig. 103, No. 33a)** Pewter dish fragments, from a second-century cremation vessel. The foot-ring was physically reconstructed and from other fragments a reconstructed drawing was possible.
	S.F. 14.	Flint flake. (Not illustrated.)
	S.F. 21.	Fourteen corroded iron nails, four with heads; some are re-corroded. (Not illustrated.)
	S.F. 48.	Nine iron corroded hobnails, some with calcined bone attached. (Not illustrated.)
Burial 36	S.F. 13.	**(Fig. 104, No. 36a)** Copper alloy object, probably incomplete.
Burial 38	S.F. 30.	Small copper alloy fragments. (Not illustrated.)
Burial 40	S.F. 9.	**(Fig. 104, No. 40a)** Pipe-clay figurine. Dr F. Jenkins writes: 'This type of statuette moulded in white pipe-clay portrays a dignified matron seated in a high-backed basket chair, but now lacks the head. Although her true identity is not known, it is virtually certain that she is a mother-goddess and, by reason of the fact that she is suckling two infants, she is usually identified as the *Dea nutrix*. She is attired in a robe worn over an ankle-length skirted *tunica*. The skirt of the undergarment hangs in deep V-shaped folds and the hem consists of two moulded bands in relief divided by an incised line presumably to represent the stitching of the double thickness of the cloth.

There is nothing to show that the robe worn over the *tunica* opened down the front or that it was secured by any kind of fastening. It seems to have consisted of a single piece of rectangular-shaped cloth with a circular hole cut in it for the collar, and designed to hang from the shoulders at the back and front. It is evidently sleeveless and open down each side, and is gathered together in front to hang down in deep loop-like folds between the knees, to expose the breasts while suckling the infants. This style of robe is exclusive to the *Dea nutrix* type of clay statuettes produced in the Central Gaulish potteries, whereas the garments worn by the nursing mothers from the Rhine-Mosel industry are entirely different. It seems, therefore, that this distinctive garment is a Central Gaulish version of the maternity robes worn by provincial Roman nursing mothers.

A noteworthy feature of the Cranmer House statuette is the hand of the infant at the left breast which is at a higher level than that of the infant at the right breast. This is also found on a wide range of statuettes of this type, but it is curious that it is not confined to one particular mould.

The basket chair on which the goddess is seated is a piece of furniture which is exclusive to the Central Gaulish statuettes of the *Dea nutrix*. It has a rounded back which supports the goddess up to the level of her shoulders, and the sides are curved round to the front to form the arms. It was evidently designed to stand on the ground on a semicircular base without feet. The weave of the wickerwork and the outlines of the vertical canes supporting it are visible. The pattern of the weave is rather stylised being represented by short obliquely incised lines arranged in herringbone fashion in raised vertical bands up the back and the sides of the chair. Similarly incised lines represent the plaited band outlining the edges of the back and the sides of the chair. The date when this type of basket chair first appeared in western Europe is uncertain, but by the second century of our era it had been firmly established on the carved stone monuments of the western Roman provinces, to which period the clay statuettes of the *Dea nutrix* belong.[223]

The front and the back of the statuette were cast in separate moulds, and then the two parts

223. J. Liversidge, *Furniture in Roman Britain* (London, 1955), 16–24.

were luted together, and the joint was concealed by smoothing the clay with some kind of tool. As the interior of the statuette is hollow, and is sealed at the base by a separate D-shaped flat pad of clay, a small hole is provided through the side of the chair in one place to allow the expanding gases within the statuette to escape at high temperatures during the firing process in the kiln, and thus prevent its disintegration.

An unusual feature is that this statuette has a surface coating which is of a yellow-brown colour. This seems to be the original slip coating and not the result of staining by the soil in which the statuette was buried.

The presence of clay statuettes as wasters and the moulds for them on the sites of the kilns in the Allier district proved conclusively that the *Dea nutrix* types were a speciality of the potters in that part of Central Gaul.[224] It is possible that the Canterbury example is one of the numerous mass-produced inferior copies of the better-quality *Deae nutrices* made by Pistillus, who seems to have had his *officina* at Autun (Saône-et-Loire) and reproduced the wicker work of the basket chairs more realistically.[225]

At the present time the chronology of the development of the Central Gaulish industry is not fully understood, because the kilns were discovered many years ago and the contemporary reports do not set forth the evidence for dating them. The dating of individual statuettes found elsewhere is complicated because of the lack of this information, and by several other unknown factors – the date when a statuette reached the British market; the subsequent shelf-life before purchase; the length of time which elapsed between its purchase and when it was either discarded in rubbish or was deliberately buried for cult purposes.

As the production of clay statuettes was allied to that of samian ware in Central Gaul, and the potters ceased the production of the latter at the end of the second century, it is reasonable to think that the export of statuettes to Britain had also ceased. Evidence from recently excavated British sites, where clay statuettes have occurred either in dated stratified deposits or in graves with associated datable material, suggests that they were in popular demand in this country somewhere between A.D. 120 and 180.

The Cranmer House statuette is the seventh example found at Canterbury and the second example to come from the extensive Roman cemetery which is located across the River Stour to the north-west of the city wall, in the area roughly bounded by St. Dunstan's Street, London Road, Rheims Way and the river.[226] A fragment of another was found in this area but was not associated with any burial.[227] The occurrence of this type of statuette in cremation burials has been previously noted at Snodland, Kent,[228] at Arkesden, Essex[229] and at Welwyn, Herts., the latter being one which suckles one infant.[230] These burials clearly belong to the Hadrianic-Antonine period and evidently before the year 190.

It is not known how the Cranmer House example lost the head, but it is possible that it was deliberately broken off at the time of the burial, thus following the known practice of ritual breakage, the purpose of which was to release the in-dwelling spirit so that it could accompany the dead into the other world.'[231]

224. M. Rouvier-Jeanlin, *Catalogue des Figurines en Terre Cuite gallo-romaine du Musée des Antiquités nationales*, Editions du Comité National de la Recherche Scientifique, XXIVe Supplément à 'Gallia' (Paris, 1972).
225. H. Vertet, and J. Vuillemot, *Figurines gallo-romaines en Argile d'Autun* (Autun, 1974), 15–33, Pls. 1–2.
226. F. Jenkins, 'The Cult of the "*Dea nutrix*" in Kent', *Arch. Cant.*, lxxi (1957), 38–46, Pl. I(a).
227. Found in excavations directed by F. Jenkins on the site of the Rheims Way north-west of Whitehall Road in 1959. See his unpublished Ph.D. thesis, University of Kent, 295, No. 007.
228. Found in 1961 and now in the British Museum, Acc. No. 1962–4–3.3. unpublished.
229. R.C. Neville, *Sepulchra Exposita*, 40 ff. Downing Street Museum, Cambridge, 48.815.
230. *Current Archaeology*, No. 3 (July 1967) Fig. No. 78.
231. F. Jenkins, *op. cit.*, note 226, for discussion of cult associations.

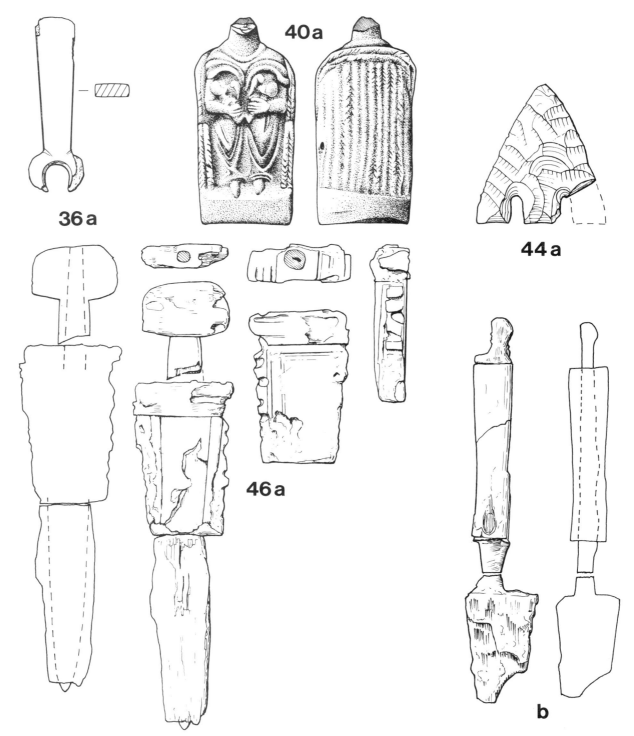

Fig. 104.   Small finds from Cranmer House: Cremation burials 36, 44, 46 (Scale: $\frac{1}{1}$) and 40 (Scale: $\frac{1}{2}$)

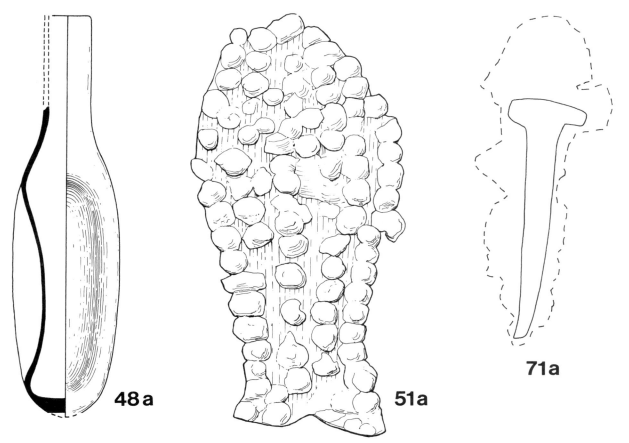

Fig. 105.   Small finds from Cranmer House: Cremation burials 48 (Scale: ¼) and 51 (Scale: ½), and Saxon inhumation
burial 71 (Scale: ½)

	S.F. 28.	Four corroded iron nail shanks and fragments. (Not illustrated.)
	S.F. 31.	Four corroded iron nails, two with heads. (Not illustrated.)
Burial 44	S.F. 34.	**(Fig. 104, No. 44a)**. Flint arrowhead, incomplete. P. Blockley writes: 'A Beaker/Early Bronze Age barbed-and-tanged arrowhead of pale–mid mottled grey flint. Pressure-flaking in the form of invasive scale retouch, was employed on both obverse and reverse surfaces to produce a 4 mm. thick arrowhead. A few of these flakes terminated in hinge fractures. Finer, steep retouch was used to remove irregularities and strengthen the edges. The barbs and tang were formed by pressure-flaking two parallel grooves 8 mm. long from the base of the sub-triangular flake. One barb is missing.'
Burial 45	S.F. 36.	Lead plug from cremation vessel. (Not illustrated.)
Burial 46	S.F. 40.	**(Fig. 104, No. 46a)**. Miniature iron sword and scabbard. Dr S. Greep writes: 'Three adjoining fragments of bone retaining an iron tang (120 mm. long) and fragment of scabbard. Although this is a particularly large example of its type, there is little doubt that it belongs to a group of model swords.[232] The Canterbury piece includes the hilt-guard, a rectangular element originally with two protruberances, only one now surviving, imitating a rare type of full-size

232.   S. Greep, 'A model Sword from Bucklersbury House, London', *Transactions of the London and Middlesex Archaeological Society*, xxxii (1981), 103–6.

guard[233] and unlike those on other model swords of this group which are more usually decorated with a horizontal groove. The scabbard is a tapering section of compact bone, decorated with longitudinal grooves, in this instance apparently both front and back, and with the remains of ?suspension loops just below the guard. It retains a long, flat, iron blade. The chape is made from a separate piece of bone and is joined to the scabbard by an iron pin. In other model swords the chape is carved in one with the scabbard, the end being blocked by a small bone plug.

The Canterbury model with its slightly unusual elements is an important addition to the known list of such objects. Despite being badly preserved, it is the most complete example so far recorded from Britain. Fragments of such models have been recorded only from Verulamium, Colchester and London, although they are more common on the Continent.[234] The Canterbury model is only the second recorded from a funerary context, the other being from a grave near Rheims. In her recent paper Faudet[235] offers a votive explanation for these forms though the example from Argentomagus she lists is the only piece to be recorded from such a context. The individual elements of these models bear varying relationships to their full-size counterparts. Closest is the handle, typically an almost exact copy of the early Roman ribbed *gladius* handle.[236] The hilt-guard on the Canterbury piece appears to be a close copy of larger Roman examples (see above) but such a comparison is not possible on other models with guards surviving. On all such models the chape is most unlike that found on any Roman weapon but is more reminiscent of those found on Iron Age swords.[237] Perhaps rather than the *gladius*, auxiliary weapons are intended?

Stylistically these forms are likely to belong to the early Roman period, a date confirmed by pieces from Verulamium (Antonine), London (*c.* A.D. 50–150), Argentomagus (mid first century) and now Canterbury.'

S.F. 54   **(Fig. 104, No. 46b)**. Iron knife with bone handle. Dr S. Greep writes: 'Triangular-bladed iron knife, 33 mm. long with a cylindrical bone handle. The handle, 71 mm. long and much worn, displays traces of what may have been quite elaborate decoration, most of which is now lost. The tang of the knife runs throughout the length of the handle.'

Glass vessel, incomplete. Dr V. Tatton-Brown writes: 'Lower part of body and neck of unguent bottle; broken and mended, a number of fragments not joining. Originally shaped like a candlestick with long neck and flattened body. Colourless with many small bubbles in the glass; dulled. Free blown. Height as restored 6.5 cm; diameter of base 7.5 cm.

'Candlestick' unguent bottles were very common and again were particularly popular in the western Roman Empire. Most examples of this variety, with no constriction at the base of the neck and with a flat conical body, date from the second half of the second century, although the type originated in the first century and lasted into the third.'[238] (Not illustrated.)

233. J. Curle, *A Roman Frontier Post and its People* (Glasgow, 1911), Pl. LXXIV, 4.

234. S. Greep, *op. cit.*, note 232, and I. Faudet, 'Miniature "*ex-voto*" from Argentomagus (Indre)', *Britannia*, xiv (1983), 97–102.

235. I. Faudet, *op. cit.*, 97.

236. H. Chapman and A. Johnson, 'Excavations at Aldgate and Bush Lane House in the City of London, 1972', *Transactions of the London and Middlesex Archaeological Society*, xxiv (1973), 1–73, Fig. 22, 12.

237. S. Piggott, 'Swords and Scabbards of the British Early Iron Age', *PPS*, xvi (1950), 1–28.

238. Morin-Jean, *La Verrerie en Gaule sous l'Empire romain* (Paris, 1913), 77–9, Form 24; C. Isings, *Roman Glass from dated Finds* (Groningen, 1957), 99, Form 82B(2); C. Isings, *Roman Glass in Limburg, Archaeologia Traectina*, ix (Groningen, 1971), 66, No. 15, Fig. 15; E. Welker, *Die römischen Gläser von Nida-Heddernheim, Schriften des Frankfurter Museums für Vor- und Frühgeschichte*, iii (1974), 50, Type 10; K. Goethert-Polaschek, *Katalog der römischen Gläser der Rheinischen Landesmuseums Trier, Trier Ausgrabungen und Forschungen*, ix (Mainz, 1977), 117–8, Form 72.

S.F. 35.   Two corroded iron nails, one with a copper alloy head. (Not illustrated.)

S.F. 59.   One iron hobnail. (Not illustrated.)

Burial 48   (**Fig. 105, No. 48a**). Glass. Indented glass vessel, incomplete. Dr V. Tatton-Brown writes: 'Body and part of neck of unguent bottle; tube-shaped with rounded bottom; body decorated with indents. Colourless; many small bubbles in the glass. Free blown with tooled indents. Height as restored 85 mm.

Unguentaria with deep indents on the body are common in the Western Roman Empire. The type is mainly of the second century A.D. although it began in the first and continued into the third.[239] Many examples are tube-shaped like ours and the rim is normally folded outwards, downwards and inwards (e.g. Colchester,[240] examples from the Rhineland[241] and from Trier[242]). Occasionally such *unguentaria* have the rims knocked off and ground, as in an example from Nida-Heddernheim.[243] Another example from Britain found in a second-century context in London has a slightly more rounded offset shoulder[244] and this is further emphasised for examples from the Continent.'[245]

S.F. 44.   Three small fragments of iron nails. (Not illustrated.)

Burial 51 S.F. 60.   (**Fig. 105, No. 51a**). Part of the left sole of a shoe or sandal studded with iron hobnails – the leather is mineralized.

Burial 52 S.F. 45.   Three small fragments of iron nails. (Not illustrated.)

Feature 63 S.F. 43.   Two corroded iron nails and a few fragments.

Feature 67 S.F. 51.   Flint flake. (Not illustrated.)

Feature 68 S.F. 8.   Anglo-Saxon *sceatta*. Dr D.M. Metcalf writes: 'Series B. 0.71 g. The obverse has a bust rather than a head, and this makes it BI, B. The obverse die is not included in Rigold's corpus[246] nor in his Addenda[247] but is similar to BI, B7. The reverse, with two dots and two annulets around the cross is by the same hand as BI, B6/i and 8/i. It reads [. . .] MVΛII Voo Mint: (?) London/Essex. Date: *c.* A.D. 700–20.'[248]

Burial 69 S.F. 56a and b.   (**Fig. 114, Nos. a, b**). Two glass palm cups. Dr V. Tatton-Brown writes: '(a)   Palm cup with conical body, rounded base and tubular rim folded upwards, outwards and downwards. Greenish-blue glass. Broken and mended, one fragment now missing from the body and two from the rim. Many small bubbles in the glass but little visible weathering apart from a few patches of brown film. Blown. Height 6.2 cm; max. diam. 11.4 cm.
(b)   Fragment of palm cup similar to (a) above.

The palm cup has been rightly described as one of the 'normal forms' of Anglo-Saxon

239.   Cf. C. Isings, *op. cit.*, note 238, 100, Form 83.

240.   As T. May, *Catalogue of the Roman Pottery in the Colchester and Essex Museum* (Cambridge, 1930), 281, Grave 100/71, No. 410, Pl. LXXXVII.

241.   F. Fremersdorf, *Das naturfarbene sogenannte blaugrüne Glas in Köln. Die Denkmaler des römischen Köln*, iv (Cologne, 1958), 26–7, Pl. 23.

242.   K. Goethert-Polaschek, *op. cit.*, note 238, 122, Form 76a, No. 668, from Trier.

243.   As E. Welker (1974), 130–1, Type 26, No. 294, from Nida-Heddernheim.

244.   Royal Commission on Historical Monuments, *An Inventory of the Historical Monuments of London* 3 (London, 1928), 157, Fig. 64.22.

245.   F. Fremersdorf, *op. cit.*, note 241, 26–7, Pls. 22, 24 1–2; K. Goethert-Polaschek, *op. cit.*, note 238, 122, No. 667, Pl. 53.

246.   S. Rigold, 'The two primary Series of Sceattas', *British Numismatic Journal*, xxx (1960/61), 6–53; id.

247.   S. Rigold, '–, Addenda and Corrigenda', *ibid.*, (1966), 1–6.

248.   Dr Metcalf discusses this coin at greater length in a corpus report on *sceatta* finds in Canterbury, which will be published in *The Archaeology of Canterbury*, vol. vi, forthcoming.

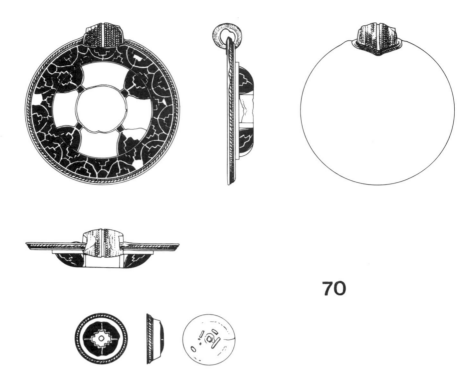

70

Fig. 106.   Small finds from Cranmer House: The Saxon Gold Pendant. (Scale: ⅟₁)

glasses[249] of which examples are as common in Britain as on the Continent.[250] The Cranmer House cups are of the plain variety with folded rim which is unknown before the seventh century A.D. In Britain the majority of plain palm cups close to ours have been found in Kent.'[251]

Burial 70 S.F. 23.   **(Fig. 106, No. 70)**. The gold pendant. Dr L. Webster writes: 'The pendant is of gold, inlaid with *cloisonné* garnets and decorated with filigree wires. The body is circular, surmounted by a

249.   D.B. Harden, 'Glass Vessels in Britain and Ireland, A.D. 400–1000', in (Ed.) D.B. Harden, *Dark Age Britain: Studies presented to E.T. Leeds* (London, 1956), 142.

250.   F. Rademacher, 'Frankische Gläser aus dem Rheinlande', *Bonner Jahrbücher*, cxlvii (1942), 301 ff.

251.   Half of those in Harden's check-list of 1956 (Harden 1956, *op. cit.*, 164–5, Type b) come from Kent – the rest are from various different counties; of the two in Canterbury Museum, which are close to ours in size, colour and condition, as well as type, one certainly (No. 957; height: 70 mm.; diameter: 106.5 mm.), and possibly also the other (No. 954; height: 65 mm.; diameter: 105 mm.), was presented about 1900/1906 by Alderman Francis Bennett Goldney, F.S.A., honorary curator and sometime Mayor and M.P. for Canterbury, having originally been bought as part of the Wilkie Morris collection named after the collector/dealer who lived in Faversham. Since 1956 only a few palm cups have been recorded and the reports do not describe them in sufficient detail to identify the type to which they belong (cf. Harden in *Med. Arch.*, xxii (1978), 2, 21, note 6).

I would like to thank Dr D.B. Harden for his help and advice and Mr K. Reedie, who kindly gave me his facilities to study the palm cups in Canterbury Museum and provided the information about their acquisition.

barrel-shaped suspension loop: the overall diameter is 40 mm. The decoration consists of an outer zone of garnet inlay in stepped and curved shapes. The central area of the pendant consists of a convex cruciform design in which the now-empty arms of the cross were originally inlaid with a form of calcite, probably shell. The semi-circular spaces between the curved arms of the cross are inlaid with convex garnet settings and are connected to the central boss by small square garnet cells. This boss consists of a separate garnet-inlaid domed stud in a filigree wire collar. It is now loose, but was originally soldered to a concealed gold support fixed to the back sheet. The whole pendant is edged with beaded and twisted wires and the heavily-worn suspension-loop is decorated with pseudo-plait filigree. The back is plain, but bears the impressions of the cell-work soldered to its other side; among these are the marks left by a circular support for the central stud, which was later drastically cut away. This, together with other signs of modification on the base of the stud itself, and the general wear on the pendant's loop and upper edge, suggest that the pendant was of some age when buried.

The metal of the pendant has been analysed in the British Museum Research Laboratory. Its composition is as follows:

Back plate: 85 per cent gold, 13 per cent silver, 1.5 per cent copper.
Loop: 84 per cent gold, 14 per cent silver, 2.2 per cent copper
Boss: 85 per cent gold, 13 per cent silver, 2.1 per cent copper

These results are consistent with a contemporaneous manufacture for the component parts of the pendant.

Despite such wear and minor damage, the pendant is one of the most complex and splendid pieces of Anglo-Saxon jewellery to have been found since the discovery of the Sutton Hoo jewellery in 1939. Pendants of various kinds emerged as a major jewellery form early in the seventh century, as a native adaptation of Byzantine fashion. They quickly supplanted brooches as the principal female article of jewellery and continued in use into the last quarter of the seventh century. The more elaborate among them were decorated with inlaid and filigree decoration of a high order. The Canterbury pendant's geometric elegance can stand comparison with the very best of these, such as the Wilton and Ixworth pendant crosses;[252] and like them displays an expressly Christian motif. However, its overall effect is very different from both of these and from simpler contemporary pendants. The distinctive use of an outer zone of stepped and curved garnet inlay, and the domed central area with its white inlay and collared boss are much more typical of the great series of Kentish composite disc brooches which belong to the first third of the seventh century; for example, the well-known pieces from Gilton, Sarre (I and II) and Kingston:[253] The Canterbury pendant is in effect just such a brooch translated into a pendant, and must surely be a product of a workshop which also dealt in these prestigious brooches.

As the parallels with the composite brooches and the cruciform pendants suggest, the pendant, like them, must belong to the first third of the seventh century; in all probability it was made around the 620s like those related pieces which can be approximately dated by their association with coins, the Wilton pendant and the Sarre I brooch.[254] The relatively high gold content of the piece is also consistent with such a date for its manufacture.[255] The evidence of alteration to the pendant and the considerable wear on the loop and upper edge, however,

252. R. Jessup, *Anglo-Saxon Jewellery* (London, 1974).
253. R. Avent, *Anglo-Saxon Garnet Inlaid Disc and Composite Brooches*, 2 vols. *B.A.R.* British Series, No. 11 (Oxford 1975).
254. S.E. Rigold and L.E. Webster, 'Three Anglo-Saxon Disc Brooches', *Arch. Cant.*, lxxxv (1970), 13–17.
255. P.D.C. Brown and F. Schweizer, 'X-Ray fluorescent Analysis of Anglo-Saxon Jewellery', *Archaeometry*, xv (1973), 175–92.

suggest that the date of burial could be several decades later, around the middle of the century.

The significance of this new find for Canterbury itself is of equal interest. The discovery of well-equipped Anglo-Saxon burials a quarter of a mile west of the City walls implies the existence of a hitherto unknown cemetery of considerable status, re-using like so many east Kentish Anglo-Saxon cemeteries, an earlier known burial ground. As only traces of the graves were found, it is impossible at this stage to say whether the remains of the burials discovered, all of them apparently seventh-century, lie on the outer edge of a large cemetery in which they represent the latest phase of a long-lived burial ground, or whether this is one of those Anglo-Saxon cemeteries newly established or re-sited in the seventh century. It does however, suggest the existence either of an extra-mural settlement west of Canterbury between the city and Harbledown, a mile away, or even of seventh-century settlement in the western part of the city of Canterbury itself. Although apparently contemporary with the extensive Anglo-Saxon settlement centred on the Marlowe site in eastern Canterbury, it could not have served such a distant community, which must have buried its dead on that side of the town, where contemporary burials are known east of the walls at St. Augustine's Abbey and St. Martin's Church.

Only further excavation can clarify these points; meanwhile, the new find is clearly of major importance not only for the hint it gives us of the scope and quality of Anglo-Saxon settlement in and around the early seventh-century Centerbury, but also as a splendid and revealing addition to the *corpus* of Anglo-Saxon jewellery.'[256]

Burial 71 S.F. 27 (**Fig. 105, No. 71a**). One of six large iron nails (lengths ranging from 90–170 mm.), all with their heads knocked at an angle. There is no trace of mineralised wood.

C. THE POTTERY by R.J. Pollard

The Roman wares represented at Cranmer House have all been described in the Marlowe Car Park pottery report (Pollard forthcoming). The acid soil has caused extensive deterioration of the surfaces of many vessels, causing doubt about the presence or absence of slip, burnish, or decoration. In such cases (e.g. BB2) general considerations of form and fabric have been taken into account in determining to which ware the vessel should be assigned.

The following fabric code numbers have been allocated to the pottery wares present at Cranmer House in order to abbreviate the report. These are not intended as a type-series of broader scope. An appropriate date is indicated for each group. Thanks are due to Mark Ellam and Rebecca Mair for illustration of the Romano-British wares and the Saxon vessel respectively.

I	Belgic grog-tempered: soft or hard, exhibiting 'Belgic' traits of style.
II	Belgic grog-tempered/Native Coarse Ware 'transitional': soft, exhibiting Native Coarse Ware traits of style.
III	Native Coarse Ware: generally very hard, though soil acidity reduces this to hard: high-fired, with a 'ring' when struck.
IV	Reduced sand-tempered wheel-thrown.
V	Oxidised sand-tempered wheel-thrown.
VI	Pink-buff and buff sand-tempered wheel-thrown.
VII	Pink-buff and buff fine sandy and smooth/powdery.
VIII	Fine reduced.
IX	Fine oxidised.
X	Fine oxidised, white slip.

256. The pendant was conserved by Karen Webster of Kent County Museums Service and analysis undertaken by Mavis Bimson and Mike Cowell of the British Museum Research Laboratory. I am grateful to them and to Paul Barford and Tim Tatton-Brown of the Canterbury Archaeological Trust for information and valuable discussion.

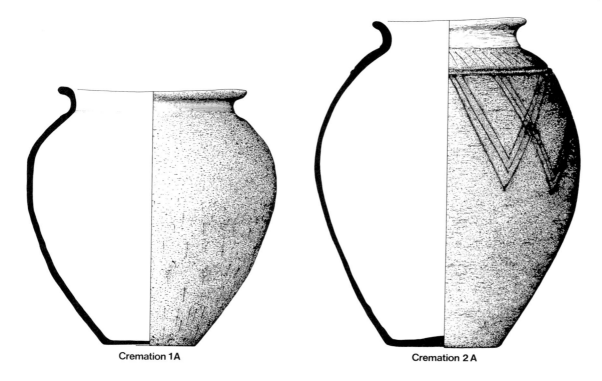

Cremation 1A   Cremation 2 A

Fig. 107.   Roman pottery from Cranmer House: Cremation burials 1 and 2 (Scale: ¼)

(i)   THE CREMATION BURIALS

The pottery burial groups are listed in order. In each case, the funerary urn is indicated thus: (*).

Burial 1	A: Fabric III(*) **Fig. 107, 1A**.
	B: Fabric IV. Necked jar with short-everted rim.
	C: Fabric VIII. Body sherd.
	Date: Mid second to third century.
Burial 2	A: Fabric III(*) **Fig. 107, 2A**.
	B: Fabric VII. Flagon, one handle, squared-bead rim.
	C: Fabric VIII. Base; bowl?
	D: Fabric V. Base; jar?
	E. Fabric VII. Body sherds; flagon?
	F. Fabric IV. Body sherd; bowl?
	G. Fabric IV. Base; jar?
	Date: Mid second to third century.
Burial 3	A: Fabric II(*) **Fig. 108, 3A**.
	B: Fabric VIII. Flask with cordon at girth. Cf. Ospringe 314. Possibly Antonine to third century.
	Date: Mid second to third century.
Burial 4	A: Fabric III(*) **Fig. 108, 4A**.
	Date: Mid second to third century.

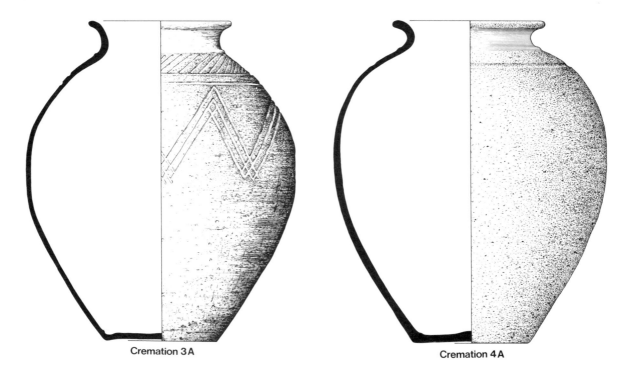

Cremation 3 A   Cremation 4 A

Fig. 108.   Roman pottery from Cranmer House: Cremation burials 3 and 4 (Scale: ¼)

Burial 5   A: Fabric III (*?). Necked jar with everted rim.
                  B: Samian, Central Gaulish, Dr. 37, base and lower body. Hadrianic-Antonine?
                  C: Fabric IV. Necked jar with roll-rim.
                  D: Fabric IV. Body sherds; jar?
                  Date: Mid second to third century.
Burial 6   A: Oxfordshire brown colour-coated ware. Flagon (?) – slip on exterior only.
                  B: Fabric VIII. Body sherds.
                  C: Fabric IV. Body sherds.
                  Date: Mid third to early fourth century.
Burial 7   A: Fabric VIII (*?). Base; jar.
                  Date: Flavian to early fourth century.
Burial 8   A: Fabric IV. Necked jar with triangular everted rim (*?) cf. Canterbury I, 311. Late second
                  to fourth century.
                  B: BB2. Dog-dish, undecorated, groove below rim. Canterbury I, 408–9. Hadrianic to early
                  fourth century in Canterbury, but mostly late second century plus.
                  C: BB2. Pie-dish, perhaps undecorated. Gillam 313? (c. A.D. 190–240).
                  D: Fabric VIII. Beaker, 'miniature' of Gillam 137, with tooled acute lattice. Mid second to
                  early fourth century at Canterbury.
                  E: BB2. (? deteriorated surface). Gillam 143. Late second to early fourth century in
                  Canterbury.
                  Date: Late second to third century.
Burials 8A and 8B   A: Fabric IV. Necked jar with roll-rim.
                  Date: No close date.

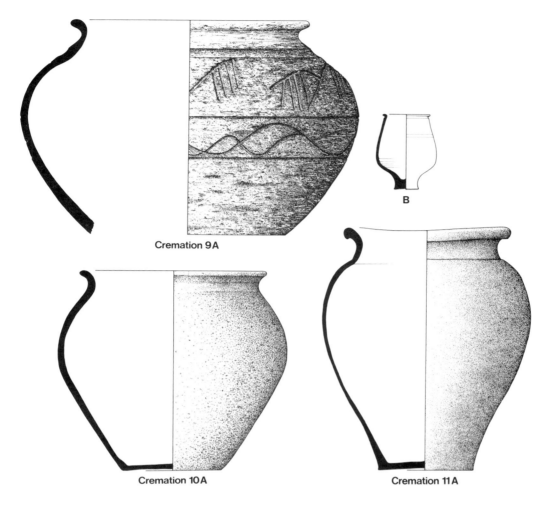

Fig. 109.   Roman pottery from Cranmer House: Cremation burials 9, 10 and 11 (Scale: ¼)

Burial 9	A: Fabric II(*). Light oblique combing overall on body, with tooled decoration over, and corrugated neck. **Fig. 109, 9A.**
	B: Fabric as 15E. Gillam 90, dated therein to the mid third century, but cf. 23D here also. **Fig. 109, 9B.**
	Date: Late second to third century.
Burial 10	A: Fabric III (*) **Fig. 109, 10A.**
	Date: Mid second to third century.
Burial 11	A: Fabric IV(*) Necked jar with roll-rim. **Fig. 109, 11A.**
	Date: No close date.
Burial 12	A: Fabric IV(*?). Base; jar.
	B: Samian, Central Gaulish, Dr. 33. Second century.
	C: Fabric VIII. Rouletted 'poppy-head' beaker. Canterbury V, 211; Ospringe 256; Tyers 52. Late second to third century.
	Date: Late second to third century.

Burial 13 A: BB2? (deteriorated surface)(*). Gillam 143/144. Date as 8E above.
      Date: Late second to early fourth century.

Burial 14 A: Fabric II (*). Wide-mouth storage jar, form as 15A, with wiped lower exterior.
      Date: Second century.

Burial 15 A: Fabric II(*). Wide-mouth necked everted-rim storage jar, burnished shoulder, wiped
        lower half of body. **Fig. 110, 15A.**
      B: Fabric II. Jar, wiped exterior and base below shoulder. Late first to first half of second
        century; Canterbury V, 209, 220. **Fig. 110, 15B.**
      C: Fabric V. Flagon, ringed-disc rim. Cf. Dane John 46, but one-handled. Second century
        broadly. **Fig. 110, 15C.**
      D: Fabric VIII. Necked jar, rim sherd, cf. Canterbury V, 335. Possibly same vessel as 15J
        below.
      E: Lower Rhineland, or possibly Nene Valley, black colour-coat on white fabric. Colchester
        392, Gose 185. *c.* A.D. 150–mid-third century. See Anderson *et al.* for discussion of
        sources of this ware. **Fig. 110, 15E.**
      F: Fabric VII. Base, flagon?
      G: Samian, Central Gaulish, Dr. 40. Late second century. **Fig. 110, 15G.**
      H: Fabric VIII. As 21A. **Fig. 110, 15H.**
      J: Fabric VIII(*). Necked jar, probably within mid second to early fourth century (Pollard
        forthcoming, Canterbury V). As (e.g.) Ospringe 114. **Fig. 110, 15J.**
      Date: Second half of second century (possibly early third century).

Burial 16 A: Fabric III(*?). Necked storage jar with triangular-rolled rim.
      Date: Mid second to third century.

Burial 17 A: Fabric VIII, with moderate quantities of fine quartz roughening the surface (deterio-
        rated)(*). cf. 27G. Late second to early fourth century? **Fig. 110, 17A.**
      B: BB2? (deteriorated). Dog-dish. Possibly undecorated. **Fig. 110, 17B.**
      Date: Late second to early fourth century.

Burial 18 A: Fabric VII(*). Two-handled large flagon. Cf. Whitehall 22; Dane John 41–43, 45, 46.
        Possibly a Canterbury product of the second century. **Fig. 111, 18A.**
      Date: Second century.

Burial 19 A: Fabric II. Base of jar; (*), or an unintended incorporation in the pit fill.
      B: Fabric VII. Flagon. *c.* A.D. 130–200/250, e.g. Canterbury I, 379; Canterbury V, 230;
        Canterbury VII, 90; Dover 558, 702. **Fig. 111, 19B.**
      C: BB2. Dog-dish, arguably a 'miniature' (10 cm. diameter at rim: see Pollard 1983). Gillam
        328 with groove below rim as 8B above. *c.* A.D. 130–200. **Fig. 111, 19C.**
      D: Samian, Central Gaulish, Dr. 31. Fragment of name-stamp, illegible. Mid to end second
        century, **Fig. 111, 19D.**
      E: Fabric VIII. Beaker base, with tooled lattice on body. Parallels 8D above.
      Date: Mid second to mid third century.

Burial 20 A: Fabric II(*). Impressed/slashed decoration on shoulder. **Fig. 111, 20A.**
      Date: Second century.

Burial 21 A: Fabric VIII. Undecorated bag-beaker, as 15H. *c.* A.D. 150 – mid (?) third century. **Fig.**
        112, 21A.
      Date: Second half of second to third century.

Burial 22 A: Fabric II(*). Base and lower body only survived. Storage jar, wiped exterior wall and
        base.
      B: Fabric VII. Body sherd; flagon?
      C: Samian, Central Gaulish, Dr. 31. Mid to end second century.
      D: Fabric IV. Body sherd.
      Date: Mid second to third century.

Burial 23 A: Fabric II(*). Decoration as 20A. **Fig. 112, 23A.**
      B: Fabric VIII. Flask. Ospringe 389.

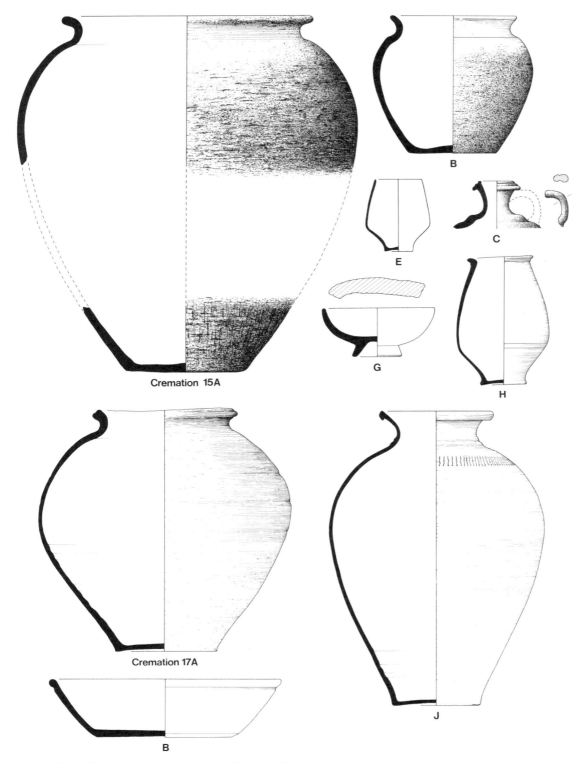

Cremation 15A

B

E

C

G

H

Cremation 17A

B

J

Fig. 110.   Roman pottery from Cranmer House: Cremation burials 15 and 17 (Scale: ¼)

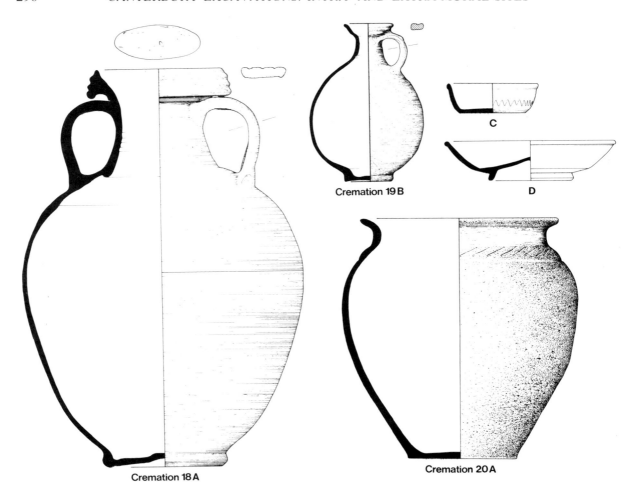

Fig. 111.   Roman pottery from Cranmer House: Cremation burials 18, 19 and 20 (Scale: $\frac{1}{4}$)

C: BB2. Pie-dish, Gillam 310; *c*. A.D. 120–210. **Fig. 112, 23C**.

D: Fabric as 15E above. Cornice-rim; Gillam 86. Late second to mid third century. **Fig. 112, 23D**.

E: Fabric V. Jar, form as 1B, with two grooves in the shoulder.

F: Fabric VIII. Beaker, as 8D above, possibly undecorated.

G: Fabric V. Lamp. Loeschcke Type IX with ring-handle. Second century. (D. Bailey). **Fig. 112, 23G**.

Date: Late second to early third century.

Burial 24   A: Fabric II(*). Sherds of storage jar.

Date: Second century.

Burial 25   A: Fabric II(*). Sherds of storage jar.

B: Fabric IV. Body sherd; necked jar?

Date: Second century.

Burial 26   A: Fabric III(*). Sherds of storage jar.

Date: Mid second to third century.

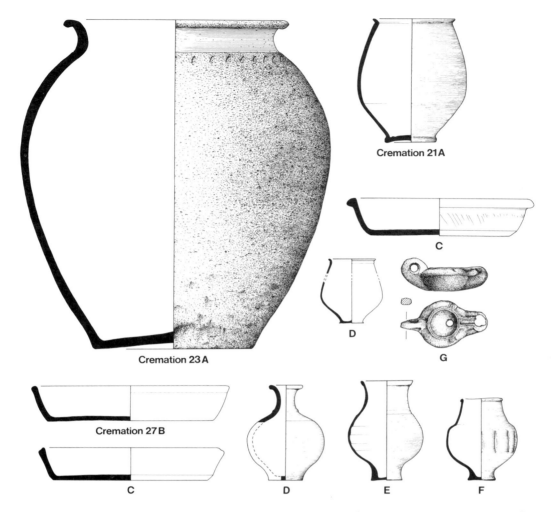

Cremation 21A

Cremation 23 A

C

D

G

Cremation 27 B

C

C   D   E   F

Fig. 112.   Roman pottery from Cranmer House: Cremation burials 21, 23 and 27 (Scale: ¼)

Burial 27   A: Fabric II(*). Identical to 23A above.
                        B: BB2. Dog-dish, as 28B below, but possibly without chamfer. Dating as 8B above. **Fig. 112, 27B**.
                        C: BB2. Dog-dish with groove on top of lip. Identical to vessels produced at Higham, Kent (Pollard 1983, Form II). Late second to early fourth century. **Fig. 112, 27C**.
                        D: Fabric VIII. Flask. **Fig. 112, 27D**.
                        E: Fabric VIII. Bulbous beaker. **Fig. 112, 27E**. Late second to early fourth century.
                        F: Central Gaulish 'Rhenish' colour-coated ware. Bulbous beaker, Gillam 45. *c.* A.D. 150–200. **Fig. 112, 27F**.
                        G: Fabric IV. Cf. the larger 17A above; probably of the same date range. Cf. Ospringe 656.
                        Date: Late second to third century.
Burial 28   A: Fabric III(*). Possible 'whorl' on base suggests cut from wheel. **Fig. 113, 28A**.
                        B: BB2. Dog-dish. Dating as 8B above. Inverted over urn as cover, as illustrated. **Fig. 113, 28B**.

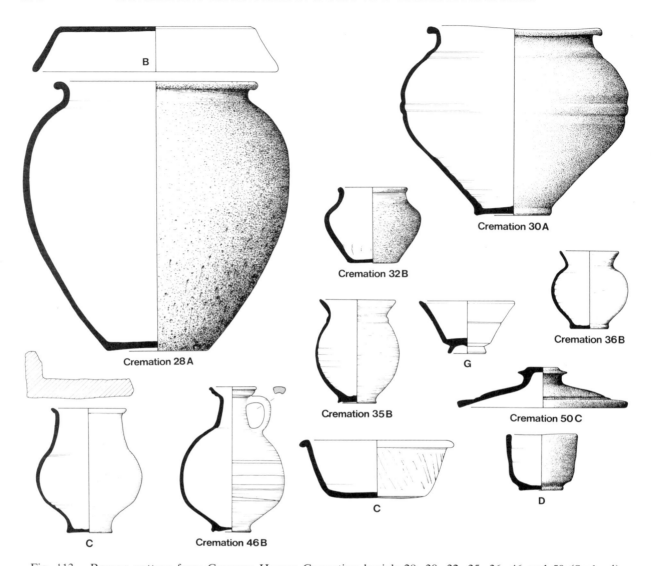

Fig. 113.   Roman pottery from Cranmer House: Cremation burials 28, 30, 32, 35, 36, 46 and 50 (Scale: ¼)

	C: Fabric VIII. Bulbous beaker, as 27E. **Fig. 113, 28C.**
	Date: Late second to third century.
Burial 29	A: Fabric IV. Bulbous-bodied bowl(*), cf. Richborough 215, 228. Late first to early second-century type. Rim missing. A Canterbury product almost certainly.
	Date: Mid first to early second century.
Burial 30	A: Fabric IV(*). Probably pre-Flavian to Hadrianic, derived from a 'Belgic' grog-tempered form (Canterbury I, 81). **Fig. 113, 30A.**
	Date: Mid first to early second century.
Burial 31	A: Fabric IV(*). Probably a jar, but little could be recovered.
	B: Fabric I. One sherd of a corrugated-neck jar. Incorporated in backfill of pit?
	Date: No close date.

Burial 32   A: Fabric IV, possibly 'Stuppington Lane' ware (Bennett *et al.* 1980, 267–289; Pollard forthcoming) of mid first-century date. A lid-seated rim from a jar or bowl, cf. Bennett *et al.* 1980, Fig. 7, No. 62.

        B: Fabric I. A small beaker or cup. Cf. Canterbury I, 33. **Fig. 113, 32B**.

Date: Mid to late first century.

Burial 33   A: Fabric VIII(*). Possibly a jar.

        B: Fabric VIII. Flask, as 23B.

        C: Fabric as 27F. Small rim sherd, cf. Gillam 46–8. Date as 27F.

Date: Late second to early fourth century.

Burial 34   A: Small fragments of grey-buff South Spanish Dressel 20 amphora.

Date: No close date.

Burial 35   A: Fabric III(*). Form and decoration as 2A.

        B: Fabric VIII. Undecorated (?) globular/sub-globular 'poppy-head' beaker; cf. Canterbury I, 380; Canterbury VII, 495; Tyers 57, 58, 63, 64. Probably mid or late second to third century. **Fig. 113, 35B**.

        C: Fabric VIII. Form as 35B, also undecorated. (?).

        D: Fabric VIII. Beaker, globular/sub-globular shape as 35B and 35C.

        E: Fabric VII. Body sherds; flagon?

        F: Fabric IV. Jar base.

        G: Samian, Central Gaulish, Dr. 33, second century. Illegible name-stamp. **Fig. 113, 35G**.

Date: Late second to third century.

Burial 36   A: Fabric IV. Necked jar with roll-rim(*).

        B: Fabric VIII. Undecorated 'poppy-head' beaker. A variant, slightly shouldered, without cordon; Ospringe 172; Tyers 51, 56. Dating as 35B probably. **Fig. 113, 36B**.

        C: Fabric X. Flagon, cupped plain mouth, round-section handle. Cf. Canterbury I, 373; Bennett *et al.* 1980, Fig. 13, no. 3; Ospringe 124. Mid second to early third century probably.

Date: Mid second to mid third century.

Burial 37   A: Fabric IV(*). Necked jar with everted, cupped rim, cf. 48 below; Canterbury I, 258; Canterbury V, 348; Ospringe 488. Late second to fourth century.

        B: Fabric IV. Base, vessel form uncertain.

Date: Late second to fourth century.

Burial 38   A: Fabric II. Body sherds; jar?(*).

        B: Fabric VI. Base; flagon?

        C: Fabric IV. Body sherds.

Date: No close date.

Burial 39   A: Fabric IV(*). Base, storage jar.

        B: Fabric VIII. Body sherds.

        C: Fabric IV. Body sherds.

Date: No close date.

Burial 40   A: Fabric IV(*). Base, jar.

        B: South Spanish Dressel 20 amphora, body sherd.

        C: Fabric X. Body sherds, flagon?

        D: Fabric VIII. Base, segmental bowl.

        E: Samian, Central Gaulish, Drag 31. Name-stamp abraded and illegible. Mid to end of second century.

        F: Fabric IV. Necked jar with roll-rim.

        G: Fabric III. Body sherds, jar.

        H: Fabric VIII. Body sherds, beaker or flask?

Date: Mid second to third century.

Burial 41   A: Fabric II(*). Base, storage jar.

Date: No close date.

Burial 42   A: Fabric IV. Base, jar.

B: Fabric V. Four-rib handle fragment, flagon?

C: Fabric IV. Body sherd.

Date: No close date.

Burial 43   A: South Spanish Dressel 20 amphora(*). Probably neck and handles broken off prior to interment (as in Burials 45 and 46). The type was imported from at least the mid first to early third century.

B: Fabric VIII. Body sherds, ovoid or globular, flask? Shoulder cordon, with rouletted band below.

C: Flint-tempered body sherd, Iron Age? Abraded, featureless, c. 10 mm. thick.

Date: No close date.

Burial 44   A: Fabric IV(*). Base, jar.

B: Fabric X. Body sherds, including one with 'fingernail-impressed' row. Flagon?

C: BB2. Dog-dish, as 28c above.

D: Fabric IV. Body sherds, jar?

E: Fabric III. Base, jar, wiped. Possibly incorporated in the backfill of the pit.

Date: Mid second to third century.

Burial 45   A: South Spanish Dressel 20 amphora(*), complete except for neck and handles, broken off prior to interment and not recovered.

B: Fabric IV. Body sherds.

Date: No close date.

Burial 46   A: Amphora, as 45A, also with neck and handles missing, broken off in antiquity(*).

B: Fabric VII with white slip. Flagon, cf. 19B, but with wide middle 'ring', probably same date range. **Fig. 113, 46B**.

C: BB2. Pie-dish, Gillam 222, A.D. 120–210. Possibly oblique tooling only (cf. Gillam 310). **Fig. 113, 46C**.

D: Fabric III. Body sherds, jar.

E: Fabric IV. Body sherd.

Date: Mid second to early third century.

Burial 47   A: Fabric VI. Body sherds of a thick-walled ?flagon. Grooved wavy-line decoration on the body of the vessel.

Date: No close date.

Burial 48   A: Fabric IV. Necked jar(*). See 37A for discussion.

Date: Late second to fourth century.

Burial 49   A: Possible Lower Rhineland Fabric I. Undecorated bag beaker, cf. Anderson *et al.* 1980,
(Reported by   Fig. 8, No. 6. Importation to Britain ceased *c.* A.D. 165/70.
M. Green)   B: Fabric VIII. Fragments of a necked flask or jar.

C: Fabric VII. Single rim sherd of a flagon, cf. Fig. 111, 18A.

Date: Second century.

Burial 50   A: Fabric IV(*). Necked jar with roll-rim (fragmented), cf. 11A.

B: Fabric IV. Necked jar with triangular-rolled rim, small sherds, possibly incorporated into burial pit backfill.

C: Fabric IV. Lid, possibly cover to A. Cf. Canterbury I, 60, 195, 352. Lids in this fabric date generally to within the mid first to late second century in Canterbury, though some later usage is attested (Pollard forthcoming, Canterbury V) **Fig. 113, 50C**.

D: Fabric IV. Cup. Possibly made for ritual purpose as parallels are not forthcoming from the city and the pot is heavily-built. **Fig. 113, 50D**.

E: Samian, Central Gaul, Dr. 37. Second century (M.J.G.)

Date: Late second to fourth century.

Burial 51   No pottery was recovered from this burial.

Burial 52   A: Fabric VIII. Biconical bowl or jar, rim missing (*), cf. St. Dunstan's 710 and Pollard 1981, No. 1 for possible parallels. Mid Flavian to early Hadrianic.

B: Fabric VII. Base, flagon?

Date: Late first to early second century.

Burial 53   A: Fabric II(*). Necked jar with everted rim, and wiped lower exterior.

B: Fabric VIII. Base, beaker. Possibly incorporated into backfill of pit.

C: Fabric IV. Necked jar with everted rim. One sherd, possibly incorporated into backfill of pit.

Date: Second century.

(ii) 54–61 THE ROMAN TOPSOIL AND MISCELLANEOUS SCATTERS

Sherds of first- and second-century date, and undiagnostic Romano-British sherds which cannot be closely dated, were collected from the Roman topsoil and from various scatters of sherds thought not to relate to burials. These included some amphora sherds in a fine, powdery fabric containing very fine quartz, white mica, iron ore and calcite inclusions. Surfaces are buff with either grey or deep pink cores. These are the only amphora sherds from Cranmer House not in the grey-buff South Spanish fabric most commonly associated with Dressel 20.

Miscellaneous sherds in Fabrics II, IV, V, VII, VIII and IX were also recovered. They include a rim in VII identical to 18A and a pedestal base possibly from a beaker in IX.

(iii) 62 PIT

A: Fabric V. Necked jar with triangular-rolled rim, cf. Canterbury V, 320. Late second to fourth century?

B: Fabric I, or possibly late Roman grog-tempered (see Pollard forthcoming, Canterbury V) necked jar with bead rim, rim sherd only.

C: Fabric I. Base, jar, two small sherds.

D: Small, featureless sherds in several fabrics, II, IV, V, VI, VIII and 'chaff-tempered'. The last indicates that the content of Pit 62 almost certainly incorporates material from the backfill of the pit (see Macpherson-Grant 1980).

Date: Late second to fourth century.

(iv) 63 THE POSSIBLE *USTRINUM*

One rouletted sherd in Fabric VIII, not closely datable. 64 and 65 (associated post-holes) contained no pottery.

(v) 66 THE DITCH

A small assemblage was recovered. This included:

A: A sherd of mould-decorated samian, probably second century Central Gaulish, Dr. 37.

B: Fabric IX. Finger impressed triangular roll-rim fragment. Possible *tazza*.

C: Miscellaneous sherds in Fabrics III, IV and VIII.

Date: Close dating of the assemblage is not possible owing to the undiagnostic nature of most sherds, but it includes second-century pieces (A and possibly B) and Fabric III of the late second century or later. The entire assemblage could date to the period of the Roman cemetery on the Cranmer House site, i.e. the mid first to third century.

(vi)   67 THE CLAY QUARRY

The Roman pottery from this feature dates from the mid first to at least the mid third century, if not into the fourth. The upper secondary fill also included sherds of Saxon pottery (see below). The nature of the excavation did not allow precise recording of the stratigraphic relationships of the Roman pottery.

A: Samian: sherds of three vessels.
    (i) Dr. 18/31 and 33, both from Les Martres-de-Veyre, and of probable Trajanic date.
    (ii) Probably Ritt. 9, South Gaulish and pre-Flavian.

B: Colour-coated wares:
    (i) One sherd in Lyon ware, a beaker with external sand rough-casting, dated *c.* A.D. 43–70 in Britain.
    (ii) A pedestal base, possibly from a beaker, in Oxfordshire brown colour-coat. Mid third century or later (Young 1977).

C: Mortarium. A body sherd in Hartley's Fabric 2B (Hartley 1982). The only certain sherd from a mortarium from the excavation.

D: South Spanish Dressel 20 amphora: body sherds.

E: Miscellaneous wares. These included three rims in Fabric IV: an everted jar, a necked jar (cf. 62A) and a triangular-rim lid, cf. St Dunstan's 706 and Canterbury I, 217. The remainder were either body sherds, in Fabrics II, III, IV, VIII and X, or bases, in Fabrics II (a jar) and in BB2. The last comprised two dishes, one with a chamfered base normal for the ware, the other with an exaggerated chamfer resembling that of the BB1 dish, Gillam 219–221. The latter is assigned to BB2 on consideration of fabric and technique, although it is clearly an aberrant form, presumably of second-century date if derived from the BB1 types.

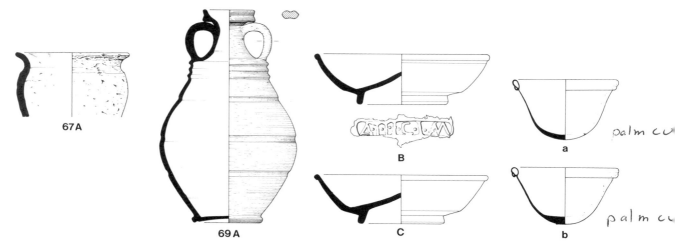

Fig. 114.   Roman pottery from Cranmer House: Feature 67 and possible Saxon cremation burial 69 (Scale: ¼)
Samian stamp (Scale: ½)

(vii)   THE SAXON POTTERY by N.C. Macpherson-Grant (Fig. 114, No. 67A)

The upper fill of the clay quarry produced part of a small pot in grass tempered ware (Saxon Fabric Group 4). A small jar, in fairly soft, smooth ware, reduced black/dark-brown. Moderate organic temper. Fabric contains little or no sand, and has noticeable fine mica. Irregular burnish on neck, lip and inner rim. Moderate degree of wear, mostly internally.

Similar small everted-rim jars are known from occupation-levels within the City, dated broadly to the mid sixth century (e.g. Frere forthcoming, from excavations east of the Marlowe Theatre, CXIX E VIII 5: *Archaeology of Canterbury*, vol. v, Part II). Unfortunately, this piece cannot be directly linked to the discovery nearby of an early seventh-century pendant, *sceatta* and palm cups (above pp. 281–2). The *sceatta* has been dated 690–710 and indicates activity in the area during the late seventh/early eighth century, at least. A date in the second half of the seventh century would not be out of place for this vessel.

(viii)   THE SAXON FEATURES

68 Pit		No pottery was present in this feature.
69 ?Cremation burial	A:	Fabric VII. Flagon, grooved body. The 'pulley rim' is generally a first- to second-century form in southern Britain, e.g. Canterbury I, 413, Canterbury VII, 59A, 59B; Dover, 848; Verulamium 574; Aldgate 225. **Fig. 114, 69A.**
	B:	Samian, Central Gaul, Dr. 31 with a stamp of Atticus ii of Lezoux, Die 2b, dated to A.D 150–70 (B. Dickinson) **Fig. 114, 69B.**
	C:	As 69B. No stamp. **Fig. 114, 69C.**
70 'Grave' cutting	A:	One body sherd in a dark grey fabric containing frequent grey and white flint temper, up to 2 mm. in grit size, and smoothed externally; of indeterminate date.
	B:	One body sherd, fabric as 15E above.
	C:	South Spanish Dressel 20 amphora; body sherds.
	D:	Miscellaneous wares. Sherds in Fabrics III, IV, V, VI (a two-rib handle) and VIII and a jar base in Belgic or late Roman grog-tempered ware (see Pollard forthcoming).
		Date: The material is not closely datable except by fabric alone.
71 Inhumation burial	A:	Fabric VIII. Base, beaker or flask?
	B:	Fabric VII: Body sherds.
	C:	South Spanish Dressel 20 amphora body sherds.

(ix)   UNSTRATIFIED POTTERY

The unstratified collection includes post-medieval sherds and a clay-pipe stem deriving from the farm itself, and Roman forms and fabrics falling within the range occurring in the interments and other excavated features. Some sherds are derived almost certainly from burials disturbed during machine excavation, others, such as a samian Dr. 35/36 possibly of South Gaulish origin, may have been deposited before the designation of the area as a cemetery.

(x)   THE CLAY 'SQUEEZE'

The backfill of the clay quarry incorporated fragments of sandy grey hard clay, kneaded into a shapeless 'squeeze'. This suggests that some preparation of the extracted clay from this or some undiscovered quarry took place in the vicinity of the Cranmer House site. Pottery kilns of first- to second-century date are known downhill of this site, in Whitehall Gardens (Jenkins 1960), to which period the 'squeeze' may belong in view of the date-range of the associated sherds from the quarry and the expansion of the cemetery into this part of the site probably by the latter half of the second century.

(xi) DISCUSSION OF THE POTTERY

Chronology of the Burials
The pottery dating of the burials agrees well with that of the small number of independently datable objects – glass, the coin and the figurine. Forty-two of the fifty-three Roman interments can be dated to within two centuries, of which only three (29, 30, 52) belong to the mid first to early second century and only one (6) need be later than the early third. The main period of burial was, therefore, the mid second to third century, which period fits in well with the history of Romano-British burial practice so far as it is understood; the period being predominantly one of cremations.

Comparison with the Telephone Repeater Station Burial Ground
The Cranmer House cemetery, taken as a whole, presents a contrast with the Telephone Repeater Station burial ground to the east (Whiting 1927), from which some eight to ten cremations were recovered. One of these, represented by pots 714–716, is almost certainly first-century (714 is a post-Conquest 'Gallo-Belgic' copy grey sandy platter), while the others could all be fitted into the Flavian to early Antonine period. Thus, only three of the Cranmer House burials need overlap in date with the interments from the Repeater Station.

It is dangerous to make strong inferences from the small Repeater Station collection (twenty-one vessels worthy of illustration), but at least one worthwhile observation can be made. Five of the large jars ('urns') are of the grooved-rim, bag-shape or sub-globular type which is one of the characteristic forms of the Canterbury potteries of the Flavian to early Antonine period (Pollard 1982b). This type is absent from Cranmer House, a fact which provides support for the view that the pottery industry of Canterbury underwent marked changes in the latter half of the second century, involving at the least a radical revision of the formal range manufactured, if not the experience of decline and dislocation on an irreversible scale (*ibid.*).

'Belgic' Grog-tempered Ware and 'Native Coarse Ware': the Transitional Period
It is probable that the latter developed out of the former, with three major changes taking place over the course of the late first and second centuries. First, the fabric became generally harder, with 'Native Coarse Ware' vessels almost invariably having a 'ring' when struck: this is one of the main criteria for assigning pottery to this ware. Secondly, the range of 'Belgic' forms was severely curtailed, with only recurved-rim storage jars, simple recurved/everted-rim jars and 'S'-profile bowls being at all common in the second century 'transitional' ware and in 'Native Coarse Ware' proper. The cemetery material falls entirely outside of the first-century 'Belgic' ware, which is here represented by a handful of sherds from the backfill of burial pits and other contexts (e.g. 31B). Thirdly, in concert with the reduction in the range of forms, decorative and finishing traits were revised. 'Corrugation', or multi-grooving of the neck, was almost totally abandoned (Cranmer House 9A and Ospringe 212 are exceptions). Horizontal fine combing was gradually abandoned. 'Furrowing' with a thick-toothed comb or similar tool was supplanted by a heavy wiping and/or knife-trimming of the central, lower and basal exteriors of the pot (e.g. 15B). 'Comb'-stabbing (e.g. Canterbury VII, 119) was abandoned, and to a lesser extent 'stick' and 'finger-nail' impressed decoration (e.g. Ospringe 193 for the former; Cranmer House 20A, 23A for the latter) were also discarded from the repertoire of decoration. In both 'transitional' and 'developed' 'Native Coarse Ware' tooled motifs can be perceived as predominant, as the series of funerary urns from the cemetery and from Ospringe (e.g. 193, 212, 332, 387) demonstrate. The styles originated in the first century A.D. (or perhaps even late first century B.C.) 'Belgic' pottery, and while free-style motifs can be found (e.g. the four Ospringe pots cited above, and Cranmer House 9A) a degree of standardisation is suggested by the repeated occurrence of the 'double-groove and tooled chevron', often with an additional, oblique tooled *motif* on the shoulder. This style is illustrated by Cranmer House 2A and 3A and occurs elsewhere in the city both in occupation (e.g. Canterbury VII, 203; Canterbury V, 235) and funerary (e.g. Bennett *et al.* 1980, Figs. 12, 1 and 13, 2) contexts. It is widespread in east Kent generally, examples being found at Eastry (Pollard 1982a, 1), Dover (738), and Ospringe (163) for example, of second- to third-century date (see Pollard 1982b for general discussion).

It is considered that the transition from 'Belgic' to 'Native Coarse Ware' was complete by the last quarter of the second century, if not somewhat earlier in that century.

2. NO. 7 PALACE STREET AND NO. 44 BURGATE[257]

A. THE SMALL FINDS FROM NO. 7 PALACE STREET compiled by P. GARRARD

(i) OBJECTS OF COPPER ALLOY by P. Garrard and D. Mackreth

1.	10 (25)	Roman brooch. D.F. Mackreth writes: 'Badly bent, corroded and in three pieces, the wings and the catch-plate of this brooch are missing. The piece is recognisably a Colchester by the manner in which both the hook and the spring are integral with the body of the brooch, but its condition precludes further description. It does not suggest an early date and the later part of the Colchester date-range is more likely, *c.* A.D. 25–40/5, and it may have survived in use until *c.* A.D. 50–60.' (Not illustrated.)
2.	12 (u.s.)	Pendant fitting, tinned; the wire loop-ends swivel in their sockets.

(ii) OBJECTS OF LEAD by P. Garrard (Fig. 115)

3.	4 (14)	Irregular disc-shaped object, with what appears to be a handle, square in section, weight 80 gm.
4.	5 (14)	Cylindrical object, possibly a weight with a loop at the top. A strip of lead has been applied around the shoulders perhaps to make up to the correct weight (250 gm.)
5.	3 (14)	Folded lead-sheet scraps, forming an irregular lump. Weight 125 gm. (Not illustrated.)
6.	2 (14)	Pool of melted solidified lead. Weight 1.630 kg. (Not illustrated.)

(iii) STONE OBJECTS by P. Garrard

7.	15 (36)	Fragment of lower greensand quernstone re-used as hone stone. Iron stained on working surface. (Not illustrated.)
8.	14 (13)	Fragment of quernstone of lower greensand, hollowed from wear. (Not illustrated.)

(iv) OBJECTS OF WORKED BONE by P. Garrard (Fig. 115)

9.	1 (1)	Hinge.
10.	6 (1)	Counter, Greep Type 1[258] with graffito.

(v) TECHNOLOGICAL FINDS by J. Bayley (Fig. 115)

11.	13 (19)	Crucible. The fabric is fairly porous and contains little mineral temper. It is dark grey in colour, except for a far paler grey band just below the outer surface. X-ray fluorescence analysis detected copper and zinc plus a trace of lead in an area of corrosion-products in the thickness of the crucible wall and also high levels of zinc on the inner surface of the crucible (nearly twenty times the level detected on the outer surface). This crucible is probably a more complete example of the similar fragmentary material recovered from the Castle Street site in

---

257. The published material is numbered consecutively under each main heading, each item being followed, where appropriate, by its small find number and layer number in brackets. The specialist reports and detailed context-related catalogues of the finds have been deposited with the excavation records in the Royal Museum, Canterbury. All the reports were edited by Mrs. Pan Garrard.
258. *The Archaeology of Canterbury*, vol. v (forthcoming).

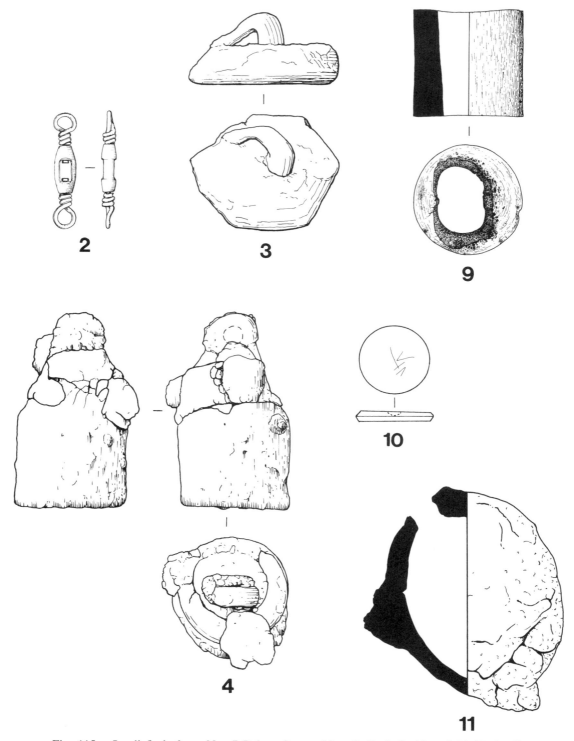

Fig. 115.   Small finds from No. 7 Palace Street: Nos. 2, 3, 4, 9, 10 and 11 (Scale: ⅓)

1976 which may have been used in brass-making.[259] Possibly earlier than the second-century A.D. suggested context.

12. (14)/(16)/(20)   A small group of iron smithing slag together with some hearth lining and a few pieces of badly corroded iron. (Not illustrated.)

13. (20)   ?Smithing slag. (Not illustrated.)

B.   THE POTTERY FROM NO. 7 PALACE STREET by M.J. Green

Due to conditions on site and the initial haphazard recovery of the material, total site-assemblage quantification is of little real value here. However, enough pottery was recovered from general clearance by workmen, and later in a more systematic fashion, to enable some assessments to be made.

There is nothing in the material to suggest a date later than the second century and much of the activity probably occurred in the middle and second half of that century.

Clearance levels (1) contained both first- and second-century material and included 'Belgic' grogged wares, samian, 'Canterbury' coarse reduced sandy wares (of late first and second centuries), fine reduced wares (Upchurch type) and many large fragments of amphorae, mostly Dressel 20, the globular oil amphora commonly imported in the second century (but ranging from the first into the third century); one or two of these sherds showed signs of burning. Mortaria were present in two forms;[260] both in a cream fabric with flint trituration grits, probably products from Gaul or south-east England[261] and possibly from Canterbury. It was noticeable in this and all other levels how well the sherds had survived; they had apparently been little disturbed, many were large, especially those of amphorae and mortaria, in general showing little sign of wear.

Two contexts have relatively large assemblages and are believed to be uncontaminated; these have been quantified by sherd count.

(14) Banded Deposits within the Building and Sealing Phase III Floor
A total of 154 sherds was recovered including 26 of BB2 comprised of five decorated pie-dishes (three examples of Gillam 222 and two of Gillam 310)[262] and one decorated dog-dish (Gillam 328). Dr Pollard's work on the Marlowe Car Park and elsewhere in the city by others has shown these decorated types to be typical of the Hadrianic-mid Antonine period at Canterbury (Pollard, forthcoming).[263] Fine reduced ware is represented by 26 sherds with fifteen conjoining to form a small, near-complete 'poppy-head' beaker (**Fig. 116, No. 1**) decorated with rectangular panels of barbotine dots;[264] a further seven sherds of another such beaker were in a fine purple-grey sandwich fabric with an external off-white slip, again with rectangular panels of dots; two remaining sherds are in a fine buff fabric.

Fine imported wares are represented by three sherds of samian, one example of the dish form Dr. 18/31 or 31 and one of cup Dr. 33, both second century.

259. For a full discussion, see J. Bayley (1984) 'Roman Brass-making in Britain?', *Hist. Metall.*, 18 (1), and *The Archaeology of Canterbury*, vol. vi (forthcoming).

260. Cf. M.R. Hull, Types 496 and 497, the latter type dated by him to the late second century. *The Roman Potters' Kilns of Colchester*, Reports of the Research Committee of the Society of Antiquaries of London, No. xxi (Oxford, 1963).

261. K.H. Hartley, Fabrics 1A and 1B, 'The Mortaria' in Bennett *et al.*, *Excavations at Canterbury Castle, The Archaeology of Canterbury*, vol. i (Maidstone, 1982).

262. J.P. Gillam, *Types of Roman Coarse Pottery Vessels in Northern Britain* 3rd edition (Newcastle-upon-Tyne, 1970).

263. R.J. Pollard, 'The Late Iron Age and Roman Coarse Ware Pottery', in *The Archaeology of Canterbury*, vol. v, forthcoming.

264. P. Tyers, 'The Poppy-head Beakers of Britain and their Relationship to the Barbotine Decorated Vessels of the Rhineland and Switzerland', in (Eds.) P.A. Arthur and G. March, *Early Fine Wares in Roman Britain*, *BAR* British Series, No. 57, (Oxford, 1978).

Dressel 20 was again in evidence as two large fragmentary sherds.[265] Mortarium sherds, two conjoining in a cream fabric with flint and quartz trituration grits, are likely to be Hartley's Fabric 1A or 1B. The remainder of the assemblage is composed of one fine cream flagon sherd, one oxidised coarse sandy sherd, 59 coarse reduced sandy ware (the majority of these are probably products of the Canterbury kilns of the Flavian/Antonine period), twelve of the 'Belgic' grogged ware and thirteen of 'Native Coarse Ware' (see Pollard this volume p. 298 for discussion of this fabric). Some of the sherds from Palace Street illustrate what could be the 'Belgic'/Native Coarse Ware transition period.

A date-range of mid to late second century is suggested for this assemblage.

(20) Occupation Layer within Timber Building and overlying Phase II Clay Floor
The layer contained 97 sherds. 'Native Coarse Ware' was represented by 27 sherds forming at least two storage jars. Fine reduced ware accounts for twenty sherds, sixteen of which are from a beaker/jar with burnished lattice body decoration. Most of the amphorae from the site are of Dressel 20 type and here there are two sherds fragmented and burnt. Again, Hartley's Fabric 1 appears in a single mortarium flange with flint trituration grits extending over the upper surface.

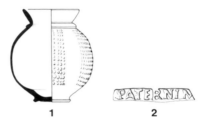

Fig. 116.   Roman pottery from No. 7 Palace Street: No. 1 'Poppy-head' beaker (Scale: ¼) and No. 2 samian stamp on Dr. 31R (Scale: ½)

Fine wares occur as two sherds of a fine, white, grey slipped ware with clay rough-casting, probably from the Lower Rhineland area; one of these, a globular beaker can be dated to *c.* A.D. 120–165/70, the upper end of the range indicating the termination point for the importation of this ware to Britain.[266] Samian accounts for 21 sherds, one example of cup Dr. 27 and two of Dr. 33, one dish Dr. 35/6 and one dish Dr. 31R with a potter's stamp **PATERNIM** (**Fig. 116, No. 2**); the Castle site produced a stamped Dr. 31 of Paternus III of Lezoux (Die 1b) identified by Brenda Dickinson and dated by her to *c.* A.D. 135–150.[267] It is not known at this time whether the Palace Street stamp is of the same die.

Of the remaining sherds, there is one BB2 dish fragment, one sherd of fine purple/grey ware with white external slip, two coarse reduced sandy sherds (probably local) and two other reduced coarse ware sherds. 'Belgic' grogged ware (eighteen sherds) completes this assemblage which can be assigned a similar date range as (14).

In conclusion, something should be said about the possible function of the timber building. A considerable amount of metalworking waste was recovered from the site, especially from Pit 19 – this together with the possible hearth is suggestive of industrial activity; layer 14 contained two conjoining base sherds of 'Belgic'/Native Coarse Ware (?jar) with one clear hole piercing through and evidence of three others, some type of iron deposit adhering to both internal and external surfaces. However, one would not expect to see such a wide range of domestic pottery occurring on such a site, a range which encompasses coarse kitchen dishes and bowls, storage jars, fine tableware, amphorae and

265.   Paul Arthur has made an analysis of all amphorae excavated from Canterbury sites over a period of four years; he concludes that Dressel 20 represents 68 per cent by weight of the studied material (Arthur, *Britannia* xvii (1986), 239 ff.

266.   A.C. Anderson, *A Guide to Roman Fine Wares*, Vorda Res. Ser. 1, (1980), cf. Fig. 8, no. 2.

267.   B.D. Dickinson, 'The Stamped Samian' in *Excavations at Canterbury Castle, op. cit. supra,* note 261, 131.

several mortaria. Perhaps, then, the industrial activity took place on a small scale within what was principally a domestic building.

C. THE LOOM-WEIGHTS FROM NO. 44 BURGATE, by P. Garrard (Fig. 123A)

One complete late-Saxon loom-weight and part of another were found by workmen in the construction trench of the medieval cellar during the cutting of a new foundation pit, under Burgate Street, immediately outside no. 44 Burgate. Both are of rust-coloured brickearth, well baked; diameter approximately 120 mm. The complete loom-weight has well-worn grooves from the cord which suspended it from the loom.

D. THE POTTERY FROM NO. 44 BURGATE by M.J. Green and N. Macpherson-Grant

THE ROMAN WARES by M.J. Green

Coarse and fine wares recovered from the Roman levels range in date from the late first to the late third or even fourth century; the upper date limit is indicated by the presence of an Oxfordshire mortarium sherd and another of a later Nene Valley type colour-coated beaker or bowl. The majority of the material is, however, assignable to the Flavian-Antonine period. The small sample of 32 sherds includes first-century samian (with fragments of a Dr. 37 mould decorated bowl), 'Belgic' grogged ware, probably Lower Rhineland colour-coated ware and sherds of four different amphorae. Two and perhaps three of these are Dressel 20 types, one example represented by three large body sherds displaying deep finger or tool impressions on the interior; this feature has been noted on other Dressel 20 amphorae, on the upper interior surface and no doubt indicates how the vessel was drawn up in its manufacture.

THE LATE SAXON AND EARLY MEDIEVAL WARES by N. Macpherson-Grant

The post-Roman material came from a large pit truncated by the foundations of a late twelfth-century cellar (documentarily dated *c*. 1180–1200). The pottery falls into two groups – Late Saxon and Early Medieval. The Late Saxon sherds consist of four coarse sandy ware pieces with external burnished trellis decoration from two possibly three, large spouted pitchers. All are almost certainly local copies of probably tenth-century north French imports and a welcome addition to the growing number of such examples from city excavations. Also present was an angular-necked, knife-trimmed, small cooking-pot, definitely local and characteristic of the period *c*. 950/75–1025. The decorated sherds might be marginally earlier.

The second group contains sherds from a large Early Medieval cooking-pot in coarse local sandy ware and is typical of the late eleventh/early twelfth century.

3. MARLOWE AVENUE AND ST. JOHN'S LANE SITES[268]

A. THE SMALL FINDS FROM MARLOWE AVENUE
compiled by P. Garrard

(i) THE ROMAN COINS by I. Anderson

1.	1 (7A) VIII	Vespasian, A.D. 72–73, RIC 740.
2.	94 (65) V	Trajan, A.D. 103–111, RIC 523.
3.	102 (69) VIA	Postumus, A.D. 259–68, RIC 65.
4.	38 (u.s.)	Gallienus, A.D. 260–68, RIC 300.
5.	113 (98) IIC	Regular radiate, *c.* A.D. 260–90. *Rev.* illegible.
6.	85 (61) VIA	Claudius II, A.D. 268–70, RIC 16.
7.	170 (167) V	Claudius II, A.D. 268–70, RIC 266.
8.	92 (65) V	Victorinus, A.D. 268–70. *Rev.* illegible.
9.	114 :98; IIC	Victorinus, A.D. 268–70. *Rev.* illegible.
10.	99 (68) VIA	Tetricus II, A.D. 270–73, as RIC 272.
11.	110 (75) IIC	Barbarous radiate, *c.* A.D. 270–90. *Rev. Pax.*
12.	93 (65) V	Barbarous radiate, *c.* A.D. 270–90. *Rev. Salus.*
13.	173 (169) IIC	Barbarous radiate, *c.* A.D. 270–90. *Rev. Salus.*
14.	59 (46) VIII	Barbarous radiate, *c.* A.D. 270–90. *Rev. Sol.*
15.	118 (86) IIC	Barbarous radiate, *c.* A.D. 270–90. *Rev. Sol.*
16.	78 (57) VIA	Barbarous radiate, *c.* A.D. 270–90. *Rev. Virtus.*
17.	143 (74) VIA	Barbarous radiate, *c.* A.D. 270–90. *Rev. Virtus.*
18.	60 (48; VIA	Barbarous radiate, *c.* A.D. 270–90. *Rev.* illegible.
19.	98 (65) V	Barbarous radiate, *c.* A.D. 270–90. *Rev.* illegible.
20.	151 (97) IIC	Barbarous radiate, *c.* A.D. 270–90. *Rev.* illegible.
21.	174 (170) IIC	Barbarous radiate, *c.* A.D. 270–90. *Rev.* illegible.
22.	195 (171) IIC	Barbarous radiate, *c.* A.D. 270–90. *Rev.* illegible.
23.	82 (62) VIA	Diocletian, *c.* A.D. 300–7.
24.	189 (171) IIC	Crispus, A.D. 321, RIC VIII, Lyons 133.
25.	146 (77) IV	Constans, A.D. 341–46, HK 143a.
26.	61 (45) VIB	Constantius II, *c.* A.D. 355–65. Copy as CK 25.
27.	168 (167) V	Constantius II, *c.* A.D. 355–65. Copy as CK 25.
28.	171 (169) IIC	Valens, A.D. 367–75, CK 312.
29.	178A (173) IIC	Honorius, A.D. 394–95, CK 570.
30.	178B (57A) VIA	House of Theodosius, A.D. 388–402. As CK 162.
31.	157 (57A) VIA	House of Theodosius, A.D. 388–408. As CK 796.
32.	73 (57) VIA	Bronze coin, illegible. Late third to fourth century.
33.	119 (101) IIC	Bronze coin, illegible. Late third to fourth century.
34.	178C (173) IIC	Bronze coin, illegible. Late third to fourth century.

268. The published material is numbered consecutively under each main heading, each item being followed, where appropriate, by its small find number, layer number (in brackets) and period. The specialist reports and detailed context-related catalogues of the finds have been deposited with the excavation records in the Royal Museum, Canterbury. All the reports were edited by Mrs. Pan Garrard.

(ii) THE MEDIEVAL COINS by M. Archibald

1. 80 (57) VIA   Henry III, 1216–72.
Penny, Long-cross type, class IIIb, *c.* 1250.
Mint: Newcastle. Moneyer: Adam.
Weight: 1.54 g. (23.7 gr.).
Ref: North 987.
This coin could have been deposited at any time up to 1280.

2. 77 (57) VIA   Henry III, 1216–72.
Cut-halfpenny, Long-cross type, class Vb, *c.* 1252.
Mint: London or Canterbury. Moneyer: Nicole.
Weight: 0.59 g. (9.1 gr.).
Ref: North 992.
Deposition as above.

(iii) THE POST-MEDIEVAL COINS by I. Anderson

1. 145 (12) VII   George II farthing. 1749.
2. 14 (10) VIII   George III halfpenny. 1797.

(iv) OBJECT OF GOLD by J. Cherry (Fig. 117, No. 1)

1. 63 (54) VIA   This decorative gold ring set with an irregularly-shaped sapphire has a hoop of circular section. The setting of the stone in a simple 'pie-dish' form of bezel as well as the shape of the ring suggests an early thirteenth-century date.

    The ring was analysed by X-ray fluorescence and the following composition obtained: Gold 65 per cent, silver 19 per cent and copper 16 per cent. No evidence was discovered of a low density core, and it seems most likely that the hoop and bezel of the ring consist of solid gold alloy. Although the ring has a low gold content, this may be paralleled by two other rings both of early thirteenth-century date. One found at Cannington, Somerset (BM 1925, 1–13, 1) has a composition of gold 61 per cent, silver 30 per cent, copper 9 per cent and the other found at Wiston in Sussex (AF 1887) has a composition of 63.5, 23.0 and 13.5. Since analysis of other rings, which may reasonably be assigned to this date, shows a much higher gold content, it is not possible to use a low gold content as in indicator of an early thirteenth-century date.

    The ring has a weight of 2.249 gm. and the diameter of the ring is 22 mm.

(v) OBJECTS OF COPPER ALLOY by P. Garrard (Fig. 117)

Roman
2. 169 (115) IIB   Cable bracelet fragment, three strands. Late Roman. Compare a similar example from the Marlowe Car Park excavations.[269] (Not illustrated).
3. 125 (120) IIB   Nail cleaner. Roman. Compare a similar example from the Norman Staircase.[270] (Not illustrated).
4. 121 (107) IIB   Disc, diameter 20 mm., 2 mm. thick. Possibly a weight – half ounce (7.9 g.). (Not illustrated).

269. *The Archaeology of Canterbury*, vol. v (forthcoming).
270. *The Archaeology of Canterbury*, vol. iii (forthcoming).

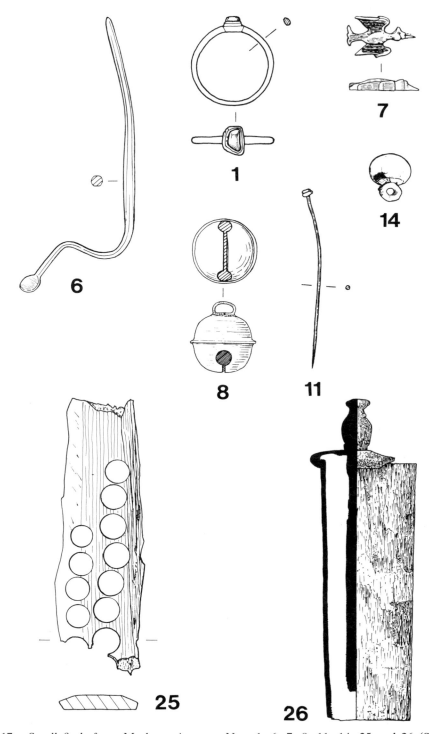

Fig. 117. Small finds from Marlowe Avenue: Nos. 1, 6, 7, 8, 11, 14, 25 and 26 (Scale: ¼)

5. 172 (169) IIC   Finger-ring, broken; plain oval section band, diameter 15 mm., 1 mm. wide, 0.5 mm. thick. (Not illustrated).

6. 109 (74) VIA   Spatula. Residual. Roman.

Medieval

7. 103 (74) VIA   Small mount depicting a bird with open wings, gilded.

Post-medieval

8. 47 (43A) VIB   Rumble bell.

9. 49 (43) VII   Spur, incomplete; second half of seventeenth century. Compare a similar example from the Marlowe Car Park excavations.[271] (Not illustrated).

10. 88 (64) VIA
11. 62 (43A) VIB   Four similar wire pins, the heads formed by two twists of wire. 5 mm. long, diam. 3–4 mm.
12. 51 (43A) VIB   No. 11 is illustrated.
13. 66 (55) VII
14. 30 (10) VII   Spherical hollow button.

(vi)   OBJECTS OF IRON by P. Garrard (Fig. 118)

Roman

15. 181 (95) IIC   Socketed point. Drawn from x-radiograph.

Medieval

16. 218 (63) VIA   Key. LMMC[272] Type III. (Not illustrated).

17. 217 (63) VIA   Whittle-tang knife, incomplete and very worn. Cf. Goodall[273] 1981, 56, Fig. 55. (Not illustrated).

18. 150 (163) VII   Whittle-tang knife, complete. Length 116 mm. Cf. Goodall, *ibid*. (Not illustrated).

19. 219 (63) VIA   Scale-tang knife, incomplete. Cf. Goodall, *ibid*. (Not illustrated).

20. 70 (55) VII   Scale-tang knife, incomplete. (Not illustrated).

21. 188 (55) VII   Scale-tang knife, incomplete. (Not illustrated).

22. 67 (47) VII   D-shaped buckle; rectangular section frame. 70 mm. x 52 mm. See a similar example from the Marlowe Car Park excavations MII S.F. No. 783.[274] (Not illustrated).

(vii)   OBJECTS OF WORKED BONE by P. Garrard (Fig. 117)

Roman

23. 201 (63) VIA   Pin, incomplete. Greep Type B2.3.[275] Residual. (Not illustrated).

Medieval and post-medieval

24. 64 (53) VIA   Two pieces of waste bone used for making buttons or beads: the holes are 6 mm. diam. No.
25. 69 (55) VII   25 is illustrated.

26. 7 (10) VIII   Syringe, broken. The distal end is grooved inside for a screw threaded fitting to be attached, probably a nozzle.

271. *The Archaeology of Canterbury*, vol. v (forthcoming).
272. *London Museum Medieval Catalogue*, 4th Impression (1975).
273. Ian Goodall, 'The Medieval Blacksmith and his Products' in (Ed.) D.W. Crossley, *C.B.A. Research Report No. 40*, 1981.
274. *The Archaeology of Canterbury*, vol. v (forthcoming).
275. *Ibid*.

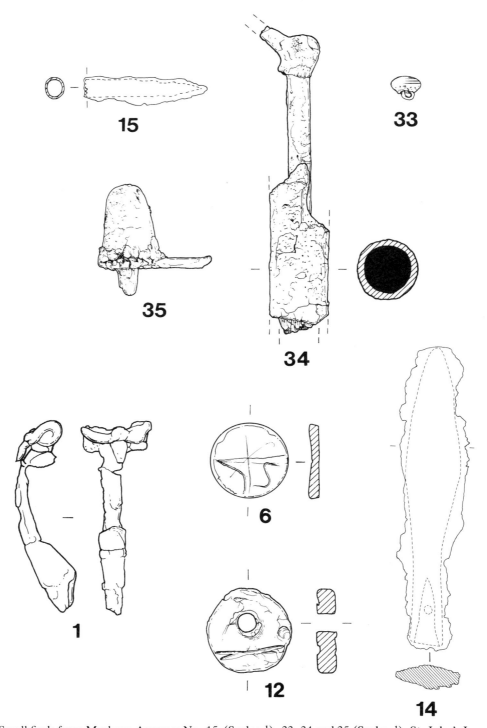

Fig. 118.   Small finds from Marlowe Avenue: No. 15 (Scale: $\frac{1}{2}$), 33, 34 and 35 (Scale: $\frac{1}{1}$); St. John's Lane: Nos. 1, 6, 12, 14 (Scale: $\frac{1}{1}$).

27. 5 (10) VIII ⎫ Three similar disc-shaped buttons, 2 mm. thick, diam. 19 mm., 12 mm. and 15 mm., pierced
28. 83 (10) VIII ⎬ by a central hole. These discs would subsequently be padded, often with sheep's wool, and
29. 22 (10) VIII ⎭ then covered by fabric, which would either be embroidered or left plain. (Not illustrated).

(viii)   MISCELLANEOUS OBJECTS by P. Garrard (Fig. 118)

Roman

30. 209 (171) IIC Shale bangle fragment, round in section, 6 mm. thick. Compare a similar example from the Marlowe Car Park excavations, *ibid*. (Not illustrated).

31. 212 (97) IIC Shale bangle fragment, D-shaped in section, 8 mm. thick. Compare a similar example from the Marlowe Car Park excavations, *ibid*. (Not illustrated).

32. 116 (97) IIC Honestone, complete, of fine sandstone, 100 mm. × 45 mm. × 35 mm. The faces are well worn. (Not illustrated).

Post-medieval

33. 76 (57) VIA Small button of opaque dark blue glass with integral copper alloy wire loop. Seventeenth century. Intrusive.

34. 25 (10) VIII Syringe of pewter, fragmented and incomplete. Probably similar to No. 26, Objects of Worked Bone, above.

35. 3 (10) VIII ⎫ Two similar objects of lead, possibly stoppers, pierced by wooden rods. No. 35 is illustrated.
36. 15 (10) VIII ⎭

(ix)   THE STRUCK FLINTS by P. Blockley

A small number of fractured flint fragments with secondary working and use were recovered from Period I and IIA levels.

The presence of cortex on many pieces suggests that the fragments were produced from the fracturing of small river-rounded flint nodules.

Very few of the pieces were made on properly struck flakes, the greatest percentage being on angular fractured flint. Where bulbs of percussion were present, they were large and prominent with a steep angle between the bulb and the striking platform suggestive of hard-hammer striking.

The majority of pieces were of multi-tool form with several working edges and the most prominent form of 'tool' was the notch with steep retouch. A few serrated edges, possible scapers and knives were also present on some edges, occasionally with traces of 'polishing' produced by use.

It would be difficult to assign the pieces a date bracket since no diagnostic assemblage is represented. A few similarly fractured and worked flints were located on the St. John's Lane excavation.

A full report will be published when the Watling Street Car Park is excavated, since a larger area of the deposit containing the flints is expected to be exposed.

B.   THE POST-MEDIEVAL POTTERY FROM THE CESS-TANK (Pl. XXXIII)[276]
by S. Morgan

Most of the pots from this cess-tank are unusually complete and give an insight into the type of china in use in a middle class family in the early part of the nineteenth-century; dinner services in creamware and later in the popular

276. Mrs. Morgan examined the entire assemblage, with the exception of the combed slipware platter and red earthenwares; her work is much appreciated. The group comprises some 125 complete vessels; a condensed catalogue is presented here and selected vessels have been photographed (Pl. XXXIII; left to right: white feldspathic stoneware jug with moulded decoration and blue enamel, black basalt cream jug, underglaze blue transfer printed bowl, on-glaze printed cup and underglaze blue transfer printed cup.)

blue shell-edged pearlware, and teaware printed with underglaze blue patterns. Surprisingly there is no bone china; was it too expensive for every day use and so kept for special occasions only, and consequently more carefully used? The porcelain cup, white feldspathic jug and the black basalt bowl and cream jug are the only items from the more expensive end of the ceramic market.

The large group of creamware is of the light shade produced in the late eighteenth century. Several pieces have impressed numerals which are workmen's marks. There is no distinctive moulding on the wares except for the twig and leaf handle on the square tureen cover which is typical of the simple, elegant style of Wedgwood. The impressed 'CH' is not identifiable.

The pearlware dinner service would have replaced the creamware one at the turn of the century. Several manufacturers are represented in this equally large group, each one using a slightly different shade of blue on the almost identical moulded shell-edging to the plates, etc.

The small teapot and tea bowl with polychrome decoration are typical products of the early nineteenth century. The Enoch Wood jug of c. 1830–35 is over-decorated by comparison.

The underglaze blue printed wares form a large proportion of the group as one would expect, but only seven items are decorated with the standard willow pattern. The rest are equally divided between Chinoiserie-style prints and the slightly later English landscape and flower designs. Several of the prints are copies of well-known designs; Wedgwood's Paeony, Spode's Tall Door and Mason's Boy at the Door, but with small differences in the detail. The Village Church pattern (maker unknown) was obviously liked by the family.

The stone chinas are printed with the Brosely pattern, another very popular Chinoiserie-based design made by many potters.

The black and brown underglaze prints are of floral and landscape subjects.

Unfortunately, the on-glaze bat prints have worn badly, but sufficient remains to identify one as a print of West Wycombe Park, a more exact copy of the original than the one used by Spode.

The only item of porcelain is a coffee cup with gilt line decoration of c. 1800, with an underglaze blue crossed swords mark on the base.

The black basalt bowl has a recess inside the rim and may be the lower half of a covered sucrier. Rivet repair holes suggest a treasured possession.

A large white feldspathic stoneware jug with moulded decoration and touches of blue enamel, is most likely of Castleford, Yorks., manufacture, having several features in common with marked pieces.

The date-range of the entire group would appear to be c. 1790–1835.

THE CATALOGUE

Creamware	Thirty-eight items; fifteen plates, ten bowls, two drinking vessels, seven chamber pots, one cover, a soup tureen and ladle and an ewer; one marked 'Wedgwood' and one 'CH'. c. 1780–1790.
Pearlware	Underglaze blue painted shell edging, thirty-six items; five oval serving plates, twenty-five round plates, one bowl, two sauceboats and three covers. Six items marked 'Rogers', four marked 'I.H.' and one marked 'ASTBURY'. c. 1790–1814.
Pearlware	Polychrome decoration, three items; one teapot, one tea bowl and one jug, the jug with impressed mark of 'Enoch Wood & Sons', in olive green with applied leaf decoration. c. 1810–35.
Earthenware	Underglaze blue transfer printed, thirty-one items; five willow pattern tea plates, six saucers, five cups, two mugs (both with the village church pattern) eight bowls, one cover, one sauceboat, two chamber pots (also village church pattern) and one large jug. Two saucers are marked 'Stone China' within an octagon containing imitation Chinese writing. c. 1807–30.
Earthenware	Underglaze colour printed, three items; two bowls, one saucer. c. 1820–30.
On-glaze bat printed	Four items; three saucers, one bowl. c. 1800.
English porcelain	One item; coffee cup with mark of crossed swords (Derby?)
Black basalt	Two items; one bowl, one cream jug.

White feldspathic   One item; large oval jug. *c.* 1790–1820.
   stoneware

Red earthenware   Five items; two chamber-pots, three small dishes.

Staffordshire combed One item; sub-rectangular platter complete and dated generally to the eighteenth century
   slipware   and probably late seventeenth.

Salt glazed stoneware One item; small jug. *c.* 1820.

C. SMALL FINDS FROM ST. JOHN'S LANE compiled by P. Garrard

(i) THE ROMAN COINS by I. Anderson

1. 70 (71) II   Trajan, *As* A.D. 98–99. RIC 395.
2. 42 (47) III   Trajan, *Dupondius.* A.D. 98–99. RIC 382.
3. 3 (2) VI   Septimius Severus, *Denarius,* A.D. 200–210. *Rev.* illegible.
4. 23 (19) V   Tetricus II, A.D. 270–73. *Antoninianus.* As RIC 270.
5. 15 (5) V   Barbarous radiate, *c.* A.D. 270–290. *Obv.* Tetricus II portrait. *Rev. Fides.*
6. 7 (13) V   Constantine I. *Follis* 313–15. RIC VII; Trier 42.
7. 24 (u.s.)   *Urbs Roma,* A.D. 335–37. HK 409.
8. 11 (11) V   House of Constantine, A.D. 335–41.
9. 13 (5) V   Constantius II, *c.* A.D. 355–365. Copy as CK 25.

(ii) THE POST-MEDIEVAL COIN by I. Anderson

1. 1 (1) VI   France. Napoleon III. 5 centimes. 1857.

(iii) THE BROOCH OF COPPER ALLOY by D. Mackreth (Fig. 118, no. 1)

1. 76 (72) II   Colchester Type. The brooch is now in two pieces. The whole is very corroded and, while the form may be made out, there is no sign of any decoration; the proper bow-section is unclear, but had a wide face to the front, is thin and seems to have a flat back. The hook is long and may have continued over the marked 'kick' at the head of the bow. The catch-plate is obscured by corrosion products and may have had a ridge across the top; the detail is best seen on the back.

    The brooch belongs to a sub-group based in Kent and isolated by the writer: although the decorative details, if there were any, cannot be seen, the flat section of the bow, the high 'kick' at its head and what seems to have been a very long hook are all diagnostic. One has been published from the Rosemary Lane Car Park site[277] and a further five from Canterbury (two from Cakebread-Robey site,[278] two from the Marlowe sites (*The Archaeology of Canterbury,* vol. v, forthcoming) and one from Highstead[279] serve to emphasise the bias of the distribution. The most far-flung example known to the writer comes from Cirencester (to be published). A

277. P. Bennett *et al.* 'Excavations in the Rosemary Lane Car Park' in *The Archaeology of Canterbury,* vol. i.
278. *The Archaeology of Canterbury,* vol. vi, forthcoming.
279. Highstead Excavations, forthcoming.

study of the make-up of the assemblages of early brooches from both Cirencester and Chichester[280] reveals that that from the latter place is highly individual and that the assemblage from the former, if it reflects the origin of the military there, shows that the army units were at least partly drawn from the Lower Thames Valley; but a single brooch is not enough to show that any element should have come from Canterbury itself. The dating of the variety is to be discussed in the report on the Marlowe sites and the conclusion there will be that it is unlikely to be very early in the first century A.D., but may have been made before A.D. 40.

(iv)   OBJECTS OF COPPER ALLOY by P. Garrard

Roman

2. 51 (62) III   Rim fragment of *speculum* mirror, convex; fine eysared line decoration at 10 mm. from and parallel to the bevelled edge: diam. 200 mm. Very corroded. (Not illustrated)

3. 8 (7) V   Facet-headed pin, head 6 mm. cube. Broken and corroded. Common Roman type. Residual. (Not illustrated).

(v)   OBJECTS OF WORKED BONE by P. Garrard (Fig. 118)

Roman

4. 33 (23) III ⎫
5. 10 (6B) V   ⎬ Two pin-stems with swelling shafts. (Not illustrated).
                 ⎭

6. 64 (47) III   Counter, Greep Type 1.[281] Incised graffito on reverse.

7. 38 (34) IV   Similar counter to No. 6, no graffiti. (Not illustrated).

8. 92 (13) V   Pin, incomplete. Greep Type B1.1.[282] (Not illustrated).

9. 18 (5) V   Needle, incomplete. Greep Type 3.[283] (Not illustrated).

(vi)   MISCELLANEOUS OBJECTS by P. Garrard (Fig. 118)

10. 17 (5) V   Fragments of a baked clay bun-shaped loom-weight, tempered with fine flint grits. Marks made by the suspending cord. Hurst Type III. (Not illustrated).

11. 106 (68) III   Glass counter, very dark cobalt, opaque. Diam. 18 mm. Roman. (Not illustrated).

12. 71 (71) II   Disc-shaped object of lead, possibly a stopper.

13. 108 (66) II   Hone-stone, shaped, incomplete. Fine grey sandstone. 24 mm. wide x 5 mm. thick. (Not illustrated).

14. 39 (34) IV   Socketed leaf-shaped spearhead of iron.

280.   A. Down, excavations forthcoming.
281.   *The Archaeology of Canterbury*, vol. v, forthcoming.
282.   *Ibid*.
283.   *Ibid*.

4. NO. 15A DANE JOHN[284]

A. THE SMALL FINDS compiled by P. Garrard

(i) THE BELGIC COIN by D. Nash

1. 50 (22) VB Bronze coin, 2.52 g.
Obv.: Young male head to right with long hair which turns up at the neck. Ring-and-dot ornaments in front; eyelet ornament behind.
Rev.: Stylised bull walking to left on a distinct ground line. The bull appears to wear a girth. Pellet and ring-and-dot ornaments above, behind, in front and below. Border of dots. This appears to be an unpublished type. It seems to be of British rather than Gaulish origin: the ornament behind the head on the obverse, and the bull's nose portrayed as a pair of rings, can both be paralleled in developed British coinage. The general style of engraving and decoration seems to place this coin in or near Kent; cf. bronzes of Dubnovellaunus such as Mack[285] 291, or gold British LY staters (Mack 293). Its types seem to be inspired by Belgic silver coinage struck in Gaul during and after Caesar's conquest; the obverse has affinities with silver of Roveca of the Meldi struck in the fifties B.C. (Scheers,[286] Fig. 199) or with silver of the Belgic Caledu struck in the forties or thirties B.C. (Scheers, Figs. 307–9). Silver of Atleva Vlatos (Scheers, Figs. 305–6), whose otherwise similar bull adopts a different stance, may have provided a general model for the reverse. It seems likely therefore that this uninscribed bronze coin was struck in or near Kent during the final quarter of the first century B.C.

(ii) THE ROMAN COINS by I. Anderson

1. 391 (165) I   Vespasian. *As* A.D. 69–79. *Rev.* illegible.
2. 345 (156) I   Vespasian. As *dupondius* A.D. 76–78. *Rev.* illegible.
3. 322 (u.s.)   Domitian. A.D. 86. RIC 335.
4. 379 (159) II   Domitian. A.D. 90–91. RIC 397.
5. 60 (3) VD   Trajan. A.D. 103–111. RIC 512.
6. 252 (105A) IIIB Trajan. A.D. 112–114. RIC 292.
7. 323 (130) II   Antoninus Pius. A.D. 139. RIC 553.
8. 337 (u.s.)   Valerian I. A.D. 258–259. RIC 12.
9. 350 (154) IIIA   Gallienus. A.D. 259–268. RIC 238.
10. 178 (68) VA   Postumus. A.D. 259-268. RIC 373.
11. 358 (22) VB   Illegible. *c.* A.D. 260–273. *Rev.* uncertain.
12. 72 (27) VD   Illegible. *c.* A.D. 260–273. *Rev.* illegible.
13. 88 (18) VD   Victorinus. A.D. 268–270. RIC 78.
14. 287 (121) II   Victorinus. A.D. 268–270. RIC 116.
15. 170 (41) VB   Illegible. *c.* A.D. 268–273. *Rev.* uncertain.
16. 253 (105A) IIIB Illegible. *c.* A.D. 268–273. *Rev. Spes Publica.*
17. 280 (113) IIIB Illegible. *c.* A.D. 268–273. *Rev. Pax.*

---

284. The published material is numbered consecutively under each main heading, each item being followed, where appropriate, by its small find number, layer number (in brackets) and period. The specialist reports and detailed context-related catalogues of the finds have been deposited with the excavation records in the Royal Museum, Canterbury. All the reports were edited by Mrs. Pan Garrard.
285. R.P. Mack, *The Coinage of Ancient Britain* (London, 1975), 3rd edition.
286. S. Scheers, *Traité de Numismatique celtique II: La Gaule belgique* (Paris, 1977).

18. 14 (6B) VD   Tetricus I. A.D. 270–273. RIC 127.
19. 31 (16) VD   Tetricus I. A.D. 270–273. *Rev. Salus.*
20. 35A (22) VB   Tetricus I. A.D. 270–273. *Rev. ?Pax.*
21. 81 (5) VI   Tetricus I. A.D. 270–273. RIC 100.
22. 279 (107A) IIIB Tetricus I. A.D. 270–273. *Rev.* illegible.
23. 321 (146) IIIB Tetricus I. A.D. 270–273. *Rev. Laetitia.*
24. 342 (150) IIIB Tetricus I. A.D. 270–273. RIC 117.
25. 332 (163) II   Tetricus II. A.D. 270–273. RIC 254.
26. 239 (102) IIIB Tetricus II. A.D. 270–273. RIC 270.
27. 327 (142) IIIB Barbarous radiate. *c.* A.D. 270–290. *Rev. Spes.*
28. 141 (u.s.)   Barbarous radiate. *c.* A.D. 270–290. *Rev. Spes.*
29. 36 (22) VB   Barbarous radiate. *c.* A.D. 270–290. *Rev.* uncertain.
30. 251 (107) IIIB Allectus. A.D. 293–296. RIC 124.
31. 274 (113) IIIB Illegible. Second half of third century A.D. to fourth century A.D.
32. 122 (9) VA   Illegible. Second half of third century A.D. to first quarter of fourth century A.D.
33. 63 (11) VB   Illegible. Second half of third century A.D. to first quarter of fourth century A.D.
34. 119 (9) VA   Illegible. Last quarter of third century A.D. to first quarter of fourth century A.D.
35. 232 (51) IV   Constantine I. A.D. 330–335. HK 65.
36. 3 (6) VD   Constantine I. A.D. 330–337. HK 184/185.
37. 52 (22) VB   Constantinopolis. A.D. 330–341. Copy as HK 52.
38. 290 (u.s.)   Constantine II. A.D. 330–335. HK 56.
39. 42 (22) VB   Constantine II. A.D. 330-335. HK 64.
40. 51 (22) VB   House of Constantine. A.D. 335–341. As HK 87.
41. 150 (u.s.)   Constans. A.D. 341–346. HK 155.
42. 257 (105A) IIIB Constans. A.D. 341–346. HK 140A.
43. 175 (66) VA   Constans. A.D. 341–346. *Rev.* illegible.
44. 261 (109) VB   Constantius II. *c.* A.D. 350–360. Copy as CK 25.
45. 64 (19) VB   Valentinian I. A.D. 364–367. CK 484.
46. 243 (104) IIIB Valens. A.D. 367–378. CK 526.
47. 330 (146) IIIB Valentinian II. A.D. 378–392. *Rev.* illegible.
48. 137 (50) VB   House of Theodosius. A.D. 388–408. As CK 796.

(iii) MEDIEVAL COINS by M. Archibald

1. 255 (106) IV   Edward I–II
   Penny, class X (late); class X struck, *c.* 1300–10.
   Mint: London.
   Wt. 1.23 g. (19.0 gr.).
   This coin is unclipped and not much worn and so was certainly deposited before 1351 and probably around 1320–30.
2. 249 (106) IV   Anglo-Gallic 'Henry IV' 1399–1413.
   Hardi d'argent, type 2.
   Obv. Here almost illegible but should read: +E'RIC'R/XAGLIE, three-quarter length figure of the king holding an upright sword under a small canopy.
   Rev. FRA CIE DNS AGI Long cross with leopard and lis alternately in angles (lis end in annulets).
   Wt. 0.61 g. (9.4 gr.) broken.
   Although Hewlett[287] attributes all of this issue to Henry IV, recent work has shown that they

---

287. L.M. Hewlett, *Anglo-Gallic Coins* (London, 1920), 161, hardi No. 2.

extend into the reign of Henry V. It should be borne in mind that it was probably struck rather later than Hewlett suggests.

Anglo-Gallic coins did not circulate in England since, although struck for the kings of England, they conformed to their own standards of weight and fineness which did not fit the English pattern. Occasional isolated finds have, however, been made in England, e.g. a *denier d'argent* also attributed to Henry IV, but probably later, found at Kingston-upon-Hull and exhibited at the British Museum in 1976.

3.   1. (u.s.)   Henry VII, 1485–1509.
Half-groat, closed crown type, no initial mark.
Mint: Canterbury, King and Archbishop jointly (?), *c.* 1490–1500.
Wt. 1.37 g. (21.1 gr.).
Ref. North 1711.

This coin is now heavily corroded but was probably not much worn when lost, so was probably deposited by *c.* 1520 at the latest.

(iv) THE POST-MEDIEVAL COINS AND JETTONS by M. Archibald and I. Anderson

The Coins

1.   11 (13) VII   Elizabeth I, 1558–1603
Threepence, initial mark, eglantine, 1575.
Mint: London.
Wt. 1.14 g. (17.6 gr.).
Ref. North 1998.
This coin is very heavily worn and was probably deposited well into the seventeenth century, say *c.* 1620–50.

2.   184 (49A) IV   James I, farthing, 1614–1625. Peck 79.
3.   180 (41A) IV   Charles I, farthing, 1625. Peck 121.
4.   212 (u.s.)   Charles I, farthing, *c.* 1638–1644.
5.   17 (6A) VD   Charles I, farthing, *c.* 1638–1644. Peck 329.
6.   7 (9) VA   Charles I, farthing, *c.* 1638–1644. Peck 340.
7.   427 (21) VC   Illegible, halfpenny. Late seventeenth century to eighteenth century.
8.   2 (7A) IV   William III, halfpenny. 1698–1699.
9.   130 (50) VB   George II, farthing. 1737.
10.   61 (19) VB   George II, halfpenny. 1746–1754.
11.   329 (6) VD   George III, halfpenny. 1771.
12.   121 (11) VB   George III, halfpenny. 1773.

The Jettons

1.   206 (85) VB   French jetton. Fifteenth century as Barnard (France) 46.
2.   8 (9) VA   Jetton. Nüremberg. Sixteenth century as Barnard (Germany) 82, but fictitious legend.
3.   108 (43) VB   Jetton. Nüremberg. Sixteenth century as Barnard (Germany) 82, but fictitious legend.
4.   193 (82) VA   Jetton. Nüremberg. Sixteenth century as Barnard (Germany) 82, but fictitious legend.
5.   129 (49) IV   Jetton of Hanns Krauwinckel. Nüremberg. *c.* 1580–1610 as Barnard (Germany) 84.
6.   112 (43) VB   Jetton of Hanns Krauwinckel. Nüremberg. *c.* 1580–1610 as Barnard (Germany) 84.
7.   160 (41) VB   Jetton of Hanns Krauwinckel. Nüremberg. *c.* 1580–1610 as Barnard (Germany) 84.
8.   336 (134) VD   Jetton of Nüremberg type. Marion Archibald writes: 'Very little of the types of this jetton remain but the legends are certainly those found on the *doubles* of Charles II of Gonzaga, Duke of Mantua as Sovereign Prince of Arches in the County of Nevers, France.

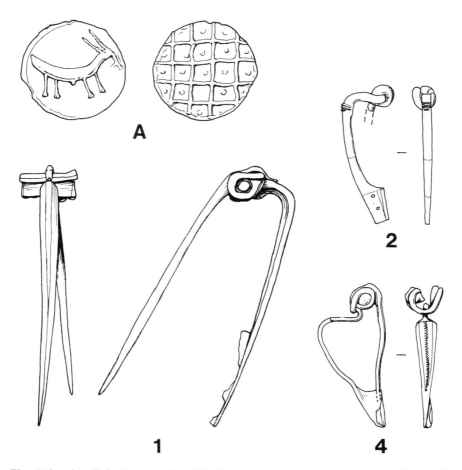

Fig. 119. Small finds from No. 15A Dane John: Nos. A, 1, 2 and 4 (Scale: ⅓)

Arches (France).
Charles II of Mantua as Sovereign Prince of Arches in County of Nevers, 1601–37.
Obv.: (CHAR)LES II (DUC D MANT S DAR) Bust to right (here illegible).
Rev.: (DOUBLE D LA) SOV DA(R 1639 or 42)
Wt.: 1.15 g.
Ref.: J. Neumann.[288]
(The very thin flan and brassy metal of this piece is certainly that of a reckoning counter of the Nüremberg type rather than that of the *doubles* of the French principalities which are of thicker fabric and often more coppery in metal.)'

(v) THE UNOFFICIAL TOKEN OF LEAD by G. Egan (Fig. 119)

A. 92 (21) VD   Bifacial. Rectilinear grid with pellets in the squares // quadruped with long ears (crudely executed). Unworn.
Diameter 28 mm.
Weight 7.890 gm.

288. J. Neumann, *Beschreibung der bekannesten Kupfermünzen*, vol. i, 646–7.

(vi) THE BROOCHES by D. Mackreth (Fig. 119)

All are made from a copper alloy. All are residual.

Colchesters

1. 339 (63) VB   73 mm. long. The spring has six coils. Each wing has a vertical groove at its end. The hook is neatly formed and relatively short. The bow has a flattened hexagonal section, is plain and has an almost straight profile with a sharp bend at the top. The catch-plate is largely missing, but parts of two piercings are visible. The whole is well finished and the normal manufacturing marks on the back of the bow have been removed.

   The brooch betrays no habits which show directly that it ought to be considered to be of Continental origin or late in the type's series. The only element of doubt arises from the groove in each wing but, weighing that against the style of the item and its generally excellent quality, more stress should be placed upon other indicators. In this case, attention may be drawn to the profile of the bow and to the shortness, amongst British brooches, of the hook – had it been of Continental origin, the hook should only have been long enough to have touched the head of the bow. The profile matches that to be expected in Augustan times and which, in Britain, is replaced by the more familiar curve at a later time. The impression given is that it ought to be dated to before A.D. 15–25.

Unclassified

2. 273 (113) IIIB   Now in three pieces, the brooch retains half of its four-coil internal-chord spring. The bow has a thin circular section with a quadrant bend at the top profile. At the base of the curve are two thin mouldings which run round the bow and, beneath these at the front, a small projection which is curved forward like a beak. The catch-plate has two small circular holes, one above the other.

   This brooch is a small – only 4 cm. long – example of a group dealt with by Stead.[289] The chief feature which declares the brooch's relationship is the moulding, including the 'beak', at the top of the bow. However, the small size, the internal chord and the two circular piercings in the catch-plate place the brooch in a later typological group than the bulk of those assigned by Stead to his Welwyn phase of the Aylesford culture (*ibid.*, 412), the second half of the first century B.C. The present specimen lies at the end of that development, but should not date after the reign of Augustus.

Nauheim Derivatives

3. 282 (117) IIIB   In three pieces, the spring is incomplete and the catch-plate is missing. The brooch has a wide bow tapering towards a, presumably, pointed foot. Beneath the corrosion on the upper bow can be seen a line of rocker-arm ornament down the centre with a suggestion of an incised line down each side. (Not illustrated.)

4. 343 (146) IIIB   The spring is now separate from the bow and there may have been an iron bar through the coils. The bow has the same basic form as that of brooch No. 3 and with a similar, but finer, line of rocker-arm decoration down the centre. There is a definite incised line on each side.

   These two brooches pose problems which are not yet capable of solution. Discussion of the Nauheim and Nauheim Derivatives from the Marlowe sites[290] draws attention to the

289. I. Stead, 'The earliest Burials of the Aylesford Culture' in (Eds.) G. de G. Sieveking, I.H. Longworth and K.E. Wilson, *Problems in economic and social Archaeology* (London, 1976), 401–16.

290. *The Archaeology of Canterbury*, vol. v (forthcoming).

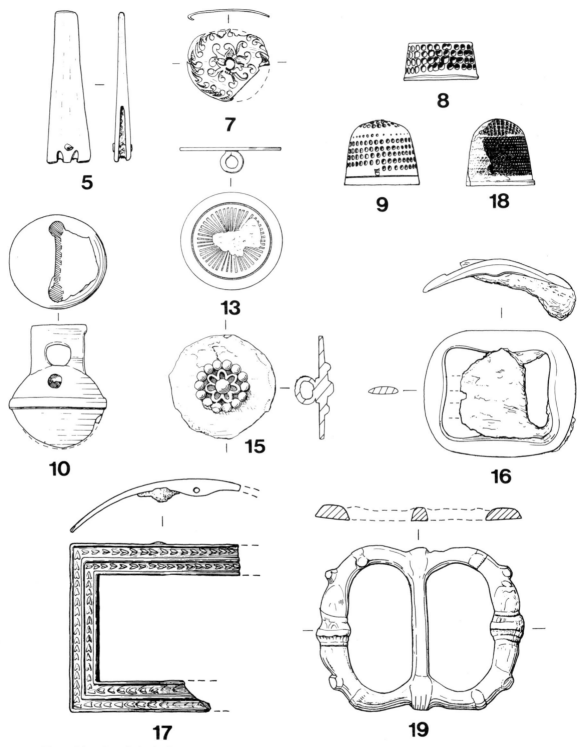

Fig. 120.   Small finds from No. 15A Dane John: Nos. 5, 7–10, 13, 15–17 and 19 (Scale: ½)

difficulties of identifying a Nauheim if the catch-plate is missing. The note continues to discuss the successors of that type and, in cases such as brooches Nos. 3 and 4 – assuming that No. 3 is not a Nauheim – while there may be a temptation to see in them the early stages in the long process which leads to the Derivative forms of the middle of the first century A.D., this has to be resisted. Until there is more evidence to place brooches in the period *c.* 25 B.C. to *c.* A.D. 50, these two brooches can only be given a first-century date with an end-date of *c.* A.D. 80–90. The probability is, however, that they do not date after A.D. 75 as survivors-in-use and there is a possibility that they may date to before A.D. 25, but the proof is lacking.

(vii)   OBJECTS OF COPPER ALLOY by P. Garrard (Fig. 120)

Medieval

5.	309 (23) IIIB	Strap-end. Late medieval.
6.	39 (23) IIIB	Netting needle. Compare a similar example from the Marlowe Car Park excavations.[291] (Not illustrated).

Post-medieval

7.	349 (51) IV	Button cap with impressed decoration.
8.	215 (51) IV	Open-end thimble, used for leather and canvas work.
9.	79 (7B) IV	Thimble, spiral pattern pits, and a maker's mark.
10.	196 (72) VA	Rumble bell. Incomplete.
11.	149 (41) VB	Button embossed with basket-work pattern. Diam. 21 mm. Cf. I. Noël Hume,[292] Fig. 23, Type 4. (Not illustrated.)
12.	107 (33) VC	Similar button to No. 11 above. Diam. 17 mm. (Not illustrated.)
13.	12 (11) VB	Disc-shaped button, gilded, with a stamped design. Cf. I. Noël Hume, Fig. 23, Type 9.
14.	29 (19) VB	Disc-shaped button with applied rosette, probably gilded. (Not illustrated)
15.	32 (19) VB	Similar button to No. 14 above.
16.	99 (21) VC	Buckle for knee-britches; the iron prongs have corroded. Cf. I. Noël Hume, Fig. 20, No. 9.
17.	110 (44) VC	Rectangular (incomplete) shoe buckle, once silvered.
18.	24 (21) VC	Thimble, rolled edge.
19.	168 (64) VB	Buckle.

(viii)   OBJECTS OF IRON by P. Garrard and B. Ellis (Figs. 121 and 122)

Medieval

20.	409 (121) II	Whittle-tang knife, angled back and inlaid with alternating design of copper and brass.
21.	422 (144) IIIA	Three small whittle-tang knives; all are broken and incomplete.
22.	432A (168) IIIA	(Not illustrated.)
23.	432B (168) IIIA	
24.	319 (44) VC	Whittle-tang knife.

Post-medieval

25.	398 (51) IV	Decorative knife handle. First half of seventeenth century.
26.	229 (51A) IV	Key. LMMC[293] Type VIIA. (Not illustrated.)

291. *Ibid.*
292. I. Noël Hume, *A Guide to Artefacts of colonial America* (New York, 1980).
293. *London Museum Medieval Catalogue*, Fourth impression (London, 1975).

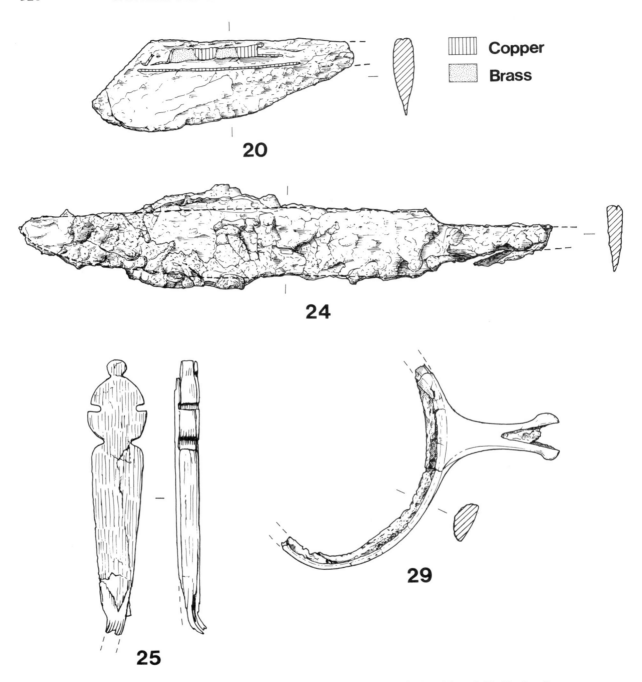

Fig. 121. Small finds from No. 15A Dane John: Nos. 20, 24, 25 and 29 (Scale: ½)

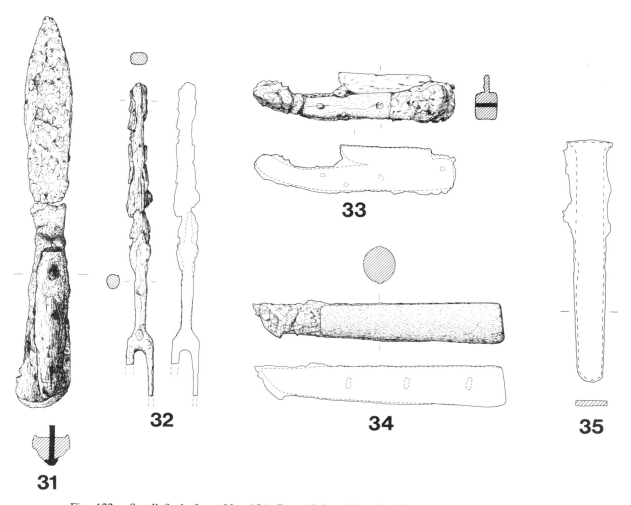

Fig. 122.   Small finds from No. 15A Dane John: Nos. 31, 32, 33, 34 and 35 (Scale: ½)

27.   153 (41) VB   Key. LMMC Type VIIB. (Not illustrated.)
28.   185 (49A) IV   Rowel spur. The rowel is missing. Similar to No. 29 below. (Not illustrated.)
29.   15 (15) VC   Rowel spur. Blanche Ellis writes:
'Iron rowel spur fragment of small proportions, its outer surfaces thickly plated with tin or silver. The spur retains 60 mm. of one straight side and a stump of the other. They are 11 mm. deep behind the wearer's heel, the longer one tapering to 6 mm. deep at its broken front end. Both terminals are missing. The oval section straight neck swells out at the junction of the sides without a defined join, and tapers towards a very slender little rowel box with rounded rowel bosses now pulled apart. The rowel pin and rowel are missing. Overall length of fragment now 73 mm. Length of neck 30 mm. Length of rowel box 14 mm. Two separate small lumps of corroded rust and soil are with the spur and were part of it. Typological date: second half of the seventeenth century.

Spurs with straight, tapered sides were already established by the mid-seventeenth century, for example those found in a forge used in the 1645 siege of Sandal Castle.[294] As the century progressed, spurs tended to become very small, such as those worn by King William III in the equestrian portrait of his landing at Brixham by Jan Wyck dated 1688, in the National Maritime Museum, London.

Silver and tin were both frequently used for the plating of spurs. Professor E.M. Jope has discussed the tinning of iron spurs.'[295]

30.   207A (72) VA   Rowel spur, similar to No. 29 above. Not tinned. The rowel is missing. (Not illustrated.)
31.   310 (21) VC   Scale-tang knife with wooden handle. (The blade is broken).
32.   426 (21) VC   Two-pronged fork with balluster haft and wooden handle.
33.   441 (21) VC   Swivel-blade knife, pivoting on an iron rivet through the tang: the handle is mounted with bone plates secured by iron rivets.
34.   318 (44) VC   Knife handle made from two halves of bone, enclosing a scale-tanged knife blade by three copper alloy rivets.
35.   425 (21) VC)
36.   375 (21) VC)   Three identical flat staples. No. 35 is illustrated.
37.   365 (28) VB)

(ix)   OBJECTS OF WORKED BONE by S. Greep (Fig. 123)

Roman

Types are as described in the report on worked bone from the Marlowe Car Park excavations.[296]

38.   346 (153) IIIA   Pin of Type A1. 58 mm. long, broken. (Not illustrated.)
39.   351 (146) IIIB   Pin of Type A2.1 42 mm. long, broken. (Not illustrated.)
40.   419 (160) IIIA   Pin of Type A2.2. Single groove. 34 mm. long, broken. (Not illustrated.)
41.   256 (u.s.)   Pin (?) with a large, round, deeply incised head above seven well cut collars. Tapering stem. 44 mm. long, broken.
42.   248 (105) IIIB   Type 1 gaming counter, 21.6 mm. diam. 3 mm. thick. IX lightly incised on reverse.
43.   308 (23) IIIB   Fragment of the slider, or back, of a bone scabbard chape of late second- or third-century date (e.g. Philp, 1981, Fig. 43, 242).[297] The front portion of such a chape was recovered from the Marlowe Car Park excavations (M.I S.F. No. 1473). 62 mm. long, broken.

Medieval

44.   250 (106) IV   Turned pin-pricker, 61 mm. long, broken, the point being lost. A number of other examples of these forms have been recovered from Canterbury (MIIA S.F. No. 9).[298]

(x)   THE CLOTH SEALS by G. Egan (Fig. 123)

45.   126 (49) IV   Incomplete seal for a coloured cloth, probably first half of the seventeenth-century.

A, (IN) CVCH(INEL) around // (disc missing) incomplete personal mark.

The missing parts of the legend (given in brackets above) and of the personal mark are

294.   B. Ellis in P. Mayes and L.A.S. Butler, *Sandal Castle Excavations 1964–1973* (Wakefield, 1983), Nos. 9–26.
295.   Professor E.M. Jope 'The Tinning of Iron Spurs: A continuous Practice from the tenth to the seventeenth Century', *Oxoniensia*, xxi (1956), 35–42.
296.   *The Archaeology of Canterbury*, vol. v (forthcoming).
297.   B. Philp, *The Excavation of the Roman Forts of the Classis Britannica at Dover, 1970–77* (Dover, 1981).
298.   *Op. cit. supra*, note 296.

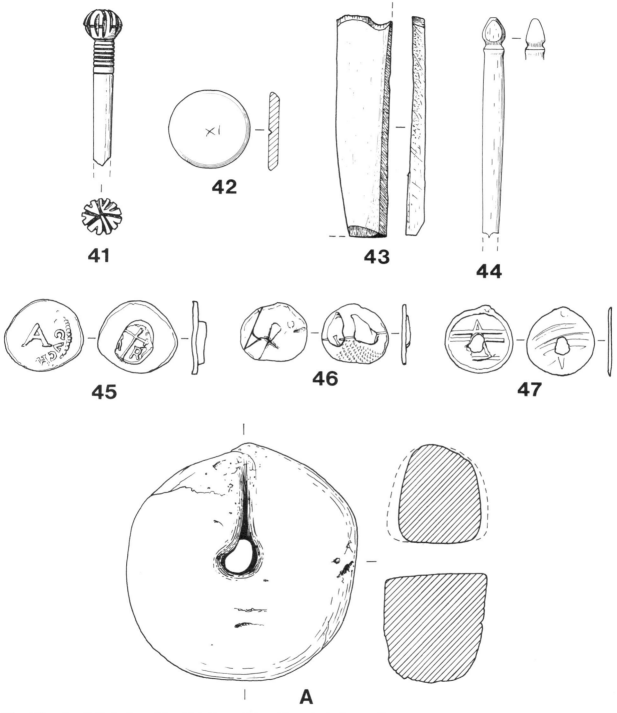

Fig. 123.   Small finds from No. 15A Dane John: Nos. 41–7 (Scale: ¼) and No. 44. Burgate No. A (Scale: ½)

seals with closely similar stamps found in London.[299] The present example is the only one recorded on which these two stamps appear together.

The extensive series of seals to which this one belongs is connected with dyeing. Most examples have a stamp on one side indicating the particular dye used on the textile to which each was attached – (dyed) 'in cochineal' in this case – and the other side usually has a personal mark – here that of someone with the initials AR. Other seals with 'in cochineal' have different letters in the centre of the stamp – P, S, and PE over C; their significance, like that of the central A on the present seal, is unknown.

Cochineal gives a pale red colour, or if a solution of pewter as a tin mordant, dissolved in *aqua fortis* (nitric acid) is added, a brilliant scarlet is produced.[300] The latter technique was developed in the earlier seventeenth century. It is not clear whether AR, whose identity is not known, would have been the dyer or an official of the dyers' guild who would check the evenness and fastness of the colour in the newly-dyed cloth.[301] Apart from the present example, seals with this stamp have only been found in London – some of them have legends which indicate that they originate in the City. One of them is dated 1614.[302]

It seems likely that this is an earlier seventeenth-century London seal which was put on a textile dyed red.

46. 228 (70) VA   Incomplete seal with two rivets. Scratched ⋎꓾ device, possibly a personal mark or letters // (disc missing) traces of lettering from a stamp on the rivets. There is an imprint on the inner surface of the disc of a plainwoven textile with *c.* 7 to 8 tightly spun threads per 5 mm. in each system. This imprint indicates a medium or lightweight fabric, perhaps a linen or cotton textile, or a worsted or mixed one, but not a pure woollen.[303]

Several broadly similar seals (i.e. having two rivets, but slightly smaller discs), have been found in London and elsewhere.[304] None is from a closely dated context, and, with the exception of one found in London (private collection) which may have part of the word 'Tournai', none of the devices gives any clue which might allow the origin to be identified.

299. A number of dies with similar stamps were in use; none of the following has definitely identical stamps to the Dane John seal. For 'in cuchinel' stamps, cf. Museum of London collection, no. 81.522/21 and 22, and Department of Urban Archaeology, Trig Lane site (layer 82), no. 3069. The last (incomplete) seal was found with several others of different types in a drain which possibly came from a dyer's premises. Although this feature is not closely datable, external evidence from parallels to the seals suggests that it may be from the reign of James I. For the AR mark, cf. J.E. Hodgkin, *Rariora*, vol. i (London, 1902), Pl. with pp. 101–3, No. 57, and Museum of London collection, No. 81.534/14.

300. F.W. Gibbs, 'Invention in Chemical Industries', in (Eds.) C. Singer *et al. A History of Technology*, iii (Oxford, 1979, reprint), 695.

301. The 'mark of a true dyed cloth', presumably a deal of this general type, was at one time applied to the cloth by the dyer himself, though this would be a very weak point in the regulation of the industry were it not supplemented by some kind of checking; P.E. Jones, 'The Guilds of the City of London with special Reference to the Worshipful Company of Dyers', in *Journal of the Society of Dyers and Colourists*, 71 (1955), 499. Officers of the Dyers' Company had overall responsibility for quality control in London in the seventeenth century; J. Hubner, 'Early History of Dyeing', *op. cit.* above, jubilee number (1934), 4. The seals have the same kinds of devices for at least twenty years from 1613, implying no change during this period in the administration of the sealing system.

302. Wembley History Society collection no. 46 (Grange Museum, Neasden).

303. Thread counts and comments on the textile are by Frances Pritchard.

304. Cf. Museum of London collection no. 81. 534/12, and Department of Urban Archaeology MFS 76 area 16/+, no. 111. For a different textile imprint on a somewhat similar seal, cf. W. Endrei and G. Egan, 'The Sealing Cloth in Europe with special Reference to the English Evidence', in *Textile History*, 13, 1 (1982) 64, Fig. 11. The type of seal is illustrated in Hodgkin, *op. cit.*, in note 16, 102 (at bottom).

Somewhat larger seals with two rivets were widely used in the Low Countries, and in England by Dutch immigrants such as the community at Colchester,[305] in the later sixteenth and seventeenth centuries. This seal is thus typologically in a Continental tradition but, in the present state of knowledge, it is not possible to suggest a firmer attribution than that it is likely to be either from an imported textile, or from one woven here in an immigrant community.

47. (unstratified)   Probably an incomplete cloth seal, or possibly a token, with some excess metal from the channel of the casting mould still attached.
Series of parallel arcs // (?cast) ⬜ device, possibly part of a personal mark.

(xi) OBJECTS OF FIRED CLAY by P. Garrard

48. 439 (114) I   Spindle-whorl of a body sherd, grog-tempered Roman coarse ware; diam. 38 mm. Only half remains. Imperforate central hole: diam. 7 mm. (Not illustrated.)
49. 340 (110) IIIA   Spindle-whorl, body sherd of grog-tempered Romano-British combed ware; diam. 56 mm. Perforated central hole 9 mm. Residual. (Not illustrated.)
50. 407 (110) IIIA   Baked clay 'bun' type loom-weight fragments, sparsely tempered with fine crushed flint grit; diam. 140 mm., height 63 mm., central hole approx. 20 mm. Compare a similar example from Church Lane.[306] (Not illustrated).

305. Endrei and Egan, *op. cit. supra*, note 304, 65–6.
306. *The Archaeology of Canterbury*, vol. ii, 149, Fig. 82, no. 43.

APPENDIX 7

SUMMARY OF 'GALLO-BELGIC', ROMAN AND LATE ROMAN IMPORTS FROM THE MARLOWE AVENUE, ST. JOHN'S LANE AND NO. 15A DANE JOHN SITES
by M.J. Green

A table (combining all three sites) of quantified fabric types is presented here (Table 1). Where it was thought useful to expand on certain fabrics, e.g. variants and pieces rare to Canterbury, footnotes have been added.

It is Trust policy to publish samian more comprehensively, i.e. a full report of all material from the Roman periods and selected pieces from post-Roman contexts. Due to unforseen changes in publication plans, a full report for St. John's Lane cannot be included in this volume.

It is intended that Volume V of this series (the Marlowe Car Park excavations) will include full reports on 'Gallo-Belgic' fine wares, Roman and Romano-British fine wares (late-Roman in particular) and *Eifelkeramik* (imported German coarse ware). An extensive study of the city's amphorae by Paul Arthur has now been published in *Britannia*, xvii (1986), 239–58.

Fabrics in Table 1 were identified by the following members of the Trust: Marion Green (Roman and Romano-British fine wares, mortaria), Andrew Savage ('Gallo-Belgic' fine wares, amphorae) and Maggy Taylor (St. John's Lane samian). Joanna Bird's reports for the Marlowe Avenue and 15A Dane John samian are gratefully acknowledged.

TABLE 1

SUMMARY OF 'GALLO-BELGIC', ROMAN AND LATE ROMAN IMPORTS

(Quantified by sherd count. Notes: cc = colour-coat; SG, CG, EG and NG = South, Central, Eastern and Northern Gaul respectively; TR = *Terra Rubra* and TN = *Terra Nigra*.)

TYPE	FABRIC	MAV	SJL	DJ
'Gallo-Belgic'	TR 1(B)	–	3	2
	TR 1(C)	2	1	2 prob.
	TR 2	–	1	1 prob.
	TR 3	–	?1	3
	TR 3(A)	–	2	2
	TR 3(B)	–	–	12
	TR 3 Type[307]	–	–	6
	?TR[308]	–	–	1
	TR : Micaceous	–	–	1
	TN : Micaceous	–	–	3
	TN : Non-Micaceous	–	10[309]	10

307. Beaker body sherds (four conjoining and two conjoining): TR 3(A) exterior surface but with buff interior (instead of the more normal pale orange-pink), cream-buff fracture, finely sandy with tiny red ?haematite inclusions.

308. Platter base: pink-buff fracture, grey-buff exterior with very pale cream-pink interior surface ?TR 1 (A).

309. Includes four conjoining platter base sherds with triple radial stamp.

TYPE	FABRIC	MAV	SJL	DJ
	?TN[310]	–	–	1
	TN/TR : Non-Micaceous	1	–	–
	Eggshell TN	–	1	?1
	Rigby Fabric I–IV[311]	2	14+1 prob.	13
	Pompeian Red:[312]			
	Peacock Fabric 2	–	–	1
	Peacock Fabric 3	–	1	–
	?Peacock Fabric 4	1	–	–
	White Wares[313]	1	19+?1	5
	?'G.B.' Fine Ware	–	2	–
Roman and Romano-British Fine Wares				
Pre-Flavian	Lyon	–	2	–
c. Late first to second				
century	Colchester/NG cc	1	16+?1	2
	Colchester cc	–	?2	2 prob. + ?2
	Lower Rhine Fab.1	1 prob.	6+?2	1+2 prob.
	L. Rhine/Early Nene Valley cc	–	9	1
	L. Rhine/CG cc	–	–	1
	Fine Marbled Ware (?London. Prob. Early Roman)	–	2	–
c. Mid second to third century	*Moselkeramik*	–	1	2
	CG cc	1	3	2+1 prob.
	Moselkeramik/CG cc	1	1	–
Third to fourth century	Nene Valley cc	7	5+?2	7
	Nene Valley Type cc	11	–	10
	?Nene Valley Parchment	–	–	2
	Oxfordshire cc	40+1 prob. + ?2	15+?2	101+1 prob.
	Oxfordshire/Nene Valley cc	–	2	1
	Oxfordshire Parchment	–	–	2
	'Streak-Burnish'[314]	3 + ?1	1 + ?2	3
	Other red cc	1	–	–
	German Marbled	–	–	1
	A l'Éponge	–	1 + ?1	2
	Argonne (roller-stamped)	–	–	2
	Prob. Hadham (oxidised)	–	4	–
	Unidentified wares (Prob. Late Roman)	–	3	–

310. Platter base: surfaces and fracture grey-cream; moderate coarse sand content resulting in 'pimply' surface appearance.

311. Val Rigby's Fabrics I–IV relate to white/buff/grey fine grained wares occurring primarily in form *Camulodunum* 113/Rigby 2–3 (butt beaker) and a later form, Gillam 42/Rigby 4–5 (pentice-moulded beaker); undiagnostic body sherds may belong to either form type. At the time of writing, Miss Rigby is preparing a typology of these wares.

312. Some of these may extend beyond the first century.

313. *Ibid.*

314. See M.J. Green, 'Romano-British "Streak-Burnished" Ware', K.A.R. Winter, 1981, for fabric description and discussion of this ware; also *The Archaeology of Canterbury*, vol. v, forthcoming.

In addition to the above fine wares, six sherds of Rigby 'Boneware' were present. These pieces in a fine reduced ware are very similar in fabric and form to a small number of buff-coloured cups produced by other city sites and identified by Val Rigby as 'Boneware'; as yet, examples are few and cannot be usefully dated.

Samian – Decorated	SG	1	11	12
	CG	2	10	28
	EG	–	8	3
– Plain	SG	62	147	247
	CG	24	159	130
	EG	4	5	12
	Argonne	3	1	2
Roman Coarse Wares				
	Eifelkeramik	–	–	–
Mortaria	Fab. 1	4	21	10 + ?1
	(Kent/S.E. England/Continent)			
	Fab. 2 (Kent)	–	17	5
	Fab. 3 (Oxfordshire)	3	–	6
	Fab. 4A (Oxfordshire)	2	1	7
	Fab. 4B (Oxfordshire)	1	2	7
	Fab. 5 (Nene Valley)	–	1	2
	?Fab. 6/7 (Rhineland)	–	–	1
	?Fab. 8 (Verulamium region)	–	1	–
	Unidentified	–	2	–
Amphorae	South Spanish	8 + ?2	3 + ?3	5 + ?4
	Dressel 20	?3	37 + ?4	24 + ?6
	?Dressel 30/Pelichet 47	3	9	16
	Dressel 2–4	–	–	1
	?Dressel 7–11	–	2	–
	Prob. Dressel 1B[315]	–	6	–
	Unidentified	4	29	15

315.   Probably all one vessel.

APPENDIX 8

THE SAMIAN FROM MARLOWE AVENUE AND NO. 15A DANE JOHN
by J. Bird and B. Dickinson

(i) THE PLAIN AND DECORATED SAMIAN FROM MARLOWE AVENUE by J. Bird

Notes: (2 ex.) = two examples.
SG, CG, EG: South, Central, East Gaulish.

All the samian from Periods I–III is presented below. Selected pieces, i.e. stamps, decorated, those attributable to a potter or workshop and particularly early examples only, are presented from the post-Roman periods.

Period I

(147)	Dr. 27, SG, first century.
	Dr. 18/Ritt. 1, SG, Claudian.
	Curle 11, CG, early second century.
(154a)	Dr. 24/25, SG, pre-Flavian.
	Dr. 18/Ritt. 1, SG, Claudian.

Period IIB

(108)	Dr. 18, SG, second half first century.
	SG platter, mid first century.
	Dr. 27, SG, pre- or early Flavian.
	Dr. 33, CG, second century.
(109)	Dr. 18, SG, early-mid Flavian.
	SG sherd.
	Dish base, probably Dr. 36, CG, early second century.
(109a)	Dr. 27, SG, second half first century.
	SG sherd.
(111)	Rouletted platter base, SG, first century.
	2 SG sherds.
(114)	Dr. 18, SG, Flavian.
	Dr. 27, SG, mid first century.
(115)	Dr. 37, CG. Fine beads, figure, circle in the field. *c.* A.D. 100–125.
	Dr. 37 or lower frieze of Dr. 29; SG. Shallow scroll winding over arrowheads. *c.* A.D. 65–85.
	Dr. 33, SG, pre- or early Flavian.
	Dr. 27, SG, Flavian.
	Dish, probably Walters, 79 etc., CG, later second century.
(116)	Curle 11, SG, Flavian.
	Dr. 36, SG, Favian (2 examples).
	Dr. 35 or 36, SG, Flavian.
	Ritt. 8, SG, pre-Flavian.
	Dr. 27, SG, pre- or early Flavian.

Dr. 18, SG, pre- or early Flavian.
Dr. 18(R), SG, Flavian
Dr. 33, SG, Nero-Flavian.
Rouletted platter sherd, SG.
Platter sherd, SG.
2 SG sherds.

(120)   Dr. 18 or 18R, SG, pre- or early Flavian.
(143)   SG sherd, mid first century; burnt.
(146)   Dr. 27 probably, SG, first century.
        SG sherd.
(173a)   Dr. 46, Argonne, late second century – early third century; abraded.
        Dr. 31, CG, Antonine.
(176)   Dr. 18/Ritt. 1, SG, Claudian.

Period IIB/C

(98)   Rouletted platter base, SG, first century.
(99)   Dr. 27, SG, second half first century.
(106)   Dr. 27, SG, second half first century.

Period IIC

(97)   Dr. 45, EG (Rheinzabern), late second century – mid third century; worn.
        Dr. 45, EG (Trier), late second century – mid third century; worn.
        Dr. 45 (or 43), CG, late second century; very worn.
        SG sherd.
(97a)   SG sherd.
(103)   Dr. 18/31–31, CG, Hadrianic-Antonine.
        Dr. 37, CG, Hadrianic-Antonine; edge of ovolo.
(173)   Dr. 27, CG, Hadrianic-early Antonine.
        SG sherd.

Period V

(167)   Dr. 33 (stamp no. 1, Fig. 124).

Period VIII

(7a)   Dr. 37, SG, edge of ovolo; Flavian-Trajanic.
(55)   Dr. 37, CG. The figures are a seated Apollo and a Diana and hind (Oswald[316] 83 and 106).
        Hadrianic-early Antonine.

(ii)   THE SAMIAN POTTERS' STAMPS FROM MARLOWE AVENUE by B. Dickinson (Fig. 124)

Notes: The entry gives the potter's name, the die number of the stamp and the form number of the vessel, followed by a reading of the stamp itself and finally the production centre.
c – pottery inferred from distribution, fabric or other factors.

316. F. Oswald, *Index of Figure-types on Terra Sigillata (Samian Ware)* (Liverpool, 1936–7), reprint 1964.

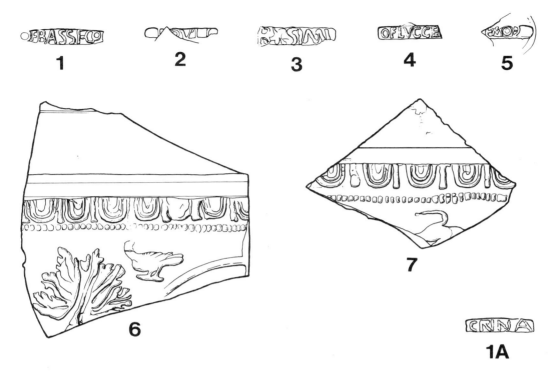

1   2   3   4   5

6   7   1A

Fig. 124.   Samian stamps and decorated samian from No. 15A Dane John: Nos. 1–7 (Scale: ½) and a samian stamp from Marlowe Avenue: No. 1A (Scale: ¼)

Period V

1.A.   (167)   **(Fig. 124, No. 1A).** Crina(?) 1a. 33. **CRINA** Lezoux[c].
                    The potter's name is far from certain. C(e)nna or C(i)nna may be intended, or the stamp may be illiterate. Only two other examples are known, from Vichy and Ickham, Kent. Antonine.

        (iii)   THE PLAIN AND DECORATED SAMIAN FROM NO. 15 DANE JOHN by J. Bird (Fig. 124)

Notes: (2 ex.) = two examples.
        SG, CG, EG: South, Central, East Gaulish.

        All the samian from Period I is presented below. Selected pieces, i.e. stamps, decorated, those attributable to a potter or workshop and particularly early examples only, are presented from the post-Roman periods.

Period I

(156)   Dr. 18, SG, pre- or early Flavian.
                   Curle 11, SG, Flavian.
                   SG platter base.
                   Dr. 18, CG, early second century.
(171)   Dr. 37, CG, early second century; top of ovolo survives.
(178)   Dr. 15/17 or 18 (2 examples, stamp nos. 1 and 2).

Period II

(124) Dr. 37, SG. Wavy line borders, figure (not certainly identifiable). Flavian.
Dr. 29 or 30, SG: part of a small lobed leaf. Pre-Flavian.
Dr. 37, CG. Grass tuft used by the Sacer-Attianus group[317] *c.* A.D. 125–50.

(144) Dr. 33 (stamp no. 3 – see below).
Possibly a Dr. 17 variant,[318]; SG, Tiberio-Claudian.

(168) Dr. 30, CG, by Cinnamus (= 146 below). The wreath and beads are on Stanfield and Simpson,[319] Pl. 159, no. 26, the Perseus on Pl. 160, no. 41, the robed figure on Pl. 158, no. 16, and the leaf tips on Pl. 161, no. 50. The *motif* in the wreath is not certainly identifiable. *c.* A.D. 150–80.
Dr. 37, SG. Wreath at base. Early Flavian.

Period III

(29) Dr. 24 or 27 (stamp no. 5 – see below).
(101) Dr. 37, SG. Part of ovolo, Flavian.
(102) Dr. 37, SG. Stubby blurred leaves round the base. Flavian.
Dr. 29, SG. Upper frieze scroll with arrow terminals; scrollery in lower frieze. *c.* A.D. 70–85.
(102a) Dr. 29, SG. Triple wreath at base. *c.* A.D. 70–85.
(102a) Dr. 29, SG. Triple wreath at base. *c* A.D. 70–85.
(113) Dr. 37, CG. Cinnamus group ovolo 3a. *c.* A.D. 150–70.
(136) Dr. 15/17 or 18 (stamp no. 4 – see below).
(136a) Dr. 37, CG. Free-style scene with horseman and deer. Antonine.
(146) Dr. 30. (= 168 above).
Dr. 37, Rheinzabern. Probably with arcade or medallion.
Later second to mid third century.
Dr. 37, CG. Part of Jupiter Ammon mask. Antonine.
(181) Dr. 37 by Julius II – Julianus I of Rheinzabern. Ludowici and Ricken[320] Taf. 206, nos. 1, 2, 9, 10 and 15, all have the same arrangement of the ovolo, cross and arcade. First half third century. The slip is apparently incompletely applied on the interior.

Period IV

(13) Dr. 29, SG. Fragment of scroll with corded *motif.* Pre-Flavian.
Dr. 37, SG. Coarse wavy line border. Flavian.
(106) Dr. 37, SG. Trident tongued ovolo. Flavian.

317. J.A. Stanfield, and G. Simpson, *Central Gaulish Potters* (London, 1958), Pl. 83, No. 10.
318. F. Oswald, and T.D. Pryce, *Introduction to the Study of Terra Sigillata* (London, 1920), Pl. 42, No. 10 (there is no evidence here of decoration).
319. *Op. cit. supra,* note 317.
320. W. Ludowici and H. Ricken, *Die Bilderschüsseln der römischen Töpfen von Rheinzabern, Tafelband* (Speyer, 1948).

Period V

(6a)   (**Fig. 124, no. 6**). Dr. 37, CG. The ovolo is probably Rogers B209,[321] which is not assigned to a named potter; the other *motifs*, notably the leaf Rogers H72, suggest the work of the Sacer-Cinnamus group.
Early-mid Antonine.

(9)   (**Fig. 124, no. 7**). Dr. 37 by Cobnertus I of Rheinzabern. The ovolo is LRF.E44, which was shared by several potters; the beadrow has no exact parallel in LRF. but occurs on bowls in Cobnertus style and with this ovolo (Museum of London collection). The fabric is not the typical Rheinzabern ware, but the London bowls are in the same fabric. Mid-later Antonine.

(22)   Dr. 29, SG. Arrowheads in upper frieze. *c.* A.D. 70–85.

(41a)   Dr. 37 by Paternus II of Lezoux. Stanfield and Simpson,[322] Pl. 107, no. 26, has the ovolo, beads, peacock and similar scrollery. *c.* A.D. 160–190.

(43)   Dr. 37, SG. Part of ovolo. Flavian.

(iv)   THE SAMIAN POTTERS' STAMPS FROM NO. 15A DANE JOHN by B. Dickinson (Fig. 124)

Notes :   a – indicates a stamp known at the pottery.
b – indicates a stamp not itself known at the pottery but used by a potter of whom other stamps are known there.
c – pottery inferred from distribution, fabric or other factors.
The entry gives the potters' name, the die number of the stamp- and the form number of the vessel, followed by a reading of the stamp itself and finally the production centre.

Period I

1.   (178)   Bassus i – Coelus. 5b. 15/17 or 18. **OFBASSI C°** La Graufesenque[a]. A stamp used mainly on rouletted dishes and occasionally on form 29. The decoration of the latter is consistent with a date *c.* A.D. 55–70.

2.   (178)   I. . .OVI C on form 15/17 or 18, South Gaulish.

Period II

3.   (144)   Chresimus. 4d. 33. [C–] **RESIMI** Montans[b]. SG. Stamps from both this and some of his other dies occur in Antonine Scotland.[323] *c.* A.D. 115–145.

Period III

4.   (136)   Lucceius i–Va–. 1a. 15/17 or 18. **OFLVCCEI[VA]**. La Graufesenque[c]. The lettering of this stamp suggests that this Lucceius is the potter who stamped form 29s. Va- is probably the beginning of another potter's name, though cf. some stamps of Ardacus, Capito, Licinus and Martialis i which have the same two letters appended. No obvious explanation occurs. The decoration associated with stamps of Lucceius suggests a date *c.* A.D. 50–65.

5.   (29)   Modestus. i. 4c. 24 or 27. **[O]FMODES** La Graufesenque[b]. There is no site-dating for this stamp. Some of the decorated bowls with his other stamps fall within the range *c.* A.D. 45–65, and this date would cover his plain ware, too.

321.   G.B. Rogers, *Poteries sigillées de la Gaule Centrale, 1: Les Motifs non-figurés, Gallia,* Supp. No. 28 (Paris, 1974).
322.   *Op. cit. supra,* note 317.
323.   For a discussion of second-century Montans ware, see *Britannia,* iii (1972), 42–5.

ERRATA IN VOLUME VII

p. 196   First heading. Delete '*Nos. 28–29*' and read '*Nos. 29–30*'.

p. 203   Nos. 111, 112, read 'cf. No. 29'.

p. 261.   No. 539, read 'similar to No. 537' and 'Cf. No. 526'.

p. 271   Heading before No. 639 should read 'POTTERY FROM C XIV SITE N'.

p. 275   No. 43. Delete 'bronze'. Add 'This object was analysed in 1958 by the British Non-Ferrous Metals Research Association, by courtesy of the Director, Mr. G.L. Bailey, at the request of Dr H. Cleere. 'The object consists almost entirely of litharge (lead oxide) though there is a small amount of tin present and traces of many other metals including copper and iron. The surfaces of the object have been converted to lead carbonate, and this is what one would expect in course of time. No actual metallics seem to be present. Other constituents were small amounts of chloride and phosphate with a little sulphate. From its shape the object appears to have been melted in some kind of vessel. It may possibly be the skull left behind in a pot used for melting lead.' Dr Cleere adds that the high litharge content suggests that this might be the bottom of a crucible or furnace used for refining silver or desilvering lead by the cupellation process.

p. 277   Read '678, 679'.

p. 285   No. 752 should read 'Dark grey grass-tempered ware, hand-made with irregular burnished surfaces, probably sixth or seventh century'.

p. 305   No. 905. Add 'Mid to late seventeenth century'.

PLATE I

(Photo.: C.A.T.)

Old Park Stone Building.

PLATE II

(Photo.: C.A.T.)

The Conduit House.

PLATE III

(Photo.: C.A.T.)

Cathedral Water Supply: the mid nineteenth-century Timber Conduit.

PLATE IV

(Photo.: Entwistle)

Whitehall Road: rectilinear Belgic Building below Watling Street (Scale in feet)

PLATE V

(Photo.: Entwistle)

Whitehall Road, Belgic Pit below Watling Street (Scale in feet)

PLATE VI

(Photo.: Entwistle)

Whitehall Road, sunken Belgic Hut (Scale in feet)

PLATE VII

(Photo.: S.S. Frere)

Whitehall Road: latest Hearth in Belgic Hut (Scale in inches)

PLATE VIII

(Photo.: C.A.T.)

Cranmer House, London Road, working Photograph.

PLATE IX

(*Photo.: C.A.T.*)

Cranmer House, London Road, Burials 4 and 3 (Scale: 1 m.).

PLATE X

(*Photo.: C.A.T.*)

Cranmer House, London Road, Burial 15 (Scale: 50 cm.).

PLATE XI

Cranmer House, London Road, Burial 28 (Scale: 50 cm.).

PLATE XII

Cranmer House, London Road, Burial 36 (Scale: 50 cm.).

PLATE XIII

(Photo.: C.A.T.)

Cranmer House, London Road, Burial 45 (Scale: 50 cm.).

PLATE XIV

(Photo.: C.A.T.)

Cranmer House, London Road, Burials 46 and 50 (Scale: 50 cm.).

PLATE XV

(*Photo.: C.A.T.*)

Cranmer House, London Road, Inhumation Burial 71 (Scale: 50 cm.).

PLATE XVI

(Photo.: C.A.T.)
Cranmer House, London Road, Saxon Gold Pendant
(Scale: 2:1)

PLATE XVII

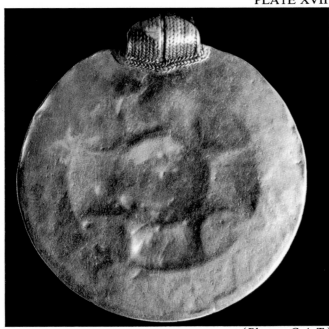

(Photo.: C.A.T.)
Cranmer House, London Road, Saxon Gold Pendant, back view
(Scale: 2:1)

PLATE XVIII

(*Photo.: S.S. Frere*)

St. Peter's Lane, medieval drain (Scale in feet)

PLATE XIX

(Photo.: S.S. Frere)

St. Peter's Lane, tiled Hearth (Scale in feet)

PLATE XX

(Photo.: C.A.T.)

King's Bridge Gas Trench, looking West showing Stone Paving of the medieval Bridge
(Scale: 1 m.).

PLATE XXI

A. The Chapel.
B. The School Master's House
C. King's Arms.
D. Tablet of the late Arch Bishop's Arms.
E. Ditto of A.B. Juxon's.
F. King's Bridge.

A View of East Bridge Hospital, Canterbury, taken from King's Mill.

(*Photo.: Canterbury Museums*)

Print of the East Bridge Hospital and King's Bridge *c.* 1780.

PLATE XXII

All Saints Church

(Photo.: Canterbury Museums.)
Mid eighteenth-century Print of All Saints' Church.

PLATE XXIII

(*Photo.: Entwistle*)

Roman Gravel below the County Hotel (Scale 2 feet)

PLATE XXIV

(*Photo.: S.S. Frere*)

Hypocaust Arch in the Fleur-de-Lis Yard (Scale in feet)

PLATE XXV

(Photo.: C.A.T.)

The High Street Sewer Tunnel.

PLATE XXVI

(Photo.: C.A.T.)

No. 9 High Street, Roman Portico Paving and Drain (Scale: 50 cm.).

PLATE XXVII

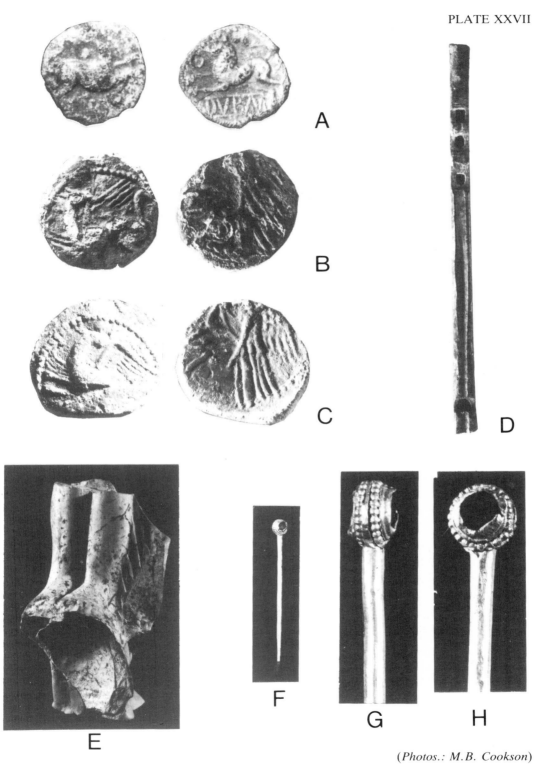

(Photos.: M.B. Cookson)

A–C, Belgic Bronze Coins (Scale: 2:1); D, Bone Flute (Scale: 1:1); E, Pipe-clay Figurine
(Scale: 1:1); F, Saxon Gold Pin (Scale: 1:1); G–H, Saxon Gold Pin (Scale 4:1)

PLATE XXVIII

(*Photo.: M.B. Cookson*)

Fleur-de-Lis Yard, Marble Fragments (Scale: 1:3·5)

PLATE XXIX

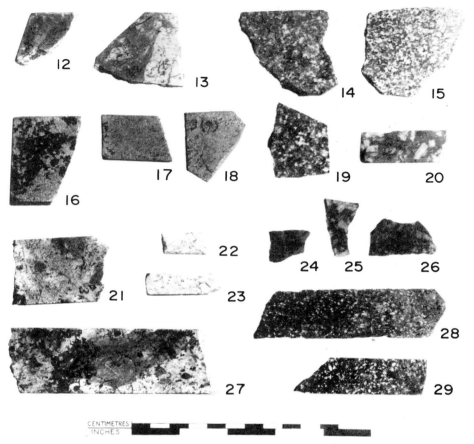

(*Photo.: M.B. Cookson*)

Fleur-de-Lis Yard, Marble Fragments (Scale: 1:2).

PLATE XXX

(Photo.: M.B. Cookson)
Andenne Ware Jar (Height: 38·8cm.).

PLATE XXXI

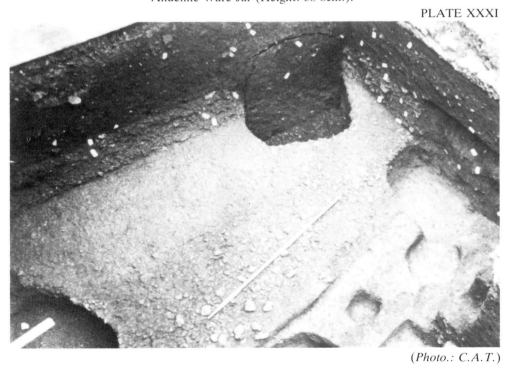

(Photo.: C.A.T.)
Marlowe Avenue, the primary Roman Street (Scale: 2 m.).

PLATE XXXII

(Photo.: C.A.T.)
Marlowe Avenue, late eighteenth-century Cess-tank (Scale: 2 m.).

PLATE XXXIII

(Photo.: C.A.T.)
Marlowe Avenue, some post-medieval Pottery from the Cess-tank (from colour slide).

PLATE XXXIV

(*Photo.: C.A.T.*)

St. John's Lane, late Roman Wall Foundation (Scale: 2 m.).

PLATE XXXV

(Photo.: C.A.T.)

The Dane John Mound looking South-east with Excavation in the Foreground.

PLATE XXXVI

(*Photo.: C.A.T.*)

No. 15A Dane John, early Norman Ditch looking East (Scales: 2 m.).

GENERAL INDEX

(Compiled by S. Stow)